BRITISH INDIA &
BRITISH SCOTLAND,
1780–1830

SERIES ON INTERNATIONAL, POLITICAL,
AND ECONOMIC HISTORY

Jack Gieck, *Lichfield: The U.S. Army on Trial*

John M. Knapp, *Behind the Diplomatic Curtain: Adolphe de Bourqueney
and French Foreign Policy, 1816–1869*

Martha McLaren, *British India and British Scotland, 1780–1830:
Career Building, Empire Building, and a Scottish School of Thought on
Indian Governance*

BRITISH INDIA & BRITISH SCOTLAND, 1780–1830

Career Building, Empire Building, and a Scottish School of Thought on Indian Governance

MARTHA McLAREN

THE UNIVERSITY OF AKRON PRESS

AKRON, OHIO

All inquiries and permissions requests should be addressed to the publisher, The University of Akron Press, Akron, OH 44325-1703

LIBRARY OF CONGRESS CATALOGING-IN-PUBLICATION DATA
McLaren, Martha, 1939–
British India and British Scotland, 1780–1830 : career building, empire building, and a Scottish school of thought on Indian governance / Martha McLaren.
p.   cm. — (Series on international, political, and economic history)
Includes bibliographical references and index.
ISBN 1-884836-73-9 (cloth : alk. paper)
1. India—History—British occupation, 1765–1947. 2. India—Politics and government—18th century. 3. India—Politics and government—19th century. 4. East India Company. I. Title. II. Series.
ds463 .m267 2001
325'.341'095409034—dc21
2001002846

Manufactured in the United States of America
The paper used in this publication meets the minimum requirements of American National Standard for Information Sciences—Permanence of Paper for Printed Library Materials, ANSI z39.48—1984. ∞

First edition 2001

Contents

Preface   vii

Introduction   1

PART I. As Actors. *Building Careers and an Empire*

1. Scottish Families, 1760s–1790s: Status, Patronage,
   Education, and Wealth   15

2. India, 1780–1801: Knowledge and Self-Help   29

3. India, 1798–1812: Knowledge Rewarded   43

4. Britain, 1808–1817: Home Leave, Accomplishments,
   and Frustrations   68

5. India, 1812–1819: The Formation of a Leadership Cadre   78

6. 1819–1830: Recognition   95

PART II. As Writers. *Scottish Ideas and Indian Government*

7. Philosophical Historians   119

8. Moral Philosophers   129

9. Religious Moderates   145

10. Systems of Government: Seeking an Equilibrium
    between Authority and Liberty   160

11. A Scottish School of Thought: Political Economy
    and the "Munro System"   192

PART III. Representations

12. Orientalist Representations   227

13. Historiographical Representations   240

14. British Scotland, British India   249

Abbreviations   255

Notes   257

Glossary   283

Bibliography   285

Index   299

Preface

In the course of researching and writing this book I have been helped along the way by far too many people for all, unfortunately, to be mentioned. The research was made possible initially by a generous grant from the Social Sciences and Humanities Research Council of Canada; it was made enjoyable as well as enlightening by the patience and expert knowledge of the staffs of the Oriental and India Office Collections at the British Library in London, the National Library of Scotland, Edinburgh, and in the Special Collections departments of the libraries of Simon Fraser University, the University of British Columbia, and the University of Washington. The readers and editors for The University of Akron Press provided numerous helpful comments on the manuscript. Enid Fuhr and Hannah Gay, at different stages in the process, provided invaluable "moral" support, as did my tolerant and good-humored family from start to finish. The book would have been neither started nor completed without the unflagging encouragement of Edward Ingram, whose discerning and constructive criticism, he will be surprised to hear, was always appreciated. Finally I thank my husband Allen, not only for sharing the adventures of the better part of my life, but also (more lightly) for possessing the necessary computer skills to save the text from annihilation due to technical glitches (rare) and my own ineptitude (often). Responsibility for errors of fact and flawed interpretation is entirely mine.

Note on transliteration

The actors in the history of British India as well as the historians who write about it have utilized a confusing variety of forms in transliterating Indian names and words into English. I have retained, for the most part, the spellings used by my three subjects. Where the form they use seems uncomfortably archaic I have adopted either fairly standardized nineteenth and twentieth century spellings (Sindhia, not the modern Shinde), or modern spellings (Awadh, Pune). This practice, I hope, will be accepted as common sense rather than inconsistency.

India, 1780 – 1830
Places mentioned in the text

Sikhs

Peshawar

Punjab

Lahore
Multan
Sutlej R.

Baluchis

Indus R.

Cis-Sutlej
Sikhs

Jumna R.

Rajputana

Delhi

Aligarh

Smd

Chambul R.

SINDHIA'S
TERRITORIES Gwalior Gohad

Ganges R.

Benares

Malwa

Bengal

HOLKAR'S
TERRITORIES Mehidpur

GAEKWAR
TERRITORIES

Indore

Nerbudda R.

Calcutta
(Fort William)

Baroda

RAJA OF BERAR'S
TERRITORIES

Burhampur Ellichpur Gawilgarh

Nagpur

Argaum

Ellora Assaye

Bassein

Godaveri R.

Bombay

PESHWA'S
TERRITORIES

Puhe

Satara Sholapur

Hyderabad

Northern Circars

Vizgapatam

Southern
Jagirdars

NIZAM'S TERRITORIES

Kistna R.

Masulipatam

Tumbudra R.

Ceded
Districts

Arabian Sea

Ballari

MYSORE

Coromandel Coast

Bay of Bengal

Carnatic

Vellore

Bangalore

Madras
(Fort St. George)

Kanara

Seringapatam

Salem

Kaveri R.

Tanjore

Malabar Coast

Coimbatore

Indian Ocean

Introduction

*T*his book is about three eminent Scotsmen, Thomas Munro (1761–1827),
John Malcolm (1769–1833), and Mountstuart Elphinstone (1779–
1859). All three men were raised in Scotland between the 1760s and
1790s—the period notable in intellectual history as the golden age of the
Scottish Enlightenment—and employed in India between 1780 and 1830,
the period notable in imperial history for the remarkable process by which
a company of British merchants became the rulers of an Indian empire.
Their careers and thought provide an important link between Scottish
and Indian history. Munro, Malcolm, and Elphinstone took part in all
the major events of their time in India, rising from junior positions in the
East India Company's service to become the governors of Madras and
Bombay. They accomplished this through their military and diplomatic
contributions to the expansion of the company's territory and their key
roles in setting up the company's administrative system. They won the respect and friendship of important political figures, including the Duke of
Wellington and his brother, the Marquis Wellesley. Munro, Malcolm, and
Elphinstone are recognized by historians as an important leadership cadre
and as the main proponents of the dominant school of thought in the
formation of Indian policy in the early nineteenth century,[1] a school of
thought that remained influential throughout the period of British rule in
India.

Every historian writing on early nineteenth-century British India from
the 1830s to the present has had to consider the work of Munro, Malcolm, and Elphinstone, but most have assumed, wrongly, that in cultural
terms Scotsmen should be equated with Englishmen. The careers and
thought of these three distinguished men have never been examined with-

in the dynamic social and intellectual context of the Scotland in which they were raised, an omission that has led to misinterpretations of aspects of their professional lives and, more important, of their approach to Indian government. This approach is usually described as conservative and pragmatic; Anglo-Irish political thinker Edmund Burke is credited with inspiring the conservative elements while, in apparent contradiction, the word "pragmatic" is used to imply an absence of any ideological commitment at all. Expediency—the pursuit of short-term practical goals for political and/or economic reasons—and the preservation of traditional Indian ways of doing things are seen as the main determinants of the three men's policy recommendations. A close examination of their extensive writings on Asian societies and their recommendations on British Indian government, however, reveal the pervasive influence of ideas developed and publicized by leading writers of the Scottish Enlightenment. These were men like David Hume, Adam Smith, William Robertson, Adam Ferguson, and John Millar, some of whose ideas foreshadowed and influenced nineteenth-century Utilitarianism and liberalism.

Like most Europeans, Munro, Malcolm, and Elphinstone took with them to India a cultural luggage which colored their general perceptions of Asia and to which they turned for guidance when confronted with the problems of governing India. This does not mean they merely invoked ideas and principles to give a cloak of respectability for their ambitions, as Sir Lewis Namier and his disciples claimed to be the case in eighteenth-century English political circles. As H. T. Dickinson points out, by treating all expression of ideas as mere ex post facto rationalizations of political action, Namier and his followers failed to explain why particular ideas or principles are chosen over possible alternatives.[2] Scottish Enlightenment ideology was "chosen," although not adopted wholesale or uncritically, by Munro, Malcolm, and Elphinstone because it provided conceptual tools they could use as a framework for their analyses of Asian cultures and theories of progress they could apply to the problems of Indian government.

Although Munro, Malcolm, and Elphinstone are of particular interest as individuals for their prominent roles in the expansion and consolidation of British India, they are also representative of the many relatively well educated, middle- and upper-ranking Scotsmen who took advantage of the career opportunities that became available to them in British India during the later eighteenth century. Although the initial object of this study was simply to explore the philosophical roots of the three men's ideas on Indian government, it soon became evident that their ideology cannot be adequately explained without taking into consideration the connection between their use of career-building techniques—for example, their deliberate acquisition of professional qualifications in the form of knowledge of Scottish Enlightenment social and economic theory, and Indian languages, society, and politics—and the development and written presentation of their ideas. Elphinstone was sufficiently well connected to have risen in the company's service relatively effortlessly. But Munro and Malcolm, lacking adequate patronage, sought other routes to advancement. At a time when many Scotsmen with professional qualifications, particularly doctors, engineers, and teachers, were taking advantage of union with England to pursue more lucrative career opportunities south of the border than were available in Scotland, Munro and Malcolm worked to acquire professional qualifications of their own that they hoped would attract favorable attention in British India. When Elphinstone too became frustrated by the leisurely pace of advancement, Malcolm encouraged him to follow his example and to acquire and demonstrate in books and official reports a knowledge of Indian affairs.

Expert knowledge and writing skills gained a new importance in the late eighteenth and early nineteenth centuries in association with the gradual bureaucratization of the middle levels of British Indian government. The staffs of the British government's board of control for India and the East India Company in London began to include men like James Cumming, William M'Culloch, and James Mill, who either gained or maintained their jobs as a result of their specialized knowledge.[3] At the same time, company officials in India found that while expertise did not supercede either patronage or seniority as a sure route to career advancement, it did provide a possible alternative route for able, ambitious, junior officials with inadequate connections. Written communication of information, explanation, and opinion was becoming crucial to the decision-making process both within the company organization in India and between India and the Home government. The relatively rare official who could produce well-written reports, provide logical analyses of problems, and recommend solutions in well-argued form with morally and practically acceptable rationales gained attention and respect. Literary accomplishments, the mark of the cultivated gentleman, were also useful adjuncts to the curriculum vitae of an ambitious company official.

In the interests of their careers, therefore, Munro, Malcolm, and Elphinstone studied Asian languages and wrote about Asian history and politics. These writings, which include Malcolm's and Elphinstone's published works of earlier and contemporary history as well as the minutes, reports, and official correspondence of all three men, were composed not merely to provide useful information but, more importantly, to impress the men who decided Indian appointments and Indian policy. The writings, however, also provide evidence of the shared assumptions that lay behind the three men's approach to Indian governance—assumptions that derived from shared roots that were firmly embedded in the political, economic, social, and intellectual "soil" of Hanoverian Scotland.

By the 1760s, the role of the Hanoverian monarchy had been defined in a way that was generally, if reservedly, accepted in both Scotland and England, and a degree of toleration had been achieved which eased the politico-religious tensions that had disturbed both countries during the previous century. The Act of Union of 1707, although not popular on either side of the border, provided a settlement which eventually helped free the energies of both English and Scots for new challenges, not the least of which were economic opportunities provided by agricultural "revolution," the early stages of industrialization, and the expansion of Britain's empire. But the Act of Union called only for political and financial integration. In the later eighteenth century, although union with England was creating the political stability and economic opportunities that Scotland's ruling classes had hoped for, developments within the country's religious, legal, and educational institutions remained separate. Scottish intellectual life, particularly the intelligentsia's preoccupation with moral philosophy and the science of man, owed more to Scotland's own intellectual traditions and to its historically close relationship with continental Europe than to English influence. And it is in their attitudes to religion, law, and the issues encompassed by the term "moral philosophy" that the most distinctive features of Munro, Malcolm, and Elphinstone's thought on India are to be found, while their respect for education and their pursuit of knowledge provided the main impetus for the practical advancement of their careers.[4]

In comparing intellectual life in England and Scotland in the second half of the eighteenth century one might point out that no books have ever been written on "The Golden Age of the English Enlightenment"; France and Scotland were the guiding lights of the western intellectual tradition at the time. Scottish culture, of course, was made up of many strands and, from the point of view of the history of ideas, the Scottish philosophes differed on many issues. Certain methodologies and modes of thought, however, attracted widespread attention and formed the core of what may, perhaps, be termed the unique ideology of the Scottish Enlightenment. Its most distinctive characteristics included the secular but not anticlerical approach to religion favored by the Moderate group within the Church of Scotland; the protosociological theories that earned Adam Ferguson the title "father of sociology"; ideas about political economy that encompassed moral as well as economic progress; the application of the concept of sensibility to the study of alien cultures; and the use of philosophical and conjectural history as a medium for transmitting to the general reading public the *common sense* rather than *rationalist* approach to man and society which was the hallmark of the Scottish philosophes. Interest in theories of man and society was not, of course, confined to Scottish intellectual circles. The evidence indicates, however, that Scottish sources provided much of the inspiration for Munro, Malcolm, and Elphinstone's interpretations of Asian culture and ideas on Indian government.

Scotland's intelligentsia, although proud of their own intellectual achievements, tended to see England's experience as the exemplar of modern political and social liberty and they approved and encouraged participation in the joint exercise of "Great Britain." But not all Scots shared this enthusiasm. Some feared that the price of becoming "British" might prove to be the loss of valued Scottish traditions and a Scottish sense of identity—one that had been painstakingly constructed over many centuries, partly at least in response to English disparagement. There was concern and resentment in some quarters that Scotland was becoming a quasi-colony of England. As political radical James Thomson Callender put it in 1792, "To England we were for many centuries a hostile, and we are still considered by them as a foreign, and in effect a conquered nation." Most Scots wanted their country to be acknowledged, in practice as well as principle, as a completely equal participant in the Union, but they often, paradoxically, accepted at face value English assessments of England's achievements and Scotland's supposed inferiority.[5] Many Scotsmen who built successful careers in British India, including Munro, Malcolm, and Elphinstone, struggled to reconcile their dual British/Scottish identities. In private correspondence with family and compatriots their affections—and affectations—remained Scottish. (Munro, whose command of literary English was exemplary, was apt to lapse into an exaggerated form of Scots when corresponding with Glasgow friends.) Professionally, however, all three men made clear their loyalty to Great Britain.

The Scottish and Indian arenas in which the three men spent their childhood and professional lives were connected in that both Scotland and British India were parts of what is sometimes termed "the Second British empire," and were subject, ultimately, to the authority of Britain's predominantly English, socially and politically exclusive ruling elite. Patronage determined the election, by a very limited franchise, of the sixteen peers and forty-five members of Parliament who, after 1707, represented Scottish interests at Westminster. There were two hundred and six seats in the House of Lords and five hundred and sixty-eight seats in the House of Commons at the time. Scotland's representation, calculated on the basis of a population ratio of one to five and a wealth ratio of one to forty (measured in terms of yield from land revenue, customs, and excise) had a negligible influence on a government that was largely indifferent to, and ignorant of, Scottish concerns. By the middle of the eighteenth century, however, both parties found it convenient to make use of an unofficial "manager" who would promote and explain Scottish political interests to the government while doing his best to ensure that the tiny percentage of his countrymen with votes exercised them in support of the government.

Tory member of parliament Henry Dundas, who played the managerial role from the mid-1780s until his impeachment in 1805, provided a steady stream of East India Company appointments for the sons of middle- and upper-ranking Scottish families in return for a guaranteed majority of Scottish votes in support of the government.

The British India of the early 1780s to which these young men went, usually between the ages of fifteen and seventeen, was a different place than the India of a century later, so lucidly depicted in the writings of Rudyard Kipling. A quick death from disease was highly likely and was made more likely by overindulgence in food and drink. With few European women to marry (supposing a young man could afford matrimony anyway), liaisons with Indian women were common, and many, including Munro, fathered children to support whose mothers were Indian. Indebtedness was common, resulting from participation in unprofitable trading activities to augment meager company salaries or from social aspirations above and beyond what those salaries could support. Both Malcolm and Elphinstone got into debt during their early years in India. In 1780, trade, not government, remained the priority of most company directors and most of their employees in India, although that was to change following the passage of the India Act by the administration of William Pitt (the younger) in 1784.

The company at this time controlled only the ex-Mughal province of Bengal, two small territories around Madras and Bombay, and a number of even smaller, scattered trading bases. But since its acquisition of Bengal and the decline of Mughal power in the mid–eighteenth century, the company had become one of several state-building rulers who were endeavoring to enhance their military capacity, power, and wealth in the Indian subcontinent by means of more centralized forms of government and more efficient systems of taxation—military fiscalism.[6] The company's main competitors were the ex-Mughal provinces of Awadh and Hyderabad, now independent Muslim-ruled kingdoms in eastern and south-central India; the Hindu Marathas in western and central India, who had successfully expanded their territories during the seventeenth and early eighteenth centuries at the expense of the weakening Mughal regime; the Sikhs in the northwestern region known as the Punjab; and Haidar Ali, a

Muslim soldier-adventurer who had seized the southwestern Hindu state of Mysore in 1761 and was successfully enlarging its power.

The East India Company's involvement in the economic life of India began in the seventeenth century with the company's participation as customer, supplier of specie, and maritime carrier in Indian trade and banking, and expanded through business partnerships between company officials and Indians. The company's involvement in Indian politics and military affairs developed rapidly from the 1740s, when trade rivalry between France and Britain in India was ignited into military conflict by war between the two states in Europe. Necessity and experience improved the company's military capacity to a point at which its potential as an ally was recognized by Indian rulers as well as by merchant groups seeking protection.[7] By 1765, participation in the economic, political, and military affairs of eastern India had brought Bengal under company control. Its subjection of the major Indian powers in the south and west of the subcontinent, which originated again in the official and unofficial involvement of company agents in Indian economic matters, was largely achieved during the governor-generalships of Wellesley and Hastings by a combination of diplomatic maneuvers and expensive military campaigns in which Munro, Malcolm, and Elphinstone were intimately involved.

Recent scholarly works on Great Britain, India, and the British empire provide a useful historiographical context for this study. The research on eighteenth-century Britain of John Brewer and Linda Colley in particular has thrown light on the increasing numbers of Scotsmen pursuing Indian careers. Brewer, in broad terms, accepts the claims made by scholars in the 1980s that the long-held perception of eighteenth-century British society as uniquely open and liberal was largely a myth, and that the aristocracy, in fact, retained an almost complete domination of British political and social life throughout the century.[8] But he presents evidence, nevertheless, that demonstrates that the British state's needs during its ongoing conflict with France opened some new routes to advancement for those outside the traditional corridors of power. Britain's rise from a minor, peripheral state to the first fiscal military state and a major international power rested largely on the improved ability of its supposedly weak central government to organize the collection and allocation of resources. The conse-

quent growth of the public administration produced new professional opportunities for middle-ranking men, but mostly for Englishmen. Scotsmen, Irishmen and, to some extent, Welshmen still faced formidable barriers to advancement and turned to the empire to improve their lot.[9] As
the East India Company expanded its directly ruled territories, the collection and allocation of Indian resources were, of course, as crucial to the
company's interests as the collection and allocation of resources at home
were to the interests of the British government, and many Scots, including
Munro, improved their career prospects by becoming students of political
and military economy.

Colley discusses the large-scale exodus of Scotsmen to the empire in
her acclaimed book, *Britons: Forging the Nation, 1707–1837*. In her examination of the way the people of Scotland, Ireland, Wales, and England were
brought to acknowledge a common British identity during these years, the
catalyst again was war with France; the means was a careful cultivation of
an image of France as an oppositional other against which the diverse
peoples of the British Isles were encouraged to define themselves collectively. Patriotic behavior, she argues, represented acceptance of a common
British identity, and served as a vehicle for different groups and interests
to claim their right to participate fully in British political life.[10] Malcolm,
a dedicated exponent of the empire's importance to British power, demanded that the patriotism of imperial service should justify his own and
other Anglo-Indian claims to public recognition and high office.

Quoting Sir Walter Scott's observation: "I was born a Scotsman and a
bare one, therefore I was born to fight my way in the world," Colley observes that this expression gets exactly right the connection between economics and aggression on the part of Scotsmen.[11] But improved social
and political status was also a powerful motive force behind Scottish imperial service. Malcolm's drive and tenacity in career building was not directed solely, or even primarily, towards economic gain. In his study of
Anglo-Persian relations in the early nineteenth century, Edward Ingram
provides a masterly account of the tangled web of British, Indian, company, Imperial, and, most important, personal interests which affected poli-
cymaking in India and towards Persia, and makes clear how much imperial
expansion took place, particularly during the governor-generalships of

Marquis Wellesley (1798–1805) and the marquis of Hastings (1812–23),[12] to serve the subimperial interests of ambitious, status-seeking individuals.[13] Territorial expansion and the administrative responsibilities that went with it meant the company needed more and more employees with Indian language skills and some understanding of Indian society and politics, a situation Munro, Malcolm, and Elphinstone were particularly successful at exploiting.

In recent decades several leading imperial historians have reassessed the character of British colonial rule during the expansionary years from the 1780s to 1830 and in doing so have challenged the influential pioneering work done by Vincent Harlow in the 1940s and 1950s. The passage of the India Act in 1784 reflected, first and foremost, practical anxieties in Britain about the company's insolvency and recognition by the ruling elite in Britain of the company's importance to the British economy. But public interest in the obligations as well as the opportunities of colonial governments had been raised by the recent American Revolutionary War and the impeachment of company governor-general Warren Hastings for corruption and tyranny. Under the terms of the act, the company's government in India had been made responsible to Parliament for the well-being of its Indian subjects and for maintaining certain standards of integrity in its administration. The company's court of directors had also insisted on a clause prohibiting further territorial expansion. Harlow interpreted these developments as harbingers of a more "liberal" form of imperialism whose progress he traced to the granting of internal self-government to the white settlement colonies in the mid–nineteenth century, a period he saw as one of growing responsibility in Britain towards the welfare of its overseas subjects.[14] Today's historians, however, stress the dominance of Tory authoritarianism during these years.

C. A. Bayly argues that the period saw not liberalization, but rather an effort by the British to centralize power, increase executive authority, and remove all natives from positions of authority in its colonies, and a deliberate attempt to set up despotic forms of government similar to the neoabsolutist regimes of contemporary Russia and Austria. Where Bayly identifies a western form of despotic government as the model, Burton Stein suggests that in South India an Asiatic form of despotism probably provided the immediate inspiration. He uses Max Weber's model of "Sultanism" as the basis for his claim that Munro's ideas on government were influenced by the authoritarian system of military fiscalism developed by Tipu Sultan of Mysore. Both historiographical interpretations recognize the central role of the army in maintaining British power. This assumption was virtually unchallenged within the British community in India in the late eighteenth and early nineteenth centuries and it provides the foundation for Douglas M. Peers's claim that the Anglo-Indian military community, by demanding priority access to Indian resources on the ground that the company's empire was dependent on its army, created a type of militarism that helped promote authoritarian rule. The possibility that Scottish authoritarian proclivities in general, and the sympathy of ex-Jacobites for royal authority in particular, may also have played a part in the development of a despotic form of rule is raised by Colley, who points out that many Scots who served the empire in the eighteenth century had had Jacobite connections, and that Scotland's contribution contained an aggressive and unscrupulous side as well as the splendid and cosmopolitan legacy of the Enlightenment.[15] The more splendid facet of Scotland's legacy, however, is emphasized by John M. MacKenzie who draws attention to the success of Scotsmen in many different colonies in transferring what he calls a distinctively Scottish concept of civil society to the empire—a social ethic developed and promoted by Scotland's most renowned philosophers that owed much to their country's independent intellectual life.[16]

These works provide an invaluable historiographical context in which to examine the careers and thought on British Indian government of Munro, Malcolm, and Elphinstone. It will be argued here, however, that the authoritarian elements in their school of thought fit neither the neoabsolutist, sultanist, militarist, nor Jacobite models. Their approach to government, formulated from oral and written information they obtained largely from Indian, Persian, Sikh, and Afghan sources, was filtered through a screen of Scottish ideas and assumptions. It recommended, instead, a *stage* of authoritarian government, supported by a strong army, to eradicate the quasi-feudal elements and enhance the influence of the middling ranks in Indian society and politics. The authoritarian stage, however, was to be merely a temporary measure to establish the necessary social order for the evolution of a more progressive India that could be administered, with the tacit consent of most Indians, according to contemporary Scottish views on civil society and political economy. It was an approach that was progressive in intent and owed more to the influence of social and economic theories emanating from Scottish Enlightenment thinkers than to either Burkean imperatives, practical expediency, or Asian or European "models."

In discussing the philosophical and intellectual origins of Munro, Malcolm, and Elphinstone's thought I have tried to avoid using labels. Since the mid–nineteenth century, the three men have been described at different times as liberal conservatives, conservative liberals, romantic imperialists, conservative romantics, liberal conservative imperialists, and conservative orientalists. The confusion stems from applying nineteenth- and twentieth-century terms to men whose thought did not derive from nineteenth- and twentieth-century culture. There are elements in their ideology which are conservative and others which anticipate liberalism, romanticism, and also utilitarianism. They are imperialists in the literal sense that they helped acquire and administer an empire, but they lacked both the presumption and racist assumptions of today's stereotypical imperialist. They are orientalists, but require a unique, not generic, definition of that contentious term to accommodate their representations of Asia. Above all, they are successful careerists who used their ability as thinkers and writers as well as their practical competence as actors in the stirring events of the time to improve their status as citizens of Great Britain. If their ideology is to be given a label it should be, simply, the "Scottish School."

PART I

AS ACTORS

Building Careers and an Empire

Scottish Families, 1760s–1790s

Status, Patronage, Education, and Wealth

We always retain a partiality for whatever we have been once accustomed
to but more particularly if we have been so in youth.
—*Thomas Munro*

The years from the 1760s to the 1790s, the formative years of Thomas
Munro, John Malcolm, and Mountstuart Elphinstone, saw Scotland's "Age of Improvement" at its apogee.[1] For the middle and upper
ranks in Lowland Scotland it was an intellectually stimulating and culturally cohesive period, despite some religious divisions. The same issues
were discussed and the same books read by the nobility and their tenant
farmers, by lawyers, doctors, and clerics, and by merchants and manufac-
turers, mostly on subjects relating to the material and moral progress—
the "wealth and virtue"—of the Scottish people. The Munro, Malcolm,
and Elphinstone families belonged to different status groups within Scottish society—the Glasgow merchant community, the rural Kirk gentry,
and the landed aristocracy, respectively—giving them different social, professional, and political advantages. But the families were all members of

the middle and upper ranks that were most involved in and most affected by the practical and intellectual developments of the time.

Thomas Munro was born at Glasgow on 27 May 1761, the second child and second son in a family of five boys and two girls. In a "self-portrait" drawn for his mother when he was twenty-two years old, Munro describes himself as resembling a picture he has seen of Don Quixote: about six feet tall, "as lank and meagre as him with a complexion no ways inferior . . . I would say that I am a person of a grave appearance and of a discrete [*sic*] and sober deportment." Elphinstone, who was not prone to flattering people, described Munro as a man of "great natural genius" and of "sound sense . . . good humor . . . and philanthropy."[2] Munro was partially deaf, the result of a childhood bout with measles; a handicap that probably hindered his access to certain appointments during his early career. The Munros were typical but minor members of Glasgow's merchant community who did well during Thomas's childhood in the 1760s and 1770s. His grandfather, a tailor, raised the family's economic status through successful investments in American tobacco. His father, Alexander, worked in a bank before joining the family firm and acquiring a small country estate near Glasgow which provided him, albeit marginally, with the gentlemanly social status that enabled four of his five sons to enter the East India Company's service.[3] But he had few of the influential contacts necessary to oil the wheels of promotion for his boys. Once in India, they had to make their own way, hampered further by their father's bankruptcy as a result of the collapse of the tobacco trade during the American Revolutionary War.

Munro arrived in India in 1780, served with the Madras army during the Second Anglo-Mysore War (1780–84) and spent the years from 1784 to 1788 on various garrison postings. He then obtained an appointment under Captain Alexander Read in Governor-General Lord Cornwallis's intelligence and supply service, where both men remained until the conclusion of the Third Anglo-Mysore War (1790–92). From 1792 until 1799 Munro served as Read's assistant in organizing the revenue system of the Madras presidency's newly acquired Baramahal district, but he returned to intelligence and supply duties during the brief fourth and final Anglo-Mysore War in 1799, followed by a prestigious appointment as second secretary to the postwar commission for the settlement of Mysore. A term as senior revenue collector for another newly acquired district, Kanara, from July 1799 until October 1800, established his reputation as an administrator; a reputation he enhanced between 1800 and 1807 with a controversial but ultimately successful administration of a large and turbulent region that had been ceded to the company by the nizam of Hyderabad. After twenty-seven years in India, Munro returned to Britain in 1807, officially on leave although frequently consulted by company and board of control officials on matters relating to Indian governance. He returned to Madras in 1814, newly married and holding an influential and prestigious position as judicial commissioner. During the Third Anglo-Maratha War (1817–18) he commanded a reserve division of the Madras army with great success. After a brief visit to Britain in 1819, he returned to India as governor of Madras, where he remained until his death in 1827.

Like the Munro family, John Malcolm's family were impoverished, but they enjoyed greater access to patronage. Born 2 May 1769, John was the fourth son of the seventeen children of George and Margaret Malcolm of Burnfoot in Dumfriesshire. Eight years Munro's junior, he was a large, generous, versatile, and ambitious man with an ability to get on well, at least superficially, with people from all walks of life, and the industry and talent to convert a limited formal education into an honorary degree of Doctor of Letters at Oxford University. Lord Clive, while governor of Madras, described Malcolm as having "extensive knowledge, activity and distinguished excellence of temper."[4] Malcolm's father had been educated for the church but, owing apparently to a speech impediment, had to struggle to support his large family as a tenant farmer. The Malcolms, however, belonged to the landed and clerical groups which had traditionally dominated Scottish life. Despite their present reduced circumstances, they enjoyed higher social status than the Munros. John Lockhart, Walter Scott's biographer, mentions that John Malcolm's grandfather Robert Malcolm had "found refuge [at Burnfoot] after forfeiting a good estate and a baronetcy, in the *affair* of 1715," an observation which suggests that Robert Malcolm, who was a church minister, was also a Jacobite. Although Lockhart was not above including gossip as well as facts in his memoir, Malcolm confirmed that the family had moved to Burnfoot soon after the 1715–16 rebellion, telling Scott that the farm had only been "the House of the Malcolm's since 1719 A.D.!!"[5]

John's mother, Margaret Pasley, was a great-niece of Sir Gilbert Elliot of Minto, the first baronet, and the sister of Admiral Sir Thomas Pasley and of John Pasley, a wealthy London merchant. Elizabeth Elphinstone, wife of Mountstuart's uncle and patron, William Elphinstone, mentions in her diary that she was on visiting terms with the Malcolms, while members of the Johnstone family of Alva, long prominent in Scottish political life and friends as well as landlords and patrons of the Malcolms, sat in Parliament and in the proprietors and directors courts of the East India Company. According to contemporary observer Thomas Somerville, Sir William Pulteney (a member of the Johnstone family who changed his name on his marriage to the immensely wealthy heiress to the earl of Bath) introduced "all the sons of Mr. Malcolm of Burnfoot . . . into the career of prosperity." Sir William was a prominent political figure, an elder of the general assembly of the Church of Scotland and had considerable influence at India House.[6]

Malcolm's relationship with the Elliots of Minto was that of distant cousin; the two families had been joined three generations before John Malcolm met Lord Minto, the governor-general of Bengal from 1807 to 1813. The connection was tenuous but patronage was still so important at the end of the eighteenth century that advantage was taken of very remote relationships. Families were usually aware of distinguished connections, particularly if they could be useful.[7] Malcolm was of the same generation but eighteen years younger than Minto; judged by the standards of Hanoverian Britain, it was natural and acceptable for him to make the best possible use of this connection. The Malcolm family had fallen on hard times and Malcolm's ambition and self-promotion, his relentless lobbying of potential patrons, and his obsession with professional recognition probably owed something to a desire to reestablish the family's status in Scotland as well as to improve his own.

Malcolm arrived in India in 1783 and served his "apprenticeship" as a cadet and ensign in the Madras army for seven years, until his regiment was posted to support the nizam of Hyderabad's force during the Third Anglo-Mysore War (1790–92). He had learned sufficient Persian to act as interpreter to the nizam's troops, and this experience convinced him to pursue a diplomatic career. Health problems sent him to Britain in February 1794, but he returned the following year as secretary to the commander in chief of the Madras army. In 1798 he became assistant to the company's resident at Hyderabad, and towards the end of 1798 accompanied the governor-general, Lord Wellesley, on a voyage from Calcutta to Madras. He returned to Hyderabad early in 1799 in the dual capacity of political officer and infantry commander during the Fourth Anglo-Mysore War. At the war's conclusion in June 1799, he was appointed first secretary to the commission for the settlement of Mysore, with Munro as second secretary. Malcolm's great opportunity came when Wellesley appointed him envoy to Persia, a mission lasting from December 1799 to May 1801. On his return he acted as Lord Wellesley's personal political agent on several Indian missions. But on the outbreak of the Second Maratha War in August 1803, ill health forced him to relinquish to Mountstuart Elphinstone a much-valued appointment as political assistant to General Arthur Wellesley. From December 1803 until June 1806 Malcolm was engaged in negotiations with various Maratha leaders, with a brief hiatus in 1804 when he displeased Lord Wellesley. In 1807 he served briefly as resident at Mysore, an appointment he had received in 1803 but previously consigned to a deputy. He also got married. But Mysore was a career backwater and in 1808 he undertook a largely unsuccessful mission to the Persian Gulf, followed in 1809 by an equally unsuccessful mission to settle a mutiny at Masulipatam, and in 1810 by an unsuccessful mission to Persia. He spent most of 1811 at Bombay, working on his *History of Persia*, and in 1812 returned to Britain where he remained for five years, occasionally consulted by the board of control on Indian army matters. Malcolm returned to India in March 1817 and carried out both political and military duties before and during the Third Maratha War (1817–18), after which he administered a large area of Central India previously under Maratha rule until 1821. At first he had hoped to be appointed governor of either Bombay or Madras; when these prestigious posts went to Elphinstone and Munro, he hoped to be made lieutenant governor of Central India. Disappointed in this as well, however, he lived in Britain from 1822 until 1827, when he returned to India to succeed Elphinstone as governor of Bombay. Malcolm retired to England in 1830 and died there three years later.

Unlike Malcolm, Mountstuart Elphinstone had no need to search for patrons or pursue distant relationships to further his career. As aristocrats who had for centuries played leading roles in the political life of Scotland, the Elphinstones enjoyed high social as well as political status. Born on 6 October 1779, Mountstuart was the fourth and youngest son of the eleventh Lord Elphinstone. Described in later life by Lord Ellenborough as "a quiet, mild, temperate man,"[8] Elphinstone was intelligent, introspective, and moody. He suffered intermittently from depression and physical symptoms that suggest he may have also suffered from migraine-type headaches: severe head pain and "liver complaints." Elphinstone's father, a general officer, was one of sixteen Scottish representative peers in the House of Lords from 1784 until his death in 1794, and the governor of Edinburgh castle during Mountstuart's childhood. Lady Elphinstone was a niece of the third earl of Bute, George III's prime minister (1762–63). One uncle, George Keith Elphinstone, was an admiral who was raised to the peerage as Viscount Keith; another, William Elphinstone, was an influential director of the East India Company.[9]

Admiral Keith and William Elphinstone controlled a patronage network that provided access to careers in the navy and India—and also, on occasion, a formidable Whig opposition to Henry Dundas's Tory domination of Scottish political patronage. The groups in Scottish society who benefited most from such patronage were the well-educated, but often impecunious, middle and higher ranks. Although a relatively high proportion of Scottish applicants for company appointments were from landed gentry or legal families,[10] Mountstuart Elphinstone's social status was higher than most.

According to the historian of the Elphinstone family, William Elphinstone promoted the careers of five of his nephews, in particular Mountstuart, his brother James, and his cousin John Adam, all of whom went to India. They "owed their progress . . . in that service, in greater or lesser degree, to the influence and assistance of their . . . uncle," an opinion borne out by Mountstuart Elphinstone's many expressions of appreciation to both William Elphinstone and Lord Keith for their interest.[11]

Mountstuart had easy access to a coveted civil writership in the Bengal presidency, a better springboard to a successful career than a military cadetship. The Bengal civil service, headed by the Supreme government at Fort William, was more prestigious than those of Madras and Bombay and offered greater opportunities for advancement.

Elphinstone arrived in India in 1796 and was appointed to a junior writership at the company's post at Benares, where he remained until 1801. He then spent two months studying at the recently founded Fort William College before travelling to Pune to serve as assistant to the governor-general's agent at the peshwa's court. In August 1803 he replaced the ailing Malcolm as Arthur Wellesley's political assistant during the Second Maratha War, and at the end of the war obtained the post of resident at the court of the raja of Berar at Nagpur, where he remained until 1808. Elphinstone then requested and obtained the position of envoy to the court of the Afghan prince, Shah Shuja. On his return from this mission he was appointed resident at Pune, where he remained from 1810 until the outbreak of the Third Maratha War in October 1817. During the war, despite his civilian status, he was given authority to direct the conduct of the war within the peshwa's territories. Shortly after the war ended he was appointed governor of Bombay, a position he held from 1819 to 1827. When he retired from the company's service in 1827 he had spent thirty-one years in India without taking any home leave. He died in 1859 after a long and uneventful retirement spent pursuing his scholarly interests in England.

Both Elphinstone and Munro were well educated by all British and all rank contemporary standards when they went to India. Malcolm was not, but he recognized the disadvantages of his relative ignorance and took steps to educate himself. By the mid–eighteenth century, there was almost universal male literacy in Lowland Scotland, although the level of achievement varied from place to place. The original objects of Scottish education were to teach basic English literacy so that all people of all ranks could read the Bible and other morally uplifting literature and to provide a few years of instruction in Latin and Greek for those with the capacity to study for the church or the legal profession. In practice, public education was not available to all. Not all parishes had schools and in those that had, long distances and rough terrain prevented many children from attending. Small fees were charged for instruction in English, Latin, and Greek, and until the late eighteenth-century it was normal for children from all but the very highest ranks to attend the same parish schools, bursaries being provided to enable talented poor children to attend higher educational facilities available only in large towns. Teaching methods were authoritarian and creativity was discouraged. School and university curricula had traditionally reflected the dominant position in Scottish life of the church and, to a lesser degree, the legal profession. By the 1760s and 1770s, however, although Latin and Greek remained important, demand was increasing, particularly in larger towns, for subjects of greater practical utility: mathematics, geography, history, European languages, sciences, and surveying and navigation. This demand reflected the increasingly materialist and cosmopolitan interests of the middle ranks of Scottish society and was fueled by two particular economic incentives. First, the general public wanted a curriculum that would be more relevant to the likely employment of most students. In 1700 the Glasgow presbytery suggested that no one intended for trades should attend the grammar school because studying Latin was "a meer loosing [sic] of so much time, and that of their best time for learning of things that may be more useful for them"—specifically geometry, geography, and history. The second motive for change was low teacher salaries, enforced under the 1696 Education Act. Although teacher's pay became increasingly inadequate as the rate of inflation rose during the eighteenth century, pay raises were refused. Many competent men left teaching for better-paying clerical jobs in the new merchant houses and the East India Company, and it would have been difficult to recruit new teachers at all without Scotland's surplus of relatively well-educated men who lacked the necessary patronage to acquire a church living, legal office, or Indian appointment.[12] To augment their salaries, teachers gave classes in extracurricular subjects outside school hours. The subjects varied from place to place according to demand and the expertise of the teacher. The emphasis, however, was always on utility.

The Munro family placed a high value on education. Thomas attended elementary school, Glasgow Grammar School and, from the age of thirteen to sixteen, Glasgow University, where he studied mathematics and chemistry. Unlike Oxford and Cambridge, which remained largely the preserve of the aristocracy and Anglican clergy, Glasgow University catered to the sons of businessmen and tenant farmers, and was associated with the world of business insofar as professors aided and encouraged industrial inventors while engineers and businessmen provided facts for theoreticians. The late eighteenth century was not, however, an age of specialization; Glasgow students, many of whom founded and attended literary clubs similar to those patronized by Scotland's intellectual elite, were often well read on a wide variety of subjects, while Glasgow businessmen studied the theories as well as the practices of political economy. Munro was working in the accounting office of a Glasgow trading company when Adam Smith's seminal work on political economy, the *Wealth of Nations,* first appeared in 1776. He later recalled that "the Glasgow merchants were as proud of the work as if they had written it themselves; . . . some of them said it was no wonder that Adam Smith had written such a book, as he had had the advantage of their society, in which the same doctrines were circulated with the punch every day."[13]

Although Munro complained in later years of the "cold, lifeless reasoning" which students were forced, prematurely, to engage in at college, he seems to have acquired an excellent education and supplemented it with extensive reading. Soon after his arrival in Madras at the age of eighteen, he was recommended as "a learned man" to a Dr. Koenig, a disciple of Linnaeus who, three years earlier, had been engaged by the East India Company to visit Siam and the Strait of Malacca in search of plants and minerals. They discussed chemistry and Koenig asked Munro to correct the English of his botanical and chemical reports. Munro wrote to his father:

I altered most of the spelling, and . . . the arrangement of the words. He put a Greek book into my hands . . . the book did not give me much disturbance; but he talks Latin, Portuguese, and French,—his English is a mixture of all the three, which makes it very difficult to understand him. When he sees I am at a loss for any particular word, he gives me the Latin; if I still hesitate, he gives me the Greek, which is always an effectual method of making me understand.

Koenig had studied the Chinese method of reducing tin ore in Siam and Munro wrote "all the descriptions which the Doctor sends to Banks,

Solander, and Mr. Greville." He felt, however, that they added nothing to what was already known in Europe. In addition to the working knowledge of Latin, Greek, and chemistry indicated by Munro's description of this encounter, his broad familiarity with English and Scottish literature is evident from numerous allusions in his letters, and from the works he mentions reading or asks to have sent to him.[14]

Munro believed a good education was of value even in the East India Company army. In 1785, he told his father he was afraid his younger brother Alexander's educational shortcomings would inhibit his military career; his writing and spelling were bad and he had paid too little attention to history. Three years earlier, in 1782, he had recommended that if his two youngest brothers were to serve in India they should be proficient in mathematics and drawing. Technical qualifications, he acknowledged, would not in themselves secure appointments requiring technical skills, but a knowledge of both subjects was, nevertheless, "absolutely necessary" for an officer. Malcolm endorsed Munro's view in 1792, lamenting his own inadequacy in "a branch of education which never ought to be neglected in the forming an officer—a complete knowledge of mathematics and drawing."[15]

The Malcolm children attended their local parish school, which probably taught the basic traditional curriculum: reading, writing, and arithmetic for the first four years with Latin added for pupils who stayed on after the age of nine. Malcolm, who went to India at the unusually early age of fourteen, left home when he was twelve with little more than an elementary education. When he began to take his Indian career seriously in the early 1790s, however, he recognized the social and professional disadvantages of his limited schooling and, on his first furlough from India, spent a winter trying to rectify some of its deficiencies by extensive reading and by attending lectures at the University of Edinburgh. Edinburgh and Glasgow Universities permitted greater flexibility as well as providing a slightly broader curriculum than Oxford and Cambridge. The recommended course of study gave equal weight to classics, philosophy, mathematics, and physics. There were no restrictions on entry, and students paid for each class separately. The student body was extremely diverse; it included men in their twenties and thirties who might be making major changes of direction in their careers as well as boys of fourteen from the parish schools.[16]

Elphinstone, like many boys from the Scottish aristocracy, received a classical education from a tutor until he was twelve. He then spent 1791 and 1792 attending both Edinburgh High School and public lectures on moral philosophy at Edinburgh University. At fourteen he moved to London for two more years of schooling at a private academy. Elphinstone's only reference to curriculum states that, on offering him a company writership, his Uncle William told him to "leave off Greek" and concentrate on the more utilitarian skills of writing and arithmetic.[17]

The educated Scotsmen who took advantage of career opportunities in India during the late eighteenth and early nineteenth centuries made themselves useful to the East India Company in many areas requiring some technical knowledge. With the exception of doctors, Scotsmen were not recruited to the company's service for their specialized knowledge. Owing, however, to the relative poverty of the middle and upper ranks in Scottish society and the workings of the patronage system at the time, many of the Scotsmen who served in India came from upper-ranking gentry or professional families and had often attained a relatively higher standard of education than their English counterparts. This was a consideration in the rise to prominence of a number of Scotsmen in the East India Company's service. The ratio of Scotsmen to Englishmen in the company's India service roughly paralleled the ratio between the two peoples in Britain: one to five, but the ratio of Scotsmen to Englishmen holding higher appointments was weighted in favor of Scots. According to British historian John Cannon, four aspects of the education of the British upper classes were particularly helpful in supporting their political supremacy in eighteenth- and early nineteenth-century Britain. First, it prepared them for a leading role in public life. Second, it was increasingly standardized: a classical (largely Latin) curriculum provided a common code of values and a firm belief in the rightness of aristocratic rule. Third, it provided "a network of acquaintances." And, fourth, it gave the upper classes a virtual monopoly on higher education, thus both protecting and giving some justification for their dominant political position.[18] In Scotland, however, a classical education at both the secondary and postsecondary level was available to men of quite humble rank and was by no means the exclusive privilege of the rulers. Although classical learning can have been of little practical value in carrying out civil or military duties in India, it may possibly have been of value in contacts with socially, politically, or militarily higher-ranking officials, insofar as it gave an impression of intelligence, shared values, and similar modes of thought. At the same time, the emphasis on utility in Scottish education provided advantages to civil and military officers whose duties required some technical knowledge: in particular surveying for both military and land revenue assessment purposes, and accounting for those working in any area that involved land or commercial taxation.

Although they were members of different status groups and had greatly differing access to patronage networks, the Munro, Malcolm, and Elphinstone families had a common problem, financial insolvency. Munro's father had intended Thomas for a mercantile career, and on leaving university at sixteen he worked for two years as an accounting clerk for Sommerville and Gordon, a company trading with the West Indies. But this apprenticeship in accounting, which may have been useful experience for his later work in the East India Company's revenue branch, came to a sudden end when the American Revolutionary War brought bankruptcy to his father's firm, leaving the family quite dramatically in poverty.[19] Thomas's father took advantage of his slight acquaintance with Laurence Sulivan, a prominent company director, to obtain a Madras cadetship for Thomas. Despite determined efforts to reestablish himself in business, for many years Mr. and Mrs. Munro, two sisters, and two younger brothers were dependent on the funds Daniel, Thomas, and Alexander, the three eldest sons, could send home from India.

George Malcolm's financial problems, the result of unwise speculations, made it necessary for the older Malcolm boys to find employment somewhat earlier than they might otherwise have done. John's older brother, Pulteney (named, no doubt, to honor the family's patron, Sir William Pulteney), joined the navy at ten under the supervision of his uncle Thomas Pasley. John was only twelve when the Johnstone family successfully sponsored his application for a company cadetship. He left Burnfoot to receive two more years of schooling in London under the guardianship of John Pasley before leaving for Madras in 1783.[20]

William Elphinstone's East India Company connections made an Indian career a probable choice for Mountstuart. Careers in Britain acceptable to the aristocracy generally required an independent income, and Mountstuart's branch of the Elphinstone family, whose estates were encumbered with debt, had four sons to provide for. The two eldest boys obtained appointments in the Crown army and navy. James went to Bengal in the company's commercial service in 1791 and died in 1828 after an unexceptional career. Mountstuart and his cousin John Adam, who rose to high office in the company's secretariat, left together for Bengal in 1795.

There was nothing unusual about impecunious company recruits. Few families in the eighteenth century sent their sons to India if their social and economic position offered a viable British alternative. But the seemingly avaricious obsession with pay, allowances, and the spoils of war expressed in the letters home of many young company recruits, reflected not only the greed and ambition of a would-be fortune hunter, but also the anxieties of a youthful breadwinner for a "clan." When his father was expecting to be sent to a debtors prison in the 1780s, Munro assured him that he would "always endeavour to live on my pay, and remit the batta [field allowance] to you."[21] These allowances, which were often in arrears, were sometimes the only source of income for a destitute family at home. Whether or not an individual was personally ambitious, there was almost invariably strong family pressure to seek advancement.

Even within an organization of merchants, a man whose father was in trade—particularly if, as in Munro's case, he was also bankrupt—was socially inferior to the sons of the clergy and landed gentry. Unlike Malcolm and Elphinstone, Munro had no useful connections in either Britain or India, and he began his career in 1780 at a point in the company's history when there was little opportunity to acquire power, fame, or fortune by merit. He was better educated than his colleagues and, having left Scotland at eighteen (older than the average company recruit) he was not only more mature but had been subjected longer to the socializing processes of late eighteenth-century Scotland. In Madras in 1780, however, social status and connections would have served him better than his superior education and greater maturity. Malcolm's social status, access to patronage, and the fortuitous circumstance of the timing of his arrival in India in 1783 gave him greater advantages than Munro, but he was far from enjoying the opportunities available to Elphinstone. Malcolm was unapologetically ambitious, however, and worked hard to make both the old patronage system and new, more bureaucratic channels to advancement work to his advantage. Elphinstone joined the company service with impeccable social credentials, extensive connections, and fortunate timing—he arrived in India in 1796, shortly before the opportunities for men of ability grew dramatically as a result of the expansionary policies of Lord Wellesley. His family's position was sufficiently influential to have enabled him to rise steadily in the company's service with or without much ability, as long as he avoided disgrace. He discovered, nevertheless, that to attain company appointments which carried the sort of salary that would enable him to return quickly and permanently to Britain, as he desired,[22] extra qualifications were necessary. To rise quickly in the company service it was helpful to have some knowledge of Persian and Indian languages and also some understanding, or at least an ability to convey an impression of an understanding, of how Indian government and society functioned in the part of India in which you were employed or wanted to be employed.

CHAPTER 2

India, 1780–1801
Knowledge and Self-Help

*The "nepotism" of the Court of Directors did not pass beyond the portico of
India House. In India every man had a fair start and an open course. The
son of the Chairman had no better chance than the son of the Scotch farmer
. . . this was the distinguishing merit of the Company's service.*
—Sir John Kaye

Writing in the second half of the nineteenth century, Sir John Kaye
wished to present the East India Company's civil and military service as a meritocracy, but his claim that the son of the chairman had no
better chance of getting ahead than the son of a Scottish farmer was as
much of a myth as the Whig interpretation of the eighteenth-century
British aristocracy as an open elite. Munro's career proves that it was possible for a man with few connections to climb high in the company's service in the early years of the nineteenth century; the contrast between
Munro's frustrating early years and Elphinstone's privileged ones, however,
makes it pointedly clear that there was no "fair start" or "open course."

In the company army, promotion was decided by seniority, not purchase or, supposedly, patronage. Raymond Callahan mentions that for

men who lacked the wealth and interest to become commissioned officers
in the Crown army, the company's forces offered a military career organized under different rules.[1] This is certainly true. But even in the company
army a connection with the colonel, or, better still, with the commander
in chief, was likely to provide easier access to positions that paid well or
offered the greatest opportunities for making money on the side. In the
civilian service promotion was also made by seniority, up to a point; a political resident was generally succeeded by his senior secretary.[2] The right
connections in Britain were expected to provide an advantageous initial
posting for both military and civil recruits, but contacts in India were
equally, if less openly, important to further advancement. Although in
theory the members of India House had no say in the progress of their
protégés once they left Britain, a casual word from an influential director
to a newly appointed governor-general, governor, or commander in chief,
indicating an interest in the progress of a particular young man was unlikely to fall on deaf ears. Those without influential patrons could either
resign themselves to a lackluster career or seek ways to beat the system. As
the eighteenth century drew to a close and the company found itself governing more and more territory, ambitious, intelligent, and able men like
Munro, Malcolm, and Elphinstone discovered that a demonstration of
Indian expertise in a well-written book or report was an increasingly valuable passport to promotion.

Munro left Britain for India at the age of eighteen, shortly before
Elphinstone was born, and arrived in Madras in January 1780. But lacking
influential connections in the patronage-dominated, corrupt, and in-
efficient Madras government, his early career progressed slowly. He faced
poverty and loneliness with fortitude, but clearly disliked the patronage
system, probably on principle as well as from frustration, and insisted
that his brother Alexander would be better working for a Glasgow
merchant than seeking his fortune with the company: "a merchant is his
own master, he has not to comply with all the humours of men whom
he despises." He advised his youngest brother, William, to go to Bengal rather than Madras because there he would have more opportunity
"to exert his own industry."[3] Like his younger compatriot Samuel Smiles,
influential author of the best-selling book *Self-Help*, Munro believed

in self-help, but at Madras in the 1780s there was little scope for enterprise.

Between 1780 and 1799 Munro studied Persian and the local languages necessary to communicate with the sepoys of the regiments he served, and gained military experience in the company's three wars against Mysore. Having, in his own words, "mastered" Hindustani without dictionary or grammar from a teacher who spoke no word of English, he was confident of his linguistic ability and claimed that with leisure and a good dictionary, he could read "any book in any language in the course of six months." Hindustani was to become what Bernard Cohn describes as "the language of command in India,"[4] an increasingly valuable accomplishment for a company official. In 1785 Munro transferred to a regiment serving in Tanjore for the express purpose of studying Persian with a missionary there, a Dr. Swartz, who was a renowned linguist. A year earlier he had encouraged William to learn Persian and serve in Bengal because the Bengal government's relations with Muslim states provided excellent job opportunities for Persian-speaking officials.[5]

Munro was right about the value of learning Indian languages. From 1788 to 1799 he served under Captain Alexander Read, with whom his name as an administrator is closely linked. Initially Read and Munro were engaged in intelligence and supply duties, which required some fluency in local languages. In 1792 Read was given charge of the revenue settlement of the Baramahal region, ceded to Madras that year by Tipu Sultan of Mysore, and Munro went with him. The governor-general, Earl Cornwallis, told the court of directors that he would select "the most capable and trustworthy of your servants to manage the newly-acquired territories" and this meant, in addition to other considerations, men capable of speaking the local languages.[6] Believing no civilian official in the Madras presidency possessed this essential qualification, Read, Munro, and two other Scottish soldiers were given the task on which Read and Munro were to work together for seven years, and which provided the springboard for Munro's later eminence.

In the 1960s T. H. Beaglehole raised the question of how much of the credit for the revenue practices later known as "ryotwari" or the "Munro system" should be shared with Read, and in the 1990s new interest in what

Eugene F. Irschick terms the "dialogic processes" between British officials
and knowledgeable local Indians has raised again the question of how
much of the Munro system should be regarded as simply following local
ideas and practices, as explained to Munro by Indians.[7] As commanding
officer, Read had ultimate control of policy, but he consulted his subordinates and they did not hesitate to express their views quite frankly; by
means of a debate carried on largely by correspondence, Read and Munro
in particular built the foundations on which Munro constructed the system of revenue and judicial administration for which Elphinstone coined
the term, the "Munro system."[8] In regard to Indian input, Read and
Munro, for obvious practical reasons, relied on local cultivators and notables as well as local records for information on existing practices. The oral
information, the Indian "voices," which would have included justifications
and opinions as well as mere description, were probably the more influential source. Both Read and Munro, however, seem to have been genuinely
interested in current Western views on agricultural improvement, a subject
receiving much attention at the time in Scotland for the simple reason
that Scottish agricultural production was much in need of improvement.
It will be argued here that although revenue assessment and collection
practices continued to owe much to Indian ideas and experience, the recommendations Munro made to bring change for the better—not only in
terms of more resources for the company's government but also in terms
of more and more widely distributed profits for the local cultivator community—were based on contemporary Scottish ideas about progressive
agriculture.[9] Irschick mentions that in 1855, the Madras Native Association claimed that a tax settlement based on the whole village rather than
on the individual cultivator, as introduced under the ryotwari system, was
"consonant to native usage," implying that Read and Munro's system was,
to some extent at least, innovative.[10]

As the number of English-speaking Indians in rural southern India in
the late eighteenth century was negligible, "dialogue" of any sort required
British officials to have a working knowledge of the relevant vernacular
languages. Munro told his father that Read's "intimate knowledge of the
language and manners of the people . . . eminently qualified him" for revenue work. He also described Read's investigation of the revenue system

in the Baramahal as more detailed, accurate, and original than any other made by a European, but observed as well that the information was so badly arranged that the members of the revenue board would understand less than half of it. James Dykes, a later Madras administrator, endorsed Munro's judgment, writing that Read "sadly wanted that perspicuity of style which was so essential for an office that he held otherwise so worthily," but Dykes believed Read's "reasoning powers [to be] as strong and clear as his writings are weak and obscure." Munro also respected Read's enthusiasm for figures, but criticized his calculations.[11] The very fact that Read was having to make calculations and work with complex accounting processes, however, makes it reasonable to assume that a knowledge of mathematics as well as languages was useful to those employed on revenue business.

Munro, having "never met with a person . . . who knew more than a few common rules," believed mathematical skills to be rare among company officials in India.[12] His own above-average knowledge of mathematics derived from his Scottish education and this seems to have been quite typical. The records of the *Survey of India* prior to 1800 indicate that 29 percent of the men employed as surveyors were Scottish and 49 percent English but, of the fifty men whose contribution was sufficiently important to warrant more than a column of biographical information, 38 percent were Scottish and only 40 percent English. As the proportion of Scots to English in the company's military and civil service in the late eighteenth century is estimated to have paralleled the ratio between the population of the two countries: one to five, a disproportionate number of Scotsmen were employed on tasks requiring technical knowledge. It has been calculated, also, that whereas only one out of nine Scots was a civil servant and only one out of eleven served in the rank and file of the army, one in three company army officers were Scottish. It is well known that many valuable and prestigious political and administrative appointments went to soldiers at this time. That soldiers were more likely than civilians to learn Indian languages (in order to communicate with sepoys) was, no doubt, one reason; the advantage of having men accustomed to command in positions of authority was another. David Kopf, however, states that many of Fort William College's students, *"especially those from*

Scotland" (my italics), had sufficient formal education to enable them to organize data, to formulate policies on the basis of written reports, and to prepare memoranda. This seems to suggest that Scotsmen serving in India had generally received a better education than their English counterparts, and that there may be a connection between the large number of Scotsmen who obtained diplomatic and administrative appointments and the increasing need for relatively well-educated officials during the twenty years before the opening of Fort William College at Calcutta in 1801 and Haileybury College in England in 1806.[13]

Although their knowledge of mathematics played no part in the selection of Read and Munro for service in the company's revenue branch, it did help them do their job more effectively, thus enhancing their reputations. Nor was an ability to write well a prerequisite for government appointments, but concise and grammatical reports and recommendations were more likely to attract favorable attention than badly constructed, badly spelled ones. Read went on leave after the Fourth Mysore War and died in Europe in 1803, so there is no way of knowing whether his poor writing skills would have hampered further advancement. Munro's competence as a writer, however, and his ability to provide a theoretical framework for his recommendations helped him to present his ideas in a form that would promote his career as well as influence company policy. The government of Madras told the Home government in an official letter in 1814 that "every writing of Colonel Munro's is entitled to attention."[14]

Throughout his early years in India Munro supplied Scottish correspondents with acute, articulate, and sometimes scathing accounts of the military affairs of Madras. H. H. Wilson, in his annotations to James Mill's *History of British India,* regarded Munro's accounts of the company's conflict with Haidar Ali of Mysore as the most accurate available. Munro also produced well-informed analyses of the structure and potential strength of the Indian states. In an attempt to promote his son's career, Munro's father arranged for abstracts of these letters to be passed by Andrew Stuart, a close friend of Adam Smith and a prominent Scottish lawyer and member of Parliament, to politicians in London interested in the company's affairs—in particular, to Henry Dundas from 1781, to Edmund Burke in 1784, and to William Elphinstone in the 1790s. Burke observed that a paper of Munro's, given him while he was rector of Glasgow University by a Professor Richardson, "is indeed full of ability."[15]

In 1795 Munro himself made a deliberate effort to use Indian information to advance his career. His brother Alexander, who had left the Bengal army to work in the indigo business, had access to intelligence on Rajputana and on French officers serving in the armies of some Indian states. Thomas, no doubt aware of the company's need for better military intelligence,[16] requested him to discover details which he, Thomas, could pass on to the governor of Madras, Viscount Hobart. By impressing the authorities with his military knowledge he hoped to obtain a transfer back to the army from his revenue duties,[17] but his attempt at self-promotion was unsuccessful and he remained in the Baramahal until the next and final war with Mysore.

It was during his Baramahal years that Munro first met John Malcolm. In a letter to his father in 1796 Munro mentions that he has recently met a Lieutenant Malcolm, who "tells me that you were one of the last persons he saw at home—and that he had a long Crack (as he calls it) with you about Tipu." One of Malcolm's sisters seems to have been acquainted with Munro's sister Erskine, whom Malcolm mentions seeing while on leave in Scotland in 1794 and 1795, but it is not clear how Malcolm came to meet Munro's father. Two years later Munro, passing on news to Erskine of several of her friends who were serving in India, told her that Malcolm "is now a very regular correspondent of mine."[18] The two men seem to have had Scottish acquaintances in common who provided a loose link between them.

Malcolm arrived in India for the first time in April 1783 and, like many cadets and ensigns, spent his early years in India irresponsibly (Munro was an exception). By 1788, however, he had matured a little and, shamed perhaps by the contributions made to the family's finances by his older brother Robert, who was employed in the company's commercial branch, and by the rapid advancement of Pulteney, who had been promoted a naval lieutenant at the age of fifteen, he wrote a contrite letter home, paid off his debts and began to take his career seriously. His first military action came during the Third Mysore War (1790–92) when he served with the troops attached to the army of the company's ally, the nizam of Hyderabad. But, impressed by the prestige and salaries enjoyed by the company's diplomatic representatives at the nizam's court, Sir John Kennaway and Graeme Mercer, he decided at this time to work toward a diplomatic career himself. Mercer pointed out the value of learning Persian and Indian languages; Kennaway probably helped him gain an appointment in 1792 as Persian translator to the military detachment serving with the nizam, which he held for nearly two years. It was during this period that Malcolm began his study of Indian history, recording his research and thoughts on the nature of Indian society and politics in a collection of manuscript books which unfortunately have been lost.[19]

This career-oriented program of study was curtailed in 1794 by an illness serious enough to drive Malcolm to Britain to recuperate. He recovered on the voyage, however, and spent his ten-month stay trying to improve both his career prospects and his education. His visit coincided with a well-publicized debate on new regulations for the company's army and, after a brief visit to Scotland, Malcolm went to London to take part in it. In a thoughtfully written letter to the *North Briton,* he presented forceful arguments for the resolution of three major grievances: the regulation that no company officer could rise higher than the rank of colonel; the chronic stagnation of promotion; and the lack of provisions for leave and retirement. These issues contributed to "the extreme state of depression" prevalent in the company's forces. A system that offered neither recognition nor reward for services rendered was oppressive, Malcolm believed, and the company army would never be really effective until incentives were provided for good service. Throughout his career Malcolm suggested and promoted reforms that would provide recognition and rewards, regarding them as the psychological basis for loyal, efficient service. His concern consistently extended to Indian as well as to British company officials on the ground that human nature everywhere responded to the same incentives. His arguments often suggest self-interest or at least corporate interest, but they reflected contemporary ideas about human nature which held that insecurity and oppression crippled mankind's natural propensity for self-betterment. Malcolm stated firmly that the knowledge of Indian customs and languages possessed by company officers—their local expertise—gave them "innumerable advantages over a general immediately appointed from home"; and he argued that anyone who had demonstrated his ability should be eligible to become commander in chief at any of the three presidencies.[20]

Malcolm's critique of the company's organization was constrained by the patronage system. He concluded his letters with flattering allusions to the individual and collective wisdom of the court of directors, Dundas, and Cornwallis (ex-governor-general and Indian elder statesman), who would have the last word on any reforms and who could influence Malcolm's career prospects. These papers represent Malcolm's first, apparently successful, experiment in promoting himself as an expert on British India through writings: he returned to India in 1796 as secretary to Sir Alured Clarke, the newly appointed commander in chief at Madras.

Before returning to India, however, Malcolm spent the unusually harsh winter of 1794–95 in Edinburgh, attending public university lectures and reading widely in an effort to remedy some of the defects in his education. Impressed by the erudition of Edinburgh's intellectuals and the opportunities and incentives the city offered to would-be scholars, he told his brother Gilbert, a student at Cambridge: "as there is no place in the world where such encouragement is given to literary men [as Edinburgh], so I believe there are nowhere to be found men of more deep learning and science. Learning is a plant cultivated in proportion to demand." Malcolm makes it clear that he has studied Persian and Indian languages "more with the hope of their being useful than entertaining," and his "demand" for learning seems to stem from a perception of the utility to his career of a knowledge of history and an understanding of systems of political and social organization, rather than from intellectual curiosity.[21]

While in Edinburgh Malcolm was directly exposed to the ideas of the Calvinist Moderates on religion and history when he was introduced to Hugh Blair, and he made frequent visits to the home of the popular minister until they were curtailed by the sudden death of Blair's wife. He read Thomas Reid's philosophy and a great deal of history and returned to India with a copy of the *Wealth of Nations*, which he mentions reading when back in Madras in 1797.[22] The intellectual life of late eighteenth-century Edinburgh would have been stimulating for anyone interested, for either personal or professional reasons, in the history of different societies and forms of government.

As Malcolm arrived for the second time at Madras in early 1796,

Mountstuart Elphinstone arrived for the first time at Calcutta, his initial reception in India contrasting dramatically with that of Malcolm and Munro. Malcolm, who had his brother Robert to meet him but no other advantages, had been quickly consigned to garrison duties. Munro had been merely one of the eighty-three new cadets to begin their careers at Madras in January 1780, almost all of whom were Scotsmen "particularly recommended to the care of the general." Munro complained, dryly, that the general had an inconceivable number of "nephews, cousin-germans, etc.,"[23] but as he was not one of them, he, too, started his career with tedious years of garrison duty. Elphinstone, on the other hand, put in at Madras on his way to Calcutta and was "hospitably entertained" by the governor, Lord Hobart. Lord Keith, recently commander in chief of an important expedition against the Dutch at the Cape of Good Hope, was also at Madras in January 1796 and, on his arrival in Calcutta a month later, Elphinstone wrote home to say that as a result of his Uncle Keith's references, the governor-general, Sir John Shore, and the commander in chief, India, Sir Robert Abercrombie, had "both . . . been very attentive." Shore "was so good as to appoint" Elphinstone as assistant to the registrar at the residency at Benares in the Indian state of Awadh, so that he could be with his older brother James, who was serving at Benares in the company's commercial branch. Elphinstone's first four years in India were spent for the most part enjoying a placid routine of whist, billiards, shooting, studies, and a little business. Like Malcolm he accumulated debts but he tended to be careless of money and, unlike Malcolm, did not escape from them until 1816.[24]

Elphinstone soon became aware that a knowledge of Asian languages would be necessary to obtain the well-paying appointments in the political service to which he aspired, and he began to study Persian. He also embarked upon a program of intellectual self-improvement that he was to follow throughout his life. Elphinstone's devotion to literature rarely fails to elicit a tribute to his intellectual acumen from admiring historians, and the volume of material he read is certainly impressive. The static nature of his job allowed him to accumulate a library and left him with a great deal of time on his hands that men like Malcolm and Munro, whose duties kept them continuously on the move, rarely enjoyed. His studies and recreational reading, however, were almost certainly, in part, a form of escape from an uncongenial way of life. They provided an alternative to daydreaming. In a journal entry from 1812, Elphinstone wrote of "the visionary life I lead, spending nearly as much time in an ideal world of my own creating as in actual life." He added, gloomily, that he was "better entertained where I have everything my own way than in the disappointments and flatness of real intercourse with the world." Although he enjoyed the challenge of his job during periods of crisis, Elphinstone preferred reading, daydreaming, and hunting to the routine duties of a residency official.[25]

In his early years in the civilian service, Elphinstone was often bored but almost always safe and comfortable. Life in the military service in peacetime was often equally boring but, for a cadet, it was rarely comfortable and could be dangerous. Nine years after leaving home Munro told his sister that he had never experienced hunger, thirst, fatigue, or poverty until he came to India; since then, he was often hungry, thirsty, and exhausted, while poverty was his "constant companion." He had neither pillow nor blanket for the first three years, and his "only conveyance" when traveling was a horse, so old and frail he felt obliged to walk two-thirds of every journey. Munro was nineteen at the beginning of the Second Mysore War and twenty-one at its end. He wrote of daily marches of as much as thirty-six miles "without refreshment," with the men eating only what could be found and resting without shelter because the army failed to organize supplies. And he spoke of the frustration of rapidly aging officers, their health broken by privation and their morale destroyed by the dreary prospect of waiting sixteen or seventeen years for a promotion that, without the necessary patronage to obtain a command, would still provide only a subsistence income.[26]

In contrast Elphinstone, at the age of twenty-one, was traveling from Calcutta in the comfort of a palanquin to take up a diplomatic appointment at Pune. This journey occupied ten months of 1801; his party chose a circuitous route which took them to Madras, where Elphinstone was entertained by another governor, Lord Clive, and to Seringapatam, where he stayed with Colonel Arthur Wellesley, later the duke of Wellington and the younger brother of the governor-general, Marquis Wellesley, who was commanding the subsidiary force in Mysore. There were frequent diversions along the way to visit temples, caves, and famous sites. Elphinstone had been in India for seven years when he mentions what is apparently his first experience—at the battle of Assaye—of sleeping on the ground.[27] Munro was still in poverty after nine years in India; Elphinstone, during his ninth year, became resident at the court of the raja of Berar. Despite Kaye's claims that equal opportunity was the distinguishing merit of the company service, Malcolm and Munro did not experience the same "fair start and open course" for their careers as Elphinstone.

Munro was under constant pressure to advance his career for his family's sake, but his own ambitions are difficult to gauge. He wanted a successful military career and he allowed his father to advertise his knowledge of political and military strategy while he himself attempted to make it known by sending military intelligence to Lord Hobart. While employed in the army in 1790 he explained to his mother that, despite his conviction that it was still possible to make a quick fortune in trade, he would not leave the army to join his older brother, Daniel, in business because "I have too much obstinacy to quit the profession which I have chosen . . . and too much absurd ambition to prefer a certain but moderate rank in the world to a high station however visionary and remote the hopes of attaining it may be." But six years later, when employed on revenue business, he told his brother Alexander that "the ambition which you suspect me of possessing will not detain me in India, for as there is no chance of gratifying it, it will have as much share as anything else in carrying me home."[28] From his writings it is clear that, like Malcolm, he regarded adequate remuneration and public recognition as essential incentives for efficient government service, and he believed that his own efforts on the company's behalf warranted both. Ironically, it was public recognition of his ability as a revenue official and his views on administration, as presented in his official letters, which pointed his career in a nonmilitary direction for which he had no ambition at all.

Malcolm was openly ambitious and after his first few years at Madras, pursued advancement by whatever means he could find. Although he complained of the frustrations of the patronage system he worked indefatigably to manipulate it to suit his own interests and those of his friends, both as a client and, later, as a patron. While governor of Bombay, however, he told his nephew that he would not "do a job" for him.

This statement may or may not be sincere, but letters from Malcolm to his son and to different nephews indicate that he expected efficient service from his clients.[29] Malcolm shared Munro's convictions about the psychological and practical importance of remuneration and recognition; public recognition of his service to the empire in India became, indeed, something of an obsession.

Elphinstone admired heroic figures and, at least in his early years, was ambitious for renown. Later he claimed that he had been cured of ambition by a difficult and ultimately disappointing mission to Peshawar in 1808, which led to the writing of his *Account of the Kingdom of Caubul.* Writing in 1811, shortly after being appointed resident at Pune, Elphinstone complained of homesickness and of his dislike of India, but hastened to add that he was grateful, nevertheless, to his uncle William for placing him in a situation where it was within his own reach to make "a certain and ample fortune." He often thanked both William Elphinstone and Lord Keith for their efforts on his behalf although he rarely canvassed their interest—perhaps because he did not need to. As a patron, having "to mingle in the filthy fray" was one of the many disadvantages he saw in being a presidency governor and he was glad that his residency appointments did not involve "being obliged to promote the undeserving, to pass over the good, and to displease the presumptuous," remarks which sound priggish coming from so well-connected a man. Although Elphinstone hoped to rise quickly in the company's service, his main ambitions, as he described them to Lord Keith shortly before his appointment as governor of Bombay, had been "for a long time . . . to get home rich, and recover, or help recover, our family interest in Scotland."[30] Neither ambition was fulfilled.

Although Munro, Malcolm, and Elphinstone came from very different social backgrounds and their early experiences in India, reflecting the status of their families, were dissimilar, they did have two things in common. They all achieved high office in India and they attained it, in part at least, by discovering the same remedy for frustrated ambition: knowledge. Many East India Company servants were ignorant of Indians and India and made little attempt to gain sufficient fluency in Indian languages to enable them to rectify their ignorance. Munro, Malcolm, Elphinstone, and a few of their more energetic and ambitious contemporaries, however, recognized that knowledge could, in fact, be translated into remunerative and influential appointments—into power. From the 1770s, under the auspices of Warren Hastings, the company actively began to seek information: general information on Indian society and culture as well as political and military intelligence, without which, in Bayly's view, "the British could never have established their rule in India or consolidated the dominant international position of the United Kingdom."[31] Lord Wellesley's arrival in 1798 opened new opportunities for advancement for knowledgeable and enterprising men, which Munro, Malcolm, and Elphinstone were qualified to seize. Munro was an experienced soldier who had acquired useful experience in intelligence. He was a competent linguist; a skill to which his growing reputation as a revenue official owed much, and his perceptive analyses of the Maratha confederacy and Mysore state had been seen by men with influence. Malcolm had acquired a working knowledge of Persian; he had anticipated the government's need for men with a knowledge of the history and structure of the Indian states and prepared himself to meet it. The type of history Malcolm read during and after his self-imposed course of study in Edinburgh provided a framework of concepts as applicable to the study of Asian society and government as to European. By making himself an authority on Maratha affairs as well as on those of Hyderabad, Malcolm, as K. M. Pannikar points out, made himself indispensable in 1803, when the Second Maratha War broke out.[32] Elphinstone had recognized since his days at Benares that to have any chance to make money and achieve renown in the civil service he needed some specialized skills. After obtaining his appointment as an assistant at the residency at Pune in 1801, he complained of insufficient time to read Homer and Virgil because "my debts and my duty compel me to learn Persian and Hindi."[33] Language skills were indispensable to a career in the political service. A knowledge of Persian, as Munro, Malcolm, and Elphinstone all discovered, was as necessary for ambitious company servants in the late eighteenth and early nineteenth centuries as it had been for Hindu officials under Mughal rule.

CHAPTER 3

India, 1798–1812

Knowledge Rewarded

*Favour effects less in this country, and competency more,
than in any other scene of equal magnitude. There is an
interminable field for individual exertion.*

—John Malcolm

"*Individual exertion*" in pursuit of career advancement had been encouraged by Warren Hastings, governor-general of India from 1773 to 1785, who made appointments in Bengal on the grounds of qualification as well as interest—a disproportionate number of them to educated Scotsmen.[1] He also provided financial inducements to company employees to learn Indian languages and encouraged the study of Indian culture. Lord Cornwallis (1786–93), in imposing the new standards of efficiency and integrity required under the India Act (1784), gave more opportunities to men with specialized knowledge, and promoted the study of Persian and Indian vernacular languages by giving civil writers an allowance to hire an Indian tutor.[2] But it was Lord Wellesley (1798–1805) who expected his military and civilian staff to acquire, maintain, and justify an Indian empire, who gave the greatest impetus to the professionalization of the company service.

The Wellesleys became a great aristocratic family in the nineteenth
century, but when Richard, Arthur, and Henry Wellesley went to India in
the last years of the eighteenth century—as the governor-general of India,
a colonel in the Crown army, and the governor-general's private secretary
respectively—they had much in common with Munro, Malcolm, Elphinstone, and many other young men who were dissatisfied with their own
and their family's wealth and status and hoped to use service in India to
improve them.[3] The Wellesleys, of course, were well above the Munros
and Malcolms in the British hierarchy, but an Elphinstone might regard
them, justifiably, as beneath him.

Lord Wellesley came to India determined to provide a stage on which
he and his brothers could make their reputations. The Wellesleys were to
be empire builders, and the contemporary European context—the wars
with revolutionary France—provided their opportunity. French influence
was to be both exaggerated and eliminated and British influence expanded
to the point at which the company would dominate the political life of
India. In pursuing this objective Wellesley enlarged the company's territory and, in association, the number and importance of military, diplomatic, and administrative appointments available to company employees. But
the obligations in regard to the new appointments were not entirely one-
sided. Wellesley knew more about the Roman empire than about Indian
states. He knew, no doubt, that Hannibal had taken elephants across the
Alps but required someone with better local knowledge to tell him that a
military campaign against Mysore in the monsoon season was less feasi-
ble.[4] Similarly, while a classical education was an admirable preparation
for a European diplomatic career, negotiations with Indian rulers were
more effective when conducted by Persian-speaking British officials than
by Indian intermediaries acting as interpreters. Investigations of local land
tenure practices and the extraction of Indian resources for the purposes of
the company state were also facilitated by a collector's ability to communicate directly with landholders and cultivators and to keep accurate accounts.

Wellesley, who believed most company employees were inadequately
educated to administer an extensive empire, founded a college at Calcutta
that officials from all three presidencies could attend. The curriculum at

Fort William College included "useful" subjects: the laws, languages, and history of India and the new laws enacted by Britain's governors-general-in-council. It also included subjects deemed necessary by Wellesley to the general education of imperial officials: jurisprudence, political economy, classical and modern European languages, European history, and natural philosophy. Although the college, a casualty of the governor-general's power struggle with the court of directors, became merely a school of languages for Bengal after the foundation of the East India Company's Haileybury College in Hertfordshire in 1806, Wellesley's initiative represented a trend that helped men like Munro, Malcolm, and Elphinstone build successful careers in India.

The most significant feature of the government's new concern with Indian culture was the linking of monetary rewards and privileged access to future elite appointments to the mastery of Indian languages, customs, and laws. Wellesley declared that from 1 January 1800, no civilian official would be "nominated to offices of trust and responsibility until it should be ascertained that he was sufficiently acquainted with the laws and regulations . . . and the several languages, the knowledge of which is required for the due discharge of the respective function of such offices."[5] Wellesley, however, could not afford to wait for the charter students of his college to graduate; he had to make do at first with men who, from ambition, intellectual curiosity, or boredom, were already proficient in Indian languages and knowledgeable about India. Most of the men who attained high office in the company's service during Wellesley's regime were accomplished linguists; some were also scholars or at least wrote books or papers on subjects of use to the government. Barry Close, Henry Colebrooke, Samuel Davis, Richard Jenkins, William Kirkpatrick, Charles Metcalfe, and Mark Wilks, as well as Malcolm and Elphinstone, were among the competent linguists who combined scholarly research and authorship with their official duties. Munro, who did not write books, was a good linguist who studied and wrote many reports on South Indian affairs.

From 1797 Munro corresponded regularly with Malcolm, who after his furlough in Britain to recover his health and improve his education was employed as secretary to the commander in chief at Madras, Lieutenant-

General James Harris.[6] Munro, however, was only one of many men with whom Malcolm corresponded on the closely related subjects of Indian politics and his career. Although Malcolm believed Harris, Lord Hobart, and Sir Alured Clarke, now commander in chief, India, paid a "friendly attention" to his interests, he also requested Sir John Kennaway, now in Britain, to lose no opportunity of mentioning him to important officials coming out to India, and offered to provide them with "much arranged information" on India—an exchange of information for patronage. Several memoranda he submitted to the Madras government received "flattering notice," encouraging him to persevere with his research and writing on Indian matters.[7] When Lord Wellesley put in at Madras on his way to Calcutta in April 1798, Malcolm showered him with information on the Indian states and was rewarded with the diplomatic appointment he had long coveted. He was appointed assistant to the resident at Hyderabad, Captain James Kirkpatrick.

In making the appointment, Wellesley told Malcolm he had been governed by his knowledge of "the zeal, activity, and diligence" with which Malcolm had pursued "the study of the native languages, and . . . the political system of India." Wellesley sent two of Malcolm's papers—on the state of Tipu Sultan's army and resources, and on his general view of the British position in India—to Henry Dundas at the board of control, observing that "the latter is curious, as Captain Malcolm had not seen any of my letters or minutes on the same subject, . . . I had no knowledge of Captain Malcolm, nor was he recommended to me before I met him at Fort St. George. He is a very promising young man."[8] Wellesley was surprised by the similarity between his own and Malcolm's views on British India, but it is unlikely that the similarity was coincidental. Malcolm, intent on promoting his career, was prepared to go to considerable lengths to obtain inside information as well as expert knowledge.

At Hyderabad, Malcolm assisted Kirkpatrick in a successful and bloodless dissolution of the nizam's French-commanded regiments. Summoned to Calcutta by the governor-general, he took with him the French colors; when welcomed into Government House circles, he hastened to demonstrate again that his ideas on the political future of India matched Wellesley's. Late in 1798 Malcolm accompanied the governor-general to

Madras, but when negotiations between Wellesley and Tipu Sultan broke down (as Wellesley probably intended them to do) and war became imminent, Malcolm returned to Hyderabad with instructions to accompany the nizam's auxiliary force to Mysore and to report on its organization, discipline, and morale. This broadly defined commission was the first of many appointments Malcolm was to receive from Wellesley and, later, from the marquis of Hastings to act as the governor-general's confidential political agent. Arthur Wellesley, who had sailed to India in 1795 in a ship captained by Pulteney Malcolm, commanded the King's 33rd Regiment which had been selected to serve with the Hyderabad force, and Malcolm and Arthur began what was to become Malcolm's most important and useful lifelong friendship.[9]

The Fourth Mysore War lasted three months, ending with the death of Tipu Sultan on 4 May 1799 during the siege of Seringapatam. Tipu's Mysore was not, as it was long depicted, "a decaying eastern despotism," but rather, as Bayly points out, an attempt by an Indian ruler to use European "weapons"—state monopoly of power and an aggressive ideology of expansion—to contend with European power. Tipu failed largely because Britain's access to Indian resources was expanding more rapidly than his own.[10] Munro, who had been happy to return to army duty for the duration of the war, had the critical but rarely rewarded task of obtaining and distributing these crucial Indian resources.

General Harris, Colonel William Kirkpatrick (military secretary to the governor-general), Colonel Barry Close (adjutant general at Madras), and Arthur and Henry Wellesley were appointed commissioners for the postwar settlement of Mysore. With the possible exception of Close, all were to some extent Malcolm's patrons and he was made first secretary to the commission. Munro was appointed second secretary. His settlement work had attracted favorable notice from Arthur Wellesley, who observed that it was "a well-known fact" that in all British India there was no region in which British authority had been so effectively established or in which "the country itself, its people, the amount, and the sources of its revenue, are so well known as in the Baramahal."[11] Malcolm, who described Munro as an "uncommon clever" man, may also have recommended him to the governor-general.[12]

As the work of the Mysore Commission drew to a close, Munro wrote to his sister Erskine describing an evening he had spent with Malcolm discussing her poetry and listening to Malcolm read poems of his own—disappointingly expressing no opinion on the merits of either. He told her, however, that Malcolm had gained much credit with the authorities for his excellent management of the nizam's troops during the war and from "making them instead of an incumbrance a most serviceable body of auxiliaries."[13] "The very conspicuous part" Malcolm had played in the war was officially recognized by General Harris and unofficially by Arthur Wellesley, who described Malcolm's efforts to discipline and train the nizam's troops as "indefatigable, . . . [he] leads the life of a canister at a dog's tail."[14] Owing in part at least to these plaudits, Malcolm did not return to Hyderabad after the war but went instead to Persia as Lord Wellesley's special envoy.

Malcolm's first mission to Persia in 1800–1801 was undoubtedly the most significant appointment of his career; though thirty one-years old, he was still a relatively junior captain. The mission was part of Wellesley's policy to extend British influence in India. He wanted to use a problematic threat of an Afghan invasion, led by Zeman Shah, to frighten the ruler of Awadh into greater dependence on Britain, and decided to give the threat more significance than it warranted by sending Malcolm to Tehran to persuade the shah to mount a diversionary attack on Afghanistan from the west. No one else took the Afghan threat very seriously, but Napoleon's invasion of Egypt in 1798, and the fear that it might lead to an overland expedition to India, provided Wellesley with extra justification for Malcolm's mission.

In Tehran in November 1801, Malcolm negotiated a defensive alliance against France and a commercial treaty which Wellesley hoped would help screen the political objectives of the mission from the attention of the directors. Neither the directors nor Henry Dundas were pleased with the slight achievements and enormous expense of the embassy, but Wellesley claimed that Malcolm's negotiations ensured "Future advantages of considerable importance, both to the political and commercial interests of the British government."[15] From Malcolm's point of view, the immediate importance of the mission lay in its publicization of his name in British political and diplomatic circles. Henry Wellesley, back in India after a brief visit to London, informed Malcolm that the Prince of Wales would be delighted to receive him whenever he should return to England;[16] a gratifying indication that he was rising in the world. In the longer term, the opportunity the mission provided for obtaining information about Persia proved equally useful.

Back in India in May 1801 Malcolm continued to work directly for the governor-general, first as Wellesley's temporary private secretary, then as his confidential representative on a sensitive mission to Madras, and then as his representative at Bombay where the shah of Persia's envoy had been murdered. Malcolm appeased the shah with conciliatory letters and an indemnity that delighted the parsimonious Persian ruler but disgusted the equally parsimonious company directorate. He then accepted an appointment as resident of Mysore, but rightly considering the post as a professional backwater, he installed a deputy in his place and in March 1803 joined Arthur Wellesley's army to serve again as the governor-general's agent.

While Malcolm moved rapidly from one important diplomatic assignment to another, Munro moved slowly from one village to another, pacifying unruly local lords and attempting to conciliate cultivators with reasonable land revenue assessments. Although the careers of the two men diverged after their work together on the Mysore Commission, they kept in touch and Munro credited Malcolm with influencing Lord Wellesley's offer, made in June 1799, of an appointment to organize the civil administration of Kanara, a region previously ruled by Tipu Sultan, which Wellesley intended to annex to the company's territories. Munro appreciated Malcolm's good intentions but initially refused the position. Read had retired and Munro hoped to be put in charge of the Baramahal; "no advantages could ever compensate for the loss of old friends and of a country [the Baramahal] to which I was much attached." A short experience of Kanara's rainfall confirmed this view, but Malcolm, unrepentant, told him that the appointment was Munro's own fault for recommending himself "to men who continue to cherish ridiculous ideas about the good of the state."[17]

In a characteristically frank and uneffusive letter Munro thanked

Wellesley "for having twice pointed me out as a person that might be usefully employed," and observed that as Wellesley had probably heard of his
reluctance to accept the Kanaran appointment, he would explain his reasons. He would have preferred to remain on the Coromandel Coast where
he had worked for nearly twenty years. Having lived in tents for most of
the last nine years, he feared the hardships of investigating the revenues of
a new country under the same conditions for two or three more would
undermine his health. He had hoped to be given charge of Coimbatore,
which he knew, from experience of a neighboring district, would yield
more than double the revenue Tipu Sultan had obtained from it, thereby
bringing great credit on the collector. Kanara, on the other hand, had
been overrated by Tipu, and the first British collector would fail to meet
the company's expectations and would suffer a loss of reputation. Despite
this, however, he felt it was his duty to go; although he would raise less
revenue than the company was expecting, he would, owing to his extensive
experience, raise more than anyone else. He mentioned the two civilian assistants he had been given, reminded Wellesley that unless they understood the local languages and possessed "great perseverance and great
temper with the natives" they would be useless, stated that he was as yet
unaware of their qualifications, and concluded, tersely, that "if I find
them deficient, I shall not fail to report to your Lordship, in full confidence that I shall be furnished with abler assistance."[18]

The tone of Munro's letter is very different from Malcolm's expression of gratitude to Wellesley in a letter written early in 1803: "Among the
various feelings which at this moment occupy my breast, I recognise with
exultation that of a personal attachment to your Lordship to be predominant; and I shall glory in every opportunity I may have of showing the nature of the zeal which that attachment inspires, and how far it places me
above the common motives which influence men who are busy in the self-
interested pursuit of fortune."[19] The final phrase, of course, is hypocrisy,
but Malcolm's general sentiments were probably sincere; he genuinely
liked and admired Wellesley, and public recognition and improved status
seem to have mattered more to him than money. But the obsequious style
would have been unthinkable for Munro, who wrote to everyone, high and
low, in the same laconic tone. This does not mean, of course, that

Munro's letters to great men were without guile; his honesty was judicious as well as disarming. After his warning, it would be difficult for the authorities to blame him for revenue shortfalls, while a reasonable collection would be greatly to his credit.

In October 1800, the Madras government informed the court of directors that, as the result of Munro's energy and ability, the company's authority in Kanara was fully established and his success in imposing order had enabled him to "pursue inquiries into the resources, administration, and history of these districts," which he had presented to the government "in one of the ablest reports" to pass under their observation.[20] Hard work, an inquiring mind, a gift for organization, and some carefully written reports enabled Munro to use this unwanted and disliked appointment to establish himself as the most successful settlement official in the Madras presidency.

Munro's success in Kanara led Wellesley to consider offering him, rather than Malcolm, the appointment as resident at Mysore. A more critical post in 1800, however, was the settlement of some districts south of the Tumbudra and Kistna Rivers which were due to be ceded to the company in October by the nizam of Hyderabad under the terms of a new subsidiary alliance—quite willingly, as the disordered state of this region tended to make the collection of their revenues more trouble than they were worth. Munro requested and obtained this challenging appointment.[21] He had spent fifteen months in Kanara from July 1799 to October 1800 and was to spend nearly seven years, from October 1800 to August 1807, in a region the size of half of England, known as the Ceded Districts. In both places he was responsible not only for establishing order and collecting the revenue so urgently needed by the company to pay for its wars, but also for the organization of supplies and transport for Arthur Wellesley's army. If Elizabeth Longford's contention is accurate that Wellesley's first involvement with the Marathas in 1803—the restoration of the peshwa of Pune to his throne—was successful in large part because he had "studied his Caesar" and prepared basket boats for his army's river crossings, and because of "a lovingly perfected bullock-train," Munro should share the credit. From 1800 Munro supplied much of the material for Wellesley's boats and, as soon as preparations for war with the

Marathas began in November 1802, he organized the continuous movement of between ten and thirty thousand transport bullocks. Writing to Alexander Read, Munro observed, "I have not only always had the purchase of the supplies, but the payment of most of the bullocks. This bullock business, together with sheep, boats, pay of boatmen, . . . and the endless disputes and correspondence about accounts, bills etc., leave me very little time for revenue."[22] The Indian army, as Bayly points out, had no organized commissariat in the eighteenth century. Munro was a leading pioneer of the more centralized, bureaucratic system of supply that developed in the early nineteenth century and which became a valuable source of knowledge on Indian resources and practices.[23] Although he continued to organize ten thousand bullocks to provision Arthur Wellesley's army after peace was restored, Munro's ability to collect revenue from the Ceded Districts was equally crucial to Wellesley's success, as land revenues remained the company's most important fiscal resource.

In his early years in the Ceded Districts Munro's career prospects were threatened by objections from the court of directors to his methods of suppressing the petty lords known as poligars (the region's most destabilizing social group), by opposition from within the company to some of his revenue policies, and by the open resentment of many members of the Madras civil service over the appointment of soldiers to civilian positions. But Munro's tough stance with the poligars brought stability. There were still few Madras civilians with the necessary language skills to handle his job, and his logistical ability in support of Arthur Wellesley's Maratha campaign helped mitigate criticism. On Munro's resignation in October 1807, the Madras government told the court of directors that his work, carried out "under circumstances of extreme difficulty," had achieved "a degree of success unequalled in the records of this, or probably of any other Government."[24]

Although officially going on leave, Munro seems to have had no firm intention of returning to India when he left for Britain. The opportunity he desperately wanted to demonstrate his ability as a military commander in the field had not been forthcoming, partly owing to lack of social rank and patronage but also because he had been indispensable in supply and administration. But he did not want to spend the rest of his career in administration and, while in Britain, he tried unsuccessfully to obtain a diplomatic or political appointment.

While Munro and Malcolm, officers of the Madras army, took part in the Fourth Mysore War (1799), Elphinstone, a Bengal civilian, remained at his first post as assistant to the registrar at Benares. Early in 1800 he was admitted to Fort William College as one of its first students, but he attended for only a few weeks before accepting a well-paid appointment on the staff of the residency at Pune. Wellesley's attention may have been directed to Elphinstone by Henry Dundas, who had promised Lady Elphinstone in 1798 that although he never "interfered" in Indian appointments, he would make known to the new governor-general "the friendly interest he took in the young writer." It is also possible, however, that by applying to the college Elphinstone recommended himself to Wellesley as an intelligent and ambitious young man; the sort Wellesley liked to patronize. This may have been misleading. Elphinstone's application probably simply reflected a desire for a more lively social life and the opportunity to study for its own sake; a view supported by his lukewarm attitude to the Pune appointment. His friend Edward Strachey had been offered the position of secretary to Colonel William Kirkpatrick, recently appointed as resident at Pune. Elphinstone was to be Strachey's assistant, but Strachey was reluctant to accept because he feared he would have "less leisure at Poona than here." Elphinstone suggested that he consult Kirkpatrick "and if he should say that it would employ the assistant constantly, the offer ought to be rejected."[25]

Like Elphinstone, Strachey was well connected. His father, Henry Strachey, had been private secretary to Robert Clive. Clive's interest enabled him to become a member of Parliament in 1768, and he held important government offices and enjoyed close ties with the East India Company until his retirement in 1807. He married Clive's first cousin and became guardian to his patron's son after Clive's suicide.[26] Henry Strachey's ward, the second Lord Clive, was governor of Madras at the time Edward Strachey and Elphinstone were deliberating about Pune. Hard work was not a high priority for such well-connected young officials, but their dilettante attitude to well-paid appointments that would establish them in the political service would have been incomprehensible to less-privileged men.

Illness prevented Kirkpatrick from taking up the appointment at Pune and he was replaced by Barry Close. Delay in choosing the new resident, however, meant there was no urgency for Elphinstone and Strachey to reach the posts they had decided, ultimately, to accept; with an entourage of one hundred and fifty servants, eight elephants, eleven camels, four horses, and ten bullocks they took nearly a year on the journey, following a circuitous route and making lengthy stops along the way. While traveling, however, Elphinstone prepared himself for his new duties by adding the Maratha language to the subjects he was studying.

The Pune residency was an important diplomatic post. After the defeat and death of Tipu Sultan of Mysore, the five main Maratha states were expected to provide the only serious threat to the security—or opposition to the expansion—of the company's position in India. Elphinstone's journal entries from Pune mention continuous negotiations with the various Maratha rulers: Baji Rao II, peshwa of Pune, Daulat Rao Sindhia of Gwalior, Jeshwant Rao Holkar of Indore, the gaekwar of Baroda, and the raja of Berar.[27] Wellesley believed a subsidiary alliance with the peshwa would allow him to regulate relations between all the different Maratha states as well as Britain's relations with the peshwa himself. Under the terms of subsidiary alliances the company supplied troops and protection to their ally in return for the cession of revenue-producing territory or, sometimes, cash. Although it pledged noninterference in the ally's internal affairs, the company expected to control its external relations, and the Maratha princes knew such an alliance would effectively end their independence. The peshwa, therefore, resisted Wellesley's offer until his army and Sindhia's were defeated in battle by Holkar in October 1802. Compelled to seek refuge in British territory, Baji Rao reluctantly signed the Treaty of Bassein, and was reinstated on his throne the following May by Arthur Wellesley, with Malcolm on his staff. Sindhia and the raja of Berar, however, failed to endorse the treaty before the expiration of two ultimatums from the company, and the Second Anglo-Maratha War began on 6 August 1803.[28]

Malcolm and Elphinstone met for the first time at Pune in May 1803. Serving again as the governor-general's confidential agent, Malcolm came to Pune with the peshwa and Arthur Wellesley, but he was in poor health and remained at the residency at Pune, where Elphinstone was a junior official, when Wellesley and the army continued north. Malcolm rejoined the army in July, but when war broke out in August he was again ill and suggested that Elphinstone replace him. Whether he was impressed with Elphinstone's ability, or merely thought it politic to do a service for a well-connected young man, Malcolm's misfortune—and patronage—gave Elphinstone a great opportunity, one he would have been unable to grasp, however, without some knowledge of Indian languages and Maratha affairs. Because he was too inexperienced to assume Malcolm's senior diplomatic role, Arthur Wellesley employed him in intelligence and as an interpreter.

Elphinstone was anxious about his linguistic skills; he feared his knowledge of Hindi might be inadequate, and when dealing with Marathas, he could not "readily understand all that is said to me, much less say all that I ought to express."[29] There were, in fact, serious intelligence failures prior to the battle of Assaye,[30] but Arthur Wellesley does not appear to have held Elphinstone responsible. Despite his civilian status, Elphinstone rode with Wellesley at the battle of Assaye, charged with the cavalry at Argaum, and mounted the breach with the storming party at the siege of Gawilgarh—martial exploits Elphinstone's nineteenth-century biographers liked to emphasize.

The taking of Gawilgarh in December 1803 brought the war against Sindhia and the raja of Berar to a close. Malcolm returned to Wellesley's camp at Ellichpur the following day, disappointed to have missed the final action but ready to take part in the peace negotiations. Elphinstone dictated the agreement with Berar to his Persian writers the night of Malcolm's arrival, and the following morning Malcolm "looked over the Persian of the treaty," which had been dictated at such speed that Elphinstone feared the quality of his Persian "must be infamous." The two men then breakfasted together and discussed Elphinstone's future prospects. There were two openings: one at the residency at the raja of Berar's court at Nagpur and one with the resident at Sindhia's court; the governor-general "graciously" allowed Elphinstone the privilege of choosing "what situation [he] wishes to fill." Prompted by Arthur Wellesley and Malcolm, Elphinstone chose Nagpur. Josiah Webbe, technically the resident there, although he had never taken up the appointment, would soon be promoted and move on and Elphinstone, as first assistant, would be first in line to succeed Webbe as resident. Collins, at Sindhia's court, on the other hand, had failed to please Lord Wellesley and was about to be replaced, which would leave Elphinstone as a mere assistant.[31]

Lord Wellesley, in fact, appointed Malcolm to replace Collins in the negotiations with Sindhia for peace, a subsidiary alliance, and the settlement of the status of Gwalior and Gohud, possessions claimed by both Sindhia and a minor Maratha chief. The terms for peace were relatively straightforward and a treaty was signed at the end of February 1804. The issue of Gwalior and Gohud, however, was more complex and Malcolm got into difficulties. He and Arthur Wellesley both acknowledged Sindhia's claim to the fortress of Gwalior and, for reasons of both policy and principle, argued that it should be returned to him. Wellesley, for reasons of policy, wished to keep it and Malcolm was censured. The governor-general's secretary informed him that "Your having shown a great disposition to admit the justice of Sindhia's right (claim) to Gwalior and Gohud is likely, Lord Wellesley thinks, to give his enemies in Leadenhall-street room to found an accusation against Lord Wellesley of injustice and rapacity in insisting upon retaining these possessions contrary to the opinion of the resident."[32] In poor health and upset over the recent death of his father as well as over the breach with Wellesley, Malcolm handed over the negotiations to Webbe and went to visit his brother Robert at Vizagapatam. Malcolm had heard of George Malcolm's death while engaged in negotiations with Sindhia at Bhurampur in February 1804, but postponed dealing with the problem of the family's debts until he had concluded his official duties. While at Vizagapatam he learned that his brother William had also died recently in Scotland.[33] Arthur Wellesley regretted Malcolm's withdrawal, telling his brother Henry that someone was needed at Calcutta with the courage to speak his mind to the governor-general. "Since you and Malcolm have left him, there is nobody about him with the capacity to understand these subjects, who has nerves to discuss them with him, and to oppose his sentiments when he is wrong."[34] Malcolm's pursuit of patronage gave him a reputation for sycophancy, but at this point in his career, Arthur Wellesley evidently believed Malcolm would be both willing and able to stand up to Richard Wellesley on matters of policy.

Lord Wellesley had intended the war with Sindhia and the raja to further his own empire-building ambitions at the expense of the Marathas, while providing an arena for his brother Arthur to advance his military career.[35] The Second Maratha War (1803–6) did eventually, although not immediately, establish Wellesley's reputation as an empire builder; it did prove to be the beginning of the end, in 1818, of the great Maratha polity; and it did provide the foundation for Arthur Wellesley's distinguished military career. It also provided opportunities for Munro, Malcolm, and Elphinstone to advance their own careers. Munro's wartime labors in the Ceded Districts established his reputation as a great administrator. Malcolm and Elphinstone both moved higher in the political service.

In 1805 Wellesley resigned the governor-generalship, preempting his recall by a Home government alarmed and angry at the costs of his wars. But before leaving India he appointed Malcolm as political agent with Lord Lake, commander in chief, India, and commander in the field in the campaign against Holkar, whose policies towards Holkar were not producing the results Wellesley desired. Wellesley had wanted war with Sindhia and Holkar in 1803, but he would probably have preferred to obtain a diplomatic solution to his problems with Holkar in 1805 to help redeem his reputation with the authorities in London. Lake, however, with a militarist agenda of his own, persuaded Wellesley that British interests in India required the eradication of Holkar's power through military victory.[36]

Lord Cornwallis succeeded Wellesley as governor-general but died soon after arriving in India. Sir George Barlow became acting governor-general until Lord Minto arrived from Britain in June 1807. Barlow accepted the terms for peace negotiated with Sindhia and Holkar by Lake and Malcolm, but added "declaratory articles" which, they claimed, reflected badly on British good faith.[37] Lake withdrew from the negotiations and Malcolm, soon after, went back to Mysore. M. E. Yapp sees Malcolm as a poor diplomatist whose negotiations with the Marathas were criticized by Wellesley and later by Hastings. He claims that Malcolm was unable to estimate the weaknesses of his adversaries, gave way on important points, and tried to buy agreements in an unsuccessful attempt to disguise the truth that he was a poor bargainer. During the Wellesley regime, however, buying agreements, as Enid M. Fuhr demonstrates, was customary: money was allocated in the budget for what were, in reality, bribes. During the campaign in Cuttack, influential chieftains were paid to remain neutral; minor chiefs were given grants of land revenues in return for support. Lake offered the Marathas, unsuccessfully, "a large sum of money" to surrender the fort at Aligarh. Arthur Wellesley, claiming that it was impossible to do business at a Maratha court without buying help, told Barry Close that he should pay Ragonaut Rao, the peshwa's minister, to provide information, and told Malcolm that it would be advisable "to bribe the prince, as well as his ministers." Elphinstone at Nagpur paid similar "allowances" to ministers of the raja of Berar.[38]

Financial inducements were an integral part of British Indian diplomacy. An integral part of Malcolm's diplomacy was his belief that trust and incentive were better methods of achieving political objectives than coercion. Elphinstone later described this approach, with little enthusiasm, as Malcolm's "confidence system," and it could be construed as weakness; Malcolm liked to be liked. Lynn Zastoupil identifies "the muted voices of Indians" behind Malcolm's consideration for the feelings of fallen princes—a consideration well known to but rarely appreciated by British Indian authorities.[39] He was, no doubt, subjected to persuasive arguments extolling the benefits of indirect rule by Indian power holders threatened with expulsion. But his reliance on the principles of conciliation and sympathy as an approach to diplomacy was consistent and probably reflects the influence of the concept of "sensibility," a form of discourse that featured prominently in late eighteenth-century moral literature. Its message, widely publicized in the Scottish press as well as in novels, sermons, and literary journals, was that an ability to identify with the concerns of one's fellow man should be the essence of modern civilization. Hugh Blair, one of the foremost spokesmen for sensibility, stated in his widely read *Sermons* (1777) that sensibility—a "humane and generous liberality" of feeling—was the "chief ground of mutual confidence and union among men," more important to the successful conduct of formal as well as informal social relationships than laws.[40]

A dispirited Malcolm returned to the professional backwater of the residency at Mysore in March 1807, intending to "draw my salary for eighteen months" and then return to Britain. He did not go to Madras the following June when Lord Minto put in there on his way to take up the governor-generalship at Calcutta because he was about to get married. But he did write to Minto's son, John Elliot, who was serving as private secretary to his father, complaining that as the Home government had ignored him, owing to his "crime of doing my duty under Lord Wellesley," he would make "the sordid motive of adding a few rupees more" to his fortune his guiding principle before returning home. He added that although still ambitious, he was now convinced that India was not the place to look for fame. Minto himself replied to Malcolm's lament, thanking him for past kindnesses to his son and explaining, soothingly, that had it not been for Malcolm's imminent marriage, he would have invited him to Madras to consult him "on the most important branches of our public affairs."[41]

Malcolm married Charlotte Campbell, the daughter of a colonel in the Crown army, on 4 July 1807. The same week a publicly more momentous contract was signed by the emperors of France and Russia at Tilsit. This alliance, in conjunction with the arrival of a French military mission in Persia, raised again the specter of an overland invasion of India by a European power and caused Minto to send missions to Persia, Afghanistan, Sind, and Lahore to arrange alliances aimed at protecting the northwest approaches to British India. Much to Malcolm's indignation, Sir Harford Jones, formerly the resident at Baghdad, was chosen by the London government to go to Persia; Elphinstone volunteered and was soon selected by Minto to go to Afghanistan.

As he had done on Wellesley's arrival, Malcolm sent a long memorandum to the governor-general soon after Minto reached India. But this time, rather than demonstrating his by now well-known knowledge of Indian politics, he tried to promote his claims to head the Persian mission instead of Harford Jones, although he included, for Minto's benefit, a severe critique of most of the members of the Supreme government. He was to do the same for Lord William Bentinck in 1828, although his portraits on that occasion were less brutal, and after several months' acquaintance with his subordinates, Bentinck congratulated Malcolm on their ac-

curacy.[42] These portraits, or in the case of the ones sent to Minto, character assassinations, were a career-building technique later disdained—at
least publicly—by Victorian proconsuls. But Malcolm's methods were
common enough at the time. His analysis of the abilities and tempera-
ments of company officials was probably meant to suggest that he had attained greater authority than the men he was describing—that he was a
superior assessing the staff. It also, and probably deliberately, gave the impression of a more intimate, or collusive, connection with the governor-
general than was warranted by Malcolm's rank.

The tactic produced results. Minto could not send Malcolm as the
government of India's envoy to Persia while Jones was there representing
the Crown, but he sent him instead to the Persian Gulf states, Iraq and
southern Persia, to dissuade the local rulers from allying with the French.
Minto justified Malcolm's mission to Robert Dundas, president of the
board of control, in enthusiastic terms: "By Colonel Malcolm, if by any
man living, we may hope to detach Persia from her hostile alliance with
our enemy, and if that benefit is no longer attainable, we shall receive
from Colonel Malcolm authentic information and judicious advice." The
shah, however, refused permission for Malcolm to travel beyond Shiraz;
little was achieved and, in July, Minto was forced to concede that Malcolm "has disappointed me exceedingly."[43]

Malcolm's efforts to use his distant relationship to the Elliots to further his career interests during Minto's governor-generalship were neither
unusual nor particularly reprehensible in the early decades of the nineteenth century. Nepotism, in the sense of extended family or "clan" loyalty in regard to professional advancement, was normal, and Malcolm himself took seriously his responsibilities as the patron of younger relatives
and protégés as well as seeking patronage for himself and his friends. He
had been in contact with Minto before the latter was appointed first to
the board of control for India and then as governor-general, and had sent
him various papers, including, in 1804, a one-hundred-and-thirty-one-
page memorandum in defense of Lord Wellesley's interpretation of the
powers of the governor-general. In his relations with Minto, Malcolm
may also have benefited from his wife's acquaintance with Minto's children. When approaching Minto on behalf of the husband of a friend in

1808, Charlotte indicated a prior acquaintance with John and Miss Elliot. By contemporary standards, Malcolm's connections with the Elliots were sufficiently close to justify the papers he showered on Minto. And he was by no means alone in what Elphinstone, irreverently, called "spunging to Gibby."[44]

On his return from Persia Malcolm was appointed to settle a mutiny of European officers in the company army at Masulipatam, but the conciliatory measures he used displeased Barlow, now governor of Madras, who favored severity, and Malcolm was replaced. In 1810 he went again to Persia at Minto's bidding and this time reached Tehran. But he became a victim of what was to become known as the "Persian dilemma," the question debated throughout the nineteenth century as to whether relations with Persia should be the responsibility of Whitehall or Calcutta. Harford Jones, with superior Crown credentials, was already at Tehran when Malcolm arrived and it was Jones, not Malcolm, who negotiated the expulsion of the French mission and a new treaty with the shah. Malcolm handled the situation badly and returned to Bombay jealous, disappointed, and bitter.

From 1798 until Wellesley's departure in 1805, Malcolm's career-building techniques had proved spectacularly successful and his performance of his duties had generally satisfied official expectations. The Gwalior controversy, however, ushered in a period in which, although actively involved in important events, Malcolm achieved little, failed to satisfy his superiors, and experienced much frustration. On his return to Bombay in November 1810, therefore, he settled down to use his pen to enhance, or perhaps restore, his reputation. By 1815, he had four publications to his name.

The first to appear was his *Sketch of the Political History of India* (1811), a somewhat rash foray into the dangerous waters of contemporary history in defense of Wellesley's governor-generalship. In a pamphlet on the crisis at Masulipatam entitled "Observations on the Disturbances in the Madras Army in 1809," Malcolm explains the grievances which led to the mutiny, dealing again with the problems of poor morale that had engaged his attention in London in 1794 while justifying his own conduct towards the mutineers on the ground that men respond more favorably to a show of confidence than to rigid discipline. The *Sketch of the Sikhs* was published in 1812. Malcolm had seized the opportunity to obtain information on Sikh history, religion, and government while engaged in negotiations with Holkar, Sindhia, and some Sikh chieftains in 1805, but explained, modestly, that his *Sketch* was merely a "preliminary study" that he hoped would both stimulate and provide a foundation for a more comprehensive work by someone "with more leisure." The book has been described as sometimes inaccurate but more profound than three earlier British works on the subject, and as particularly valuable on Sikh institutions and society.[45] Malcolm's most important literary venture, however, was the *History of Persia*, a country that was terra incognita to most Europeans. Like most Scottish historians of the time, Malcolm used an examination of the past to help him form general opinions on the present state; and the last five chapters deal with recent Persian history, providing information and analysis useful to anyone responsible for the defense of the northwest frontier of India or trying to assess the likely effect of Russo-Persian relations on European affairs. The publication of Malcolm's Persian history in 1815 brought his name to the attention of the reading public in Europe as well as in Britain, and did more to establish his lasting reputation as an authority on Persia than all his diplomatic missions.[46]

Malcolm was busy writing history when Elphinstone visited him while on his way to take up the position of resident at Pune in February 1811. Last together at Arthur Wellesley's camp at Ellichpur in December 1803, they had had many professional experiences since on which to compare notes. As a diplomat Elphinstone had been less controversial than Malcolm, but his achievements were not outstanding and he, too, was worried about his future prospects.

Although acknowledging his obligation to Malcolm for arranging his appointment with Arthur Wellesley's army and for advising him on the appointment at Nagpur in 1803, Elphinstone had not really wanted to go to Nagpur. He had wanted "idleness, society, and ladies," and dreaded a long period "at a place where I shall be so solitary." The "long period" lasted three years, from December 1803 until January 1807. New to the responsibilities of a resident, he was at first carefully coached and closely supervised, in particular by Arthur Wellesley, but after six months governor-general Lord Wellesley approved the "judgement, firmness, and ability" he had shown during the first important months after the conclusion of the Second Maratha War. In December 1804, a moment of tense Anglo-Maratha relations, he was mildly rebuked for threatening to withdraw from Nagpur; he was instructed to remain there until he could persuade the raja to request a subsidiary force. Elphinstone described the incident to Strachey: "You never saw such hot water in your days ... but all ended well. Lord W[ellesley] said that, though convinced of the raja's intention to renew the war, he believed him to have lately dropped his intention; so everything went smooth, and I got a *kudos* for 'energy and firmness'."[47] Arthur Wellesley, however, saw Elphinstone's role in a less favorable light. He believed that although peace with the Marathas was precarious, there was "a wide difference between preparation ... and an actual determination to go to war at all events; and I am sorry to observe that my friend Elphinstone was not aware of that difference. Accordingly in his despatches he has almost considered war as existing, and has created an unnecessary alarm, which will be the cause of an enormous expense."[48] Bayly has drawn attention to the frequency of what he calls "information panics" in the early nineteenth century, and Elphinstone's response undoubtedly comes under this heading.[49] His conduct at Nagpur, however, laid the foundation of his reputation as a competent diplomat. As Lord Wellesley was recalled in large part as a result of the excessive cost of his policies, Elphinstone was fortunate, perhaps, to escape unscathed from this incident. William Elphinstone's position as chairman of the company may have helped shield him from criticism; a less well-connected official might have been quietly posted to a career backwater.

During the tedious years at Nagpur Elphinstone added international law to his studies, reading works by Grotius and Pufendorf, Barbeyrac's commentaries on Pufendorf, and the contemporary works on law of R. P. Ward, probably with a view to preparing himself for the more interesting diplomatic appointments he hoped would come his way. Pursuing this object, in April 1808 he asked his cousin John Adam, who by now had some influence in the Calcutta secretariat, to try to get him appointed to one of the missions likely to be sent beyond the northwest frontier as a consequence of what Elphinstone lightly referred to as "the intended invasion of [India] by the French, with the assistance of the king of Persia."[50] Three months later Minto ordered him to Delhi to prepare for a mission to Afghanistan.

Elphinstone was pleased because he saw the mission as an opportunity to participate, albeit peripherally, in international affairs, but by the time he met Shah Shuja, the ruler of Kabul, at Peshawar in 1808, the mission's importance had declined. Napoleon's Spanish campaign removed the likelihood of a European expedition against India, while Shuja was fighting, and losing, a civil war. The Afghans treated the embassy courteously, but Elphinstone was not empowered to offer the help Shuja needed and nothing of political value emerged from their meetings. Although criticized for expense and for some of his policy recommendations, the mission, somewhat paradoxically, established Elphinstone's reputation as a diplomat. He was fortunate that Minto and the authorities in India, hoping to disguise the fact that the mission had been costly and pointless, emphasized the polished manner in which the negotiations had been conducted rather than their results. In the longer term, the book Elphinstone published as an adjunct of the mission did more for his reputation than the mission itself.

Although the diplomatic achievements of Malcolm's Persian and Elphinstone's Afghan missions were negligible, their ability as writers enabled them both to benefit from Minto's overreaction to the French invasion scare of 1808. The court of directors had decreed in 1805 that "all available information on the geography and history of India should be collected." This dictum, which could obviously be applied to any place likely to be of interest to the Indian government, provided a superb opportunity for anyone with novel and useful information and the ability to present it effectively to attract the attention of the authorities. Minto, uncertain whether the danger of invasion was over and thinking, perhaps, that information—if not alliances—might still be useful, agreed to a request from Malcolm for money to employ Persian secretaries and draftsmen and to cover house rent, on the ground that the Persian material Malcolm had collected would be useless unless "fully arranged and well-digested." Elphinstone was allowed the same privileges to work on his Afghan material.[51] Elphinstone's *Account of the Kingdom of Caubul*, like Malcolm's *History of Persia*, made his name known to the educated public in

Britain and established his reputation in government circles as a zealous, knowledgeable, and cultured official—an accredited member of British India's ruling elite.

Elphinstone enjoyed historical research and found composition tedious, but he resented the interruptions to his writing occasioned by diplomatic and social obligations. He voluntarily interrupted his writing in January 1812, however, to spend fifteen days traveling from Pune to Bombay and back to pay a farewell visit to Malcolm, who was leaving India. The journey, he observed afterwards, was worthwhile because his "conferences with Malcolm [should be] of great consequence to my future prospects," while his renewed acquaintance with William Erskine, an official of the Recorder's Court at Bombay and a keen orientalist, would be "of no small advantage to my literary plan."[52] As resident at Pune Elphinstone held a prestigious and well-paid post in the company's diplomatic service, but he was still impatient with the speed of his professional and financial progress. Malcolm had suggested "pushing with the help of my uncles for some promotion which would have expedited my return [to Britain]," a project which failed and which Elphinstone regretted, but Malcolm, who unlike Elphinstone was an optimist, had convinced him it was worth trying.[53]

Elphinstone's acquaintance with William Erskine brought more positive results. The two men corresponded regularly while Elphinstone prepared his Afghan material for publication between 1812 and 1814, and Erskine's interest in Asian history and languages provided Elphinstone, intermittently bored and depressed, with some welcome encouragement and intellectual stimulation. Erskine himself was completing a translation of the "memoirs" of the Mughal emperor Babur begun by John Leyden, a fellow Scot who had recently died. Erskine and Leyden were members of a group of Scottish orientalists that also included Alexander Hamilton, Alexander Murray, John Crawfurd, and Vans Kennedy, who attended Edinburgh university between 1784 and 1803 when Dugald Stewart was disseminating the doctrines of the Scottish Enlightenment. Jane Rendall points out that most of the Indian research of this group was directed towards discovering the cultural evidence that would enable them to place the history of Indian civilization within the interpretive framework developed by Scotland's moral philosophers.[54] Malcolm and Elphinstone might also be classed as members of the group. Both attended lectures at Edinburgh university during Stewart's time, if only briefly, and both were influenced by Scottish moral philosophy. It was no coincidence that Malcolm was reading Hume's *History of England* while writing his *History of Persia* in 1811, or that Elphinstone was reading Adam Smith while writing about the political and social organization of the Afghans.[55]

Throughout the fifty years that Munro, Malcolm, and Elphinstone spent in the east, Indian service was less recognized and less well rewarded than public service in Britain or Europe, and no one chose to spend his life in India if he had any other way of advancing his own and his family's interests. Nevertheless, a number of men, including several governors-general, were able to use India to enhance their status and wealth. Lord Wellesley, who had come to India to do just that, sought well-educated officers with a knowledge of Indian languages and politics as well as practical talents to carry out his empire-building policies, and men who possessed these qualifications found a door open to new and challenging opportunities.

Between 1798 and 1810, Malcolm was directly involved in all of the most important political events in British India. He traveled extensively between the different presidencies, throughout the Indian states, and as far afield as Tehran and Baghdad. His life was spent in professional association with members of the highest ranks of British Indian, Indian, and Persian society and, until 1805, he was Governor-General Wellesley's favored emissary and personal representative. Minto, too, was impressed—mostly due to the stream of well-argued letters and memoranda with which Malcolm bombarded him—and sent him twice to Persia. Despite Munro's extra years and Elphinstone's superior connections, Malcolm was the most prominent of the three men at this stage in their careers, owing largely to his deliberate efforts to make the system work for him, that is, to his indefatigable pursuit of patronage according to the usages of "old corruption," but also to his speedy adoption of the newer, more bureaucratic techniques of advancement—the acquisition of the expert knowledge increasingly necessary to the government of India, and the ability to present it in an articulate form. When his labors in the company service were ineffective or unappreciated, he turned to writing and published several works that demonstrated intellectual competence as well as an impressive knowledge of Persia and India. These books did as much, if not more, to establish his reputation as an expert on Asian affairs as his practical accomplishments as a political agent.

Malcolm and Elphinstone's careers were interconnected from their first meeting in 1803 until Malcolm's departure for Britain in 1812. The elder by ten years, Malcolm helped Elphinstone take advantage of the career-building opportunities that became available as a result of Wellesley's policies, and he encouraged his literary aspirations. It is possible that Malcolm hoped Elphinstone's friendship would provide access to influential circles in Britain and India, but he also helped Munro when Munro had virtually no influential connections and before his reputation, based on merit, was established. Malcolm was instrumental in obtaining two career-building appointments for Elphinstone and had helped in obtaining two for Munro. At this time he was the link between the three men; Elphinstone and Munro did not meet until 1818.

In contrast to Malcolm's high-profile career, Munro spent most of the years between 1792 and his return to Britain in 1807 in remote areas of rural India, moving from village to village, district to district, all within the Madras presidency. Apart from contacts with members of his staff, his time was largely spent in the company of the cultivators, minor officials, and petty chiefs who made up the overwhelming majority of the Indian population; his main contact with higher authority was by writing. His writing skills and ability to justify his recommendations on ideological as well as practical grounds, however, enabled him to use his reports and official correspondence to influence policy and draw attention to himself.

CHAPTER 4

Britain, 1808–1817

Home Leave, Accomplishments, and Frustrations

What I am chiefly anxious about is, what I am to do when I go home.
I have no rank in the army there . . . and as I am a stranger to the
generous natives of your isle, I should be excluded from every other
line as well as military and should have nothing to do but to lie
down in a field . . . and look at the lark.
—*Thomas Munro*

*H*ome leave was both longed for and dreaded by company servants, who were in many ways transients in both India and Britain. Munro's administrative abilities were respected by men in the government of India. Malcolm's diplomatic service, controversial in the company because of his association with Lord Wellesley, was recognized by the British government with a knighthood in 1812. Like many of Malcolm's rewards, the knighthood probably owed something to Lord Wellesley, now foreign secretary, or to Arthur Wellesley, now Lord Wellington. It came, however, only two months after Malcolm's brothers James and Pulteney received knighthoods for naval services; the awards testified at least to the Malcolms' competency as career builders. Even if the knighthood indicated a genuine acknowledgment of Malcolm's services, however, an Indian reputation did not solve the employment problem in Britain. Company army officers could not serve in Europe, even though Wellington thought the country's best interests would be served by allowing them to exchange into the Crown army, apparently so that Munro and Malcolm would be eligible to serve under him in Spain. Few company officials could hope to penetrate the overcrowded patronage networks in Britain. When Malcolm mentioned his hope of becoming ambassador to Constantinople, Wellington replied that he would be considered an interloper and advised him to go back to India or to "get into parliament if you can afford it."[1]

Men who had acquired money and reputation in India could present themselves as candidates for the company directorate, but neither Munro nor Elphinstone were interested in entering India House, while Malcolm, who toyed with the idea in 1826, soon abandoned it. The most popular option was to buy a country estate—a gilt-edged investment that provided an income on which to support a family and, equally important, a clearly defined status in British society. Many, however, found retirement difficult. Elphinstone spoke of "our best Indians," who, "In the idleness and obscurity of home . . . look back with fondness for the country where they have been useful and distinguished, like the ghosts of Homer's heroes, who prefer the exertions of a labourer on the earth to all the listless enjoyments of Elysium." Munro not only disliked having nothing useful to do, he did not even like Britain very much: "It is our native land, but . . . so cold and dark and wet and dirty that . . . no fortune I think can make it comfortable." India was a "pleasanter country."[2]

For the three years of his official leave Munro spent much of his time restless, frustrated, and often wishing he had never come home. After some months in Scotland, he made London his base, making frequent visits to friends and relatives in the country. He was a guest in the social world of the English gentry so faithfully depicted by Jane Austen, where it was "a truth universally acknowledged, that a single man in possession of a good fortune must be in want of a wife." Finding a wife seems indeed to have been Munro's top priority. He also hoped to find a patron to sponsor his nephew and ward (Daniel's orphaned son, John) to a company writership, to buy an estate, and to find something worthwhile to do.[3]

Although Munro was not the most eligible bachelor, he expected certain talents in a wife. He had what he called a "moderate competency," not a fortune. In 1814 he seems to have had about £50,000—enough to invest £30,000 to provide an annuity of £1,000 per annum for his wife in case of his death, but not, perhaps, enough to buy an estate as well. He was a colonel, but in the Indian, not the Crown army; he was nearly fifty, tall and lean but intermittently quite deaf; and he had been away from "polished society" so long that his costume and manners had become eccentric, while his conversation, even his devoted biographer the Reverend George Gleig had to admit, assumed at times "a character indicative of anything rather than an excess of refinement." No doubt he rectified some of these shortcomings while looking for a cultivated woman with a mind "above the common" and a pleasant disposition. He did not want to marry a philosopher, but neither did he want good looks to tempt him "into the hands of a silly wife." He seems to have shared the view of gender relations advocated by Francis Hutcheson, David Hume, and other eighteenth-century moral philosophers that marriage should be founded on mutual respect, companionship, and a recognition of equal, if different, spheres of responsibility.[4]

Munro's three-year leave should have ended in 1811, but at that time he had neither found a wife nor abandoned his efforts to obtain a British appointment, and he successfully requested an extension. In April of 1811 he wrote to Wellington in Spain that there was "nothing now in the world so interesting as the affairs of the Peninsula, or in which I am so desirous of having some part to play." But this broad hint failed to draw the desired response. Three months later, having heard that the marquis of Hastings would succeed Lord Minto in India, he wondered whether the new governor-general might be persuaded by his friend Henry Erskine (Munro's brother-in-law) "to employ me in some high diplomatic or staff situation." But again nothing eventuated and in September Munro acknowledged that he would have to return to India with the fleet leaving in January 1812 unless he soon found a post that would enable him to stay at home for another year, something easily "accomplished by any person having friends in the administration" but, even with a change of government, something he feared he had insufficient interest to obtain.[5]

The year 1811 was not an auspicious time to be job hunting. The company was divided over the question of whether Christian missionaries in India would provoke unrest among Indians; it was anxious about the state of its army in the aftermath of sepoy and "white" mutinies; and it was threatened by the free trade lobby and by the infiltration of private trade interests within the directorate. The British government was preoccupied by the war with France. Neither body was interested in the details of Indian administration, but, fortunately for Munro, there were individuals within both bodies who wanted to reform the Indian administration.

In preparation for the company's application for the renewal of its charter, due to come before Parliament in 1813, a committee of the House of Commons was convened to compile a report, known as "The Fifth Report," on the state of the company's government of British India. The report determined the form taken by the parliamentary inquiry. By the time it was distributed to members of Parliament in July 1812, the assessment and collection of revenue and the provision of a justice system had become the most important subjects of discussion—subjects about which Munro knew a great deal. There were increasing doubts in both India and Britain about the efficacy of the system Cornwallis had established in Bengal. The two most active members of the House of Commons committee—Samuel Davis, resident at Benares during Elphinstone's early years and a company director since 1810, and James Cumming, a member of the permanent staff at the board of control—were two of its strongest critics. Davis, who wrote the Bengal section of the report, and Cumming, who dealt with Madras, tried to construct a strong case for introducing a different revenue and judicial system into the Madras presidency. They were encouraged by the earl of Buckinghamshire, the president of the board of control, John Sullivan, a member of the board, and Thomas Wallace, assistant commissioner at the board and chairman of the House of Commons committee. Munro became their expert consultant; the inclusion of many of Munro's papers in the appendix of the Fifth Report attested to the extent of his influence on the proceedings.[6]

It is not clear how Munro became involved in the preparation of the Fifth Report, although he had advertised his expertise and kept his name before the authorities while in Britain by submitting several memoranda to the board of control on the judicial service, on the company army, and on revenue systems. Cumming, however, had been interested in Munro's recommendations for many years and was familiar with the collections of Munro's papers sent to England from Madras between the late 1790s and 1807. The most important of these, because it provides a clearly delineated alternative to the Bengal Zamindari revenue collection system, is entitled "On the Relative Advantages of the Ryotwari and Zamindari Systems." A second paper, "Trial by Panchayat," is also significant because it contains Munro's first official recommendations on judicial matters. The two papers, which are both dated 15 August 1807, were written shortly before his departure from India and represent his mature thought on the civil government of the Madras presidency.[7]

The company's revenue and judicial systems were only two of a number of subjects examined by the parliamentary inquiry of 1813, and many people were more interested in promoting British exports to India and in the issues of free trade and missionaries.[8] Both Malcolm and Munro gave evidence as expert witnesses on all these matters, but discretion was advisable and Malcolm was, perhaps, too frank. Many years later he told Elphinstone that his warnings of the danger "of over-zeal in propagating Christianity in India" had probably, among other "sins," offended Charles Grant, powerful member of the directorate, member of Parliament, and a leader of the Evangelical Clapham Sect, who, Malcolm believed, opposed his promotion because of it.[9] Munro was cautious about missionaries and kept his enthusiasm for the principles of free trade discreetly to himself, and the positive impression he made at the parliamentary hearings helped persuade the directorate to authorize a trial of his administrative methods in the Madras presidency, to be carried out under his direction. An anonymous Utilitarian pamphlet published in 1831, in which Munro's and Malcolm's views on the government of India are compared unfavorably with those of Elphinstone, states that Munro's expert evidence before the House of Commons in 1813 "contributed materially" to his later attainment of the governorship of Madras.[10]

The differences between the revenue and judicial systems introduced by Cornwallis in Bengal and recommended by Munro for Madras derived partly from different local practices but also from different principles.

Broadly speaking, under the Bengal revenue and judicial system revenue was collected by zamindars—usually local landholders—who, under Mughal rule, had the right to a percentage of the revenue collected in return for their agency in collecting the rest on behalf of the Mughal authorities. To provide support for their authority as revenue collectors they had had the right to administer justice and, as middlemen, they had handled most of the contacts between the state and the cultivators. Under Cornwallis, land*holders* were to become land*owners:* a settlement was made which helped zamindars to obtain private property rights to the land and which fixed revenue assessments in the hope that, like many British landowners at this time, they would take a greater interest in agricultural improvement if they were to be the chief beneficiaries of increased production. But their judicial powers were abolished on grounds of principle—the separation of executive and judicial authority—and were replaced by a quasi-British system of law courts which administered Indian law, but in a form incomprehensible to many Indians.

It was Munro's intention that, on the basis of an established revenue system known as ryotwari, revenue assessment and collection and the judicial system should be linked. The term "ryotwari" referred to a land tenure system widely, although by no means exclusively, practiced in parts of southern India, in which the ryots (small peasant landholders) paid revenue, according to long-established methods of assessment, directly to the ruler's revenue collector. Law was enforced by local officials including the collector and by the use of local juries (panchayats). Munro believed that to be effective, laws and legal forms must be rooted in the customs, assumptions, and values of a society—even if they were not always "just" according to western notions—and he advocated the utilization of traditional Indian legal practice, supervised by British revenue collectors who would be given the powers of a magistrate. Collectors generally had a greater knowledge of local languages and customs than the members of the company's judicial service.[11]

The East India Company's decision in 1813 to allow Munro to introduce his system in the Madras presidency was by no means unanimous. The main objections of those opposed to it were stated by John Hudleston, a prominent director, in two "official dissents" arguing that Munro's recommendations merely described what he had done in the Ceded Districts and were not a "system" at all. They should have carried no more weight, therefore, than those of Madras officials who either supported the Bengal system or suggested other alternatives to it. He also claimed that Munro's appointment as commissioner represented a usurpation of the powers of the directorate by the board of control; that Munro, a soldier, should not be appointed judicial commissioner; and that civilian members of the Madras government should not be expected to serve under him. Evidence indicates clearly that the members of the board of revenue at Madras, at least, saw Munro's recommendations as a carefully thought-out administrative system based on contemporary ideas about political economy, while his recommendations carried weight because his work had been highly, frequently, and officially praised.[12] But Hudleston's complaints of board of control interference and the preferential employment of soldiers in civilian positions were more justified. Munro's writings from 1813 include well-developed arguments to support the attempt by Buckinghamshire to change the way India was governed and to give the board of control greater influence on policy formation.[13] Surprisingly, Munro's close association with Buckinghamshire and the board of control did not prevent him from obtaining support for his system from several influential directors.

The complex process which led to the decision for administrative reform would never have taken place had there not been increasingly widespread doubts about the principles on which the Cornwallis system was based as well as about its efficiency. The company was also frustrated with the permanent nature of the Cornwallis settlement which seemed to prevent any increase in revenue.[14] Munro's system had not been developed initially as an alternative to that of Cornwallis; its basic form had been defined by Read and Munro in the Baramahal at much the same time as Cornwallis introduced his regulations in Bengal. But the system was ready, spelled out in Munro's reports, and Munro was there to be consulted and to proselytize at just the right moment.

Cumming, who was, perhaps, Munro's most dedicated disciple, described him as having had closer contact with Indians and greater opportunities for examining their institutions "than any other person," and as possessing an "uncommon knowledge of every subject connected with Indian government." Munro's reports, however, not only made his modified Indian system appear viable; they also had the inestimable advantages of being unusually well written and relatively brief.[15] Munro did not initiate the movement for administrative reform that took place between 1810 and 1814 but, once it was under way, his written submissions and personal evidence provided its instigators with the principled base, progressive direction, and economic and moral justification necessary to overcome most opposition.

A month before he returned to India in 1814, Munro married Jane Campbell of Craigie in Ayrshire, a woman he described as "extremely handsome" and with whom he formed the affectionate and friendly relationship he sought. Of his other priorities while in Britain, he did not purchase a country estate, but William Elphinstone had provided a writership for his nephew and he had found interesting employment in the London end of Indian affairs; a momentous step for his career, but one which diverted it from the military direction he would have preferred. He returned to India as judicial commissioner for the Madras presidency.

Munro and Malcolm probably met during the parliamentary hearings in April 1813 and were together in Buckinghamshire's office early in 1814 when Malcolm witnessed the apparently purely verbal agreement between Munro and Buckinghamshire about the allowances Munro would receive as judicial commissioner. When by 1818 Munro had not received his full remuneration and could not supply a written contract to prove his claims, Malcolm dealt with the matter at Calcutta before Munro had even raised the issue, a warmly appreciated service.[16] The two men, however, do not seem to have met often in Britain, perhaps because Malcolm had access to higher social circles.

Malcolm had returned from India in July 1812 and settled his family in a country house in Hertfordshire. He seems to have liked life in Britain well enough but, like Munro, was restless and spent much of his time on visits and in London. He was consulted, mainly on military matters, by the parliamentary committees preparing for the charter renewal, and wrote a long paper for Buckinghamshire recommending reforms to the company's army, reiterating many points he had made in 1794 and in his pamphlet on the mutiny at Masulipatam but which had still received no official attention. He stayed twice with Buckinghamshire and his family, visited Lady Minto, the governor-general's wife, in Scotland, and became friends with Walter Scott, who described him to a close friend as "the Persian envoy, . . . the poet, the warrior, the polite man, and the Borderer. He is really a fine fellow . . . I like his frankness and his sound ideas on morality and policy."[17] Malcolm had acquired a family connection with the Elphinstones through his brother Pulteney's marriage in 1809 to William Elphinstone's daughter, and he remained on terms of friendship with Lord Wellesley, whom he visited in Ireland, and with Arthur Welles-ley, the duke of Wellington by the end of Malcolm's furlough and now famous throughout Europe.

Wellington invited Malcolm to join him at Paris during the exhilarat-ing summer months after the battle of Waterloo in 1815. He was intro-duced to the emperor of Austria and the czar of Russia, the latter com-menting on his Persian experience. He dined with distinguished diplomats and, as a result of the publication of his *History of Persia* in July 1815, was warmly received in French literary circles. Sir James Mackintosh told Mal-colm that Lord Grenville, who had previously held "some prejudices" against Malcolm owing to the tone of Malcolm's evidence before the House of Lords on the company charter renewal, was "one of the warmest panegyrists of your history of Persia . . . he spoke of it with a warmth which is often . . . in his feelings, but very seldom in his language." Elphinstone, on reading Malcolm's *History*, wrote to a friend in what seems to be mild surprise: "Malcolm's 'History' is grave, sober, judicious, philo-sophical. Not a trace of *Jack* Malcolm in it. It seems really a work of great merit." Malcolm arranged for the translation of the *History* into French and sent an original English presentation copy of his work to the czar.[18]

In 1815 Malcolm became a Knight Commander of the Order of the Bath and, a year later, a doctor of letters at Oxford. His acquaintances were a "who's who" of eminent European society, yet social prominence failed to gain him office in Britain, or even in India at the level he wanted: the governorship of Bombay or Madras. When these posts went to politi-cal appointees whose claims and qualifications were, he believed, inferior to his own, he decided to return to the Madras army. "High on the list of lieutenant-colonels," he could expect to obtain "his regiment" quickly.[19] Short of money, disappointed, and tired of being idle, he left his young family in England—he now had five children to support—and in October 1816 departed for Madras.

Britain offered little to men who had achieved high rank and carried out difficult and important duties in India. Access to British public life was difficult. They were rarely members of Britain's ruling groups, and men who might have patronized them in India had clients with more pressing claims in Britain. Elphinstone, who took no home leave because it would have extended the time required to save enough money for retirement, would have been able to enter political or business life in Britain if he had returned at the same time as Malcolm and had saved as much money as Munro. William Elphinstone and Lord Keith were influential in Britain as well as India. His brother John, Lord Elphinstone since their father's death in 1794, had been appointed aide-de-camp to the duke of York, commander in chief of the British army, while still in his mid-twenties, and had been a Scottish representative peer since 1806 and lord lieutenant of Dumbarton since 1811. Another brother, Charles, a naval officer who had attained the rank of rear admiral at the age of thirty-eight, was a member of Parliament for Stirling. If Munro had liked Britain better and found a wife sooner, he might have found enough money to buy a small estate and settled to life as an improving landlord; he had acquired land and experimented in growing fruit in the Baramahal and the Ceded Districts and his scientific and horticultural interests were well known at Madras. His further role in British Indian history, however, was decided by his presence in Britain at a time when the Home government was concerned with administrative reform, his particular area of expertise, rather than foreign policy and army reform, Malcolm's specialties. Malcolm, a soldier-diplomat, had influential friends but could obtain no suitable appointment. By the time of his return to Madras in March 1817, however, Anglo-Maratha tension was such that foreign relations and security were again attracting attention in India, and in April 1817, Elphinstone told William Elphinstone that Malcolm was awaiting a summons to Calcutta "where his talents will be greatly required . . . and where I have no doubt he will be a welcome guest."[20]

CHAPTER 5

India, 1812–1819
The Formation of a Leadership Cadre

*Acting in countries remote from each other, and whose inhabitants differ in
language and customs as much as the nations of Europe, some [company
servants] rise to the exercise of almost kingly rule.*
—John Malcolm

*T*heir predilection for "kingly rule" has done much to highlight the authoritarian and conservative elements in Munro, Malcolm, and Elphinstone's school of thought on Indian government. But a temporary period of authoritarian, monarchical government was regarded by Scottish historians as a necessary stage in the progress of civil society in terms of political liberty, acknowledgment of certain human rights, and commercial prosperity. Concentration of the authority and resources of the state in the hands of the monarch in France and England had led to the demilitarization of the divisive and destabilizing power of the feudal aristocracy, with its antiprogressive private armies and agricultural vassalage, while providing the orderly setting and royal encouragement necessary for the growth of commerce, the empowerment of the middle ranks, and the development of rule by law. As the authoritarian "rulers" of Britain's newly conquered Indian territories, Munro, Malcolm, and Elphinstone's priorities were the demilitarization of local lordships and the imposition of the necessary law and order for agriculture and commerce to prosper—prerequisites, they believed, not simply for the maintenance of British structures of domination but also for the progress of civil society in India.

Between 1812 and 1819, Munro, Malcolm, and Elphinstone all played important roles in Indian government. But while Munro and Elphinstone's professional stature grew, Malcolm's career reached a plateau. Although promoted to higher military rank on his return to India in 1817, his important post as the governor-general's political agent was similar to posts he had held under Wellesley and Minto; it was not a step up. The careers of the three men came into direct conflict for the first time between 1816 and 1819; that their friendship survived was due partly to mutual respect and partly to shared views on policy that made them natural allies. Although they served in different theaters during the Third Maratha War (1817–18)—Munro against the peshwa's southern feudatories, Malcolm in the north against the Pindaris and Holkar, and Elphinstone against the peshwa in central Maharashtra—they were all concerned with the political aspects of the war and with the arrangements to be made for the civil administration of the conquered territories. Munro and Elphinstone were dominant figures in their areas while Malcolm, with much greater knowledge of India than either the marquis of Hastings or Sir Thomas Hislop, commander in chief in the Deccan, had considerable influence on the conduct of affairs further north.

Malcolm wrote regularly to both Munro and Elphinstone throughout 1817 and 1818, and Munro and Elphinstone exchanged frequent letters on the campaign against the peshwa from late in 1817. Although aware of each other's accomplishments, partly through their link with Malcolm, Munro and Elphinstone only met for the first time in May 1818. It is from this time that the three men may be termed an important leadership cadre and the ideas they shared may be termed a "Scottish school of thought" on Indian government.

While Munro and Malcolm were on leave in Britain, Elphinstone lived quietly at Pune, finishing his book on the Afghans, reading, hunting, and carrying out his duties as resident. Soon after taking up his post in

May 1811, he was asked by the Supreme government to prepare a comprehensive report on the history and legal status of the relationship between
the peshwa and his southern jagirdars—his "great feudatories"—and to
recommend a policy for settling disputes between them which were destabilizing central and western India and, arguably, threatening the security
of the company's territories.

In an untitled paper remarkable for its detailed information and clari-
ty of expression, Elphinstone demonstrates his expert knowledge of
Maratha history, law, and politics. He discusses all the questions—ethical
as well as practical—that the government should take into consideration,
and concludes by recommending the precise terms of a settlement. The
problem, Elphinstone believes, is that Baji Rao II is following a clearly defined scheme to remove all rivals to his authority and "draw the whole
part of the state into his own hands."[1] Although the British doubted the
peshwa's ability to do this, any exercise in state building and the centralization of power of this sort alarmed them.

The masterly presentation was Elphinstone's work but the content of
the paper, as Elphinstone made clear, owed much to Arthur Wellesley,
Barry Close, and Edward Strachey, who had analyzed the relationship between the peshwa and his jagirdars when Elphinstone was serving his apprenticeship in Maratha affairs under their supervision in 1802 and 1803.
In his report, Elphinstone cites the opinions of Close and Wellesley and
echoes their policy: a threat of military force to back a demand that both
sides maintain what British research has identified as their legal relationship. Governor-general Lord Minto praised the "force and ability" of Elphinstone's discussion of policy and, as the arguments supporting it had
been urged by such competent authorities (Wellesley and Close), observed that "little is left to be added to the subject." In March 1812 Elphinstone was given "*carte blanche* for all the disposable force of the Deccan" to impose a settlement. The threat of force, however, was sufficient
to induce most jagirdars to cooperate, and Elphinstone was soon able to
report that the settlement of the peshwa's southern territory was "in such
forwardness" that the company troops could return to their stations.[2]

The following year the peshwa, pleased with the company's solution
to this problem, requested British arbitration to settle long-standing dif-

ferences with Baroda, and in February 1814 a Barodan envoy, Gangadhar Shastri, visited Pune under a British guarantee of protection. Little had been achieved, however, when the envoy was murdered by hired assassins in July 1815 while Elphinstone, who was technically the guarantor of his safety, was away visiting the great cave temples at Ellora. His "careful intelligence work," which Bayly cites in *Empire and Information* as a major reason "for British success in the Maratha wars," seems on this occasion to have been inadequate. Elphinstone's account of the incident, which is virtually the only one, blames the murder on Trimbakji Danglia, the peshwa's favorite. It has been suggested that the evidence against Trimbakji was not convincing and that the murder may have been arranged by a rival Barodan faction rather than by someone from Pune; even Elphinstone admitted to being uncertain about Trimbakji's "ultimate design in the murder." The victim, however, was a brahmin, assassinated at a place of pilgrimage. There had been a public outcry on his death, and it was important for the British that justice should be believed to have been swiftly administered. There was circumstantial evidence which could be used to implicate Trimbakji and, as Elphinstone makes eminently clear in his report on the way in which he handled the crisis, he seized the opportunity to remove from an influential position someone who strongly opposed British interference in the peshwa's affairs.[3]

It was standard practice for an official to draw attention to his accomplishments and to justify his proceedings in his reports, but Elphinstone's ability as a writer gives a rare subtlety and polish to his account of the crisis. The events are presented to demonstrate his foresight in anticipating every possible contingency and every likely response by the peshwa or Trimbakji, and hints are dropped of the difficulties under which he worked in the tense atmosphere of Pune where the peshwa's ministers, he claims, were intimidated, indeed terrorized, by the peshwa's favorite. Elphinstone received the "unqualified approbation" of the new governor-general, the marquis of Hastings, for his spirit, energy, decision, and judgment.[4]

During the winter and spring of 1813–14, when the jagirdars were coming to terms and before the negotiations with Baroda reached a crisis, Elphinstone had worked hard to finish his book on the Afghans, and on 7

June 1814 the manuscript, entitled *An Account of the Kingdom of Caubul,* was
sent to England. It was less well received on publication than Malcolm's
History of Persia but Elphinstone remarked, in response to a friend's account of its reception in England, that "this unanswerable proof of the
dullness of my works had no effect but that of giving me a very hearty
laugh."[5] The book nevertheless made Elphinstone an expert on Afghanistan in the eyes of both the reading public and the Home government and
in the long term is probably the more widely read book.

Two weeks before Elphinstone's book began its journey west, Munro
had received his commission to return to the east. On 16 September 1814,
he arrived at Madras with his new wife and a mandate, as he describes it,
"to revise the internal administration in the Madras territories." This
meant arranging the assessment and collection of the revenue along ryotwari lines and the gradual introduction of a judicial system which gave
the collector the powers of a magistrate, employed Indian judges in minor
cases, and used panchayats (juries) in civil trials. The Bengal-style courts
were to be retained for criminal cases and for appeals. There was fierce opposition from officials in the Madras and Supreme governments, particularly from the members of the judicial department who had most to lose.
The importance of the judicial service itself, as well as the number of judicial appointments, would be reduced when revenue collectors and Indian judges were given judicial responsibilities. Munro found it necessary to
insist that instructions from London were phrased as orders; if they began "It is our wish" or "We Propose," Madras officials disregarded them.[6]
Although the job was nearly complete by the summer of 1817—within the
three years specified in Munro's commission—he made powerful enemies,
and his difficulty in obtaining men and supplies from the Madras government during his military campaign against the Marathas in 1817 and 1818
was probably due to deliberate obstruction.

The third and final war against the Marathas developed out of a campaign mounted to eradicate the Pindaris, seen by the British as predatory
robbers but described more accurately by Biswanath Ghosh as "armies
without masters." For centuries there had been a large "military labour
market" in India, drawn not only from traditional Hindu and Muslim
warrior castes but also from peasant cultivators and pastoralists who re-

garded casual military service as an invaluable additional source of income.[7] The subordination of Hyderabad, Mysore, and the Maratha princes to indirect British control had reduced the military employment available to these groups and many had joined Pindari bands. These sometimes fought as auxiliaries with Maratha armies, but as often they subsisted by pillaging Maratha territories. Between 1812 and 1816 Pindari raids were extended into the company's territories at a time when the British were becoming increasingly irritated at the failure of the Maratha princes to conduct either their internal or external affairs in conformity with the alliances they had signed. Lord Hastings used the incursions to gain the support of his initially reluctant council and the Home government for his policy of establishing the company's hegemony in India.[8] For this he required, partly for the sake of appearances, the cooperation of the Maratha rulers against the Pindaris. Military action, if fought in alliance with the Indian princes, might avoid the stigma of outright aggression, so during 1816 and 1817 negotiations were initiated with four of the five principal Maratha rulers, ostensibly to gain their support. Holkar refused to negotiate, but new alliances were imposed on Sindhia and the peshwa. Elphinstone, who conducted the negotiations with the peshwa, had to threaten force to obtain the latter's signature and felt the new demands were so humiliating that, if enforced, they would probably lead to war. All the Maratha rulers resented the company's power and no British official was surprised—or disappointed—when the campaign against the Pindaris in 1817 precipitated a final effort by the princes to recover their independence.[9]

Malcolm returned to India from Britain in March 1817, just in time to take part in the hostilities. He had been promoted to brigadier general; but before taking up his command under General Hislop, he was ordered to visit various Indian states as the governor-general's agent to report on the "disposition" of their rulers. He went first to Madras, however, and after consultations with the presidency government in July 1817, remained a few days longer to await Munro's return from the country.

Eight months earlier Munro, whose work as judicial commissioner was nearly complete, had unsuccessfully requested a military command in the forthcoming campaign against the Pindaris. To his disappointment,

Hastings had appointed him instead to supervise the civil arrangements
of the districts adjacent to the Madras presidency which Baji Rao II was
expected to cede to the company under the terms of Elphinstone's new
treaty. Malcolm, however, was also disappointed at Munro's civil appointment as he had been hoping to be assigned to control these districts himself. At the same time, Munro was annoyed that Malcolm, among other
colonels with less seniority and less active Indian military experience than
he, had been promoted to brigadier general and given command of a division or brigade ahead of him.[10] These areas of possible friction, however,
do not seem to have troubled the two men when they met in Madras in
July 1817. Malcolm was resigned to his new appointment as the governor-
general's agent and had already written to John Adam, political secretary
to the Supreme government, extolling Munro's abilities: "The Marathas
will neither cheat nor beat Munro, and, besides, he will be the best man in
the universe to look after the jagirdars . . . it is important a master hand
should be the first to touch them." Munro recommended to Hastings an
"able" report by Malcolm on the various Maratha states.[11]

After his meeting with Munro at Madras in July, Malcolm went to
Pune. In the previous May, when relations with the peshwa were particularly tense over the issue of the new subsidiary alliance, Elphinstone had
suggested to the Supreme government that Malcolm, whom Baji Rao
trusted, should replace him as negotiator. The government, however, who
favored coercion rather than conciliation to achieve its ends, rejected the
suggestion. On 13 June 1817, Elphinstone finally induced the resentful
peshwa to sign the new alliance. The following day Elphinstone learned
that Hislop was to take command in the Deccan, in both the Pindari
campaign and any operations which might result from company pressure
on the peshwa. Malcolm, who would benefit by it, had suggested this
arrangement to Hastings; Elphinstone, who would not, was annoyed.
Shortly before Malcolm's arrival in Pune he recorded in his journal that
he had been "out of humour" since hearing that he was to be superceded,
and he blamed "a push of Malcolm's to add everything he could to his
own credit." When Malcolm reached Pune in August, however, the two
men talked frankly and Elphinstone conceded that, although Malcolm
had unintentionally injured him, "a plan of mine, by securing the com-

mand of the southern army to General Smith, unknowingly frustrated Malcolm's views."[12]

Perhaps to make amends, Malcolm wrote to William Elphinstone praising his nephew and urging him to support an Indian government proposal to reward Mountstuart financially for his services. This friendly gesture led Elphinstone to review his own services and "pretensions" to reward and recognition. In his journal he concluded that "it would be a most liberal allowance to place myself in that respect where Malcolm was in 1806, and to think that my conduct affords good hopes of my turning out as well, if I have an opportunity."[13] The two men remained on good terms, although Malcolm's social ease and garrulousness always irritated Elphinstone, who was uncomfortable in society and a reluctant public speaker.

Malcolm's purpose in visiting Pune had been to obtain intelligence of the peshwa's intentions, and he listened patiently to both the prince's complaints and his professions of loyalty to the company. He pointed out, however, that the peshwa's best chance of retaining power lay in the company's alliance and encouraged him to demonstrate his will to cooperate with the British by helping them against the Pindaris. Malcolm was confident Baji Rao II would remain loyal. Elphinstone, who had been keeping a careful record of the activities of the peshwa's spies,[14] was doubtful, but he deferred to Malcolm's "sound judgment and great store of knowledge, derived both from reading and observation" and allowed the British force, which had been sent to keep an eye on the peshwa, to move out of Pune.[15]

It was a mistake. On 5 November 1817, as Sindhia reluctantly signed his new alliance with the British, the peshwa, who had used the excuse of cooperating in the war against the Pindaris to assemble his troops, stormed the Pune residency. Elphinstone and his staff were forced to take refuge with the company force outside the city where, greatly outnumbered, they were attacked by Baji Rao. The Maratha force was driven off, however, and the peshwa spent the next six months alternately harassing or eluding two British forces under Elphinstone's direction that were supposed to bring about his submission. The sack of the residency at Pune precipitated a general war against the Marathas.

The outbreak of war brought Munro rapid promotion to the rank of brigadier general—Malcolm's rank—but his command over the reserve division of Hislop's army was worded ambiguously. He told Elphinstone he had been ordered originally to defend the company's frontier and the nizam of Hyderabad's dominions, but these instructions had been superseded by a recent order "directing the reserve to be held at your disposal," for operations against the peshwa.[16] In December 1817, Elphinstone was made sole commissioner for the settlement of any territory taken by the company from the peshwa, and he was given authority to direct all the company forces in the field against him. This arrangement made Munro, an army officer for thirty-seven years and one of the most experienced and highly respected administrators in the company's service, subordinate in both military and civil matters to Elphinstone, a civilian diplomat who was eighteen years his junior. Remarkably, there is no evidence to suggest that he resented Elphinstone's authority, while Elphinstone's lack of self-confidence, ready acknowledgment of his own inexperience, and apparent respect for Munro enabled an arrangement that might have been undermined by personal rivalry to work well. The two men did not meet until the end of May 1818, but Elphinstone bombarded Munro with requests for advice on every aspect of the military, political, and administrative problems of his new job. Munro accepted the role of mentor gracefully.

From November 1817 to April 1818, Munro, who was barred by the presence of troops loyal to the peshwa from moving north to join the division he had been ordered to command, conducted a highly successful campaign of his own devising against the forces of the peshwa's southern jagirdars. Malcolm, generous as always with his tributes to Munro's ability, describes his unusual strategy.

We shall all recede, as this extra-ordinary man comes forward. We use common vulgar means, and go on zealously, and actively, and courageously enough; but how different is his part in the drama! Insulated in an enemy's country, with no military means whatever (five disposable companies of sepoys were nothing,) he forms a plan of subduing this country, expelling the army by which it is occupied, and collecting the revenues that are due to the enemy, through the means of the inhabitants themselves, aided and supported by a few irregular infantry, whom he invites from the neighbouring provinces for that purpose. His plan, which is at once simple and great, is successful in a degree, that a mind like his alone could have anticipated. The country comes into his hands by the most legitimate of all modes, the zealous and spirited efforts of the natives, to place themselves under his rule.[17]

Another contemporary, Captain James Grant, explained that Munro's irregulars, sent to the right and left of his column of march, "occupied the villages, fought with spirit on several occasions, stormed fortified places, and took possession in the name of 'Thomas Munro Bahadur.'"[18] "Bahadur" was a courtesy title indicating high respect and meaning, literally, "invincible."

A friend of Munro's in the Crown army once observed that to Munro, "the business of the field . . . [was] relaxation or most agreeable amusement." General Dunlop, who had known Munro since they worked together in the Glasgow accounting office of Sommerville and Gordon in the 1770s, understood that the science of war appealed to Munro more than the conventional lure of valor and glory. Warfare, whether strategy, tactics, or logistics, was a series of mentally challenging problems, like mathematical puzzles, to which solutions must and could be found. Munro's intellectual interest in the science of warfare is evident in many of his writings. The reports on the company's political and military relations with the Indian states, which Munro's father had forwarded to the Home government in the 1780s and 1790s, demonstrate Munro's comprehension of many aspects of Indian warfare, as does his correspondence with Arthur Wellesley on the Second Maratha War. The relish with which he tackled the organizational problems of the First Burma War in the 1820s, at a time when he wished and expected to leave India, indicates his appreciation of the central importance of the organization of resources, as well as strategy, tactics, and leadership, to the successful conduct of war.[19]

Despite Munro's inferior military and social rank, Arthur Wellesley respected his opinions. Munro criticized quite severely Wellesley's conduct of the battle of Assaye in 1803, but Wellesley, describing Munro as "a judge of a military operation," was anxious to secure his good opinion and provided the older man with a detailed defense of the action. Munro responded that he would endorse Wellesley's action, but he did not entirely withdraw his criticism. He disliked "the practice of carrying on war with too many scattered armies" and analyzed the considerations which would have made him hesitate to follow Wellesley's course, offering an alternative plan of operation. He did, however, concede that although the mode of attack was not the safest, it "was undoubtedly the most decided and heroic."[20] Arthur Wellesley's continuing respect for Munro's military competence is evident in a comment made in 1825 to Sir Charles Wynn, president of the board of control at the time of the First Burma War. By this time duke of Wellington and Britain's pre-eminent military authority, Wellington observed that on examining a box of papers sent from India on the war, "The only paper which shows in the writer any knowledge of his subject is Sir Thomas Munro's minute . . . and it is curious how all appear to have chimed in with his simple proposal, just as a pack of hounds do to the voice of the experienced dog."[21] For Munro, military campaigns presented problems to be analyzed and solved. His campaign in the southern Maratha country during the Third Maratha War was an unorthodox but intelligent (and cheap) solution to a military problem.

Munro gained control over the resources of three thousand square miles of the peshwa's territory, thus denying Baji Rao men and money in his struggle with the British. He created a broad corridor of company-controlled territory between the Madras presidency and Pune. And he did all of this while holding what he called "a subaltern command" and at virtually no cost to the Supreme government because he collected the land revenue as he went along.[22] Malcolm took credit for having recommended Munro: "Confess," he demanded of John Adam, "that I have a right to exult in the eagerness with which I pressed upon you the necessity of bringing forward this master-workman." However there is no evidence that Malcolm's recommendations influenced Hastings's decision to promote Munro and allow him to return to the army. Elphinstone told a friend who had been "liberally dispensing praise and censure" on the conduct of various individuals during the war that Munro was the real hero: "the great claimant to praise for enterprise and talent, and for retaining his zeal and good humour in every circumstance."[23]

In devising his strategy Munro had taken into consideration the history of the Marathas and the social structure and organization of the region. He had also applied what was to him the psychologically important principle of self-help. Writing five years later about a different war—the

Greek struggle for independence from the Ottoman Empire—he observed to George Canning that the Greeks should emancipate themselves,
without foreign aid, because the struggle would "give them a national
character and a spirit to defend their liberty."[24] There were many ethnic
and linguistic groups in addition to Marathas in the region Munro took
from the peshwa; by giving them a role in their own "liberation" from
Maratha rule, they might become useful supporters of the British, whatever regime was set up after the war.

While Munro worked his way through the southern Maratha country
in 1817 and 1818, leaving amildars (local revenue officers) to administer the
districts he had conquered, Elphinstone traveled the peshwa's territories,
sometimes with the force attempting to bring Baji Rao II to bay, at other
times with a second force which was capturing, one after the other, the
hill forts south of Pune. Satara was taken in February 1818 and, on 10
April, the raja of Satara, the titular chief of the Maratha princes who had
been held in captivity by the peshwa from the beginning of the war, was
installed by Elphinstone as a Maratha figurehead in "a sovereignty sufficient for [his] comfort and dignity."[25] A month later Munro defeated a
force of the peshwa's infantry outside Sholapur and a few days later concluded his campaign by capturing the fortress at Sholapur, bringing to an
end the war in southern Maharashtra.

Malcolm, after leaving Elphinstone in Pune in August 1817, went to
Hyderabad to arrange the supply and movement of the company's army
into the Deccan for General Hislop, who was ill. He then concluded his
duties as political agent by visiting Nagpur to make sure the raja of Berar's contribution of supplies to the campaign against the Pindaris would
be forthcoming, before taking up his own regimental command. Two
months later the campaign was virtually over. But fighting continued
against Holkar and Sindhia in the north, and Malcolm joined Hislop's
army in time to take part in a pitched battle against Holkar at Mehidpur
on 21 December 1817. He led a force of cavalry against enemy horse
threatening British troops at a river crossing and then, somewhat rashly,
led a charge against the enemy's batteries. Luck and the skill and courage
of the sepoys allowed him to take the batteries with a bayonet charge
while under heavy fire. It was a dramatic but orthodox engagement of the

type that reaped conventional military acclaim and honors, and Malcolm was delighted to have been part of it. When Munro heard the news, he congratulated Malcolm on his success in a battle "as severe as Assaye," but wondered why the army "did not instantly follow up the victory, instead of halting four days to sing Te Deum, and write to your grandmothers and aunts how good and gracious Providence had been." He was pleased that Malcolm had played so conspicuous a part in the drama, however, "both on your own account, and on that of the honour of the coast [Madras] army."[26] The rivalry for respect and rewards between the Bengal and Madras armies was intense.

From December 1817 to early May 1818, Malcolm was occupied with negotiations with Holkar and with coercing and cajoling various Pindari chiefs into submission, but in May an emissary from the peshwa arrived unexpectedly at his camp. The peshwa was moving north at the head of an army, relentlessly pursued by British forces, and wished to discuss with Malcolm possible terms of surrender. There was little doubt that Baji Rao II would soon be defeated in the field, but Malcolm preferred, in the interest of long-term stability, that the prince should be seen to abdicate voluntarily rather than lose his throne to the British in battle. Made a prisoner, he would become an object of sympathy and a potential figurehead for revolt. Killed in battle he might become a martyr and the discontented might rally around "a real or pretended heir to his high station."[27] Abdication, Malcolm felt, would put an end to any threat the peshwa might pose to British power.

For two weeks Malcolm was engaged in tense negotiations with Baji Rao II. He made it immediately clear that the Supreme government would reject even a nominal sovereignty, and that its generosity would be proportional to the speed at which the war was concluded. But the likelihood of attaining an outcome satisfactory to Britain's interests depended largely, Malcolm states, "on passing events" in other areas that raised or lowered the peshwa's hopes. "The complete defeat of the peshwa's troops at Sholapur" by Munro was particularly helpful.[28]

When Malcolm's offer of a lavish pension of eight lakhs of rupees in return for an immediate end to the war was accepted by the peshwa, he was censured by the Supreme government for extravagance. But Munro and Elphinstone both endorsed Malcolm's justification of his terms. Munro observed that "The amount of the pension, and I believe also the principle of granting [the peshwa] any terms whatever, have been disapproved of. I certainly think differently; I think that great allowance should be made for a native Sovereign, reduced to a state of degradation by a foreign power." He also mentioned that Baji Rao II had made overtures previously to Elphinstone but that Elphinstone had rejected them because he had been instructed to accept nothing but unconditional surrender. Malcolm had been given no instructions at all—Baji Rao had not been expected to travel so far north—and had done what he could according to his own assessment of British interests.[29]

To console Malcolm, Munro told him that if the peshwa had approached him, he would probably have offered ten lakhs rather than eight because the peshwa's surrender, which deprived the disaffected of their leader, was the key to the rapid restoration of peace and the smooth settlement of the country. He also said that he, himself, would rather have taken Baji Rao than the Bombay government, and he hoped that Malcolm would soon be "the taker of both." Munro told Elphinstone that what the British called the peshwa's "treachery" should be neither resented nor punished because it was natural; any sovereign controlled by a foreign subsidiary force in his own domains must become timid, cunning, and treacherous. "We ourselves induce the treachery we punish."[30] Munro consistently criticized the subsidiary alliance system for its debilitating moral effects and unfortunate practical consequences.

In the spring of 1818, Hastings asked Munro to undertake the postwar settlement of the peshwa's southern territories in cooperation with Elphinstone in the north. But Munro had already decided to return to Britain on account of his increasing deafness and deteriorating eyesight.[31] Elphinstone, whose administration of the area around Pune had begun before Baji Rao's surrender and deposition, was given control of the whole region. He learned of Munro's decision in April 1818 and expressed his qualms at being left to handle the task alone in an anxious letter to the older man.

I really do not see how we are to fill the blank that you will leave . . . I had calculated on receiving much instruction from you on the management of the rest of the country, either by minute communications or in the capacity of a joint commissioner . . . I now find that you will be quitting the scene at the time when the settlement of the country north of the Kistna will just be beginning and I really feel some uneasiness at the prospect of under-taking alone a task on which so much is to depend.

He sent a palanquin with a strong escort to bring Munro to Satara for a meeting at which he took careful notes.[32]

Elphinstone's debt to Munro has long been recognized by historians,[33] but the extent of Munro's influence on Elphinstone's administration of the peshwa's territories has become more evident from papers acquired by the Oriental and India Office Collection in the British Library in the 1970s, which were unavailable to earlier historians. Until November 1817 Elphinstone was employed as a diplomat. He had no administrative experience and there is no indication that he had given thought previously to the problems of maintaining civil order, collecting revenues, or administering justice. So between January and April 1818, while he and Munro were still fighting the Marathas, he sought Munro's advice on a multitude of subjects including the disposition of the forces he was directing against the peshwa, the appointment of civil collectors, and how to treat the different classes of jagirdar. Munro confided to Malcolm that Elphinstone wanted his aid only because he overestimated the difficulties of settlement work. He recommended that William Chaplin, the collector of Bellari and one of his disciples, should replace him in the southern territories and that Elphinstone should be provided with an experienced revenue official as his secretary.[34]

Munro and Elphinstone met for the first time at Satara at the end of May 1818, and Elphinstone noted in his journal that he was greatly impressed with the older man's good sense, frankness, and benevolence, and that he had gained much instruction from him.[35] Throughout the summer Elphinstone continued to solicit Munro's advice in letters which included numerous phrases such as "I am extremely obliged for your answer to my queries . . . They will be very instructive," and "I shall not fail to attend to what you say . . . and shall modify the orders," or "What you propose . . . seems the best course." In August 1818, Munro, now staying with friends at Bangalore, sent Elphinstone a comprehensive report on the condition of the southern Maratha lands, and he continued to respond patiently to

Elphinstone's requests for advice on questions of policy until early in 1819 when he set sail for Britain.[36]

Although inexperienced and, according to Munro, lacking in self-confidence, Elphinstone was intelligent and a very successful company servant; it is unlikely he would have sought or accepted Munro's advice so consistently if he had not been in sympathy with the principles on which Munro based his administrative policies. Elphinstone was responsible for the administration of the peshwa's former territories from December 1817 until he moved to Bombay in October 1819. His approach to administration, as he describes it in his *Report on the Peshwa's Territories*, had much in common with what might be termed the central pillars of the Munro system: regenerating rather than replacing existing revenue and judicial systems, adapting necessary reforms to the stage of development of local society, protecting a graduated social structure, and giving Indians a role in the government of their country.[37]

These criteria were also applied by Malcolm during the four years from 1818 to 1822, during which he was responsible for the settlement and administration of Malwa—territories taken from Sindhia and Holkar and organized by the company as the Central Indian agency. He told Sir Walter Scott, with obvious pride, that he was governing a territory "as large as England and Scotland," where the "large folks are quiet" but the great problem is "to keep the Rob Roys under."[38] There were no important towns in the region and Malcolm seems to have spent much of his time moving from district to district, again alternatively cajoling and coercing the more unruly local lords into accepting British rule. He also spent much time gathering and analyzing information obtained from oral and written Indian sources on the history and administrative system of Malwa, which he presented in a report to the government in 1822 and expanded into a two-volume *Memoir of Central India*, published after his return to Britain. Malcolm hoped his report and book would demonstrate to the authorities how well qualified he was, in terms of knowledge of India, for a top appointment. But he also believed such historical research was a necessary preliminary to the development by the British of a form of administration suited to the conditions and needs of the local people.

The Third Maratha War was the catalyst in bringing the three men to-

gether as a leadership cadre; potential rivalries were smoothed over by mutual respect, a similar approach to policy issues, and, perhaps, by cultural
solidarity—a tinge of Scottish partisanship. The war was also, in many
ways, the apogee of their careers. Their Indian expertise and their all-
around talents were tested to the full. Their achievements were officially
recognized when George Canning, the president of the board of control,
announced that although the court of directors, since the India Act of
1784, had preferred to select British aristocrats or politicians as their presidency governors, he was nevertheless "disposed to concur in the appointment of either Sir John Malcolm, Mr. Mountstuart Elphinstone or
Colonel Thomas Munro as Governor of Bombay."[39] Malcolm was enjoying the extensive civil and military powers he had been given to settle Malwa and Munro was on the high seas expecting never to return to India
when Elphinstone learned, on 12 February 1819, that he rather than Malcolm, his patron, or Munro, his mentor, had been appointed governor of
Bombay.

CHAPTER 6

1819–1830
Recognition

*The subordinate governments . . . present no employment so interesting
as securing and regulating a new conquest with ample powers, civil
and military, with plenty of troops, and the most liberal support
from the governor-general.*
—*Mountstuart Elphinstone*

The subordinate governments—the governorships of Madras and Bombay—were to be the pinnacle of the careers of Munro, Malcolm, and Elphinstone in terms of status and prestige. Munro was considered for, but not offered, the governor-generalship of India in 1825. Elphinstone declined an offer of the governor-generalship in 1834, ostensibly on the ground of ill health. Malcolm would have jumped at the opportunity of serving as either acting or permanent governor-general but was never considered. To win renown as a governor was difficult because the overriding authority of the governor-general and the checks imposed by presidency councils, boards of revenue, and judiciaries seriously inhibited freedom of action. Neither Munro, Malcolm, nor Elphinstone expected the post to be particularly rewarding—except, perhaps, financially. Elphinstone's view that the settlement of newly conquered territories was a more interesting appointment than ruling a presidency was shared by Munro and Malcolm. However, neither Madras nor Bombay, which at this time carried a lower salary and less prestige, was likely to be declined by a company official. Since 1784, as Canning had pointed out, these appointments had generally been held by men with political connections in Britain and a higher social status than that of most company officials—although not necessarily more ability—and the nominations were an honor.

During the years from 1820 to 1827, when Elphinstone and Munro governed Bombay and Madras and Malcolm, for most of the time, was in Britain, the three men kept in touch by correspondence. Their experiences during the Third Maratha War and their similar views on governance, more evident after Malcolm and Elphinstone moved from diplomacy to administration, brought them closer, increased their mutual respect, and established them as the leading spokesmen of a particular approach to Indian government. If Malcolm regretted promoting his friends' talents during the fifteen years when he was the most prominent of the three, he gave no sign; but in the 1820s Munro became their "elder statesman." Sound administration now took precedence over diplomacy, and both Malcolm and Elphinstone sought Munro's advice and approval. He encouraged Malcolm's literary activities and advised Elphinstone on his administrative policies.

Although their nineteenth-century biographers stressed devotion to duty in explaining why the three men accepted appointments for which they had little enthusiasm, other considerations were more important. A governorship offered a relatively liberal salary and public recognition—in Britain as well as British India. It was a practically and emotionally satisfactory culmination to a distinguished career for a company official because it confirmed his improved social and political status.

As early as 1801, Elphinstone was wondering what he could "do honourably to get money to go home with even for a time?" In 1813 going home for a time was a temptation he must resist because it would extend the time it would take him to save enough to retire on permanently. Shortly before his appointment to Bombay, after thanking his uncle for his "warm interest" in his career, Elphinstone told Lord Keith that "my ultimate view is to get into quiet retirement, which I should do tomorrow if I had £1,500 a year."[1] A month after taking office at Bombay in October 1819, Elphinstone told Malcolm that equipping himself for the governorship would "run away with" at least one, possibly two, year's allowances. Malcolm, he claimed, "was never in better luck" than when he "escaped Bombay," where he would never have been able to save a farthing, while in Central India "you have Rps.50,000 clear or nearly so." In 1822 Elphinstone was still complaining of debts. But by May 1827 he had accumulated enough money for a comfortable country retirement, occasional travel in Britain and Europe, and the pursuit of his literary interests, despite having taken responsibility for some of his brother James's debt of Rps.47,000.[2] For Elphinstone, a governor's salary and his obligations to the relatives who had promoted his interests were probably the decisive considerations in accepting the appointment. There is no mention of a duty to the company or the people of India.

Munro liked both the climate and country of India better than those of Britain and told his friend Lady Liston that he "would rather wander over this country in a tent than live soberly in any town in my native land." But he would miss British friends and the stimulating culture of Europe and was ambivalent about returning to India in 1819. He claimed to feel obliged to go, although it is not clear whether his obligation was to India, to men in the company and the British government who had supported him and his policies, or to his family. A desire to consolidate his administrative reforms may have provided an inducement and the salary of £10,000 was also, no doubt, persuasive; his first son had been born during the voyage to Britain in 1819 and, at the age of fifty-eight, he found himself with a family to provide for. (A second son was born in 1823.) In 1821 he told his friend and financial agent George Brown that he had been too slow in making money ever to make "what is called a respectable appearance in the world," but with economy he hoped to save £6,000 a year while at Madras. His relatively humble origins may have enhanced the attraction of a governorship and the knighthood that went with it, but they were honors he felt he had earned. Munro judged everyone, including himself, by merit. At the time of his death six years later, a lifetime of careful attention to money and a thrifty style of life had enabled him not only to provide ongoing financial support for many years for many relatives, but also to leave an estate worth £126,648. Munro was poorer and more poorly connected when he joined the company than either Malcolm or Elphinstone, but by the end of his life he was the wealthiest and, arguably, the most respected of the three.[3]

In 1820 Malcolm told Munro he would have about £50,000 by the end of the year, which would enable him to retire to Britain and provide "Porridge and Butter for me and the weans" if he were not, as he was hoping, appointed lieutenant governor of Central India. Seven years later, when he was about to take over from Elphinstone at Bombay, he told Wellington that the prize money he had received recently from the final division of the spoils of the Third Maratha War, in addition to his former means, had made him "very independent" and he would not stay long at Bombay unless he was also given authority over Central India. Bombay alone would provide no chance of adding to his reputation, and the £15,000 to £20,000 he would make was insufficient to compensate for the hazards of serving again in India. Malcolm had more children to support and a more expensive lifestyle than Munro and his frequent insistence that money was not a determining consideration where appointments were concerned needs to be treated with caution. William Elphinstone told Munro in 1820 that Malcolm "cannot afford to come home to live in comfort with his habits, and an expensive family to bring up."[4] Money, however, seems quite genuinely to have mattered less to him than recognition. His private letters allude more frequently to a desire for renown than for wealth; they indicate that, after his first irresponsible years in India, it became of the greatest importance to him that his parents, brothers and sisters, and later his wife and children, as well as his country, should be proud of his achievements. Throughout his career he longed for public acknowledgment in Britain of his services to the company and, as he saw it, to the British empire.

Malcolm, Elphinstone, and Munro were nominated by Canning for the governorship of Bombay as a gesture of recognition for the recent achievements of the company's officials in general, as well as of those of the three men in particular. Canning intended his nomination of company officials rather than British political figures as a conciliatory move to reduce tension between the British government and the court of directors.[5] Naming Malcolm and Munro as well as Elphinstone as candidates for Bombay, however, was probably meant to indicate an equal appreciation for the past services of all three, not that he considered them as equal contenders for this office. If Canning hoped to appease the company, Malcolm's appointment to a governorship was out of the question, owing to his unpopularity with the directorate for what was regarded as the excessive cost of many of his diplomatic achievements. Munro was never a genuine contender for Bombay because he was wanted for Madras.

Because Bombay became vacant before Madras, and because in the later nineteenth century Bombay became the more important posting, Elphinstone's promotion ahead of the two older men has attracted much attention and added not inconsiderably to his reputation. Munro's appointment to Madras, however, was decided upon at the same time and, at a time after the Maratha War when efficient administration and reduced costs were priorities, was probably the cornerstone of the arrangements. As Sir John Kaye points out, Madras was "the higher and more advantageous appointment" in the 1820s. According to Malcolm, William Elphinstone, Sir Alexander Allan, and John Sullivan, three men with great influence over Indian affairs in London, had been working since 1812 to "support Munro's pretensions to a government." By 1818 there was a "strong and respectable" party determined to give a full trial to Munro's judicial system.[6] These statements are supported by the fact that the directorate made sure Munro would be able to implement his system by appointing George Stratton, William Thackeray, and Henry Graeme to the Madras council and James Cochrane as president of the board of revenue—all men who supported Munro's policies and with whom Munro was on good personal terms. John Ravenshaw, an active and articulate member of the company, told Munro that the directors were determined there should be no "factious opposition during the whole of your reign." Munro probably knew more about the Madras presidency and its Indian subjects than any contemporary British official. If company servants rather than British political figures were to be the next presidency governors, he was the natural choice. Although Munro was not actually appointed to Madras until the summer of 1819, George Gleig (author of the official biography of Munro prepared in association with Ravenshaw and other members of the directorate) stated that it had been decided that Munro would be asked to succeed Hugh Elliot as governor of Madras when Canning first made his nominations in the summer of 1818.[7]

A group that was sufficiently influential to obtain Munro's appointment to the more prestigious post at Madras because they were determined that his system should be given a "full trial" were likely to favor a candidate for Bombay who was known to hold similar views. Although Elphinstone attributed his appointment to the fact that no one in London knew anything about him and, therefore, had no grounds on which to object to him, this modest explanation was given to console Malcolm. The Home government knew enough about Elphinstone's administration of the peshwa's former territories to recognize Munro's influence. Canning, who played a role in both appointments, seems to have asked Munro to report to him on how Elphinstone was managing when Munro and his wife visited Bombay en route to Madras in May 1820. This commission implies a close understanding between Canning and Munro, a possibility supported by the mutually respectful tone of the correspondence between the two men and Munro's genuine regret when Canning left the board of control.[8]

Bargaining and maneuvering between the government and the company over appointments was customary. On this occasion, however, the usual priorities—political interest and patronage—seem to have been relatively unimportant. Policy pointed to the selection of Munro and Elphinstone in preference to Malcolm. Malcolm, of course, was disappointed. He accepted Munro's superior credentials, telling his wife: "Ambitious as I am, and impatient as I have become of slight, I do not know that I should not have had conscience enough to vote against myself [in regard to Madras]." But he resented the fact that Elphinstone, his "junior by twelve years in the political line" and his subordinate at the beginning of the Third Maratha War, was pushed ahead of him by the company.[9] The governor-general, Lord Hastings, attempted to make amends to Malcolm in 1819 and 1820. Observing that the directors might be prepared "to do something" for Malcolm, Hastings asked Elphinstone what he thought of detaching "an adequate extent" of the peshwa's former territory from the

Bombay presidency and installing Malcolm, for a time, as lieutenant governor of the region,[10] a proposal obviously designed solely to please Malcolm. Elphinstone's response is curious. He mentions that on his appointment to Bombay, he himself had seriously considered recommending the appointment of a commissioner for the peshwa's former territories under Bombay's authority. A lieutenant governorship would do what he had in mind, and Malcolm, with "his enlarged views of policy, and his liberal principles towards the natives," was well qualified to conciliate a newly conquered people. Elphinstone, however, also tells Hastings that Malcolm should be given a council to deal with civil administration, implying that Malcolm's enlarged views and liberal principles might need curbing. Put beside a letter Elphinstone wrote to Malcolm at much the same time, the council suggestion appears mildly malicious. Elphinstone told Malcolm: "It is a great annoyance to a person who is used as we are (or rather as we were and you are) to have his word law and to have nobody to satisfy of the propriety of a measure but himself, to be obliged to explain his motives to a council." Elphinstone thoroughly disliked having to work with a council.[11]

In concluding his reply to Hastings, Elphinstone questions whether it would be advisable to remove Malcolm from Malwa. "However quiet that country may be at present, it must retain, in the habits of its inhabitants, and in the character of the many petty governments of which it is combined, great materials for disturbance ... [and] every disturbance of the public tranquillity is to be dreaded." If Hastings knew "a fit person" to succeed Malcolm in Malwa, or if the country was sufficiently pacified that strong rule was no longer required, then, in Elphinstone's opinion, Malcolm could be moved. One wonders why Elphinstone thought a council so necessary for the government of the peshwa's former territories, but not for Malwa. Neither Hastings nor Elphinstone raises the question as to whether the lieutenant governor should be placed under Bengal or Bombay. If Bengal, Elphinstone would lose a large slice of the territory he was governing; if Bombay, he would be in the uncomfortable position of being Malcolm's superior. Colebrooke observes dryly: "we can readily understand that the correspondence went no further."[12]

Unaware, no doubt, of Elphinstone's lack of enthusiasm, Malcolm would have rejected the appointment in the peshwa's former territories anyway, on the terms Elphinstone suggested, as Elphinstone probably knew. If appointed lieutenant governor, Malcolm expected to have complete civil and military authority. A solution would have been to give Malcolm the rank of lieutenant governor in Malwa and the Central Indian agency, which comprised lands previously held by Sindhia, Holkar, and some minor chiefs. These regions had suffered badly at the hands of the Pindaris, were politically unstable and potentially rebellious, and there was some justification for Malcolm's claim that they needed to be ruled by a man with autocratic power. Munro supported this claim, telling Canning in May 1820 that Malcolm "ought undoubtedly to be kept in Malwa for some years," but his recommendation had no effect. Although polite words were spoken about Malcolm's dedicated service, no one in either London or Calcutta was willing to employ him at this time.[13] The Supreme government made no attempt to create a lieutenant governorship, and Malcolm returned to Britain in 1821 with his ambitions frustrated.

Malcolm's reputation had been established as a diplomat and as the political agent for several governors-general. Although he wielded the broad powers he had been given in Malwa with apparent success, events were working against him. With the defeat of the Marathas in 1818 Britain was indisputably the paramount power in India, but the war had been expensive and the government wanted retrenchment. In this setting, two of Malcolm's more attractive attributes, his generosity—the company thought of it as extravagance—and his sensibility, became liabilities rather than assets. His liberal pension for Baji Rao II was fresh in everyone's mind, recalling the exorbitant cost of his first Persian mission and the indemnity he had authorized after the murder of the Persian envoy in Bombay in 1802, which had prompted the shah to remark that a dozen envoys might be killed if the British would pay for them all at the same rate. Moreover Malcolm's bargain with Baji Rao II, a financial millstone the company would carry for many years, contrasted starkly with Munro's conquest of the peshwa's southern territories, which was paid for from the revenues of the territories themselves and cost the company virtually nothing.

A less obvious but nevertheless important "flaw" was Malcolm's respect for the feelings of defeated rulers. His knowledge of Indian politics and affable relationships with Indian princes had been useful to the diplomatic branch in the past, but the company expected to be dictating to rather than negotiating with Indian rulers in the future, and Malcolm's sympathy and generosity might be inconvenient. Short of money and with much more territory to govern, the Home government preferred proven administrators to men with broad vision and liberal principles.

Malcolm wanted a governorship badly. He had, in fact, been working quite hard for fifteen years to obtain one, not only by trying to influence patrons but also by acquiring the qualifications he believed were required for the job—career-building techniques that had served him well in the past. He had first risen in the company's service by attracting the Home government's attention with his thoughtful report on the organization of the company army in 1794. His next step up had followed Wellesley's receipt of his knowledgeable report on the Indian states in 1798. In preparation for a governorship he had spent much time while in Britain between 1812 and 1816 studying the workings of the British government and its relationship with the East India Company, because he felt there could be only one rational objection to the appointment of a company official to a governorship—his probably inadequate knowledge of the government of his own country, "or in other words ... being *too Indian.*" This view was shared by Wellington, who supported Malcolm's claims to a governorship a few years later. He told the president of the board of control, Charles Wynn, who preferred British public servants to company officials as governors, that Malcolm was an exception. He had spent much time in Britain, "and to great advantage. He has a thorough knowledge of men and affairs here."[14]

Munro and Elphinstone, however, had been selected for their knowledge of Indian rather than British men and affairs. This led Malcolm to write indignantly to his wife in 1820, asking,

Has not the whole government, in all its parts, been my constant study? ... Has not my life been given to all the details of revenue settlement and judicial proceedings, native as well as European modes of administering justice, and the most minute investigation of everything relating to the rules and institutions ... of this and neighbouring countries?

They shall ere long see all this in a report, which will enable me to ask my friends whether I am or I am not, fit for a civil government.[15]

Malcolm believed his broad knowledge of Asian politics and society qualified him for a governorship, and between 1819 and 1823 his determination to demonstrate his expertise—to prove that faction, not lack of knowledge or ability, had caused his exclusion—led to an almost obsessional preoccupation with his report on Malwa.

Lynn Zastoupil points out that Malcolm obtained much of his information on Malwa from local oral and written sources; he cites, in regard to Malcolm's advocacy of the conciliation of local elites, a quotation that Malcolm attributes to "the hereditary zamindar of Indore" to demonstrate that "A clearer example of how Indian ideas were refashioned into early British policies can hardly be found."[16] Indian ideas, of course, emerge quite clearly from many of the policy recommendations of Munro and Elphinstone as well as Malcolm because, unlike many later British officials, all three recognized much that was viable in Indian forms of governance. They favored the continuing utilization of some Indian practices. Malcolm, in particular, used Indian "voices" to support policy recommendations that reflected his own values and assumptions in the same way that he used examples of the undesirable consequences of what he saw as "bad" Indian government, also derived from Indian and other Asian historical sources, as didactic warnings to the British of how not to govern.

Malcolm sent his report on Malwa to Munro for criticism, chapter by chapter, in manuscript form. In May 1819 he rejoiced at Munro's praise of his revenue chapter—praise highly valued because Munro was "not in the habit of giving Balloon Draughts." But by 1821 Munro was becoming concerned that Malcolm was undermining his health with "over-exertion and unceasing occupation"; despite serious and repeated attacks of fever, no one could persuade him to leave India until he had completed what Munro now dubbed "the Malwa Encyclopaedia."[17]

Malcolm remained in Malwa until the end of 1821, moving between a number of temporary camps or small towns, restoring order, setting up a revenue and judicial system, listening to the concerns of the local population, and writing letters. He was partly consoled for his failure to obtain a lieutenant governorship with a promotion to major general and the honor of being made a Knight Grand Cross of the Order of the Bath, and with a salary equal to that of Elphinstone as governor because he received army pay in addition to his stipend as a political officer. Shortly before Malcolm left, at last, for England, Munro, who now had a copy of all the chapters of the report, told him how impressed he was by the mass of information it contained. In his official position as governor of Madras, Munro also suggested formally to the directorate that the company should express appreciation of Malcolm's distinguished service in general orders. Elphinstone's regard for Malcolm was more ambivalent. He attended a farewell banquet for Malcolm at Bombay, observing afterwards that although he appreciated Malcolm's "kindness, friendship, and good sense and good humour" and admired his "inexhaustible spirits and imperturbable temper" (qualities he felt he himself lacked), he confessed to a "want of tolerance for the single defect [egotism] of one of the first and best men I know." Elphinstone, himself, was not egotistic, but he was very self-absorbed. Numerous journal entries minutely chronicle, analyze, and criticize his own feelings and behavior.

Back in Britain Malcolm divided his time between a sociable home life in England and travel to Ireland, Scotland, and continental Europe. As he had done during an earlier period of career frustration, he turned to writing to keep his name before the public eye and promote his opinions. He revised his report on Malwa for publication under the title *A Memoir of Central India . . .*, expanded his earlier *Sketches of the Political History of India* into *A Political History of India*, and wrote *Sketches of Persia* (1827).[18]

The latter was a compilation of stories and anecdotes drawn from his own experiences in Persia and from Persian sources that he published in response to James Morier's *Adventures of Hajji Baba*, which had appeared in 1824. Malcolm's deceptively light and allusive introduction to his own book makes it clear that his main intention is to ward off any challenge to his position as the preeminent British authority on Persia. He also makes the claim, however, that his *Sketches* provide a more accurate picture of Persia than the one painted by his rival. Morier recounts the adventures of Hajji Baba in the first person singular and every event is seen, ostensibly, through the hero's eyes. Orthodox western values, however, are subtly im-

posed on all Hajji's activities, and a brutal indictment of the moral bankruptcy of Persian culture lies as a subtext beneath an entertaining veneer.
Malcolm implies that Morier's work should be treated as imaginative literature rather than as a genuine representation of Persian life, and stresses
that in his own work, "the sense, the nonsense, the anecdotes, the fables,
and the tales, all . . . with the exception of a few sage reflections of my
own, do actually belong to the good people amongst whom they profess
to have been collected." In other words, primary sources are required to
produce a true representation. Although himself intensely critical of Persian government and what he regarded as its deplorable effect on the national character and moral integrity of the Persian people, Malcolm
rather liked the vitality and quick intelligence of the Persians, and his
Sketches provide, in some respects, a more tolerant view of Persia.[19]

Malcolm did not send his *Sketches of Persia* to Munro but he sent the
additions and revisions of the *Political History* to him for his comments, as
he had done with the report on Malwa. Malcolm had described the last
chapter of the *Political History* to Walter Scott as "My brains . . . upon
every large question of our administration at home and abroad." He received Munro's endorsement of his views in June 1826, when the latter declared it to be "by far the most valuable book in our language on our Indian empire, to every person who takes any interest in its stability." The
final phrase probably alludes to Malcolm's main competition, James Mill's
History of British India, which had appeared in 1817 and was beginning to
have some influence on British attitudes towards India and British Indian
government.[20] In his preface to the 1970 edition of the *Political History*, K.
N. Pannikar points out that in addition to its contemporaneity, which en-
titles Malcolm's work to be treated as an original source, Malcolm was
one of the first British writers on India to make extensive use of government records. "Intimacy and authenticity are, hence, the hall-marks of his
works." Holden Furber, writing in 1933, claimed the best treatment of Sir
John Shore's administration was still that given by Malcolm in his *Political
History*, while more recently, Malcolm's accounts of the Indian Army in
the *Political History* have been praised by Raymond Callahan.[21]

In addition to his approval of the opinions expressed in Malcolm's literary works, Munro also encouraged his friend to continue to work for a

governorship, offering to let him know in advance when he was going to retire from Madras so that Malcolm could "take measures" to be appointed to succeed him. Munro first submitted his resignation as governor in September 1823. In the same year Malcolm declined an offer of an appointment as resident at Tehran, ostensibly because the government would not give him Crown rather than company credentials, and he thought the shah's perception of the inferior status of an Indian government representative would curtail his influence in Persia. It is likely, however, that Malcolm declined the Persian appointment because he was hoping to succeed Munro. The governorship of Madras was a greatly superior appointment to the company's residency at Tehran; when Munro's resignation became known in London in January 1824, Malcolm hastened to apply for the post. Soon afterwards a letter from Elphinstone in Bombay told the directors that he, too, wanted the higher Madras post, but war with Burma began before a dispute between the directors and the government over Munro's successor had been settled. In the light of the Burman crisis, Munro agreed to stay on.[22] Malcolm turned his thoughts, briefly, to entering the directorate or standing for election to Parliament, but Munro told Malcolm he could do far more good as the next governor of Madras than as a member of Parliament and that nothing would please him more than to have Malcolm as his successor.[23] Elphinstone, however, resigned from Bombay at the same time and Malcolm went to Bombay, while Stephen Lushington, the Liverpool administration's candidate, went to Madras.

Like Malcolm, Elphinstone sent written work to Munro for comments and, as he had done while commissioner for the peshwa's territories, sought advice as well as information. During Munro's first months as governor in the summer of 1820, Elphinstone asked for his opinions on a draft of a minute he was writing on the development of a legal code, in particular about the expediency of developing judicial regulations compatible with the ryotwari revenue system. He asked for information on the way the Madras College was being organized, arranged to have all Munro's minutes on "general subjects" sent to him by Munro's secretary, and later thanked Munro for his "particularly instructive" information. In 1822, on hearing that Munro had instituted a "Native Board of Revenue" at Madras, he asked Munro to explain it to him, as it seemed an excellent way of opening the door to "the employment of natives in high and efficient situations." He wanted to know whether Munro was thinking of doing the same for the judicial or any other branch of the service.[24]

The continuous passage of written material between the two presidencies allowed Elphinstone to benefit both from Munro's extensive experience and from the administrative lessons learned at Madras. On the other hand, Elphinstone's popularity with the directorate and his polished writing style made him a valuable advocate and publicist for the general principles of government on which the two men agreed. In a letter to Elphinstone in April 1823, Munro observed that Elphinstone's and Chaplin's "valuable works . . . will one day be considered all over India as the best guides for the internal administration of our provinces."[25]

Munro was made a Commander of the Order of the Bath in 1818, promoted to major general in 1819, and made Knight Commander of the Order of the Bath on accepting the governorship. In 1825 he was made a baronet in recognition of his services during the First Burma War and for the help he had given to the governor-general, the inexperienced Lord Amherst.[26] As a compromise candidate for the governor-generalship, Amherst received little political support from either the company or the government, making it difficult for him to maintain his authority over Bengal's opinionated military and civil officials. In the autumn of 1825 there was a movement in London to recall him, ostensibly because of his conduct of the war, but probably, as Douglas M. Peers suggests, because he had failed to please the directorate while at the same time becoming politically expendable to the government. In October the prime minister, the earl of Liverpool, asked Wellington whether he thought Amherst should be recalled and, if so, by whom he should be replaced. Wellington believed Amherst should be supported; if he had to be replaced, however, Wellington was "clearly of the opinion" that Munro should be appointed governor-general, "because he is peculiarly conversant with Indian warfare; and, in fact, the only intelligent papers which I have seen on the subject of this Burmese war have come from" him. Towards the end of October, Wynn told Wellington the company was going to insist on replacing Amherst with either Munro or Lord William Bentinck and supposed that, given the war, Munro would be the better choice. He wondered, however, whether Munro's authority would equal that of a nobleman sent from England, whether he would be capable of cutting staff appointments and allowances in the army, and whether his unpopularity in Bengal owing to his support for "ryotwar and judicial reform" would undermine his position. His age was also against him; Munro was sixty-four. Differences between the company and the government delayed a decision, however, and Amherst remained in India, largely owing to the powerful support of Wellington. Munro also defended Amherst.[27]

John Ravenshaw kept Munro fully and candidly informed about the debate and Munro was confident that if called upon to be governor-general, he would have no difficulties. Had he been offered the post ten years earlier, or even as recently as 1823 when Amherst replaced Hastings, he would "have been delighted with it." He had served the company for forty-six years, however, and ought, "according to all ordinary rules, to have been dead seven years ago." Only his excellent health and "great temperance" had enabled him to endure the rigors of Indian service so long. If appointed governor-general he could expect to remain no more than two years—too short a period to do any good.[28] He never states, however, that he will decline the appointment if it is offered.

The war with Burma ended early in 1826 and Munro, Elphinstone, and then Amherst all asked to be relieved. Amherst and Elphinstone returned to Britain, replaced, respectively, by Lord William Bentinck in 1828 and by Malcolm in November 1827. Munro died of cholera in July 1827 before his successor, Lushington, arrived. He was sixty-six years old. One of his closest associates in the Madras government, chief secretary, David Hill, paid tribute to Munro in a letter to Holt Mackenzie thanking him for joining the long list of people "disposed to pay honour to our late incomparable Ruler."

His, without question, was the greatest mind which ever applied itself to the practical study of Indian affairs; and it is infinitely to be rejoiced at that his sentiments upon every branch of them are upon record. Officially and privately he has written I imagine much more on the subject than any other individual: I am sure with much more accurate information and profound and enlarged views. I hope that his writings will be collected, as an inestimable treasury of wisdom and experience to Indian statesmen.[29]

Many of the writings which demonstrate Munro's views on Indian government were published three years later in G. R. Gleig's highly selective *Life of Major General Sir Thomas Munro.* In a journal entry from early 1830, Elphinstone mentions reading and being "quite enchanted" with Gleig's compilation of Munro's letters, which in Elphinstone's view, demonstrate that Munro's "judgment and sagacity at nineteen were as superior to those of ordinary people as they were to those of his contemporaries when his reputation was more extensive."[30]

As governors of Bombay, Elphinstone's and Malcolm's judgment and sagacity were directed mainly toward the problems of civil administration, but both were expected to produce some reduction in military expenditures. Elphinstone held office for eight years while Malcolm stayed for only three, but the opportunities and problems were similar for both. They had two main responsibilities. The first was the effective governance of the native inhabitants of the presidency; the second was the organization of the civil and military employees of the company in such a way as to achieve the first object as cheaply as possible. Land revenues were the main source of income for the government but the Bombay territories were not very productive; paying for the civil service and army absorbed most of the revenue and sometimes exceeded it. In regard to the assessment and collection of the revenue, both Elphinstone and Malcolm followed, in principle, Munro's system: an accurate survey of the land and collection of revenue from individual cultivators. Land tenures in the regions governed from Bombay, however, often differed from those under Madras and collectors were allowed to choose whether they would use the ryotwari system or modify it to suit local practice. In administering justice, Munro's precepts were again used as a framework. Civil cases were tried first by Indian judges; panchayats, although not common in the Bombay territories, were introduced if practicable. Both Elphinstone and Malcolm tried, on grounds of principle, to increase the role of Indians in the revenue administration and judiciary, although they justified the practice to the Home government on grounds of cost.[31]

Elphinstone's most notable accomplishments as governor were his efforts to develop a code of laws that would be compatible with both Western principles of justice and Indian custom and tradition—a daunting task—and his championship of public education in the vernacular languages, as opposed to the English language education recommended by westernizing, Anglicist reformers. Elphinstone believed in organic rather than abrupt change and recognized the value of "engrafting" Western education onto Indian roots as well as the importance to British claims to legitimacy of continuing government support for Indian educational institutions.[32] Malcolm was more interested in improving communications; he encouraged road construction in India and a steamship link between Bombay and Egypt. But he also tried to improve the efficiency and lower the cost of the public service, arguing invariably in both his published and unpublished writings on government that British rule "must be cheaper and simpler; it should be a government of supervision in its civil branches, not a direct agency"; this, by extension, meant employing more Indians.[33]

Both men came into conflict with British judges serving on the newly established (1823) Bombay supreme court. Elphinstone's differences with chief justice Sir Edward West began in 1823 in a dispute over Elphinstone's friend William Erskine, recorder of the court. Erskine had been ill and had allowed a clerk in his office to carry out the business. Some fees had been obtained, illegally, by both Erskine and his deputy, and Erskine's neglect of his duties while still collecting his salary were considered by West to be grounds for dismissal. Erskine accepted the court's verdict and left Bombay, but Elphinstone became involved in the issue when, in his capacity as president of the Bombay literary society, he moved a vote of thanks to Erskine on the society's behalf for his past services as secretary. Elphinstone concluded his motion with a profession of "esteem and respect" for Erskine which West thought unsuitable under the circumstances. Erskine's misdemeanors were relatively mild compared to much that went on among the British legal fraternity at Bombay, but the Home authorities wanted to improve the integrity of the judicial service. West, who had arrived only recently from Britain, believed, probably rightly, that he had been sent out with a mandate to do just that. Wynn, at the board of control, reprimanded Elphinstone for his untimely compliments to Erskine, calling them prejudicial to the public interest because they exposed disagreement between the government and the judiciary.

The issue would probably have been forgotten if Elphinstone had not given personal offense to West by failing, possibly deliberately, to adhere to protocol at a Government House dinner, thereby publicly insulting the chief justice. Protocol mattered because it indicated status and public respect and, if violated, could cause unpleasant repercussions throughout Bombay's inward-looking and faction-riven British community that were likely to undermine the prestige of the rulers. From this point the differences between Elphinstone and West degenerated into an acrimonious quarrel that lasted until Elphinstone left Bombay in 1827. West is usually described as a difficult man who quarreled with other members of the British community, but his unpopularity is largely attributable to his efforts to enforce stricter standards of professional ethical conduct. Elphinstone vacillated between trying to conciliate West and supporting his Bombay friends.[34]

Aware of the differences between West and Elphinstone, Malcolm went to some pains, with some success, to establish an acceptable working relationship with West, but he got into difficulties with another judge, Sir John Grant, after West's sudden death in August 1828. The jurisdiction of the supreme court was confined to the city of Bombay and its immediate environs and to the white community, Eurasians, and a few Indians who had close professional dealings with the white community. Grant, in an attempt to expand the court's jurisdiction, tried to intervene in a case involving a high-status Indian youth from Pune—one of the "privileged sirdars" who were under the special protection of the government. Malcolm opposed Grant's move and the issue erupted into another inglorious dispute between government and court. West would probably have accepted the case as outside the jurisdiction of the supreme court,[35] but Sir Charles Chambers, the third judge at Bombay, supported Grant until he, too, died suddenly two months after West. Eventually the dispute came before the privy council in London which declared in favor of the Bombay government, and Malcolm could claim victory. But Grant asked to be allowed to resign and move to Calcutta to practice at the bar, a move Malcolm interpreted as an attempt to convey the impression "that he resigns because he was not supported, not that he is recalled because his conduct was disapproved." The case had already caused dissatisfaction among Indi-

ans, Malcolm claimed, because they believe "he goes to exercise greater influence in these affairs and probably to rise to higher rank." Grant's recall
was necessary to show that "intriguing and venal men"—Europeans as
well as Indians—could not use the court to excite opposition to the government. A minute of Munro's indicates that at Madras, also, the judicial
branch was attempting to expand its jurisdiction at this time.[36]

Elphinstone's rift with West, insofar as principles were involved at all,
concerned the imposition of British standards of professional conduct
upon the British community in Bombay. The challenges to Malcolm and
Munro concerned differences between them and would-be westernizing
reformers whose numbers and influence in British India were increasing
rapidly. Although Malcolm's desire to limit the jurisdiction of the supreme court stemmed at least in part from his perception of Grant's action as a threat to his personal authority as chief executive officer of the
presidency, he did have grounds of principle on which to defend his position. He argued that the jurisdiction of all the presidency supreme courts
should be confined to a few miles beyond the capitals at which they were
located, because the people the courts were intended to protect—British
subjects, Eurasians, and "natives who are associated by their ties, their interests, and their occupations with English laws and usages"—formed a
community quite different in its attitudes and practices from those of the
small towns and villages of India.[37] Munro, Malcolm, and Elphinstone all
opposed the extension of British-type courts of law into the Indian countryside because they believed legal process should be comprehensible and
relevant to the population it served, and British-style courts and British-
style justice, which were meaningless to most Indians, were a slow, expensive, and generally unsatisfactory way of administering justice.

Elphinstone's administration of Bombay is generally regarded as more
distinguished than Malcolm's. Kaye claims that "no one ever brought with
him from India a higher reputation." R. D. Choksey, who discusses Elphinstone's failure to lower the excessive demands for land revenue, reduce
unemployment, or solve other problems which produced widespread
"economic ruin" in the Deccan, refrains from criticism and directs the
blame to the legacy of Elphinstone's predecessor, Baji Rao II. Elphinstone's handling of the presidency's financial affairs, however, was certain-

ly less than distinguished. Recent research by Peers shows that Bombay's
accounts for the years 1823 to 1827 indicate a rise in total expenditure of
23 percent, despite the fact that the Bombay presidency was at peace and
taking on no new responsibilities. Madras under Munro, by contrast, bal-
anced its books, despite making a major contribution in terms of men
and resources to the First Burma War.[38] The finances of British India were
of keen interest to the Home government. Although no detailed figures
have been established for Malcolm's short administration, in general his
conduct of the government was approved. Ravenshaw, who supplied
Bentinck as well as Munro with a great deal of confidential information,
complained in 1827 that Lushington, whom he had backed for Madras,
had made "a bad start," but Malcolm "on the contrary is exceeding all expectations formed of him by our council." Ravenshaw had little liking for
Malcolm but later told Bentinck again that Lushington had done everything wrong and in the wrong spirit, but that Malcolm was "getting on
very much and generally to the satisfaction of all the authorities at home.
I confess myself most agreeably disappointed and if he would only leave
others to see his merits without thrusting them before your eyes upon all
occasions, he would with me be second only to Munro."[39]

Malcolm's long-hoped-for governorship was probably somewhat anti-
climatic. Before leaving Britain for Bombay in 1827, he had described to
Wellington a "day-dream" in which he was made acting governor-general
because Amherst wanted to leave India before a successor could be decided upon, and the measures he executed proved so beneficial he was appointed to a full term of office. He recognized the "almost insurmount-
able obstacle" to the fulfillment of this fantasy, however, and publicly
welcomed Bentinck's appointment. Malcolm was disappointed also that
Central India was not annexed to Bombay. He would have liked to make
his acceptance of Bombay contingent on this happening but was in no
position to bargain. The question continued to be debated between the
board of control, the directorate, the Supreme government at Calcutta,
and Malcolm long after he had arrived in India. In 1828 Lady Malcolm
asked Wellington to support her husband, but to no avail. The Home
government ultimately left Bentinck to make the decision and he found
the Calcutta bureaucracy so hostile to the idea that he had no choice but

to reject it even though he regarded Malcolm as a friend.[40] Malcolm resigned the governorship in December 1830, following Wellington's resignation as British prime minister. He was sixty-one years old. In April of the
following year he was elected to Parliament as a Tory, for Launceston, a
seat in the gift of an acquaintance, the duke of Northumberland. His
stand against parliamentary reform, however, lost him the seat in 1832 and
he spent the last year of his life improving his newly purchased estate in
Berkshire. He died in London in May 1833.

Elphinstone had left India in November 1827, almost immediately after Malcolm's arrival at Bombay. He traveled home by way of Egypt, the
Ottoman Empire, Greece, Italy, and France, arriving in England in May
1829. Ellenborough mentions consulting him from time to time on matters relating to India, and notes in his diary that Wellington thought Elphinstone should accept another term at Bombay "with the expectation
of afterwards going to Madras," and also that Wellington had "an idea of
making him governor-general" in the future.[41] Elphinstone was offered the
post of resident at Tehran, and a concerted effort was made by his relatives and family friends to persuade him to stand for Parliament in Lan-
arkshire as a Whig. In 1834 he was offered the governor-generalship of India—unlike Munro and Malcolm he had the requisite aristocratic status
for the appointment—and posts as undersecretary to the board of control and as a special commissioner to Canada, but he declined them all.
Neither duty, money, nor ambition could persuade him to reenter public
life, and he spent thirty years in secluded retirement. In 1834, as he began
work on his *History of India,* he received an honorary degree from Oxford
University at the instigation of Wellington, who was chancellor. He later
began work on a manuscript published after his death as *The Rise of British
Power in the East* but died before completing it, in November 1859.[42]

PART II

AS WRITERS

Scottish Ideas and Indian Government

CHAPTER 7

Philosophical Historians

I believe this to be the historical age and this the historical nation.
—David Hume

Although Malcolm and Elphinstone's historical works were written in the early and mid–nineteenth century, when fashions in historical writing were changing, they wrote history that was typical of the Scottish Enlightenment. Historians have paid little attention to these works because the two men, who intended their books to be read by the general public as well as by men with a professional interest in India and its neighbors, presented their interpretations in the broadly philosophical style that had been popularized in Scotland by David Hume and William Robertson, and utilized the technique known as "conjectural" history, favored particularly by Adam Ferguson and John Millar, to explain the evolution of Asian institutions and to describe historical periods for which there was inadequate documentary evidence. These genres were popular in the late eighteenth century but more recently have been regarded as insufficiently objective or accurate to be considered historical.[1] Although this verdict may be justified, Malcolm and Elphinstone's published works provide, nevertheless, the ideal source for identifying their personal ideological assumptions, for the simple reason that philosophical historians were *expected* to intersperse their narrative with commentary and explanation based on their own values and beliefs. It was an unashamedly didactic form of historical writing and, for Scotsmen, the favored channel of dissemination for the precepts of contemporary moral philosophy. Many of the concepts Malcolm and Elphinstone applied to their historical analyses could also be applied to the problem of finding a viable form of government for British India.

History was a popular form of literature in most European countries in the late eighteenth century, but many Scotsmen believed, like Hume, that their countrymen had a peculiar aptitude for it. According to Hume, "'tis well known, that the English have not much excelled in that kind of literature." William Robertson admired Voltaire but criticized him for paying too much attention to ideas; like many Scotsmen, Robertson believed intellectual developments could not be separated from the study of society as a whole. He also censured Voltaire for failing to cite his sources: ". . . as he seldom imitates the example of the modern historians in citing the authors from whom they derive their information, I could not, with propriety, appeal to his authority in conformation of any doubtful or unknown fact." Sir James Mackintosh attributed the lack of good historians in France to "Absolute monarchy . . . [which even] in its most moderate form, is, no doubt, destructive of the free spirit which is the soul of history." This view probably influenced Malcolm's wordier observation that the Muslim "annalists of despotism" were unable to attain "any portion of that excellence which belongs to those who, living under happier auspices, have mixed the wisdom of philosophy with the facts of history." Even the Englishman Edward Gibbon, in a tribute to the work of Hume, Robertson, and Adam Smith on the "progress of European society," spoke of the "strong ray of philosophic light [that] has broke from Scotland." Whether or not such opinions were justified, they indicate a high degree of self-confidence in Scottish historiography. Until the 1790s, all the literate classes in Scotland read and discussed history, and almost everyone with literary aspirations made some attempt to write it. In the preface to his *History of Persia*, the men whose help and advice Malcolm acknowledged were all Scotsmen: James Mackintosh, William Erskine, and, in particular, Alexander Hamilton.[2]

The methodology of philosophical history, which was expected both to instruct and to entertain, called for a narrative of the events of a particular time and place accompanied by an explanation of the origins and significance of political, social, economic, and cultural developments in accordance with the philosophical beliefs of the historian. Original documents and contemporary accounts, critically evaluated, were the source material favored, as Robertson stresses, by "modern historians." Malcolm and Elphinstone diligently acquired and utilized Asian sources for their studies of Asian history and culture for reasons of principle as well as practicality. (Hume's works of history, based largely on secondary material, are exceptions to this general practice). Historians were also expected to treat their subjects with sympathy, to analyze the societies they were studying according to the standards of the stage of civilization they believed them to have reached; to be sensitive to the characteristics of place and time, and to avoid judging past societies by the values of eighteenth-century Europe.[3]

Conjectural history was justified by Dugald Stewart, who explained that most societies took important steps to progress before they kept records. With no direct evidence, historians were forced to speculate from the nature and physical situation of a particular society how it was likely to have acted. Travelers' accounts of contemporary societies in earlier stages of development could be used as "landmarks"—conceptual models—for speculation. Stewart claimed that "when we cannot trace the process by which an event *has been* produced, it is often of importance to be able to show how it *may have been* produced by natural causes."[4] Some historians, on the basis of Stewart's example of using contemporary societies in earlier stages of development as models, conflate the terms "conjectural" and "stadial" history. But not all the conjecturing was made in association with the theory of "stages" of civilization, related to "modes of subsistence," as promulgated by, in particular, Lord Kames, John Millar, and Adam Smith. Ferguson's *Essay on the History of Civil Society* and John Millar's *Origin of the Distinction of Ranks* are probably the best-known works to rest mainly on conjectural or theoretical techniques.[5] Thematic and comparative in method and universal in their scope, they explore issues such as "the decline of nations" and "the condition of women in different ages," approaching the history of society in a way hailed by some as the forerunner of modern sociology, although not today regarded as history. To contemporaries like Hume and Robertson, however, and to Malcolm and Elphinstone who modeled their histories on late eighteenth-century examples, the methodologies of philosophical and conjectural history were valid approaches to the study of past societies.

Both Malcolm, in writing his *History of Persia* and *Sketch of the Sikhs*, and Elphinstone, in his *Account of the Kingdom of Caubul* and *History of India*, discuss the strengths and weaknesses of their sources. Elphinstone complains that social and cultural matters were beneath the dignity of Persian historians and may only be investigated by examining travel accounts, laws, letters, legends, and, "above all, tales." The last are particularly useful, he believes, because they derive from the author's own observations and are adapted to suit his readers' beliefs. Chaucer, for example, depicted the way of life in Richard II's time more accurately "than the 170 volumes of Petitot do at any one period in France." Hume's rejection of fable as an historical source was cited by James Mill to justify his own rejection of Hindu myths and legends, but Adam Ferguson, like Malcolm and Elphinstone, believed fables could be helpful. The *Iliad* or the *Odyssey*, in Ferguson's opinion, revealed "the conceptions and sentiments of the age" and illustrated the genius of the people "with whose imaginations they were blended." Similarly, Malcolm maintained that the character of peoples, as well as of individuals, could often "be better appreciated from anecdotes than from mere narration of events."[6]

Ferdosi's great poem, the *Shah Nahmah*, was used as an historical source by both Elphinstone and Malcolm. Commissioned by Mahmud of Ghazni in the eleventh century, it recorded the achievements of the kings and heroes of ancient Persia. Elphinstone notes that one of its more remarkable features—one that may indicate "the taste of the age"—is Ferdosi's fondness for ancient Persian words and his "studious rejection of the Arabic." Arabic was the language of Mahmud's Muslim predecessors who, during their conquest of Persia, had destroyed the records of the events of ancient Persia that Mahmud wished to celebrate. Elphinstone also uses an anecdote about the poem's origins to illustrate aspects of Mahmud's personality, relating a story about the writing of the poem because it not only throws light on Mahmud's enthusiasm for literature but is also "improved in interest as well as authenticity by its incidental disclosure of the conqueror's characteristic foible"—avarice. Mahmud had paid Ferdosi in silver when he had promised gold. Ferdosi responded with "a bitter satire" aimed at his patron and prepared to flee the country to escape Mahmud's wrath. The ruler, however, was magnanimous; he ignored the satire, remembered only the great epic poem and gave ample remuneration to Ferdosi. But the satire survived and, as Elphinstone notes, "It is to it we owe the knowledge of Mahmud's base birth; and to it beyond doubt, is to be ascribed the presentation of the memory of his avarice, which would otherwise long ago have been forgotten."[7] Satires and stories were acceptable source materials which could provide insight into aspects of history often missing from more conventional documents.

The unsatisfactory nature of many of the sources for the early history of Persia posed problems for Malcolm. In addition to the lack of contemporary records, owing to the destructive habits of Muhammad's followers, Old Testament scriptures were unsatisfactory from the paucity of facts, the confusion of dates, and "errors arising from the proper names in different languages," while Greek historians, particularly Xenophon, used history to instruct their own rulers, and ascribed "every quality that can dignify human nature" to ancient kings and peoples whose real history they knew little about, "which allowed them to indulge their imagination to the full."[8] Like Elphinstone, Malcolm found Ferdosi useful. In Ferdosi's account of ancient Persia, the rule of Jamsheed lasts for seven hundred years and witnesses the development of social ranks, the foundation of cities, the invention of arms, the teaching of astronomy, and other progressive developments, which lead Jamsheed to become so vain that he declares himself a god. "This impiety brought disaster"; Persia, after a period of unexampled prosperity, was invaded and devastated by a savage foreign prince. Malcolm provides a classical conjectural explanation for this seven-hundred-year period:

May we not, without presumption, conclude that this is a general account of a people's history for a certain period? It describes their emerging from a savage state, in which men have few wants, and consequently few distinctions, either in rank or occupation; their division into the classes of a more civilized community; their becoming industrious, rich and prosperous; their lapsing into a state of luxury and irreligion; and consequently, falling an easy conquest to a foreign enemy. This seems a plain interpretation of the history of Jamsheed as related by Persian authors.[9]

Elphinstone provides a typical conjectural history of the probable origin of caste divisions in Hindu society, attributing them to the desire of the priestly class to perpetuate existing institutions in order to assure their own control over innovation.[10]

The desirability of taking into consideration the stage of civilization reached by a society when examining its history was an offshoot of the development of "the historical gospel of sensibility". Hugh Blair and Henry MacKenzie were two of the best known Scottish "sentimentalists,"[11] but the popular movement had been powerfully influenced by Adam Smith's more penetrating exploration, in *The Theory of Moral Sentiments* (1759), of the concept of the sympathetic "spectator" and the social and moral value of what would now be termed "empathy." Even Hume, in a letter to William Mure, endorsed the "sentimental" approach to character analysis (in the specifically Scottish sense of the word): "The first Quality of an Historian is to be true and impartial; the next to be interesting. If you do not say, that I have done both Parties Justice; and if Mrs Mure be not sorry for poor King Charles, I shall burn all my Papers, and return to Philosophy."[12] Blair and MacKenzie believed a capacity for sympathy should be the core of modern ethics. They hoped to inspire their readers with an interest in the "concerns of our brethren" so they would "feel along with them . . . [and] take part in their joys and sorrows."[13] When applied to the study of history, the concept of sympathy encouraged historians to try to see events from the perspective of the people they were studying: to understand the minds and feelings of their subjects.

In discussing the reign of Mahmud of Ghazni, who between 997 and 1030 A.D. had conquered an empire extending from the Caspian Sea to the Punjab, Elphinstone places this empire-building process in what he believes to be its correct historical context, ignored in previous accounts. Earlier European historians had treated Mahmud harshly for what they saw as his religious bigotry, while Muslim historians had taken the opposite view and accused him of religious skepticism. But in Elphinstone's interpretation, Mahmud, while attentive to the outward forms of Islam, engages in military ventures not to gain converts to Islam but simply because conquest was, "in his day," the greatest source of glory and gain.[14]

Although Elphinstone considered the context of the time in his interpretation of historical events, he felt Malcolm had sometimes given context too much weight in the *History of Persia* and criticized "the tone of apology for all the acts of cruelty and tyranny" it records. Malcolm justified his apparent sympathy for despotism on the grounds that under contemporary conditions, people were better off under a strong ruler than under a weak and divided government, and that in Asia, the punishment of crime was regarded as one of the ruler's more important duties. The executions a ruler ordered were not necessarily mere caprice and his sentences not necessarily unjust "because the forms are different from ours." To illustrate this point, Malcolm uses an analogy between Asia and Europe:

Let us imagine in the present tranquil state of our own country, that all criminals whom the laws condemn were sentenced by our king, and that the court-yard of St. James's was the place of execution. Though his sentences might be as just as those of our judges, yet the monarch would be deemed a sanguinary despot.

Adam Ferguson had made a similar analogy between European and Asian legal practice.

When a basha, in Asia, pretends to decide every controversy by the rules of natural equity, we allow that he is possessed of discretionary powers. When a judge in Europe is left to decide, according to his own interpretation of written laws, is he in any sense more restrained than the former?

Elphinstone, however, protested that "there is an immutable distinction between just and unjust, which no systems nor opinions can remove."[15]

Many anecdotes in Kaye's biography attest to Malcolm's sympathy for defeated princes, loyal sepoys, and oppressed peasants. Although Elphinstone seems to have had scant regard for what he termed Malcolm's "confidence system" where diplomacy was concerned, in a fragment written shortly after the older man's death, he acknowledges Malcolm's possession "in an eminent degree, [of] the power of gaining the attachment of those with whom he associated, and [he] was, at one time of his life, the most popular man with all classes that ever was known in India." Malcolm may not have deliberately followed the maxims he would have heard while attending Blair's sermons in Edinburgh in 1794 and 1795, but his interest in human psychology and his consideration for the way he imagined others would feel were a key part of his approach to diplomacy and administration as well as to history, and would have been appreciated by other Scottish sentimentalists. In his Bombay journal, James Mackintosh mentions that Malcolm annotated the copy of Hume's history of England's Tudor dynasty, which he was reading while writing the *History of Persia*, with the perceptive observation: "The head cannot join the heart respecting Mary; nor can the heart follow the head about Elizabeth."[16] Malcolm's use of the motifs of "head" and "heart" reflect the importance Scottish thinkers gave to people's feelings, in comparison with the greater emphasis given by many of their European counterparts to rational thought. People's feelings, not least his own, were important to Malcolm as motive forces for action.

Malcolm was more deeply influenced than Elphinstone by the moral and social thought of the sentimentalists, but the latter's reputation for sympathy was helped by comparisons between James Mill's interpretation of Indian history and his own. Mill, like other philosophical historians, provided a narrative of events accompanied by explanations of their significance in accordance with his own philosophical beliefs. He would have endorsed Elphinstone's advice to William Erskine to "be bold . . . and do not think that the History itself is of so much importance as your own opinions." He would have approved Elphinstone's criticism of Erskine's work to Sir John Kaye: Erskine's historical writing suffered from an excessive attention to detail which took up too much time and bored the general reader, who would have been more interested in listening to the author's conclusions "and the reflections they suggested." But Mill believed any society or form of government could be judged and prescribed for, from a distance, on the basis of rational principle.[17] Elphinstone defended his more empirical approach on the ground that "the excellence of histories derived from European researches alone does not entirely set aside the utility of similar enquiries conducted under the guidance of impressions received in India; which, as they arise from a separate source, may sometimes lead to different conclusions." Elphinstone excused Mill's biases, conceding that, as a proponent of a school of philosophy advancing new opinions, "Mill was obliged to resort to argument to establish his principles and destroy those opposed to him." He thought Mill's account of pre-British Indian history took "much the same view of affairs as I do, at least not more unfavourable to the actors." Its great fault, however, was its "cynical, sarcastic tone." On the British period Elphinstone felt that Mill's imagination was inadequate to deal successfully with Warren Hastings, because Mill was "a mortal enemy to all heroic propensities," and his work suffered from a harshness which lay more in his use of "sneers and sarcastic expressions" than in distorting facts. Elphinstone disagreed with some of Mill's conclusions, thought he paid too much attention to the controversies surrounding the administrations of Hastings, Cornwallis, and Wellesley and too little to their legacy; he saw Mill's "want of sympathy with great . . . characters—indeed, with anybody except men suffering injustice," to be a serious fault. And "even in this most honourable exception, it is rather indignation at the oppression than tenderness for the sufferer that Mill shows."[18] There was little room in Mill's scheme for either empiricism or sensibility.

O'Brien observes, perceptively, that Elphinstone's *History of India* "is a history manifestly ill at ease with, but unable to transcend the sociological vocabularies of the Scottish Enlightenment." But the following comments, made as late as the 1840s, seem to indicate that for Elphinstone, David Hume was the cynosure of historians, and that Elphinstone's historiographical taste had been formed by Scottish Enlightenment values.

I now see with wonder the extent and variety of his powers. Eloquent, glowing, picturesque, almost poetical, he flows on in animated and absorbing narrative, exciting all our feelings, and yet pregnant with profound reflections and impressive lessons of morality. How can one be surprised that such powers of eloquence and imagination, combined with and restrained by the soberest judgment and the calmest philosophy, should produce a History with which no modern attempt can stand a moment's competition?[19]

Similar values are evident in Malcolm's *History of Persia.* M. E. Yapp has suggested that this work is flawed by the focus on Persian customs and manners, the extra detail on eighteenth-century Persia, and the emphasis on defining the Persian national character, which indicate a preoccupation with the contemporary condition of Persia rather than with its whole history. Judged by today's standards this is no doubt true. These are, however, all aspects of Malcolm's work that would have been regarded as strengths rather than weaknesses by contemporary historians and readers of history. The first volume of Hume's *History of Great Britain* has been described as

"the vital sector . . . in Hume's campaign to educate the Whigs in political
realities, to promote 'moderation' in politics, and provide the Establishment . . . with a respectable, modern, post-revolutionary intellectual basis"—most certainly a contemporary issue. William Robertson, in his
masterly essay, *A History of the Progress of Society in Europe*, traces developments that would now be described by historians as state building and
military fiscalism, which led to the recognition of the concept of the balance of power as a regulator of international relations, a concept of enormous contemporary interest. Both Hume and Robertson enhanced their
intellectual reputations by writing history and made a lot of money from
their work.[20] Elphinstone and Malcolm were never rich or renowned
enough to disregard the financial rewards or career advantages that might
be attained by catering to contemporary historical taste.

Philosophical history was the product of a symbiotic association between history and moral philosophy. History played a curious dual role in
intellectual discourse; it was the preferred medium for the expression of
philosophical principles, but it also provided the empirical evidence from
which those principles were derived. In other words, it contributed to
both the deductive and inductive processes of reasoning that were used
interchangeably by the Scottish philosophes. Historical theories were used
to analyze contemporary conditions; historical evidence provided caution-
ary examples, and the writing of history was used, as Malcolm explains—
and as he practiced it—"to instruct future ages by [the] narration of the
events of the past."[21] It became the favored channel of dissemination for
philosophical ideas, partly because financial incentives and didactic purposes encouraged the Scottish philosophes to present their material in a
form as comprehensible to general readers, including fourteen-year-old
university students and soldiers on leave from India, as to fellow intellectuals. Malcolm and Elphinstone used philosophical history to develop
their ideas on Asian society and government, to advertise their knowledge,
and to disseminate warnings and advice to those responsible for the government of British India.

CHAPTER 8

Moral Philosophers

The ultimate object of philosophical inquiry is the same which every man of plain understanding proposes to himself, when he remarks the events which fall under his observation, with a view to the future regulation of his conduct. The more knowledge of this kind we acquire, the better can we accommodate our plans to the established order of things, and avail ourselves of natural powers and agents for accomplishing our purposes.
—Dugald Stewart

*A*lthough *the Scottish moral philosophers* spoke of their "experimental methods," their "philosophical inquiry"—their research—was based rather on "a rough, common sense empiricism" in which introspection of their own minds and the study of history provided much of the information on which they based their theories.[1] The type of explanation they provided for the development of systems of government, civil and military institutions, social structures, and gender relations, among other topics, was based on their interpretation of human psychology, a partially determinist explanation of historical change (with the exception of Robertson who believed in the power of human agency, guided by Providence, to determine the course of history), and on a secular but not necessarily atheistic approach to religion.[2] "A rough, common sense empiricism," colored by the ideas about religion, systems of government, and political

economy they had absorbed from their own culture, accurately describes
the methodological approach to the problems of Indian government followed by Munro, Malcolm, and Elphinstone.

In the context of the history of ideas, the period of the Scottish Enlightenment belongs neither to the Age of Reason nor to the so-called
Age of Belief in the Idea of Progress. Scottish thinkers believed in the
utility of reason but not in its omnipotence, in the possibility of progress
but not in its inevitability. Despite their use of stadial theory as a conceptual tool, they were interested in the decline as well as the rise of civilized
states. The most apt generic label for the period from the 1750s to the
1790s would probably be the "Age of Social Science" in the literal sense
that the Scottish moral philosophers were attempting to apply the mathematical, empirical, and experimental methods used so successfully by Isaac
Newton in the development of his scientific theories to determining the
place of man and society in a general scheme of the universe. Moral philosophy was the matrix of the social sciences. Although the Scots were
neither sociologists, anthropologists, political scientists, nor economists
in any modern sense, the social scientific aspects of general Enlightenment thought reached their most mature and sophisticated level in Scotland between the 1760s and 1790s and had a profound effect on the way
Munro, Malcolm, and Elphinstone perceived Asian societies and cultures.

Reflecting the practical preoccupations of their own society, Scotland's philosophes were concerned with both material and moral progress.
They acknowledged a necessary and desirable relationship between wealth
and power but found the relationship between wealth and virtue more
difficult to interpret. Most Scottish literature from the second half of the
eighteenth century, however, whether ostensibly concerned with history or
philosophy, astronomy or economics, or even novels, dealt overtly or im-
plicitly with morality. It was not a self-denying, world-renouncing morality because the philosophes approved of prosperity, seeing it as advantageous for the state as well as the individual. But they sought ways to foster
economic improvement without creating the complacency and corruption
which, according to their interpretations of history, had often brought
about the decline of earlier civilized states.

With the notable exception of David Hume, the philosophes were mostly churchmen, lawyers, and university professors who were closely associated through ties of kinship, patronage, and shared concerns with the most powerful sector of the political community, the aristocracy and landed gentry. They met every day at literary clubs and once a year at the general assembly of the Church of Scotland. While often differing over ways and means, they achieved a remarkably broad consensus on their main concern: the progress of civil society. David Hume and Adam Smith, Adam Ferguson, William Robertson and John Millar, and other thinkers and writers who were important at the time but whose reputations have proved less durable, examined the past and present of Scotland—and the world in general—to discover what inhibited progress and what could be done to remove the inhibitions. They discussed their ideas, wrote books and pamphlets to publicize them, and, through their close relationship with landowners, farmers, lawyers, ministers, and the teachers of the rising generation of Scotsmen, did their best to ensure that these ideas would contribute to the future progress of Scotland. Some members of this rising generation, however, spent their working lives in the empire, and saw themselves as professionally responsible for the future progress of other societies.

As a framework for their social analyses and historical interpretations, the moral philosophers sought to discover a principle of explanation to which past actions could be referred that was sufficiently all-encompassing to replace divine will or rational intent as the motive force for historical change. They, and Munro, Malcolm, and Elphinstone, found this principle in their belief in the universal character of human nature with its supposed dual natural impulses to economic and moral self-improvement, "the product of man's instinctual and unconscious programming."[3] The causes and effects of historical change were examined "to show how . . . one cause, prepared the way for another, and augmented its influence," but particular attention was paid to the unintended consequences of events. William Robertson described the Crusades as "a singular monument to human folly," but nevertheless saw them as having had beneficial consequences "which had neither been foreseen nor expected." Cultural diversity was accounted for by the widely accepted theories of stages of economic, social, and political development and by ideas about national

characteristics which were believed to have been produced by peculiar religious, political, and economic circumstances and, to a lesser degree, by
physical conditions.[4]

Malcolm states explicitly that "human nature is always the same in
whatever garb it is clothed" and that Indians, like everyone else, should be
judged "by a standard . . . suited to their belief, their usages, their habits
. . . and the stage of civilization to which the community as a whole are
advanced." In his *History of Persia* he argues that Zoroaster, in order to
achieve his objectives, adapted his ideas to the stage of development of
contemporary society, and that Zoroastrianism was an agent of progress
insofar as it was monotheistic and promoted industry, virtue, and order.
The introduction of flame as a symbol of God, however, had had unexpected and undesired consequences: the spread of superstition which inhibited further progress.[5]

The similarities rather than differences between Indians and Europeans are emphasized by Munro, indicating that he, too, believed in a universal human nature. He sees no reason to believe that Indians are inferior
to Britons in natural talent: both possess an equal mixture of good and
bad qualities. And he, too, warns of the uncertainties of cause and effect
when writing of the danger of haste in committing the government to
permanent measures "of which we cannot possibly foresee the consequences, and which may often be quite contrary to our expectations."[6]

In his last work, *The Rise of British Power in the East*, written in the
mid–nineteenth century when Whig historians liked to celebrate the
agency of great men and great ideas as motive forces for historical change,
Elphinstone saw the political involvement of the East India Company in
Indian affairs not as the result of conscious decisions to acquire territorial
possessions or political power but—as most of the Scottish philosophes
would have done—as the result of structural forces beyond the control of
individuals. Despite the fact that the company's goals had always been
strictly commercial, the "requisite intercourse with local Governments"
and rivalry with European powers had "compelled them and all others in
that age, to engage in political and military transactions." Similarly Malcolm, in regard to the subjection of India by the British, states that the
causes of great revolutions are to be found "not in the successful issue of

the complex schemes of ambitious statesmen, but in the simple operation of natural and obvious causes." These determinist explanations reflect Adam Smith's view of the processes of historical change: "On the great chess-board of human society, every single piece has a principle of motion of its own, altogether different from that which the legislature might chuse [*sic*] to impress upon it."[7]

The concept of stages of development and the historical significance of unexpected consequences were of interest to all three men, but Elphinstone, in particular, made comparisons between contemporary Asian society and earlier stages in European development. In his account of Afghan society he comments on the similar types of behavior in countries that have reached the same stage of development but are far removed from each other in time and place. "Chaucer's sompnours tale," he observes, "exactly describes the importunity of the mendicant Mullahs, [in Afghanistan] and the mixture of respect and aversion with which they are regarded." And he compares Afghan practice, in which the "masters of the country, the ruling families," do not live in the towns, to the similar situation "in England after the Norman invasion."[8]

The social theorists who influenced Munro, Malcolm, and Elphinstone's approach to Asian society tended to pay more attention to what they called moral than to physical considerations as determinants of national character. Hume categorized moral causes as "the nature of the government, the revolutions of public affairs, the plenty or penury in which the people live, the situation of the nation with regard to its neighbours and such like circumstances." The uniform system of government of a large empire would, he thought, create distinctive national characteristics despite climatic variations. Small contiguous states would develop marked differences in character and manners although, as in the case of the city-states of Athens (ingenious and gay) and Thebes (rustic and phlegmatic), they were only a short day's journey apart. Closed societies, like those of the Jews in Europe and the Armenians in the Middle East, with little in common with the nations among whom they lived, would retain their own character, as would two nations with different religions and languages inhabiting the same country. A purely republican government would produce one type of national character, an absolute monarchy another, and the nature of the dominant religion would mold the manners of the people in both.[9]

Although Malcolm allows that in Makran and Baluchistan there is little sign that the people have ever emerged from "the poor and sterile state to which they seem to have been condemned by nature," like Hume, he is more interested in moral than physical determinants of national character. In the *History of Persia*, he identifies uniform characteristics throughout the Persian empire which he believes have developed as a result of a tradition of despotic government reinforced by the tenets of Islam. This uniformity is modified among tribal groups, however, because they enjoy a more democratic form of local government which leaves them less morally debased but also less amenable to political control than other Persians.[10]

Munro, again like Hume, has little time for theories of the effect of climate on national character and complains of the "learned men" who argue that the "vertical rays" of the sun make the natives of India indolent when, in actual fact, Indian farmers are just as industrious as European ones and their women are more so. Their poverty, in Munro's estimation, derives from the system of government, not from "their idleness nor the sun."[11] But Elphinstone shared Millar's and Ferguson's interest in the influence of climate. Although the "defects" of the Hindus "arise chiefly from moral causes," Elphinstone believes they may also be ascribed to physical constitution and to soil and climate, and he points out, ruefully, that the warm climate and fertile soil which make hard labor unnecessary in Bengal "produce that state of listless inactivity which foreigners find it so difficult to resist." He adds that "the shades of character . . . in different parts of India . . . confirm this supposition," and gives as an example the vigor of the Marathas, who inhabit a mountainous and infertile region, compared with the Bengalis "with their moist climate and their double crops of rice." The dreary aspect of their surroundings explains why the Arabs sought excitement "in contemplation, and in ideas derived from within," Muhammad having particular opportunities "of indulging in such reveries."[12]

History's status as a recruit in the service of the science of man deflected attention, to some extent, from kings, politics, and wars. Hume claimed that history was neither intelligible nor instructive without an accurate understanding of the systems of government, manners (meaning social morality), economy, and degree of learning of a state. This view was endorsed by Malcolm, who saw the system of government and the manners of "the nation described" as the most important parts of its history. During the 1780s, a debate on the superiority of social morality to laws in the regulation of civil life attracted much attention in Scottish literary clubs and periodicals. Hugh Blair, whose *Sermons,* published in 1777, were among the century's most popular books, believed that "mere law" was rigid and inflexible; it was manners which really held society together. Munro's opinion, expressed in a discussion of policing in 1824, that the only efficient preventive of crime in India would be "the improvement of manners" suggests that he held similar views on the relative value of social morality and laws. Blair died in 1800 so that, unlike Malcolm in the winter of 1794 to 1795, Munro would not have heard him preach when in Edinburgh in 1808. But during his first twenty years in India he had been kept in touch with Scottish news and opinion by his father, who sent him each year every edition of the *Glasgow Courier,* while friends, obviously believing he would be interested, kept him informed of developments in Scottish literature. From James Melvil he learned in 1796 that the popular public lectures of Dr. Hugh Blair had made "a considerable addition to the corpus criticum," and that the work of Robert Burns was appreciated as lively and humorous "but sometimes too profane and saucy to the clergy for which he was genteelly reprimanded in the newspapers." He also learned that Dr. Thomas Reid (the author of *An Inquiry into the Human Mind on the Principles of Common Sense*) had recently "gone over the Intellectual and active powers of man in two different Guinea books, and has set every thing on a right footing, so that philosophers will have no trouble with human nature for the future, but may apply to the turning ice into gunpowder or any other interesting speculation." It is a comment, albeit in irreverent vein, that reflects precisely the change in direction that occurred in Scottish intellectual life in the 1790s as events in France began to inhibit freedom of thought and expression. Science was replacing moral philosophy as the focus of intellectual attention. Munro, nevertheless, bought the five volumes of Blair's *Sermons* to take with him to India in 1814.[13]

Munro, Malcolm, and Elphinstone make no attempt to explain or justify their use of the concepts of a universal human nature, stages of civilization, or national character, or the importance they placed on manners, which suggests that they take them for granted themselves and expect their readers to do the same, or that they see them as facts rather than as assumptions. These beliefs were important to their approach to government, however, because they allowed Munro, Malcolm, and Elphinstone to observe eastern societies, which they regarded as less advanced in most ways than their own, in an analytic but relatively uncritical way. Bigotry, ignorance, superstition, and other defects were believed to be universal characteristics of early nineteenth-century Asia—as they had been of medieval Europe—but they were temporary, not eternal, attributes and thus susceptible to improvement.

If human nature were much the same everywhere, an Asian could be expected to experience feelings similar to those of a native of Britain when faced with the pleasure and pain of everyday life or the approval or disapprobation of others, although this did not mean, necessarily, that he would react in the same way. Responses were thought to vary according to the same experiences and conditioning that created national characteristics. Munro, Malcolm, and Elphinstone, however, all believed that the British would have to take into consideration the "natural" feelings of Indians if their rule was to be effective. Although it is unlikely that they consciously applied the techniques of the advocates of sensibility when considering human relations in India, the priorities of Munro and Malcolm reflect their own feelings. The professional advancement of both men was frustrated in their early years by inadequate patronage. For Munro, for whom self-fulfillment, service, and morality were synonymous, the quintessential components of good government were the provision of opportunity and incentive, the chance to be "interestingly and importantly employed."[14] His professional attention was focused for much of his career on civil and administrative matters. He accepted the fact of British rule and the importance of India to Britain's political as well as commercial interests, but he believed that Indians should do things for themselves as far as possible with the object of eventually governing themselves. British rule should provide the necessary environment—opportunities as well as order and stability—in which the "human nature" of the Indian people could function in its most moral, active, and therefore most progressive way. Malcolm, whose need to recount to family and friends every instance of official commendation and every word of appreciation suggests self-doubt as well as the vanity to which it is usually attributed, believed that sensitivity to the feelings of the governed and recognition of service rendered were top priorities. His interests were political and strategic; his experience until late in his career was confined largely to diplomatic and military affairs; and his writings on India are replete with analyses and profusely illustrated with anecdotes of the "nature" and "feelings" of the sepoys, "by whose valour and attachment the great conquest has been principally achieved, and without whose continued fidelity it cannot be preserved."[15] Their prejudices and feelings should be treated with the greatest care.

The school of thought on the government of British India that is associated with Munro, Malcolm, and Elphinstone is not usually described by historians as an "ideology." All three men emphasized the importance of practical experience over theory in determining policy. Taking this at face value, historians use the word "pragmatic" to suggest that their policy recommendations were based largely on expediency. Little consideration has been given to the possibility that, like the founders of other schools of thought on governance, Munro, Malcolm, and Elphinstone turned to the assumptions and principles of their own society for guidance when faced with the practical problems of government.

On the other hand, historians have been quick to attribute to the influence of Edmund Burke any measure Munro, Malcolm, and Elphinstone advocated that may be made to fit the mold of late eighteenth- and early nineteenth-century conservative thought. The features of their ideology that appear to owe most to Burke, as Eric Stokes, George Bearce, and, more recently, Burton Stein and Thomas R. Metcalf suggest, are their appeals to the value of history and experience, their endorsement of traditional institutions, their dislike of policies based on speculative theory, and their concern with moral values.[16] Stokes speaks of the three men as bringing to the Indian problem "Burke's notion of history, that conception which regards human society as a continuous community of the past, present, and future." Bearce claims that, "Provided with [Burke's] Conservative outlook," Munro and Elphinstone began to introduce good government in various parts of India. For Stein, Munro's "basic orientation" was derived from Burke. He shared with other "post-Burkeans" a deep awareness of the "power of nationalism and of what he called 'national character' as expressing the highest order of public values," and also an appreciation of hierarchy, especially one based on merit. (Munro would have seen his "appreciation of hierarchy" in terms of a preference for multi- rather than two-class societies with most of the merit belonging to "middling" ranks.) In Stein's view, "Edmund Burke's imprimatur" was important also in regard to the "ambient moral concerns" which were "a fixture of Munro's writing on India, from early in his public career." Stein notes that Munro purchased the twelve volumes of Burke's published writings in 1814 but does not mention the five-volume set of Blair's *Sermons*,[17] another slightly different expression of conservative thought that was as widely read as Burke at the turn of the eighteenth and nineteenth centuries.

No eighteenth-century Scotsman needed Burke to point out to him the value of history or experience, custom or morality. In discussing the way in which David Hume redirected his intellectual interests from metaphysics to history, Leslie Stephen explains: "the moral which Hume naturally drew from his philosophy was the necessity of turning entirely to experience. Experience and experience alone, could decide questions of morality and politics; and Hume put his theory in practice when he abandoned speculation to turn himself to history." In a seminal work on the Scottish Enlightenment, Gladys Bryson adds: "It was the rare [moral philosopher] who did not begin his investigations with 'Experience' instead of with some large a priori afforded by 'Reason.'" Most Scottish intellectuals, who used the evidence of history as the data from which to develop theories on a variety of subjects related to man and society, believed their methodology could be classified as empirical, scientific research, not rational speculation. They would have endorsed Munro's opinion that "a few pages of history give more insight into the human mind, and in a more agreeable manner, than all the metaphysical volumes that ever were published."[18]

David Hume and Adam Smith, before Burke's thought was widely known, both publicly emphasized the value of custom and tradition. As early as 1739 Hume, in reaction to contemporary rationalist enthusiasm, wrote that men not only reconciled themselves to long-established practice but gained an affection for it that "makes us prefer it to other objects, which may be more valuable, but are less known to us." In *The Theory of Moral Sentiments* (1759), Adam Smith claimed that the traditional ranks and orders in society were necessary for stability. "It may . . . be hard to convince [the individual] that the prosperity and preservation of the state require any diminution of the powers, privileges, and immunities of his own . . . order. . . . This partiality, though it may . . . be unjust, may not . . . be useless. . . . while it sometimes appears to obstruct some alterations of government which may be fashionable and popular at the time, it contributes in reality to the stability and permanency of the whole system."[19] This type of argument, labeled "Burkean" in the nineteenth and twentieth centuries, was widely promoted in eighteenth-century Scotland before it received Burke's public endorsement, and Burke himself acknowledged the debt he owed to his older contemporaries Hume and Smith. In 1759, Hume, who described Burke to Smith, somewhat dismissively, as "an Irish Gentleman, who wrote lately a very pretty Treatise on the Sublime," sent Burke a copy of Smith's *Theory of Moral Sentiments* in the hope that it would be reviewed in the *Annual Register*. Burke was impressed, provided a glowing review, and told Smith privately that it had never cost him "less trouble to admit so many things to which I had been a stranger before."[20]

At the time Munro, Malcolm, and Elphinstone were formulating their ideas, Burke was only one of many conservative authors, most of whom wrote about moral concerns, national character, and hierarchical social structure as well as about the importance of historical continuity and traditional institutions. Burke, after all, was applauded for his championship of traditional institutions because he was expressing, albeit in incomparable language, precisely what most conservative thinkers and most of his readers already believed and wanted to have reaffirmed, not because he was developing a new or exciting concept. Inevitably, because their thought derived from a similar intellectual heritage, Burke and the Scottish philosophes shared many ideas. Burke, however, took a less secular approach to religion, was less interested in psychology and in protosociolog-

ical explanations of institutional development, and placed much less importance on the role of the "middling ranks" of society as agents of
progress—key aspects of contemporary Scottish thought which are particularly important in explaining Munro, Malcolm, and Elphinstone's approach to Asian society and government. This is not to say that any of the
three men had plumbed in great depth the work of men like Hume,
Smith, and Ferguson. But they had heard the issues discussed and read
some of the books in the way their authors intended: as analyses of social
and political organization and as explanations of principles of economics
and morality that would prepare their readers, as Francis Hutcheson put
it, for "every honourable office in life."[21] Burke's rhetorical skills allowed
him to express his views with a memorable eloquence that was entirely
lacking in the prose of the Scottish philosophes. But most of the precepts
of early nineteenth-century conservatism that are common to the writings
of Burke, Munro, Malcolm, and Elphinstone had been discussed in the
readily accessible literature of Enlightenment Scotland. And there were issues on which the three Scotsmen differed from Burke.

Munro's initial response to the French Revolution differed from
Burke's. In 1788 he told a close friend that, "I wish Louis may avail himself of the powerful engine he has in his hands, a standing army, to crush
the mutineers of his parliament; for if they carry their point of establishing a free government, commerce will become as honourable among them
as it is in England, and France will then prove by sea what she is now by
land, the greatest power in the world; and you and I may live to see Britain
stripped of all her foreign dominions." At this time he saw the possible
overthrow of the existing French government as bad for Britain because
the replacement of an absolutist system by a "free government"—one
that was similar to that of Britain—would make France stronger, richer,
and a greater threat. In April 1790, as Burke was preparing his *Reflections on
the Revolution in France* for publication in the same year, Munro told the
same friend that the situation in France was alarming because, as a British
patriot, he could not watch with indifference the restoration of French
liberty. "That nation, already too powerful, wanted nothing but a better
form of government to render her the arbiter of Europe; and the convul-
sions attending so remarkable a revolution having subsided, France will

soon assume that rank to which she is entitled from her resources, and the enterprising genius of her inhabitants."[22]

Burke's prophecies of anarchy and disaster proved to be prescient and did much to enhance his reputation. At the time he was writing the *Reflections* and Munro was writing to his friend, however, Burke saw the French Revolution as dangerous because a long-established, "customary" system of government was being overthrown; Munro saw it as dangerous because the long-established bad system of government of an enemy was being replaced with what he expected to be a better system which would make that enemy more powerful. In 1790, Munro saw the French conflict as a scene in the ongoing drama of man's struggle between authority and liberty, and his sympathy was with greater liberty. Louis's supposed "absolute" form of government represented for Munro a flawed system that retarded progress, particularly commercial progress.

In 1792 Munro, describing Tipu Sultan's loss of vigor and spirit as a result of a defeat by the company's forces, hopes that he will recover from his "fit of despair: . . . he is at present as much changed as Mr. Burke's vision." Mr. Burke's "changed vision" presumably alludes to the apparent inconsistencies between Burke's view of events in America, India, and France. In regard to America, Burke had claimed, first, that universal political disobedience should be regarded as an indication of bad government and not treated as criminal behavior and, second, that the exercise of authority should always be adapted to the nature of the subject people. In his clash with Warren Hastings, however, Burke rejected Hastings's contention that government in India had to be adapted to the nature of the subject people, appealing instead to universal principles and the law of nature. In his approach to the French Revolution, Burke no longer saw universal political disobedience as an acceptable response to bad government. Although an argument has been developed by Charles Parkin[23] to establish a basic consistency in Burke's thought, for casual readers like Munro in 1790 and 1792, the inconsistencies were most noticeable.

In 1794 Munro, no doubt aware by this time of the course the French revolution had taken, writes that he prefers Burke's opinions on it to those of James Mackintosh and Burke's other opponents because, despite "his declamations and in some places downright nonsense," Burke developed

"more of the springs by which all governments must be moved until human nature is entirely changed and men are no longer actuated by the pas-
sions." Munro now condemns the situation in France because the assembly and convention are being ruled by factions which in turn are
controlled by the leaders of the mob. The problem is now excessive liberty
and he would have agreed with Burke on its dangers. In 1817, however, he
writes that Napoleon's operations had made "most countries on the con-
tinent much more interesting than they were before." In 1823, in response
to news of friction between France and Spain, he hopes it will end "in the
expulsion of the Bourbons" from both countries.[24] Munro may not have
liked "democracy," but European ancien regimes clearly did not impress
him, either for their own sake or as the guardians of stability and tradition. Where Burke, in the interest of stability, favored traditional elites as
the dominant group in society, Munro, concerned with the progress of
civil society, favored the agency of well-educated men from the middle
ranks.

Malcolm held similar views to Burke on many issues but in regard to
India would probably have condemned him as one who tried to apply to
Indian government a standard that had been framed for a different type or
stage of society and government. Discussing the impeachment of Warren
Hastings in the introduction to his *Political History* (1826), Malcolm describes Burke as "one of the wisest men and greatest orators that England
has ever boasted"—an often-quoted statement which has been used to
give an impression that Malcolm admired Burke unconditionally. Malcolm credits Burke and Henry Dundas with bringing to the notice of the
public the unsatisfactory state of the affairs of the East India Company.
He points out that "there can be no doubt that the promoters of these
inquiries, *however mixed their motives might have been* [my italics], became entitled to the gratitude of the country." Malcolm, however, placing Hastings's career in what he believes to be its appropriate historical and geographical context, sees Hastings as a great Indian statesmen who has
served his country well. He claims that despite the "factional" or "party"
opinions expressed on the issue of Hastings's impeachment, there are several important facts on which all "dispassionate minds" are now agreed.
"Hastings, during a time of unexampled public embarrassment, and at a

moment when he had to contend against those from whom he should have derived support, showed all the active energy of a great statesman; and by his . . . extraordinary exertions, saved the interests of his country in India from . . . ruin."[25] Although he praises Hastings's response to crisis unstintingly, Malcolm concedes that the system of government at the time was corrupt. He is trying, of course, to establish Hastings's conduct as a model useful to his defense of Wellesley's governor-generalship, while recording his own opinion that the office of governor-general requires sufficient power to be able to deal with sudden crises. However, the implication that Burke, wise man and great orator though he is, is tainted by "mixed motives" and "party factionalism"—an interpretation that Malcolm retained from the emotional *Sketch of the Political History of India* (1811) in the more deliberate *Political History* published in 1826—suggests that Malcolm's regard for Burke was not uncritical.

There are no grounds at all on which it may be argued that Burke's philosophy was important to Elphinstone. Despite his extensive reading and his interesting critiques of numerous works of philosophy, history, and politics in his journals, his only comment on Burke appears to be a laconic entry for 7 February 1802, well after Burke's prophecies of the excesses of the French Revolution had proved accurate. Elphinstone notes: "Talked with Colonel Close about Burke; he is in love with him. He read some passages from the "Reflections"; the assertions seem to me as false as the language was beautiful . . . A dispute about the right of nations to remove their kings for misconduct."[26]

Although there are areas where Burke's views coincide with those of Munro and Malcolm, and even Elphinstone, when the full range of their thought is taken into consideration, their ideology is more closely aligned with the ideas and assumptions of Scotland's moral philosophers. The frequency and consistency with which their thought has been associated with Burke's name, however, has overemphasized their conservatism at the expense of their more progressive, reformist ideas.

Although most East India Company recruits, including Munro, Malcolm, and Elphinstone, arrived in India before they were twenty years old, all had been exposed to some degree to the socializing process and cultural environment of their local community and were likely, if only unconsciously, to draw on early influences for guidance in coming to terms with India. During the eighteenth century Scotland enjoyed a period of intense intellectual vitality, a period in which a combination of intellectual freedom with a "fundamental conservatism"[27] produced a philosophy of improvement that was empirical, practical, and reformist rather than speculative, idealist, and revolutionary. If, on arrival in India, the recruit proved to be ambitious, conscientious, culturally curious, or merely bored, the intellectual world of Enlightenment Scotland provided him with a theoretical framework for the study of history and contemporary society and government as applicable to an analysis of Asia's past and present condition as to Europe's.

Working from the assumption that human nature is the same everywhere, that societies pass through various stages on the path from savagery to civilization, and that national character is formed by interrelated moral and physical causes, the Scottish philosophes examined religions in the secular context of beliefs about social control, social morality, and national character. Ideas about the correct relationship between liberty and authority helped to define discussions of the practical and moral efficacy of different systems of government. Modes of subsistence and levels of prosperity were scrutinized in the light of recent ideas on political economy. Laws were assessed according to their utility, given the level of sophistication of the society concerned. Munro, Malcolm, and Elphinstone were not doctrinaire disciples of any of Scotland's philosophers, but the way they thought and the way they wrote, particularly about religion, systems of government, and political economy (the subjects of the next three chapters), owed much to the principles and methodologies commonplace in their own society.

CHAPTER 9

Religious Moderates

The aid of religion was called in to . . . subdue the ferocity of the times.
The Almighty was said to have manifested, by visions and revelations to
different persons, his disapprobation of that spirit of revenge, which
armed one part of his creatures against the other.
—William Robertson

This account of the secular use to which the powerful influence of religion
could be put appears in the Reverend William Robertson's explanation of the way in which the "rule of law" was gradually introduced in
medieval Europe. Robertson was a Presbyterian minister, and his observation that "The Almighty was *said*" (my italics) to have revealed his will to
different people in order to achieve social and political ends is startling.
By the second half of the eighteenth century, however, the harsh, theo-
cratic rigidity of Scottish Calvinism was being modified, at least for some
of the well-educated middling ranks in society, by intellectual currents
emanating from continental Europe. Robertson, together with other influential thinkers, became a leading member of the Moderate group within the Kirk.

The Moderates, as opposed to the Evangelical High Flyer group,
were the dominant party in the general assembly of the Church of Scot-

145

land from the 1760s to the 1780s. Although cautious in expressing their
opinions on contemporary Christianity, as early as 1755 the Moderates
had been sufficiently confident on the subject of liberty of conscience to
defend Lord Kames and David Hume from charges of skepticism and
heresy. When the question of compulsory subscription to the Westminster Confession of Faith became a controversial issue in the 1770s and
1780s, they argued that all creeds and confessions were incomplete because they were the product of a specific historical situation. They went
so far as to assert that Luther and Calvin, being products of their time,
were no more likely to be infallible than their Catholic contemporaries.
But this statement seriously alarmed the Evangelicals who accused them
of even extending their toleration to Muslims and to "the Alcoran."[1] The
proceedings of the general assembly were widely publicized; its members
represented a broad cross section of educated Scottish society, and the
ideas of religious Moderatism were debated, if not invariably endorsed,
throughout southern Scotland. Although Munro, Malcolm, and Elphinstone undoubtedly believed the moral and ethical precepts of Christianity to be superior to those of other religions, they were as cautious as
most of the Scottish philosophes were in revealing their own faith. The
evidence indicates, however, that their approach to both Christianity and
Eastern religions owed much to Scottish Moderatism and, in the case
of Malcolm and Elphinstone, to deism. The three men were clearly not
"High Flyers."

Munro's family were staunch Episcopalians and he attended what he
called his mother's "English Chapel" and listened to his father's fireside
sermons throughout his childhood. The Reverend George Gleig, who did
his best to represent Munro as a mid–nineteenth century middle-class
role model, believed it to be important that his subject should be seen to
subscribe to orthodox religious views, and asserted that Munro's "whole
life, both in public and private, was modelled upon the rules laid down in
the Gospel." He avoided a direct statement about Munro's faith in revelation, however, merely observing, somewhat evasively, that "he is, after all,
the most vitally religious man whose general behaviour corresponds best
with the revealed Will of God." References to religion of any sort in
Munro's papers are extremely rare and do not suggest a deep commitment

to either revelation or to a belief in man's dependence on divine will, although later in life he enjoyed reading the Bible. Munro never mentioned his own religion publicly and his only private allusions, made in the 1790s to his sister Erskine, his most intimate correspondent, were frivolous in tone. He compared his brother James's religious enthusiasm with his own "more sublime religion," insisted on his right to "liberty of conscience" in a hypothetical marriage contract, and spoke of the spiritual truths he might have discovered in the withered leaves sent by Erskine "if I were a man of devout turn of mind," implying that he was not.[2] Munro applied the adjectives "superstitious" and "bigoted" to Hindus and Muslims respectively in the technical way that David Hume applied the words "superstition" and "enthusiasm" to Roman Catholicism and fanatical Protestantism.[3]

Munro was circumspect in his public statements about the work of Christian missionaries in India. He did not object to their activities as long as Indians could not interpret them as official policy—as sanctioned by the government. As governor of Madras, however, he would not tolerate attempts at proselytization by a company official and censured and later dismissed a subcollector, one of his own protégés, for distributing within his district Kanarese translations of the New Testament and tracts on moral and religious subjects. Munro was indignant that the collector, while professing his willingness to conform to the government's directives, requested nevertheless that his opinions on converting Indians should be judged "according as they are supported or contradicted by the Word of God" as contained in passages from the Scriptures. He sent these passages to Munro as an appendix to his letter of apology. Munro regarded this as "an extraordinary kind of appeal." The collector was using his official position to work as a missionary and, when told by his superior that he was wrong to do so, "justifies his acts by quotations from Scripture, and by election, a doctrine which has occasioned so much controversy; and he leaves it to be inferred, that Government must either adopt his views, or act contrary to divine authority."[4]

Writing just before the renewal of the company's charter in 1813, when the question whether missionary activity in India should or should not be encouraged was the most contentious Indian issue in Britain, Munro observes that while primitive people seem to relinquish their superstitions quite easily, the Turks of Europe, although at an advanced stage of civilization and in close contact with Christian states, have not discarded their faith in Muhammad's teachings. In India, he maintains, change will not take place until, "by the improvement of the country, India shall abound in a middling class of wealthy men, secure in the possession of their property, and having leisure to study our best authors translated into the various languages of the country."[5] As "our best authors" did not write the Bible, the statement implies that, for Munro, economic and social development aided by reading of western literature (in translation to reach the widest possible audience), rather than Christian proselytization would be the catalyst for Indian progress.

Munro was intolerant of stupidity but not of other people's beliefs. In a letter in which he deliberately connects Hindu with Catholic superstition, he provides a sympathetic portrayal of a swami, a religious Brahmin of a class who "possess an influence not inferior to that of the Pope and his bishops and cardinals in the darkest ages." Swamis do not marry as do the pagoda Brahmins, "but must lead a life of celibacy and temperance, or rather abstinence." Unlike the "swamis" of Europe, Munro observes drily, "they have no nephews and nieces." They amass no wealth; whatever they receive they distribute to others and "They are to the full as respectable as their brethren in Europe." Munro liked diversity, including religious diversity: "give me ... the world as it now stands, with all its beautiful variety of knowledge, and ignorance,—of language—of manners—customs—religion and superstitions—of cultivated fields and wide-extended deserts—and war and peace."[6] This latitudinarian confession is compatible with Munro's open-minded approach to India but seems to reject the confining particularism of revealed Christianity. When he first came into close contact with rural Indian society as a revenue collector, Munro's religious views, like those of Malcolm and Elphinstone, seem to have been those of a Moderate.

In his biography of Malcolm, Sir John Kaye makes no attempt to detail Malcolm's religious beliefs, but the influence of Moderatism on the Malcolm family's Calvinism is indicated by the fact that Mrs. Radcliffe's *Mysteries of Udolpho* was read aloud at home, and by the young Malcolm's attendance at a London theater on his first home furlough.[7] These two activities would have been roundly condemned by Kirk High Flyers. Malcolm's approval, in his writings on Asia, of anyone he could describe as holding the "sublime general truths [of] pure deism," suggests that he also found the broad, cosmopolitan creed of the deists acceptable.

In Malcolm's estimation, the religious practices of a society should be the starting point for the historian because they help to determine the nature of the state and the character of its inhabitants, they are generally used as an agent of civilization, and they are the natural focus of man's earliest efforts at art, literature, and learning. He believes that the significance of the Koran, for example, has been underestimated by Europeans. "We can hardly (in the pride of better knowledge) venture to pronounce that to be puerile or contemptible which has so fully answered the purpose for which it was designed." Unbelievers, Malcolm suggests, should admire the skill of Muhammad's strategy in claiming that the Koran was sent complete by God but only revealed, bit by bit, by Gabriel. "No mode could have been better calculated to preserve and to promote his power. He was at once the civil ruler and military leader . . . and he drew at pleasure, from a source which they deemed divine, those laws and mandates which were to regulate their lives, and to excite them to actions of virtue and valour." Although the Arabs were divided at home and despised abroad, Muhammad's religion taught them to worship one true God and, as Malcolm points out, "they obtained strength from the political union brought about by a common creed to become masters of the fairest portions of the globe." Similarly, Malcolm approves in general of Sufism, which teaches "the equality of the relation of all created beings to their Creator." He suggests that traces of Sufism may be found everywhere: "in the most splendid theories of the ancient schools of Greece, and in those of the modern philosophers of Europe."[8]

On the origins of Sikhism, Malcolm explains that although Nanak grounded his religion on a principle of pure deism, the minds of the masses could not remain loyal for long to a creed "the most sublime general truths" of which were of a nature too vast for their comprehension. After their founder's death, his followers worshiped his name and, in direct contravention of his teaching, "clothed him in all the attributes of a

saint." It is an account that would have provided empirical evidence for
Hume's theory on the "flux and reflux of polytheism and theism." After
Nanak, Malcolm claims, the forms of Sikh devotion began to take precedence over the substance of the founder's beliefs, and, strengthened by
habit, "they become the points to which ignorance and unenlightened
minds have in all ages of the world, shown the most resolute . . . adherence."[9]

The tenets of Hinduism, in Malcolm's opinion, had been "calculated
to preserve a vast community in tranquillity and obedience to its rulers,"
but they had also the effect of making the country "an easy conquest to
every powerful foreign invader." Referring to the doctrine that forbade all
but those of the warrior castes to bear arms except in self-defense, Malcolm observes that, bound by "the chains of their civil and religious institutions," Hindu states, unlike Muslim ones, could not increase their numbers by conversion, nor "allow more than a small proportion of the
population to arm against the enemy."[10]

These observations, although they may not accurately represent the
tenets of the religions they describe, suggest that Malcolm had been quite
strongly influenced by the protosociological elements in Scottish Enlightenment approaches to the study of man and society. They recognize rational intent in regard to social control, unintended consequences, and the
symbiotic relationship between religion and the power of the state. Malcolm saw religion as an integral part of human nature—as a powerful
emotion that could also be a powerful and practical tool. He believed it
had been used by individuals and groups since earliest times, generally for
the benevolent purpose of bringing order out of chaos and aiding the
progress of civilization but, occasionally, to further the ends of power
politics. In his historical works, Malcolm consistently portrays the prophets of new religious movements as men with the capacity to conceive
the sublime nature of the creator but aware that the weakness of human
nature and the particular stage of development of their societies requires
them to adapt their doctrines accordingly. And he emphasizes the point
that, once established, the tenets of a new religion have a significant impact on the development of national character—national culture—and
"the revolutions of public affairs." In the short term, the desired objec-

tives are often met but, in the long term, unanticipated consequences sometimes occur that are of greater significance from an historical perspective. "The sacred character of religion, under whatever shape it assumes, has always given it a supreme influence over the human mind: but its effects are most remarkable when they influence the fate of nations."[11] Malcolm's examination of religious forms and beliefs was invariably made from a secularist and universal standpoint.

Elphinstone's approach to religion was similarly secularist and universal. The Elphinstones had been Episcopalian Calvinists at least until the eighteenth century,[12] but Elphinstone himself mentions no sectarian convictions. On being appointed governor of Bombay, with apparently little personal preference either way he asked John Adam: "as one must go to church ought it . . . to be [the] Scotch one or is the gov[ernor] supposed to be . . . *always of the religion established by law*[?]" In what reads like an apology for Elphinstone's views, Colebrooke observes that although Elphinstone's journals say little about religion, "when the subject is referred to they breathe a spirit of resignation and reliance on his Maker." Cotton, after pointing out that Elphinstone had once been described as "devoid of religion and blinded to all spiritual truth," defends his subject with the assertions that his "outward rule of life was based upon the maxims of Stoic philosophy" and that he passed through a period of religious skepticism in his younger days, but "experience of the world and much reading" converted him into a devout Unitarian. Nineteenth-century biographers, including Colebrooke, Cotton, Gleig, Bradshaw, and Kaye, tended to be less interested in the ideas and personalities of their subjects than in their potential as morally, socially, and in regard to India, politically useful role models. They believed, as Colebrooke put it, that in "laying the historical facts before the public [the biographer] assumes the care of the reputation of a great man."[13] Taking care of the reputation of a great man in the nineteenth century involved the biographer in the construction of a facade of orthodox Christian beliefs if the subject seemed to lack the genuine article.

The passive Christian virtues of faith, hope, and charity seem, in fact, to have been far less appealing to Elphinstone than what he saw as the more positive and active virtues of the ancients, a fact that makes a "spirit

of resignation and reliance on his Maker" seem out of character. Stoicism
enjoyed wide popularity in educated circles in late eighteenth-century Europe and the term "polite stoicism" has been used to describe the ethics
promoted by the Moderate ministers of the Church of Scotland. Elphinstone's admiration for the doctrines of Stoicism placed him in good intellectual company; they had a major influence on the thought of Adam
Smith.[14] Elphinstone's skepticism was probably confirmed, if not inspired,
by Hume.

Although Hume's *Natural History of Religion* (1757) and the *Dialogues
Concerning Natural Religion* (1777) shocked the orthodox, many educated
people accepted the view expressed in the *Natural History* that, "the whole
frame of nature bespeaks an intelligent author; and no rational enquirer
can, after serious reflection, suspend his belief a moment with regard to
the primary principles of genuine theism and religion." For Hume, however, enquirers were rarely rational, and religion, like everything else, was
determined as much by feelings as by reason. Adopting an historical-an-
thropological approach, he used the technique of conjecture to explain
how the "incessant hopes and fears, which actuate the human mind" led
men to ascribe to the activities of an invisible agent the acts of nature and
the "various and contrary events of human life" that were otherwise inex-
plicable. The idea that religion originated in human need not divine
will—that man created God rather than God creating man—was, of
course, unacceptable to orthodox Christians. Hume proceeded to demonstrate that early religions were always polytheistic; that it was natural for
mankind gradually to exalt one deity above all others, endow him with
omnipotence, celebrate his power and greatness, yet conceive of him as
vengeful and vindictive; that man needed then to invent intermediaries between himself and this terrible deity—minor gods, saints, or dervishes—
thus lapsing again into what was in fact, if not in name, polytheism. He
presented evidence to suggest that polytheism, though designated an "inferior" form of religious belief, was less harmful than theism: that it was
more tolerant, that it inspired courage rather than the personal mortifica-
tion and social deference associated with monotheistic religions, that the
symbols and outward trappings of all the "superior" religions were equally absurd and that none, however sublime its concepts, had persuaded

mankind that virtue and morality alone, not ritual adulation, could be acceptable to a perfect being.[15]

In the *Dialogues* Hume analyzes the evidence that may be discovered in the concept of "design" for the existence and benevolent nature of the Creator and for the existence of a divinely created order in the universe. It questions, in fact, his own "assumption" in the *Natural History* that "the whole frame of nature bespeaks an intelligent author." The work is inconclusive and has provided fuel for much debate over Hume's own religious views. It is undoubtedly, however, one of the most important eighteenth-century works of religious skepticism. In a journal entry for April 1801, Elphinstone mentions reading Hume's chapter on "Academical or Sceptical Philosophy" and observes that he has "finished reading the admirable dialogue on natural religion." His respect for Hume's religious views seems to match his admiration for the philosopher's approach to history.[16]

The evidence for Elphinstone's Unitarianism derives from a journal entry for 1846 in which he expresses his liking for Alexander Pope's "Universal Prayer." While considering the poem, Elphinstone muses on institutional Christianity, formal ritual, faith in orthodox doctrine, the sanctifying or deifying of human beings to create intermediaries between man and the Creator, and the social role of religion and its value as a superintendent of social duty. Although the evidence for the view of Elphinstone as a Unitarian is clear in his obvious dislike of the concept of the Trinity, in his *History of India*, which was published five years before the date of this journal entry, he approves Hinduism's celebration of the Unity of God and discusses ritual, faith, the sanctifying of human intermediaries, the social role of religion, and the dual strands of philosophical and popular religious usage in much the same way as he considers aspects of Christianity in his journal. A comparison of the journal with the *History* suggests that Elphinstone's interest in religion was directed towards the identification and analysis of the common elements to be found in all great religions.[17]

In the *Wealth of Nations*, which Munro, Malcolm, and Elphinstone all read, Adam Smith noted that two types of religion tend to develop within each society, different forms that meet the different needs of the poor and illiterate and of well-educated higher ranks. According to Smith, the reli-

gion of the lower social orders is likely to be either austere or imaginative
or maybe both, because extravagance will be ruinous and the consolation
of a beautiful afterlife is needed to compensate for the ugly realities of
their earthly existence. The wealthy and powerful, he believes, tend to be
more lax and worldly in their religious views and observances. In other
words, religious beliefs tend to be determined according to economic and
social considerations rather than in response to revelations from God.
Malcolm observes that it would be unfair to judge the people by the
records of the great, as "illustrious personages in all ages and countries
deem themselves exempt from vulgar restrictions." Elphinstone acknowledges the political importance of the clergy in a letter in which he discusses Adam Smith, whom he regarded as a man of "enlarged" views.
Smith had suggested that the clergy should be paid for practicing their
trade, "like tailors or other workmen," but Elphinstone felt they should
not enjoy such independence. "The . . . enterprise and ambition which the
clergy have shown in all times makes it absolutely necessary to keep a
strong and well-disciplined standing army of them who shall be interested in maintaining order and in fighting (in their way) against other clergy
who attack the state." Munro spoke of "pain and poverty" as two apostles
who probably converted more people to religion than "all the bishops
that ever existed"—an explanation for religious convictions that reflects
Hume's arguments in the *Natural History of Religion* as well as Smith's in the
Wealth of Nations. Elphinstone clearly accepted the concept of two forms of
religion. Although his interpretation was not quite the same as Smith's,
there are intimations of approval in his journal entry for a proper difference between the dutiful religion of a philosophical elite and the worldly
petitions of the masses, which suggest that religious practices should be
useful reminders of social obligation for the former but necessary agents
of social control for the latter.[18]

In his examination of Hindu religion in the *History of India,* Elphinstone argues that ritual has gained an undesirable although not complete
preponderance over its moral precepts. Reward and punishment is often
"well apportioned to the moral merits and demerits of the deceased" and
they undoubtedly influence the conduct of the living. But "the efficacy ascribed to faith," the emphasis on forms of devotion, and the ease with

which crimes can be expiated by penance undermine the effectiveness of Hindu principles. The contemporary state of religion suffers, he believes, from "the doctrine that faith in a particular god is more efficacious than contemplation, ceremonial observance, or good works." The elements of ritual and faith in Hinduism are, in Elphinstone's estimation, as undesirable for moral purposes as those of Christianity. Superstition irritated Elphinstone because it "debased and debilitated" the mind and was a hindrance to improvement. Brahmin morality, which fostered passive obedience rather than active virtue, also inhibited progress: the "exclusive view to repose in this world, and absorption hereafter, destroys the great stimulants to virtue afforded by love of enterprise and of posthumous fame." Religion, when it controlled law, science, and the minutiae of everyday life, inhibited a sense of free agency and reduced life to "a mechanical routine." It is hard to believe that Elphinstone could write of Hinduism in this way and still maintain a spirit of resignation and reliance on his Christian Maker. A more likely statement of his own faith appears to be his opinion that: "When individuals are left free [from religious interference], improvements take place as they are required; and a nation is entirely changed in the course of a few generations without an effort on the part of any of its members."[19]

What Elphinstone thought of as religious interference, Malcolm called religious prejudice—a concept that influenced, in particular, his explanation of the role of women in society. Elphinstone shared the view of many of the Scottish philosophes that any inquiry into the manners of a nation should include a discussion of the position of women, because their status was an accurate indicator of the stage of civilization it had reached. Munro, in giving evidence on India before the House of Commons in 1812, stated that if "a treatment of the female sex, full of confidence, respect and delicacy" indicated "a civilized people," Hindus were equal to Europeans.[20] But Malcolm, like Hume and John Millar, saw women as agents as well as indicators of progress, an important role in society they could fulfill only when society was unencumbered by religious prejudice.

Writing of the Islamic customs of polygamy and female seclusion, Malcolm observes that they "had an influence, scarcely secondary to any other cause, in retarding the progress of civilization among those nations who have adopted this faith." For Malcolm, patriarchal despotism encouraged political despotism and political despotism inhibited progress. There was nothing that affected the condition and character of a people more than the laws and customs which governed the relationship between the sexes: "On it, perhaps beyond all other causes, depends the moral state of a country and its progress and general improvement."[21]

These views were interpreted by M. E. Yapp, in an early article, as representing the feelings inspired by Malcolm's marriage, which took place shortly before he went on his second Persian mission and began to write his history of Persia. He describes Malcolm as belonging "to the depressing collection of simple, practical men who have been there," who have lived in "the romantic world of the Indian soldier," where a European woman "was a rarity to be cherished and guarded." This rosy picture of the lot of European women in India, however, was rejected by Munro who stated, twelve years before Malcolm's marriage, that India was a bad place for a British woman to look for a husband, because "the promiscuous intercourse with the sex that [British men] have all been accustomed to makes it almost impossible that they can ever become tender affectionate husbands—indifference is the only mark by which such men distinguish their wives from other women." For these reasons Munro persuaded his brother Alexander to help him provide allowances for their financially destitute sisters so that they would not have to seek husbands in the "marriage markets of Bengal or Madras." Malcolm's romantic attitude to women, however, is seen by Yapp as "the root of [his] explanation of the motivation of Persian history."[22]

It is an interpretation that seems to rest on the assumption that "simple, practical men" have no philosophical or cultural beliefs. The idea that there was a close association between the status of women and the state of civilization, however, was a popular one in Scotland, which in the late eighteenth century allowed considerable freedom of social intercourse between the sexes and saw this as a civilizing force. The letter of a visiting Englishman, written from Edinburgh in 1774, talks of "The women, who, to do them justice, are much more entertaining than their neighbours in England, discovered a great deal of vivacity and fondness for repartee.

The general ease with which they conducted themselves, the innocent freedom of their manners, and the unaffected good nature, all conspired to make one forget that we were regaling in a cellar."[23] The cellar location does not indicate a lower-class gathering: the group included Jean Maxwell, later duchess of Gordon, who presented Munro's eldest sister to Queen Charlotte in 1806, after her marriage to Henry Erskine, lord advocate for Scotland.

In the conclusion to his essay on national character, Hume observed that "the politeness of a nation will commonly much depend" on a free relationship between the sexes, and he suggested that marriages should be conducted "with perfect equality as between two equal members of the same body." Francis Hutcheson emphasized compatibility and companionship as the foundation for a right relationship and objected strongly to the double standard that tolerated infidelity in men but not women: "the powers vested in husbands by the civil laws of many nations are monstrous." John Millar claimed that when some progress has been made in the arts and men have achieved "a proportional degree of refinement," they set a value on "those female accomplishments and virtues which have so much influence on every species of improvement."[24] This opinion appeared in Millar's best known and most respected work, *The Origin of the Distinction of Ranks,* which first appeared in 1771 and ran to three more editions in 1773, 1781, and 1806. The views on gender relationships expressed by Munro, Malcolm, and Elphinstone reflect the influence of contemporary Scottish social theory.

Their views on missionary activity in India probably owed more to practical than to theoretical considerations. Malcolm's *Sketch of the Sikhs* and *History of Persia* were both written when the debate over the encouragement of missionary activity in India was causing controversy in both Britain and India, and his feelings on the issue are made clear. He uses historical narratives and explanations to warn of the danger of interference in Indian religious beliefs and practices, not only to the political stability of British India but also to its continued existence as a state.

In the *Sketch of the Sikhs,* Malcolm points out that Har Govind converted "a race of peaceable enthusiasts into an intrepid band of soldiers" out of an "irreconcilable hatred of [Muslim] oppression." In his account of Persia under Islamic rule he states, "kingdoms have become powerful, not from the inhabitants cherishing a spirit of patriotism . . . but from a congenial feeling of irreconcilable hatred to their neighbours, on account of some slight difference in the mode or substance of their paying their adoration to the great Creator of the universe." This is true "of human society in every part of the globe," but particularly so in regard to "those nations which have adopted the belief of the Prophet of Arabia." Malcolm warned that even the pacifism of the Hindus should not be taken for granted, and quoted the speech of a Hindu prince on the occasion of the invasion of his state by the Muslim leader, Mahmud of Ghazni: "My followers, who appear so mild and submissive, will, if they see no escape, or are irritated beyond their power of sufferance, soon change their character; they will murder their wives and children, burn their habitations . . . and encounter your army with all the energy of men, whose only desire is revenge and death." Malcolm warns that "the history of India abounds in similar instances" and that the speech accurately depicts the character of Hindus of the military castes.[25]

While employed in the administration of the Deccan in 1819, when missionary activity was still a controversial issue, Elphinstone was equally anxious to avoid any interference with Indian religion. He stated that he has left out of his *Report on the Peshwa's Territories* an account of the dangers that would follow upon any attempt to interfere with religious customs because they are so obvious that "we may hope they will never be braved." But he goes on to point out that "The numbers and physical force of the natives are evidently incalculably greater than ours. Our strength consists in the want of energy and disunion of our enemies. There is but one talisman, that, while it animated and united them all, would leave us without a single adherent: this talisman is the name of religion, a power so odious that it is astonishing our enemies have not more frequently and systematically employed it against us."[26] By the time Elphinstone started writing his *History of India* in the mid-1830s, however, the British were sufficiently confident to consider a program of westernizing reforms. Apparently reflecting this change, Elphinstone was now more concerned with the barriers to improvement he identified in the practices of Hinduism and Islam than in the danger of provoking rebellion.

Religious considerations are important in Elphinstone's treatment of Indian history from the first Muslim incursions to the decline of the Mughal empire and in Malcolm's account of the more recent centuries of Persian history. In both cases, however, when they are dealing with states in which Islam is the religion of the rulers, religious issues are generally discussed in relation to the system of government of the state rather than to the manners of the people. Sometime after Elphinstone's death, a correspondent of the *Times* recorded that on one occasion, Elphinstone had defended Pontius Pilate on the ground that it was his duty as governor to maintain order, and, therefore, that what he did was right. To the correspondent, "the late Mr. Elphinstone ever appears to us in his most unamiable light when he advocates the hateful doctrine [of political expediency]."[27] Religion was important for Malcolm and Elphinstone for its effects on national character, its political volatility, and its inhibiting influence on the progress of civilization—all secular interests. The well-being of men's souls, for Munro as well as for Malcolm and Elphinstone, was not the responsibility of the government of India. But their relatively tolerant and intellectually curious attitude to religion is important because it set the tone for their approach to other aspects of Asian culture.

CHAPTER 10

Systems of Government

Seeking an Equilibrium between Authority and Liberty

A great sacrifice of liberty must necessarily be made in any government . . .
yet . . . authority . . . ought never in any constitution, to
become quite entire and uncontrollable.
—David Hume

The issue of establishing a "correct" relationship between authority and liberty was at the center of western political discourse throughout the late eighteenth century. Most Scottish intellectuals assumed that European monarchy, even in its more absolute forms in Russia and France, provided a relatively satisfactory balance between freedom and oppression. It was preferable to despotism, described by Adam Ferguson as "monarchy corrupted," and also to the so-called freedom of the ancient republics, because they had rested on slavery. It was suitable for the governance of relatively large areas, and it was unlikely to degenerate into anarchy. Britain, they thought, enjoyed a superior but by no means perfect form of monarchical government. The term "liberty" rarely meant much more than the security of the persons and property of the governed under rulers whose right to govern rested ultimately on some form of tacit consent. It did not mean democracy or even representative government. Although there was wide agreement that despotic and arbitrary authority were morally degrading and discouraged the progress of civil society, it was also agreed that individual liberties could not be protected without some form of political authority.[1] When Munro, in the 1790s, and Malcolm and Elphinstone, in 1818, became administrators responsible for the *consolidation* rather than the *expansion* of British power, they all advocated a form of government for British India that would provide a balance between the authority necessary for stability and the liberty necessary for both individual and state progress.

For eighteenth-century historians the term "despotism" lacked some of the derogatory connotations it acquired in the following century—unless the word "oriental" was associated with it. In Hume's and Robertson's interpretations of the progress of Britain and continental Europe, despotism, in the sense of a centralized, authoritarian monarchy, was a stage through which the more civilized European states had necessarily passed as part of the process of their transition from feudal anarchy to limited monarchy, with its regularly constituted institutions of government. Robertson regretted that Scotland had not taken "the painful but necessary road" to strong, centralized monarchy in the sixteenth century—a road which, in Hume's interpretation, England had taken under the Tudor dynasty, while Robertson pointed, more specifically, to the reigns of Louis XI in France and Henry VII in England. This stage of despotic government had been progressive because it had provided the stable environment necessary for the "rise of commerce and the arts," the production of agricultural surpluses, and the exercise of enterprise which, in turn, had led to the development of more graduated social ranks and a gradual shift of power and authority to "middling ranks" whose particular interest it was to insist on a rule of law.[2] Munro, Malcolm, and Elphinstone acknowledged that British rule in India was despotic and saw many, but not all, Asian forms of government as despotic. Like the philosophes, however, they did not see despotism as inevitably reprehensible; it might be good, bad, or indifferent according to whether power was wielded in the interests of the community as a whole or to fulfill selfish ambitions. In their histories of past and present Asian societies, Malcolm and Elphinstone identified the strengths and weaknesses of despotism in order that they might be adopted, or avoided, by the British in India.

When Malcolm and Elphinstone wrote their books about the Sikhs and the Afghans in the early nineteenth century, Sikh and Afghan leaders had been using, for some time, the opportunity provided by the decline of Mughal power to the east and the collapse of the Safavid empire in Persia to build independent states. Malcolm traces the transformation of a passive and oppressed Sikh people into the proud and warlike rulers of a state extending through and beyond the Punjab. Elphinstone, on the other hand, traces the process by which the Afghan people, independent and egalitarian under rulers from the Abdali clan "whose government was at all times democratic," were induced to accept a more autocratic form of government by Ahmad Shah Durani.[3]

Malcolm's *Sketch of the Sikhs*, based largely on information he obtained from Sikh leaders while on a diplomatic mission in 1805, is a short book written to explain the present condition of the Sikh people. Two of its three chapters examine contemporary civil institutions and religious beliefs and practices. Institutions, for Malcolm, are the key to understanding the nature and power of any state, and he examines the historical evolution and political impact of Sikh institutions, claiming that any knowledge he can provide will be useful at a time when recent British expansion in India has brought the company into contact with the Sikhs for the first time. Much space is devoted to explaining how the tenth and last spiritual leader of the sect, Guru Govind, while upholding the religious tenets of the sect's founder, Nanak, established institutions and practices that turned an "inoffensive, peaceable sect" into a militant but unruly nation.[4]

Govind, according to Malcolm, offered equality through the abolition of caste distinctions and the constitution of a federative republic. "[He] calculated to rouse his followers from their indolent habits, and deeprooted prejudices, by giving them a personal share in the government, and placing within the reach of every individual the attainment of rank and influence in the state." His innovations were publicized through preaching and writings in which he claimed divine sanction for his mission and exhorted his disciples to valor, emulation, and sacrifice. Symbols of identity and a ceremony of initiation were devised in order to inculcate a sense of pride and particularity. In sum, he inspired "a low race, and of grovelling minds," with pride and the realization that their progress would depend solely upon their own efforts.[5]

Malcolm sets the Sikh leader's methods and objectives in a universal context. Govind possessed "many of those features which have distinguished the most celebrated founders of political communities." His praiseworthy object was the emancipation of his tribe from oppression, his means those that only a comprehensive mind would suggest. His only hope of success was "a bold departure from usages which were calculated to keep those by whom they were observed, in a degraded subjection to an . . . intolerant race" of Muslim rulers. Yet Malcolm sees the contemporary Sikh state as a failure. Govind's revolutionary constitution led to disorder and weakness. By allowing the Sikh chiefs to retain their local powers and maintain their independence—their "liberty"—he ensured that only an external threat would produce sufficient unity of purpose to render them a formidable power.[6] One of the most serious external threats to which the Sikh state had to respond was that mounted by Ahmad Shah Durani of Kabul in the early 1760s. Ahmad's power was at first overwhelming, but the Sikhs did eventually maintain their position in the Punjab owing partly to a timely resurgence of Sikh unity in the face of danger, and partly to disturbances within Ahmad's domains which drew him back to Kabul.

The Durani empire had come into existence with the crowning of Ahmad in October 1747, little more than sixty years before Elphinstone himself visited the court of Ahmad's descendent Shah Shuja al-Mulk in 1808. While in Peshawar, Elphinstone's staff collected a great deal of information on the geography and resources of what is now Afghanistan. Elphinstone himself sought information from men from all walks of life, but particularly from itinerant traders and physicians who "traverse great spaces and being everywhere welcomed, . . . have the best means for observing the manners of the people as well as the nature of the country."[7] Traditionally, the Afghan tribes had paid tribute either to the Persians or to the ruling dynasty at Delhi, or had maintained a fragile independence when their neighbors were too weak to enforce their demands. Ahmad's endeavor was the first attempt to create an Afghan state, and "he either felt, or pretended to feel, a strong attachment to his nation." According to Elphinstone, Ahmad's ideal was monarchical government on the Persian model. The forms of his court, his ministers, army, and the powers of the crown were modeled on those of Nadir Shah. But Ahmad's need to modify Nadir's arrangements points up a critical difference in their situations. Nadir, who had usurped an established monarchy, faced little internal opposition because Persians were accustomed to despotic government. Ahmad, on the other hand, was trying to impose monarchy on a republican, warlike, and independent people.[8]

In Afghanistan, those most familiar with monarchical government regarded a king as an enemy interested only in extracting tribute; they had no conception of a king as a magistrate to whom one owed loyalty in return for protection. Ahmad attached his own tribe—his power base—by providing opportunities and privileges while abstaining from interference in its internal affairs, and he gradually imposed his authority on the other tribes by noninterference and by sharing the spoils of war. Elphinstone describes the character of Ahmad in terms soon to be reserved for British imperial proconsuls. He had the "enterprise and decision" to seize opportunities and the "prudence and moderation" that was as necessary to the government of a warlike and independent people as the "bold and commanding turn of his natural genius." His military courage and ability were admired by all, yet he was by nature mild and clement; "and though it is impossible to acquire sovereign power, and perhaps, in Asia, to maintain it without crimes, yet the memory of no Eastern prince is stained with fewer acts of cruelty and injustice." If Ahmad's approach had been followed by his successors, Elphinstone believes a strong, stable government would have been established. But his successors were less able men and the dynasty's power declined. Failure to unite the tribes in support of a Persian-style monarchy, however, saved the Afghan people from the more morally damaging effects of Asian despotism.[9]

Elphinstone compares the Afghanistan of the *Kingdom of Caubul* to "ancient Scotland." In early times, Scottish kings ruled the towns and the surrounding country and exacted an unreliable tribute from nearby clans; more distant clans retained their independence. He explains that "the inordinate power and faction of the nobility most connected with the court, and the relations borne by all the great lords to the crown, resemble each other so closely in the two states, that it will throw light on the character of the Durani government to keep the parallel in view."[10]

The tribal divisions and systems of local government of Afghanistan —the latter varying from complete democracy to circumscribed patriarchy—are described by Elphinstone in detail. The defect of democratic government is its tendency to produce anarchy and disorder; its inestimable advantage is its moral impact. For Elphinstone, the great moral virtues are the enterprise, energy, and civic virtue found in ancient Greece and Rome. "However rudely formed," a popular government which provides occupation, interest, and a sense of independence and personal worth inspires courage, intelligence, and elevation of character. The Afghan tribes are described as "organised republics" which protect people from both foreign invaders and the often disorderly royal government, and this helps explain "the progressive improvement" of Afghanistan, despite twelve years of civil war, whereas Persia remains in a state of decay despite twenty years of peace.[11]

Afghan institutions, although inferior as instruments of national power to those found under a more despotic government, nevertheless afford superior materials for the construction of a "rational constitution," and Elphinstone engages in "a pleasing reverie," a conjectural explanation based on the British historical "model" of how a constitutional, monarchical form of government might evolve out of the Afghan system of self-governing tribes. A "king of genius" would cooperate with the hereditary khans. In order to consult the interests of all, a general assembly would be established—an arrangement already "congenial to the habits of their internal government." This council of the nobility would be connected with both king and people but, by custom, most khans could neither levy taxes nor adopt public measures without the consent of the elected chiefs of the tribes, and these chiefs were themselves bound to obtain the consent of their tribesmen. The inconvenience of having to leave court to persuade followers, ignorant of the requirements of the state, to contribute to the general revenue would soon suggest to the khans the idea of selecting tribal representatives: an elective assembly would be formed of individuals closely connected with their constituents. They would represent a people "accustomed to respect their chiefs, but as much accustomed to debate on, and to approve or reject, the measures which those chiefs proposed." Elphinstone, however, is forced to conclude that this is unlikely to happen. The various factions at the Afghan court have borrowed too many ideas from neighboring despotisms, and Afghan social structure possesses within itself "a principle of repulsion and disunion, too strong to be overcome, except by such a force as, while it united the whole into one solid body, would crush and obliterate the features of every one of the parts."[12] Authority and liberty coexist uneasily in Afghanistan, the capacity of the ruler determining the presence—or absence—of the equilibrium necessary for good government.

Concepts of authority and liberty are central to Malcolm's discussion of the government of Islamic Persia. Muhammad, he explains, intended his religion to unite and civilize the Arab tribes, but it contained two flaws: by endorsing domestic tyranny it fostered and entrenched political tyranny, and by glorifying proselytization and conversion by the sword it sanctified violence and oppression. These flaws affected the recent condition of Persia as well as its distant past. Malcolm believes that, "fortunately for mankind," there are few nations "where the authority vested in the chief ruler is so absolute." But he recognizes, as modern scholars do, that some checks to absolute power do exist in the high officials, provincial governors, and tribal groups, whose power base is beyond the control of the ruler and who will rebel if pushed too far, and that religious traditions and sometimes even public opinion are also restraining influences. He maintains, however, that Persia cannot progress. Where a man is accustomed only "to obey or to command, he cannot understand what is meant by individual or political freedom"; he expects his ruler to exercise the absolute power that he himself exercises over everyone under his authority and is apathetic about the form of government under which he lives. Forced by the nature of his government to resort to falsehood, deceit, and violence in everyday life, his immorality should be attributed to a "bad system of internal administration." This may excuse his behavior but destroys, nevertheless, "all social ties between the rulers and those whom they govern," leading to continuous disorder and the total absence of any sense of national unity. No Muslim, Malcolm believes, has ever made any attempt to pursue a "rational freedom" or check the absolute authority of his sovereign on grounds of principle.[13]

Despite this pessimistic conclusion, Malcolm believes the system does more moral than practical harm to the individual. Persians are reasonably prosperous and as happy as most other people. Their ignorance and prejudice may disgust Europeans, but "men are formed by habit" and their sufferings and happiness are relative. "He who has travelled over the greatest space," Malcolm wisely observes, "will be most struck with the equal dispensation of happiness and misery." Europeans, who derive their attitudes from the condition of their own society, cannot judge with any accuracy the feelings of anyone else. This was a belief Malcolm shared with Adam Ferguson, who had argued:

> Man finds his lodgement alike in the cave . . . and the palace; and his subsistence equally in the woods . . . or the farm. . . . he devises regular systems of government, . . . or naked in the woods, has no badge of superiority but the strength of his limbs and the sagacity of his mind. . . . The tree which an American . . . has chosen to climb for . . . the lodgement of his family, is to him a convenient dwelling. The sofa, . . . and the colonnade, do not more effectually content their native inhabitant.[14]

Malcolm claims that "useful and important" lessons to Britain on the crucial importance of preserving British civil liberties may be learned from studying the condition of Persia. Again echoing Ferguson he describes Britain as

> a nation who continues, amid scenes of luxury and refinement, to cherish an individual independence, and a political freedom, that are grounded upon the institutions of a race of brave, but turbulent warriors.

Ferguson had remarked of civil liberty that it

> requires a fabric no less than the whole political constitution of Great Britain, a spirit no less than the refractory and turbulent zeal of this fortunate people, to secure its effects.[15]

Munro, Malcolm, and Elphinstone would all have agreed with Dugald Stewart that "It is by the particular forms of their political institutions, that those opinions and habits which constitute the manners of nations are chiefly determined. . . . these are [intimately] connected with the progress and the happiness of the race." A few years after the publication of Stewart's book, Munro, busy setting up a form of government administration in Governor-General Wellesley's latest acquisition, Kanara, told his sister that "an excellent book might be written by a man of leisure, showing the wonderful influence that forms of government have on moulding the dispositions of mankind."[16]

For the Scottish philosophes and for Munro, Malcolm, and Elphinstone, good government, leading to the progress of civil society, required an equilibrium between liberty and authority. Bad government—too much of either—meant disorder or stagnation. For Malcolm and Elphinstone, the defects of the countries they analyzed stemmed from the nature of their government. In Persia, the problem was excessive despotic authority; among the Sikhs and Afghans, the bar to progress and power was liberty carried to a politically destructive extreme. Malcolm and Elphinstone saw precolonial Indian government as despotic, but not as typical of Oriental despotism; they recognized the existence of de facto if not constitutional limits to the power of the sovereign. All three men saw British rule in India as despotic. If India was to progress beyond despotism under British governance, however, the lessons of both European and Asian history must be learned.

The form of governance set up in British India between 1780 and 1830 has to be considered in relation to what was happening in both Europe and Asia. C. A. Bayly states that attitudes, legends, theories, and institutions as well as economic interests must be considered as determining forces in the expansion of British imperial rule during this period. He describes the process as representing not simply a hiatus between waves of liberal reform, as Vincent Harlow presents it, but as "a series of attempts to establish overseas despotisms which mirrored the politics of neo-absolutism and the Holy Alliance of contemporary Europe." The despotisms set up in the colonies, he argues, were characterized by viceregal authority and an aristocratic military system which emphasized hierarchy, racial subordination, and the patronage of indigenous landed elites. In Bayly's interpretation, constitution making for the dependencies remained evolutionary and pragmatic. Citing Burton Stein's work, he suggests that in southern and western India, the schemes set up by the British "owed much to the system inherited from Tipu Sultan by the early Scots administrators Alexander Reade [*sic*] and Sir Thomas Munro."[17]

Recent historiographical debate on the British conquest of India during the late eighteenth and early nineteenth centuries has centered around the concept of a process of competitive state building and the development of the necessary techniques of "military fiscalism" to support it. Detailed studies of various Indian regions indicate that this period should no longer be seen as one of Indian economic decline and disorder due to the collapse of the Mughal empire, but rather as one in which a "changing balance of power between centre and province led to growing regional autonomy." As D. A. Washbrooke observes, the Mughal empire was being "superceded from below by regional states more 'modern' in many of their functions." Military needs provided the motive force for the development of more centralized administrative organizations which aimed at maximizing the state's receipts from land revenue and from state-encouraged trade. This process enhanced the importance of towns and middle ranks—merchants, artisans, and service gentry—and increased the "recycling of state resources" in agriculture and commodity production and in commerce. "In a great many ways, South Asia was involved in 'the social history of capitalism' from a very early period and underwent many of the same types of social development as those taking place in Western Europe."[18] The company state was one of the several competing polities introducing centralizing forms of administration in order to maximize revenues for military purposes, and Munro's role in the building of this company state, his contribution to what Bayly calls "the politics of neo-absolutism," and his vision of empire has been examined recently by Stein.[19]

Stein relates Tipu Sultan's form of government, which he sees as the model for the system advocated by Munro, to Max Weber's concept of "sultanism." He defines this as a system in which "a primitive, premodern administrative apparatus and substantial military force [are] at the personal disposal of the patrimonial ruler," but warns that the type of ideological discontinuities between the ruler and the local lordships—discontinuities between Muslim ruler and Hindu lords—that existed in Tipu Sultan's state were not considered by Weber. There is documentary evidence of Tipu Sultan's plans and orders regarding civil administration, some of which would have been available to Munro. According to Stein, Munro criticized Tipu's system while arranging the settlement of Kanara, but later utilized Tipu's methods in his own organization of the Ceded Districts. Stein identifies the main element of continuity between the administrations of Tipu and Munro as being military fiscalism. As part of their efforts at centralization, however, both men attempted to reduce the power and the ability to appropriate resources of the petty rajas or poligars. They both replaced local lords as the link between cultivators and "the extractive state" with outsiders—in Tipu's case with Muslim officials and in Munro's with politically safe, nonmilitary Maratha Brahmins. They both sought to enlarge the tax base by expanding the amount of land under cultivation. Munro, Stein claims, established continuity with Tipu's system because it met the company's need, as a militarist state, to increase its ability to appropriate resources. He argues also that Munro's championship of indigenous institutions and "native agency" was a powerful ideology developed to justify the company's expanding appropriation of resources.[20] In identifying the continuities between Tipu's and Munro's regimes and by stressing Munro's insistence on utilizing indigenous institutions, Stein implies that Munro's system was also a form of sultanism—with ideological discontinuities between British rulers and Hindu lords. This argument, however, which proposes that Munro's administration was an essentially Indian form of government, fails to take into consideration the implications of what, in another work, Stein calls Munro's "vision of empire."

Despite the emphasis in the subtitle of his book *Thomas Munro: The Origins of the Colonial State and His Vision of Empire*, Stein allots only five and a half pages to his examination of what comprised Munro's vision of empire. The first principle of the British imperium, visualized, he claims, by Malcolm as well as Munro, was Crown rule carried out through viceregal officials (themselves). Undoubtedly they gained much satisfaction from the periods in their careers when they enjoyed relatively untrammeled authority to administer large areas of India as they thought best. But they saw their degree of authority as a temporary measure. Stein also maintains that both men considered the East India Company government to be doomed. He does not mention the sources on which his interpretation is based, and both men may have privately favored Crown rule. Malcolm, however, devotes ten pages of the *Political History* (1826) to discussing whether the company was capable of governing the type of state British India had become; he comes down firmly, in public at least, in favor of continued company government. "The foregoing arguments," Malcolm states, "are meant to show the evil effects which we may anticipate to India, and eventually to England, from the abolishing of the East India Company as a medium for the government of India." His main reasons were that the Crown would know too little about, and have too little interest in, India to govern well. According to Gleig, one of Munro's "general principles" was that "A Governor should always be a man who will maintain the system prescribed by the Court of Directors."[21]

The second principle of Munro's vision involved the idea of a system of politically separate states functioning under the hegemony of British India. This in Stein's view is neither Burkean prescriptivism nor nationalism but simply the idea that competing political units would produce a more efficient and stable order than the domination of one regime over a large geographical area. Stein identifies Munro's vision as a belief that "the Indian subcontinent could become a sphere of interacting states, just as Europe had been from the seventeenth century a self-contained political world."[22] If this is an accurate interpretation, as it probably is, it indicates that Munro saw the continuity he maintained with Tipu Sultan's regime in European, not Asian (or Sultanist), terms, as Stein argues in the paper on "State Formation."

Stein states that Munro's approach to government was partly pragmatic—coping with local conditions—and, from the time of his last two years in the Ceded Districts, partly a "precocious perception of how his pragmatism might be embedded in principles." It is always difficult to differentiate between principled action and action rationalized on grounds of principle. It will be argued in the next chapter of this book, however, that the parallels between the ideas expressed in Munro's earliest reports from the Baramahal in the 1790s and the terms of the debate on political economy, familiar to most men raised in the merchant community of Glasgow in the 1770s and 1780s, suggest that the system he developed rested from the beginning on ideological assumptions that were widely held at that time in Scotland.

The processes of state building and military fiscalism which were taking place in India in the eighteenth century are related by Stein to similar processes that took place in early modern Europe.[23] Although historical analysis of Indian state building is relatively new, the development of the European state system attracted the attention of historians in the eighteenth century. In regard to the correspondence between Munro's system and that of Tipu Sultan, it is likely that Munro recognized the same similarities between the European and Indian processes as Stein has done. An analysis of state building following the lines of William Robertson's analysis of the progress of Europe would have enabled Munro to recognize features of Tipu Sultan's system that would serve his own purposes.

There is no evidence to prove that Munro read Robertson. There is, however, circumstantial evidence that makes it probable. Munro liked reading history; Robertson was a leading—and readable—historian whose *History of the Reign of Charles V* (to which the fine essay, *The Progress of Society in Europe*, is the introduction) was an enormous success when first published in 1769.[24] History being a favorite literary form, Munro is likely to have read the work anyway. His fondness for Cervantes' *Don Quixote*, which, according to Gleig, led him to learn Spanish at the age of sixteen so that he could read the book in the original language,[25] makes it not unreasonable to assume that he would have been sufficiently interested in the historical background of Cervantes' heroes to read Robertson's work.

In the first chapter of *Progress of Society*, Robertson describes Europe from the barbarian invasions of the Roman empire to the fifteenth century, commenting on early efforts by monarchs to counterbalance the power of the nobility by conferring privileges on the towns. The phrase Robertson uses to describe the newly privileged towns is "so many little republicks." It is probably no coincidence that Munro used the term "little republicks" for what he called the "village municipal governments" of India.[26] Village governments were important to Munro's administrative scheme because he expected their leading officials, the potails and curnams (headmen and accountants), to form the core of his much desired, rising middle rank.

Although, in Robertson's view, Europe had made much progress by
the fifteenth century, government was "still far from having attained that
state, in which extensive monarchies act with united vigour, or carry on
great undertakings with perseverance and success." Unity of purpose,
Robertson believes, may be achieved only by an efficient despotic ruler or
by means of "the powerful influence of regular policy." The great eastern
empires were examples of the former, eighteenth-century European states
of the latter. The political constitutions of the European kingdoms at the
beginning of the fifteenth century, however, were different from both. The
authority of the aristocracy—local lords—circumscribed the power of
the monarch. The revenues available to the monarch were so small that
"the armies which they could bring into the field were unfit for long and
effectual service." Charles VII of France was the first monarch to undermine the power of the nobility by establishing a regular army, paid for by
the extraction of new taxes. Louis XI's maxims of rule "were as profound
as they were fatal to the privileges of the nobility": he filled all government departments with new men, enlarged the regular army, and imposed
heavier taxation to pay for it. Henry VII of England, however, who came
to the throne with a disputed title after long wars during which the nobility frequently demonstrated their ability to create or depose kings, found
it necessary to use greater caution in centralizing authority. He achieved
his objective "by introducing regulations prohibiting the nobility from
keeping the armed retainers which rendered them formidable, and turbulent." Moreover, he encouraged population, agriculture, and commerce,
brought peace, and, by accustoming the people "to an administration of
government, under which the laws were executed with steadiness," he was
successful in altering and improving the English constitution.[27]

Robertson provides a lucid account of state building and military fiscalism which, in his view, created in Europe a great political system of national states, regulating their foreign relations by means of the concept of
maintaining a balance of power. The terminology is different, but he describes processes recognizably similar to those taking place in precolonial
India. If military fiscalism is regarded as Munro's only objective, then it
might be possible to accept the view that Munro was content to take over
an Asian form of government. When his views on empire are also taken

into account, however, some further explanation is required, and here it seems possible to identify an ideological source in Adam Ferguson's thematic examination of different forms of political organization.

Ferguson's thesis was that civil society would never have come into existence without the rivalry of nations and the practices of war. He argued that if states grew too large and were successful in imposing peace throughout their territory, their people would lose "the common ties of society," their loyalty to their state, and their spirit of enterprise, and an age "of languor, if not decay" would ensue.[28] The evidence that suggests that Munro's vision of empire encompassed "a sphere of inter-acting states" similar to those of seventeenth-century Europe is contained in three papers: a letter written by Munro to Lord Hastings in 1817, a memorandum dated 1823, and as Stein indicates, the conclusion to Munro's minute "On the Employment of Natives in the Public Service." In the often-quoted letter to Hastings, Munro argues that "even if all India could be brought under the British dominion, it is very questionable whether such a change, either as it regards the natives or ourselves, ought to be desired." Such a conquest would mean that the Indian army, "having no longer any warlike neighbours to combat, would gradually lose its military habits"; but, equally important, the political stability imposed by British military power would harm the Indian people. Like Ferguson, Munro believed that security would be "purchased by the sacrifice of independence—of national character—and of whatever renders a people respectable." Subsidiary alliances, Munro claims, are even more harmful to the Indian character than direct British rule, and he suggests that, as the British are now strong enough to ignore threats of an alliance of Indian states against them, it would be better to leave the Indian states their independence. If Britain conquers the whole of India they will debase the whole people.[29]

The memorandum written by Munro in 1823 argues that each presidency should pursue the course best suited to produce improvement in its own territory. Madras, Calcutta, and Bombay, a thousand miles apart, neither could nor should be governed by means of one uniform system of internal administration. "Let each presidency act for itself. By this means, a spirit of emulation will be kept alive, and each may borrow from the other every improvement which may be suited to the circumstance of its own provinces." In the same year, in a letter to George Canning, Munro makes it clear that he admires classical Greece, with its competing city states, rather than the monolithic Roman empire. Referring to the possibility that Russia might gain territory if the Turks are driven out of Europe, he tells Canning that "it is for the advantage of a great and enlightened nation to have powerful rivals." Munro subscribed to views similar to Ferguson's on the disadvantages of large, pacified empires and the importance to the moral character of a people of a spirit of independence and emulation. Again like Ferguson, he regarded military rivalry between states as a good thing. The form of despotism he advocated was that of the rulers of early modern Europe who were contriving to build the type of "nation state" that has been seen by twentieth-century nationalists in many parts of the world as the "principal vehicle of human liberation."[30] He was not trying to establish a system that resembled those of the neoabsolutist rulers of the nineteenth-century empires of the Holy Alliance.

Munro's view of empire, located in a European rather than an Asian tradition, may perhaps be seen as bridging the gap between what P. J. Marshall has described as "the inhibitions and fears about an imperial role in Asia," which were widely held in Britain in the eighteenth century, and the gradually developing confidence of nineteenth-century Britons in the type of empire visualized by Lord Wellesley too early for his own contemporaries. While governor-general from 1798 to 1805, Wellesley's object was to subordinate the Indian states to British control and to centralize British power by reducing the minor presidencies to a similar subordination to the Supreme government at Calcutta; the latter was a policy that opposed Munro's "vision of empire."[31]

Writing in the 1840s, Elphinstone, unlike Munro, accepts the fact of a relatively unified form of imperial rule throughout the subcontinent. In his *History of India*, he seeks to identify ways to create unity of purpose rather than emulation and competition as the path to progress. In his examination of the nature of Indian government from the time of the first Muslim invasions, Elphinstone discusses why would-be conquerors who had reached Multan in the eighth century found it difficult to establish themselves in India despite the incentives of Indian wealth and Hindu passivity. He concludes that the Arabs swept easily through Persia because religion and government had not supported each other, but in India, a powerful priesthood, working with governments and revered by the people, had encouraged resistance. Religion colored the laws and manners of Indians, who had a horror of change and the sort of passive courage that was likely to exhaust an impetuous force. Even the divisions in Indian society helped protect it: the defeat of one prince did not bring about the defeat of the whole country. These facts accounted for the slow progress and relatively "mild and tolerant form" of Islam and Islamic government in India. Chiefs became "politic sovereigns" rather than "fanatical missionaries." Aggrandizement of their families rather than promotion of their faith became their object, and from rough soldiers they became magnificent and luxurious princes.[32]

The second volume of the *History of India* begins with an account of a series of campaigns which took place between the eleventh and sixteenth centuries, in which greater or lesser rulers of varying degrees of competence tried to dominate or resist domination by their neighbors.[33] Although forms of government in India were invariably despotic, Elphinstone believes that the most oppressive elements of Muslim rule were again modified by the influence of Hinduism. The peace and prosperity of each state, however, depended on the ability of the individual ruler; there was no "system" to ensure the continuance of good government during the reign of a weak, dissolute, or tyrannical king.

Although Elphinstone rarely adopts Malcolm's pontifical tone and his didacticism takes the form of a subtext rather than an explicit statement, his analysis was meant, nevertheless, to provide object lessons on governing India. His representation of pre-Mughal India emphasizes the apparent absence of religious, social, and political friction between Hindus and Muslims. There were few bigoted rulers, dynasties were founded by both Hindus and Muslims, by the high-born and the humble, and by Indians and foreigners. Religion rarely affected the continuous processes of state building: Muslim rulers rarely united to defeat a Hindu; Hindu states rarely formed coalitions to expel a Muslim rival. The intermarriage of Muslim rulers with Hindu princesses—actively promoted by Akbar in the sixteenth century—was a positive step; most important of all, Hindus were appointed to the highest military and civil offices of Muslim-ruled states.

Elphinstone's views on Indian government are most evident in his accounts of the reigns of Akbar, who raised Mughal power to its apogee, and Aurangzeb, whose reign in the late seventeenth century saw the beginning of its decline. Although Aurangzeb was the Indian ruler most admired by Muslim writers, Elphinstone's approval is reserved for Akbar, who resembled Ahmad Shah of Afghanistan in that he was a great ruler as well as a great conqueror—an appellation coveted by the British. Elphinstone begins his discussion of Akbar's reign with an account of the relative weaknesses of the power bases of India's foreign conquerors. Tamerlane was the least secure because his own country was furthest from India. The houses of Ghazni and Ghor depended on their own kingdoms, but these at least "were contiguous to their Indian conquest." Babur relied largely on a body of adventurers "whose sole bond of union was their common advantage during success." Lack of "natural support" had led to the easy expulsion of Akbar's father, Humayun. Britain was only the most recent of India's many foreign conquerors and it would be easy to recognize that her power base was more distant than Tamerlane's and that she relied on a body of sepoy mercenaries whose loyalty might depend solely on common advantage during success.[34]

Akbar, Elphinstone believes, was inspired with the "noble design" of "forming the inhabitants of that vast territory [India], without distinction of race or religion, into one community." To create a sense of unity of purpose, "he admitted Hindus to every degree of power, and Muslims of every party to the highest stations in the service, according to their rank and merit; until, as far as his dominions extended, they were filled with a loyal and united people." It was an admirable vision of empire. First, however, Akbar had had to establish his authority over rival claimants to power in the subcontinent, secure his dominions, and restore order to an administrative system disrupted by a period of disorder—a scenario familiar to anyone who, like Elphinstone, had taken part in the British conquest of southern and western India. A cultured man possessing great physical vigor, courage, and intelligence, Akbar became "sober and abstemious" with maturity, enjoyed philosophical discussion and, though constantly at war, "made greater improvements in civil government than any other king of India." Though not free of ambition, because the countries he invaded had formerly been subject to Mughal rule he would have incurred more blame than praise, judged by the standards of his time, had he not tried to recover them.[35]

It was to his internal policies, however, that Akbar owed his place, in Elphinstone's view, "in that highest order of princes, whose reigns have been a blessing to mankind." He practiced religious tolerance, encouraged research into Hindu doctrine, and sponsored translations of Sanskrit and Greek literature into Persian. Akbar's own religion was pure deism: "His fundamental doctrine was, that there were no prophets; his appeal on all occasions was to human reason." Although Akbar's religion was too abstract to appeal to the bulk of mankind, and under his successor, Jehangir, Muslim forms were restored, the "liberal spirit of inquiry" personified by Akbar continued to thrive after his death. If "extrinsic causes had not interrupted its progress, it might have ripened into some great reform of the existing superstitions." India and Indians, it is implied, could have progressed without British guidance, had it not been for the accidents of history.

Akbar had been eulogized by earlier historians for his revenue system, but Elphinstone points out that the system was not new; Akbar simply made the existing arrangements work effectively. The way in which the revenue system functioned under Akbar is described in some detail, but its main object—and the point Elphinstone emphasizes—was to reduce the amount taken from the cultivators without reducing the income of the government. This was done by diminishing the losses incurred in the process of collection—precisely what Munro tried to do as a revenue collector.[36] Akbar created a stable and prosperous society by making the existing system work well and by introducing modifications, not innovations, that in the long term and with further adjustment might have led to a process of change. Lastly, he encouraged all the diverse groups in Indian society to participate in the execution of his "noble design." He tried to unite the people of India into one community, a community that would recognize its own interest in serving the interests of the state.

Elphinstone's examination of the problems and achievements of Akbar's reign was a blueprint of empire in disguise—one that might be followed with advantage by the British as they built upon the foundations of their own. The points Elphinstone stresses are Akbar's promotion of unity, tolerance, stability, opportunity, prosperity, and the broadening of traditional beliefs and assumptions. His was a despotic rule, not progressive in itself, but one likely to lead to progress. In contrast, Aurangzeb's failures were presented as a warning.

Elphinstone wrote his *History of India* during the 1830s, when Christian Evangelicals and Utilitarian reformers were beginning to exert considerable influence on British Indian government. Religious bigotry was Aurangzeb's greatest sin. In Elphinstone's interpretation it "irritated" the Hindus "by systematic discouragement" more than it "inflamed them by acts of cruelty or oppression." But it was responsible, nevertheless, for providing the great Maratha leader Sivaji with the opportunity to rouse Hindu enthusiasm and "foster a national spirit that out-lasted his lifetime." Similarly, Aurangzeb's attempts to crush the Sikhs only strengthened their resistance. Elphinstone regards Aurangzeb's commitment to Islam as sincere and admires his physical and mental toughness and indefatigable industry. But, in addition to his bigotry, he criticizes his lack of any "generous or liberal" feelings and his inability to delegate or trust, faults which crushed the enterprise and loyalty of his subjects.[37] Writing three years after the publication of Elphinstone's *History of India*, Horace Hayman Wilson complained that "a harsh and illiberal spirit has of late years prevailed in the conduct and councils of the rising service in India which owes its origin to impressions imbibed in early life from the History of Mr. Mill."[38] Elphinstone's work was written partly to ameliorate the negative impact of Mill's depiction of Indian history and culture. He used the unfortunate consequences of Aurangzeb's "harsh and illiberal spirit," as well as his religious bigotry, as a warning of what might happen to British India as a consequence of the harsh rationalism of Utilitarian reformers and the religious bigotry of Christian Evangelicals.

Malcolm, writing in the 1820s when the East India Company—the new paramount power in India—was not yet overly confident of its ability to maintain its position, used Aurangzeb's policies as a blatant example of what an imperial government should *not* do to maintain order and consolidate its position. As Zastoupil points out, Malcolm relied heavily on both written and oral Indian sources for his *Memoir of Central India*. It would be interesting (although probably no longer possible) to discover whether Indian opinion influenced his unorthodox view of Aurangzeb as an "actor" whose early zeal for Islam was merely an expedient ruse to attract the support of strict Muslims in his contest with his more tolerant brothers for the Mughal throne.[39] Malcolm observes that despite Aurangzeb's supposed Islamic "enthusiasm," Hindus were treated as equals in the early years of his reign, again for reasons of expediency, but later, having attempted and failed to convert them to Islam, he fined them and taxed them heavily. The state's revenue had declined and Aurangzeb, Malcolm thinks, used this method to fill his treasury. It proved to be an unstatesmanlike policy, however, because it lost him the goodwill of the majority of his subjects. Aurangzeb lacked the greatness of mind to make temporary sacrifices for the sake of future gains. "Existing rule," Malcolm warns his British readers, "is always in some degree unpopular," and pressure produces resistance. The Hindu princes who had been subjected to Mughal rule had been deterred from rebellion in the past by their recognition of the overwhelming power of the Mughals, but they had also been reconciled by religious toleration and by the advantages they derived from participating in the affairs of a rich and splendid empire. The moment the imperial power faltered, however, "new enemies arose in every quarter," and the disastrous response was persecution. Tempted by weakness and provoked by injury, the Rajput princes of Jaipur and Malwa ceased to defend the empire from attack and either secretly or openly supported the Maratha rebels. In doing so, they became "the authors of their own ruin."

Malcolm describes Aurangzeb as "a prince whose attainment and exercise of power present perhaps as many lessons as the life of any monarch that ever reigned."[40] There were four lessons in particular that British readers must learn. Excessive demands for revenue would cost the government the goodwill of the majority of its subjects. Religious toleration and the provision of opportunity to play a part in government were the only ways to reconcile a conquered people to foreign rule. Interference with Indian institutions would lead to a dangerous perception of an identity of interest between discontented subjects and foreign enemies, no matter if such an alliance jeopardized the true interests of Indians. (By the time the *Memoir of Central India* appeared, the concept of a dangerous connection between internal and external enemies was providing the rationale for Malcolm's military strategy for the defense of British India.) Last, the prestige of the government must be maintained at all costs. Any suggestion that its power is faltering will lead to disaster, as it did for Aurangzeb. Without both internal order and safety from invasion, the exercise of British power to promote good government would fail.

As an example of a good Indian government, a "model" the British could usefully emulate, Malcolm allots thirty-eight pages of the first volume of the *Memoir of Central India* to the reign of the Hindu princess Ahalya Baee (Ahilyabai), widow of Maratha leader Mulhar Rao Holkar, who ruled the Holkar family territories from 1765 to 1795 to the apparently unanimous applause of her contemporaries throughout India. She was ". . . a being exercising, in the most active and able manner, despotic power, not merely with sincere humility, but under the severest moral restraint that a strict conscience could impose on human action; and all this combined with the greatest indulgence for the weakness and faults of others. Such, at least, is the account which the natives of Malwa give of Ahalya Baee: with them her name is sainted." Ahalya Baee's "first principle" of government was moderate land revenue assessments. Internal order was maintained by treating "the peaceable" with indulgence and "the more turbulent and predatory classes" with firmness and severity, tempered by justice and consideration. "The fond object of her life was to promote the prosperity of all around her; she rejoiced, we are told, when she saw bankers, merchants, farmers, and cultivators, rise to affluence" and saw their increased wealth as claim for increased protection, not heavier exactions. The tributaries of the Holkar family were "treated with an attention and moderation that made delays even in their payments unusual," while those subjects who differed from her in faith were treated with a kindness and consideration that went well beyond the natural tolerance of Hindus. Malcolm cites a favorite saying: that she "deemed herself answerable to God for every exercise of power," and concludes by observing that Ahalya Baee "affords a striking example of the practical benefit a mind may receive from performing worldly duties under a deep sense of responsibility to its Creator." There were four particular lessons the British could learn from the example of Ahalya Baee's reign. Tolerance of religious difference; responsibility and restraint in the exercise of despotic power; moderation in the extraction of resources—encouragement for, not extra exactions on, economic improvement; and the reduced need for military expenditure on maintaining internal order when one's subjects are content.[41]

Malcolm's writings, together with those of Munro, Elphinstone, and Charles Metcalfe, have been identified by Douglas M. Peers as expressing and publicizing an ideology of militarism which came to a peak in British India in the 1820s. In several papers and a persuasive book on the First Burma War, Peers sees military fiscalism as the central issue between the Home government and the Indian bureaucracy—in essence, a competition for Indian resources. Anglo-Indians, he claims, saw the army as the cornerstone of British India because the company state depended on its efficiency to defend itself from internal and external dangers, and they successfully promoted a form of military fiscalism "which argued against the company's supply-side economics in favour of demand-driven economy where the army's requirements were to be established first." Munro, Malcolm, and Elphinstone are represented as members of a group of men well placed in Indian administration who, by insisting on "the centrality of the army to the security and prosperity of the colonial state," provided intellectual justification for the appropriation of resources for military purposes.[42]

Various statements by Munro, Malcolm, and Elphinstone to the effect that the company's government in India rested on military power may indeed have contributed to the development of militarist attitudes, particularly statements made by Munro and Malcolm during the early stages of their careers. By the time of the war with Burma, however, they were all administrators, not soldiers, and a strong army was seen as a means to an end rather than an end in itself. Nor did they share, as Peers suggests, Wellington's willingness to sacrifice future progress to security. They recognized the symbiotic relationship between the two and argued that Indian economic and moral improvement would increase the security of

Britain's Indian empire just as security from internal unrest and external threats were necessary before economic and moral progress could take place. The three men believed, as Peers states, that British dominion in India was dependent upon military power. They also believed that the army must appear invincible, that the prestige of the government was of great importance and that a long period of peace might affect the efficiency of the army.[43] Everyone in India knew that a foreign trading company could not govern several previously independent and relatively well-organized states without a credible threat of force to back it. But some of the many statements asserting the dependence of the company state on military power were for the benefit of those in Britain who, influenced perhaps by Burke's indictment of Warren Hastings, might be tempted to think that newly conquered territories could be administered under a less authoritarian form of rule.

In this sense, Munro, Malcolm, and Elphinstone were militarists. This does not mean, however, that they thought military rule to be a permanently desirable system of government. Peers quotes Malcolm as saying that the army was "the only means by which we can preserve India." But Malcolm also said of British India that "of all governments, that is least likely to command respect over which a sword is always suspended, and which holds existence under respite." The attachment of the sepoys was important to Malcolm because the maintenance of order depended on them, but he did not think they could maintain order permanently if faced with widespread civil resistance. The attachment, or "consent," of the civilian population must be gained by good government. Munro is quoted by Peers as saying "our government rests almost entirely upon the single point of military power." In the unquoted lines of this passage, however, Munro observes that "there is no native [government] which rests so exclusively upon [military power]. . . . Our situation as foreigners . . . make[s] it more necessary for us to seek the aid of regular [village governments] to direct the internal affairs of the country, and our security requires that we should have a body of head men of villages interested in supporting our dominion." Again "consent," based on common interest, not submission to military force, was the object. In the early 1820s, when the general tone of the company government was quite militarist, Munro told examinees at the College of Fort St. George that everywhere, but most particularly in British India, "the good-will of the people" was the government's strongest support.[44]

Peers's contention that "it was believed by many, including Munro and Malcolm, that there was no firm and recognized tradition of civil institutions in India" is untenable in regard to Munro, Malcolm, or Elphinstone, as is the observation that there was "no widespread conviction that development in itself would lead to enhanced internal security." The belief that the company's administrative system should be built upon existing Indian institutions and that prosperity was the best means of attaching the natives were basic assumptions held by all three men. Close to the beginning of his most famous minute, "On the State of the Country and the Condition of the People," written in December 1824 at the beginning of the war with Burma, Munro states that "we must . . . frame gradually *from the existing institutions* [my italics], such a system as may advance the prosperity of the country." In the *Political History*, Malcolm claimed that "we may be compelled by the character of our government to frame some institutions different from those we found established, but we should adopt all we can of the latter into our system." Elphinstone told Malcolm in regard to his plans for the administration of the Deccan that he intended to take every precaution to preserve the institutions of the natives as he found them and to do his best to take the people with him rather than "imposing a government by force."

It is possible that, standing on its own, Munro's statement that "we always are, and always ought to be prepared for war" could be interpreted, as Peers does, as "a thinly disguised argument for expansion." But that is not what Munro was arguing when he wrote the words in 1820 in a letter to Canning at the board of control. He starts by saying "I see no reason to expect disturbances from any of the native states now surrounded by our territory. They are all too weak to give us any uneasiness. . . . The Bheels and other plundering tribes, of whom so much has been said, are a miserable race, poor and few in numbers. . . . well treated, they will in a few years become as quiet as any of our other Indian subjects." He then mentions, as quoted by Peers, that the government should always be prepared for war. His justification, however, is that "this very circumstance

gives us the best security for the long enjoyment of peace" and the opportunity, which should be seized, "to improve our own territories."[45]

The detailed research Peers has done on the finances of British India
provides a strong argument for the domination of the military interest in
the Bengal and Bombay presidencies, and both Elphinstone and Malcolm
tolerated what was happening. They may even have endorsed it; Malcolm
was certainly obsessed with military considerations insofar as they might
be expected to bring about the attachment of the sepoy troops on whose
loyalty British dominion rested.[46] Liberal treatment of sepoys, however,
while it might be a drain on the state's resources, does not indicate personal self-interest in appropriating resources for military purposes. Munro's
control of expenditures in Madras indicates not only that he may have
learned useful lessons about financial management in the accounting department of Sommerville and Gordon in Glasgow in the 1780s, but also
that he was by no means overawed by, or even particularly sympathetic to,
militarist aspirations.

Nor was he particularly anxious about security. Peers stresses the general fear of internal rebellions, external aggression, and the probable relationship between them, as Malcolm, among others, argued. Munro, however, does not seem to have shared these concerns in the 1820s. His
observations to Canning about weak "native states" and poor tribes suggests that he had little fear of Indian enemies. Further, in a letter to Malcolm written in 1825, he mentions that he has always considered a Russian
invasion of India as "impracticable, without the previous conquest of
Persia, and the quiet submission of the people to their new masters," neither of which events he thinks to be likely. He concludes somewhat flip-
pantly: "Let us get out of [Ava], and then come Russians and Persians
when they will."[47]

Peers himself points out that, like Wellington, Munro believed firmly
in the subordination of the military to the civil authority. In a memorandum written while on leave in 1812 or 1813, Munro stated that "the civil
government of India should have a greater control over the military power, than in other foreign dependencies of Great Britain. . . . the authority
of government over such an army, [composed mainly of Indians], ought
to be maintained by every means not incompatible with the respect due to

the commander-in-chief, and . . . the supreme military power should be vested in the governor-in-council." Munro had no self-interest in support-ing the superior authority of governors at this stage of his career, al-though he may have wished to stress his own nonmilitarist beliefs to the directorate, as he was hoping for an important appointment at the time. As governor of Madras in 1822, he indignantly requested the government and court of directors to express their official displeasure with the Madras military board for daring to challenge the civil government's ("the supreme authority's") decision on a matter of supply. In December 1823 and April 1825 he submitted two minutes to the commander in chief, Madras, insisting that changes in sepoy uniforms must not be made, as they had been recently, simply by directives from the office of the adjutant general. "It is the duty of the government at all times to see that its own orders and those of the Honourable Court are strictly attended to, but this duty is more especially imperious when the . . . native army is con-cerned." Munro paid close attention to every aspect of the government of Madras and fiercely defended the civil, but supreme, authority of the gov-ernor on every occasion, slight or important, on which it appeared to be challenged. Peers also mentions that Elphinstone warned that "the great problem [in Bengal] has been always to maintain the subordination of the military power to the civil," an observation which suggests that Elphin-stone also favored the supremacy of the civil authority.[48]

In regard to the conduct of the First Burma War, Munro certainly ad-vocated, as Peers points out, "a very forward policy." He had always claimed, however, that if the British were going to go to war they must, for reasons of economy, do it by means of a vigorous offensive. As early as 1794 he had maintained that "it is always bad and dangerous policy in war to be rigid in proportioning the means to the object in view—it is from this cause that our wars have always been so long and expensive." If men and money are allocated at the beginning of hostilities, "the speedy termination of the war will compensate for the additional expense of preparation." Gleig included in a list of what he called Munro's "maxims" a statement from a memorandum arguing that "nothing is so expensive as war carried on with inadequate means." Munro's frequent recommenda-tions for the allocation of extra resources for military purposes during the

Burmese war reflected principles of military economy rather than militarist enthusiasm.[49]

Insofar as they accepted a strong army as essential to the maintenance of a British presence in India, Munro, Malcolm, and Elphinstone may be designated "militarists." But in regard to their role as administrators— their responsibility for designing and putting in place the administrative structure that would consolidate Britain's hold on India—they placed great emphasis on what Munro called the "attachment" of the people and what Malcolm referred to as Indian "opinion." "[I]t must be our continual study" to improve the condition of the Indian people, Malcolm argued, because British rule cannot last "but by their means, and it is not in nature that they should contribute their efforts to its support unless they are, by a constantly recurring sense of benefit, made to feel a lively and warm interest in its prosperity and duration."[50]

The importance Munro, Malcolm, and Elphinstone attached to Indian opinion is discussed by Lynn Zastoupil in his book, *John Stuart Mill and India*, in which he devotes a chapter to examining the influence on Mill's thought of a "vision of the Raj," influential from the 1820s, which he terms "an empire of opinion." Munro, Malcolm, Elphinstone, and Charles Metcalfe are identified as the main proponents of this approach to government, and Zastoupil restates the orthodox view that the influence of Burke "looms especially large" in their school. He sees the empire of opinion group, however, as more than "a transplanted body of Whigs owning special allegiance to Burke," and stresses the role of their knowledge of Asian society and government in the development of their thought. Eighteenth-century theorists, he points out, assumed the existence of a traditional bond between the British public and its government. This, naturally, was lacking between the Indian public and the British Indian government and it was something the empire of opinion school was anxious to cultivate by governing through traditional institutions and the patronage of traditional elites. Zastoupil is interested in discovering why John Stuart Mill, who had endorsed his father's policy line during his early years at India House, began to move in a different direction in 1837. But by stressing the importance Munro, Malcolm, and Elphinstone gave to enhancing the legitimacy of British rule without considering at the same—

time the emphasis they placed on economic and social progress, he unwittingly overemphasizes the conservative aspects of their thought.[51] Indian "opinion" or "attachment," in Malcolm's and Munro's usage, meant gaining the consent of the people by governing them in a way that would bring improvement to the quality of their lives, however marginally.

The approach to Indian government of John Stuart Mill's father, James Mill, differed from that of Munro, Malcolm, and Elphinstone, although Mill too aimed at providing Indians with a better form of government. As he was a Scotsman of the same generation, a brief consideration of the differences is required. Mill (1773–1836) was four years younger than Malcolm and six years older than Elphinstone. Like them, he was raised and educated in Scotland. His philosophical assumptions, like theirs, derived from the four main intellectual sources which had influenced eighteenth-century Scottish thought: religion, rationalism, the classical world, and what was thought of as "Newtonian scientific empiricism." He believed, as they did, in the "natural faculties" of the human race and "the various stages of their career."[52] Yet his attitude towards India—indeed towards man and society in general—differed from theirs in several ways. The differences arise from the relative importance attributed to religion, reason, and experience by the four men, to the mature age at which Mill left Scotland, and to British influences on Mill to which Munro, Malcolm, and Elphinstone, isolated in India, were less exposed. The influence of Jeremy Bentham was the most important of these, although Bentham's thought would not have attracted Mill had he not been drawn to rational ideas and methods.

Mill was raised as an orthodox Calvinist, educated for the Kirk and licensed to preach. Until he discarded his Christian faith in the early 1800s, he belonged to the Evangelical High Flyer group in the Kirk. He remained in Scotland throughout the 1790s, when Moderatism was increasingly tarnished by its close association with Henry Dundas and Tory politics. Although Mill admired the work of Adam Smith, John Millar, and Dugald Stewart, with whom he had studied, his early religious training ensured his resistance to the propositions of Hume and the Moderate churchmen, while his later loss of faith and a consequent hostility to religion led him to perceive superstition as the great barrier to progress.

Upon discarding his Calvinist faith, however, Mill did not discard its austere morality, and he was genuinely disgusted by many Hindu practices.[53]

For Mill—and Bentham—rationality and self-interest, not feelings, were the prime motives for human action, and they enthroned them as the core of the utilitarian philosophy. Mill then tried to apply them to his examination of Hindu history and culture, but, as Elphinstone once told Malcolm, "You will not know what difficulty is until you come . . . to reconcile Maratha custom with Jeremy Bentham." Elphinstone was interested in Bentham's works, although by no means the disciple that a Utilitarian pamphleteer tried to make him out to be in 1828.[54] But he recognized that Maratha customs had developed out of cultural influences that were part of Indian historical experience and were irreconcilable with the precepts of European rationalism, the product of another culture with a different history. Mill's rationalism led him to suppose that Britain's military control of India, which looked more solid from Britain than from Calcutta, Madras or Bombay, had created a suitable arena for an experiment in ideal laws and administrative systems. This supposition may have prompted Munro's complaint that, "in recommending new systems, people are too apt to think that mankind are mere pieces of machinery, on which it is perfectly harmless to make experiments every day."[55]

Although Adam Smith's famous concept of "the invisible hand" played an important role in the development of Utilitarian and liberal thought, Mill rejected another aspect of Smith's thought that was accepted by Munro, Malcolm, and Elphinstone—his determinism. For Mill, economic determinism or any other determinist explanation of change— the idea of deep structural forces moving mankind in directions over which it had little control—were incompatible with his belief that the application of rational processes of thought would enable man to control both his present and future. Mill supposed a direct relationship between cause and effect; unintended consequences were unacceptable to a rational mind.

Mill's approach to man, society, and government differed from the approach taken by Munro, Malcolm, Elphinstone, and by most of the more distinguished philosophers of the society in which all four men spent their early years. The difference lay in Mill's less tolerant attitude to religion, his emphasis on rationality, his rejection of empiricism and his preference for "mind" over "feelings," and in his rejection of the precepts of "sensibility" and of an "historical principle" which insisted that events should be judged within the context of their own time and place. For Mill, man must use his intellect and powers of reason to devise institutions and systems of government that would produce, mechanically, a moral, orderly, and progressive society. Most of the Scottish philosophes as well as Munro and Elphinstone, however, would have endorsed Malcolm's view that "Great and beneficial alterations in society, to be complete, must be produced within society itself; they cannot be the mere fabrication of its superiors, or of a few who deem themselves enlightened."[56]

Munro, Malcolm, and Elphinstone, unlike Mill, were perfectly aware that India could not be treated as a political tabula rasa. Beneath the umbrella of despotic rule existed government and administrative practices as familiar and, therefore, as acceptable to Indians as their notions of rights and privileges were to the British. India also had religious and social customs, both cause and effect of Indian "national character," which would take generations, perhaps centuries, to modify. The three men never forgot that the British Indian government was a despotism, its territories acquired by the dubious right of conquest and retained by military force. As it was neither possible nor desirable that government should rest indefinitely on military power, however, policies must be devised to bring about the attachment, or tacit consent, of the people.

The necessity of some form of consent was one of Hume's "First Principles of Government." He had argued that

Force is always on the side of the governed, the governors have nothing to support them but opinion. . . . and this maxim extends to the most despotic and most military governments as well as to the most free and most popular. The sultan of EGYPT, or the emperor of ROME, might drive his harmless subjects, like brute beasts, against their sentiments and inclination: But he must, at least, have led his *mamelukes* or *praetorian bands*, like men, by their opinion.[57]

It would not have been too difficult to recognize an analogy between the sepoy army and "praetorian bands." Although consent, for Munro, Malcolm, and Elphinstone as well as for Hume, might be a passive rather than an active condition, as yet it was difficult to pretend that "opinion" was supporting the company's government. In the long term, however, it must be persuaded to do so.

There is no reason to suppose from their writings that Munro, Malcolm, and Elphinstone were uncomfortable with authoritarian rule. Malcolm and Elphinstone, however, learned much from their research on Asian history. Although the forms of despotic government that existed in pre-British India were not seen to be as oppressive and therefore as antiprogressive as those of some other Asian countries,[58] the challenge for the British was to break the cycles of despotism—excessive authority, anarchy, excessive liberty—which they saw as characteristic of Asian political systems. The progress of civil society in India required a system of political economy that utilized a "progressive," constitutionally regulated, European-type authoritarianism, which would include the centralized control of military power and fiscal resources to demilitarize quasi-feudal lords in the interests of law and order. But both military and fiscal oppression must be abjured. The need to gain the attachment of the people, the vast majority of whom (although stratified according to ritual and social status) were rural cultivators, meant restricting the amount of land revenue the state should extract. Either rebellion against oppression or the moral degradation that followed from living under oppression would prevent the social and economic improvement Munro, Malcolm, and Elphinstone sought to achieve.

CHAPTER 11

A Scottish School of Thought

Political Economy and the "Munro System"

Political economy considered as a branch of the science of a statesman
or legislator, proposes two distinct objects: first, to provide a plentiful
revenue or subsistence for the people, or more properly to enable them to
provide such a revenue or subsistence for themselves; and secondly, to supply
the state or common-wealth with a revenue sufficient for the public services.
It proposes to enrich both the people and the sovereign.
—Adam Smith

Although a few writers in the late eighteenth century were beginning to re-
strict the term "political economy" to issues relating only to the
wealth of the state, many continued to use it in discussing the political,
social, and moral value of economic policies and administrative systems
within the social setting. This broader sense of the term is applied here to
Munro's ideas: to his approach to improving the economic prosperity and
moral well-being—the wealth and virtue—of a people subjected to colonial rule, as well as to his approach to the extraction of resources for the
benefit of the colonial state, the aspect of his work that has attracted
most attention from historians.

Throughout the period of British rule, Anglo-Indian historians represented Munro's policies as merely practical solutions to specific problems. In the 1960s, T. H. Beaglehole conceded that although Munro's ideas "largely resulted from what he observed in Madras," what Munro observed was in part determined by his character and preconceptions. But more recently, Burton Stein has concluded that "we may in the end be left with little that is more profound or penetrating on the influences that shaped the life of Thomas Munro" than that he was "a great Castle-Builder" with faith in his own ability to "do something very grand."[1] More can be said than this. These interpretations owe much to a letter written by Munro to George Canning in 1823 in which he complains that the Madras records contain "a mass of useless trash," because "every man writes as much as he can and quotes Montesquieu, and Hume, and Adam Smith and speaks as if he were living in a country where people were free and governed themselves."[2] This statement is frequently cited to establish Munro's rejection of theory, yet his approach to government indicates that he shared many of Hume's and Smith's assumptions about the causes and effects of historical change and, therefore, which broad lines of policy might be expected to produce certain desired effects. The confusion stems from two considerations: first, from assuming Munro's phrase "mass of useless trash" refers to the thought of Montesquieu, Hume, and Smith, not to the writings of Madras officials who make inappropriate use of Montesquieu, Hume, and Smith's ideas; and second, from underestimating the importance Munro assigned to the fact that Indians were not free and did not govern themselves. Munro, Malcolm, and Elphinstone all seem to have seen the interpretations of earlier stages of European development by Scottish thinkers as helpful in understanding contemporary India. But they rejected, in regard to India, late eighteenth- and early nineteenth-century prescriptions for progress which derived from Britain's experience as a politically and commercially advanced society, because they believed these prescriptions were irrelevant to a country and people which had not yet reached the same stage of development and did not enjoy the same freedoms.

It is generally accepted that the philosophical assumptions behind the zamindari land revenue settlement set up by Lord Cornwallis in Bengal

had their roots in the economic theories of the Physiocrats and in Cornwallis's faith in great landowners as promoters of agricultural improvement. Confronted with the need to produce order out of the confusion of
existing revenue practices, he and his subordinates turned to ideas and assumptions that had influenced their own English society.[3] But the possibility that the ryotwari system, as it was developed initially by Munro and
Alexander Read and later by Munro alone, might bear a similar relationship to ideas and assumptions held by many contemporary Scotsmen has
not been considered. Minutes written by Munro from the 1790s on, however, indicate a process in which an early principled idealism is modified
but not eradicated by wider experience. Like Malcolm and Elphinstone's
works of history, Munro's official minutes show that his "Castle Building," when applied to state building in India, was profoundly influenced
by political, economic, and social principles taken for granted by many
educated people in the Scotland of his day, although it was based, as
David Ludden argues, on an empirical or social scientific approach to fact
gathering.[4]

    At the beginning of the eighteenth century, Scotland was a small, im-
poverished, backward country; by the end, in conjunction with England, it
had become a pioneer of capitalist development in both agriculture and
industry. Although the scientific curiosity and expensive experiments of
great landowners did much to spur agricultural improvement, it was yeoman farmers, a rural middle rank pursuing their own economic betterment, who played the leading role in maintaining the momentum of Scotland's eighteenth-century agricultural revolution. The rapidity and extent
of Scotland's transformation fostered a widespread interest in agricultural
improvement and the development of numerous theories on the subject.[5]
Two issues studied and publicly debated in Scotland in the 1780s and
1790s feature prominently in Munro's and Read's discussion of land policy for the Baramahal region: the relationship between soil fertility and
rent and between land improvement and labor. James Anderson (1739–
1809), an ardent Scottish agricultural reformer and, according to Adam
Smith's biographer, "the original proponent of Ricardo's theory of rent"
believed rent should be a premium on the cultivation of good soil, reducing the profits of its cultivator to equality with those of the cultivator of

poor soil. Both Adam Smith and his friend Robert Beatson of Fife studied the relationship between soil yield and stock (meaning capital) increase. Read was related to the Beatson family, and both Robert and Alexander Beatson, who served in the Madras army with Read and Munro, published works on agricultural improvement. Many Glasgow merchants, including Munro's father, invested their profits from trade in land, and some engaged in agricultural improvement. Even the poet, Robert Burns, wrote on the issue of soil quality: "Our lands . . . are mountainous and barren; and our landholders, full of ideas of farming gathered from the English and the Lothians and other rich soils in Scotland, make no allowances for the odds of the quality of the land and consequently stretch us much beyond what in the event we will be found able to pay."[6] The topic of agricultural improvement had a high public profile in Scotland in the second half of the eighteenth century.

Commenting on "Ricardo's Political Economy" in 1820, Munro notes that Ricardo "maintains with Adam Smith, that labour is the measure of value. . . . In the same country, double the quantity of labour may be necessary to produce a given quantity of food."[7] Thirty years earlier, Read had argued that the land survey of the Baramahal must take into consideration the fertility of the soil, while Munro maintained that land was good or bad only in proportion to the amount of labor bestowed upon it. But later Munro conceded that rents should be "proportioned to the nature of the soil." At first he also opposed Read's intention to permit Brahmins and other privileged groups to hold land on reduced terms. Stock (capital) and labor, according to Munro, determined the ability of a farmer to prosper. If a Brahmin had stock, he could manage his farm as well as any other cultivator; without stock and forbidden to labor, "whatever he receives [in the way of a remission of rent] is in fact a gratuity from other cultivators and the state." For practical reasons, however, he eventually accepted the need to allow some privileges to Brahmins. Read and Munro clearly accepted some theories of political economy as being relevant to Indian, as well as Scottish, conditions.

By 1814 the government of Madras was acknowledging Munro as the architect of the presidency's "political economy." In a letter dated 12 August 1814, the Madras board of revenue attempts to clarify the policy of the Home government towards land tenure and revenue collection, stating first that Munro's minute of 15 August 1807 contains the only "project of a ryotwar permanent settlement"; second, that the board will in future regard "the project which it contains as the permanent settlement which your honourable court would wish to introduce"; and third, that Munro's views should be given every attention owing to "the range which his mind takes through the whole science of political economy."[8]

When beginning his career as an administrator in 1792, Munro had asked his brother James to send him a copy of Adam Smith's *Theory of Moral Sentiments*. Although this work is not a "hand-book of development economics," as the *Wealth of Nations* has been described, Smith does provide models for "good" and "bad" rulers which match the general approach to government of Malcolm and Elphinstone as well as Munro.[9] Smith defines a good ruler as a man who

When he cannot conquer the rooted prejudices of the people by reason and persuasion, . . . will accommodate, as well as he can, his public arrangements to the confirmed habits and prejudices of the people; and will remedy as well as he can, the inconveniences which may flow from the want of those regulations which the people are averse to submit to. . . . like Solon, when he cannot establish the best system of laws, he will endeavour to establish the best that the people can bear.

The bad ruler is "the man of system":

very wise in his own conceit; and . . . often so enamoured with the supposed beauty of his own ideal plan of government, that he cannot suffer the smallest deviation from any part of it. . . . Some general, and even systematical, idea of the perfection of policy and law, may no doubt be necessary for directing the views of the statesman. But to insist upon establishing, and upon establishing all at once, and in spite of all opposition, every thing which that idea may seem to require, must often be the highest degree of arrogance.[10]

Munro's "system" began as a method of revenue administration developed by Alexander Read and Munro in the Baramahal region of the Madras presidency in the 1790s. They took an existing Indian method of assessment and collection that was familiar to the local population, known as ryotwari, and tried to give it, as Smith recommended, all the improvements they thought the people would bear. How accurately—deliberately or unintentionally—Read and Munro adhered to the indigenous, local form of ryotwari is difficult to determine, but Munro's friend Josiah Webbe spoke of the system "which you invented" in the Baramahal, which suggests that modifications were deliberate. Ryotwari, however, was the core not the whole of the Munro system and should not be used as a synonym for it.[11]

The four main objects of Munro's system may be identified from the many reports and minutes he wrote on administrative matters between 1796 and 1827. These papers resemble Malcolm's and Elphinstone's works of history and contemporary history in that they were written with the double intention of educating a specific audience and promoting his own career. Munro's first two objects derived from the ryotwari revenue system. The first aimed at creating a society of numerous small but independent landholders rather than a few great ones, on the ground that the widest possible distribution of the country's agricultural wealth was beneficial to both individuals and the state. The second object, which Munro hoped would develop out of the first, was the creation of more social gradations (Munro called them graduated ranks). These, he believed, would emerge as the result of different applications of skill and industry by individual cultivators. The third and fourth objects concerned the administration of justice and the employment of Indians by the government. Munro believed the company's judicial system should be comprehensible to Indians, protect the interests of the majority of the population (the cultivators) in general rather than protect specific individual rights, and it should maintain the stability of the community. He also argued strongly for the inclusion of Indians in the government of their own country. Every British official recognized the practical need to employ Indians in the lowest branches of the government service, but few beside Munro, and later Malcolm and Elphinstone, saw the employment of Indians in superior posts as a prerequisite for Indian progress.

Read's and Munro's appropriation of the ryotwari system called for a detailed survey of land in order to place a permanent value on each field. This value was a fixed fraction of what it might be expected to produce, considering the nature of its soil and its access to water, under levels of cultivation that were neither "indolent" nor "improving." Each cultivator then paid rent for the land he could stock and cultivate himself each year.

According to Munro, if left to their own exertions the cultivators would enlarge or shrink their farms according to their fortune, and in time there would be no country in the world with so many "substantial middling farmers, whose condition, though inferior to that of British landholders, would certainly be preferable to that of the great bulk of the [British] tenantry." Once assessed, the revenue could not be raised unless the productive capacity of the land was improved by irrigation provided by government. No amount of improvement through the industry or capital investment of the cultivator was to alter the assessed value, but a slight remission was allowed to Brahmins who had to employ members of an agricultural caste to plough for them, and a substantial remission was allowed to promote the cultivation of valuable cash crops. Rent in cash rather than kind was encouraged.[12] The accurate land survey made by Read and Munro, their consideration of the relationship between soil fertility and rent and between labor and land improvement, the fixed assessment, and the encouragement of specialization (cash crop production) along the lines of Adam Smith's concept of division of labor were innovations based on contemporary theory.

In a report to Read written in July 1797, Munro argues that it is undesirable for the government to have only a few great proprietors as tenants. It would be better to encourage "the multitude of small independent farmers . . . [to] extend or contract their farms according to their different success." Over time, this freedom will produce "gradations of rich and poor proprietors and large and small farms; and by leaving every man who does not choose to serve another, to set up for himself, the fairest chance and the widest scope is given to the progress of industry and population." Two months later he reiterates the argument: numerous small landholdings are in the best interest of the cultivator and of the general wealth of the state. Small farms do not produce men of "great fortunes and overgrown possessions," but they reduce the number of the poor and raise everywhere men of small but independent property who, when sure that they themselves will benefit from the extra labor, will work with a spirit that cannot be expected from the tenants or servants of great landholders.[13] Like Smith and Hume, Munro saw the advantages of providing incentives for self-help in the relationship between increased individual wealth, respect for law, and the power of the state.

The opinions of Smith and Hume on the advantages to society of a middle rank formed of small landholders are quite clear. For Smith, "to improve land with profit . . . requires an exact attention to small savings and small gains, of which a man born to a great fortune . . . is very seldom capable." Comparing the condition of the great estates held by one family "since the times of feudal anarchy" with the lands of neighboring small proprietors, he observes: "you will require no other argument to convince you how unfavourable such extensive property is to improvement." If little improvement could be expected from large landowners, even less was to be hoped for from tenants at will. A person who can acquire neither property nor a secure lease "can have no other interest but to eat as much as possible, and labour as little as possible."[14]

Hume was no democrat but he argued, nevertheless, that too great a gap between rich and poor weakened the state. Everyone should enjoy "the fruits of his own labour," because such equality is suitable to human nature and does less to diminish the happiness of the rich than to increase the happiness of the poor. Equally important, it "augments the power of the state." When wealth is in the hands of the few, they wield all the power, and "conspire to lay the whole burthen on the poor . . . to the discouragement of all industry." Elsewhere, Hume describes the problems of a society "divided into only two classes, proprietors of land, and their vassals or tenants." While landowners become petty tyrants and engage in feuds "like the ancient barons," thus throwing society into anarchy worse than the most despotic government, tenants are dependents fitted only for subjection, particularly in a society where their knowledge of cultivation is not valued. Public liberty is achieved only where "peasants, by a proper cultivation of the land, become rich and independent," where a demand for luxury goods encourages commerce and manufacturing, and where tradesmen acquire property and the middle ranks have authority. "They covet equal laws, which may secure their property, and preserve them from monarchical, as well as aristocratical tyranny."[15]

Although Munro had recognized the existence of various ranks of local notables within the structure of Indian society by the time Malcolm and Elphinstone joined him as administrators, during his early years in the Baramahal he seems to have seen Indian society as divided into Hume's two classes: landowners, who were often petty tyrants, and their vassal tenants. He refused to recognize any affinity between the higher ranks of Indian and contemporary British society. "Rajas and old zamindars . . . are not private landholders, but rather petty princes, and the ryots [cultivators] in their districts stand nearly in the same relation to them as to the sovereign." Similarly he saw "no analogy whatever between the landlord of England and his tenants and the muttadar, or new [company created] village zamindar of this country and his ryots." Although Munro stated in his evidence before the House of Commons in 1813 that Indian government in general was despotic and bore little resemblance to the former feudal institutions of Europe, he nevertheless saw rajas and zamindars, as well as the smaller chiefs known as poligars, as similar to the type of lordship, with its agricultural dependents and armed military retainers, that had existed under medieval land tenure systems in Europe. He did not see them as eighteenth-century English landowners.[16] His often reiterated desire to create graduated ranks was not only meant to foster agricultural improvement and the wealth of individuals and the state but also to establish a substantial intermediate group powerful and interested enough to support the rule of law.

Despite their greater liking for aristocracy, Malcolm and Elphinstone, like Munro, rejected the idea that the upper ranks of Indian society could be equated with English landowners. Malcolm explains that although the word "zamindar" means landholder and cultivator of the soil, in Central India at least, zamindars were originally just government functionaries, supported by a land grant. Elphinstone describes zamindars and poligars as "insurgent officers of the old government," not improving landlords.[17]

Munro disliked both zamindari and mirasi (communal) forms of land tenure because he felt both systems inhibited progress. He answered advocates of mirasi tenure, who held influential positions in the government of British India throughout his career, by arguing that, historically, the breakup of communal holdings always preceded material improvement and was only impeded by overassessment or inadequate water. The development of communal tenure, he believed, was explained by the need for communal irrigation systems. It had existed in many countries "in the rude and early stages of agriculture" but was always considered to be "hostile to improvement." It was practiced where peasants were poor and where government looked only to short-term benefits because the community as a whole had to make up individual failures, allowing the government to obtain "as much revenue from the country as is possible under its then actual condition"—implying the discouragement of progressive practices. Paying rent in kind rather than cash also inhibited progress. It was suited to the same early stage of development, however, because government always received half of whatever was produced while the cultivator was secure from demands he could not pay. Protection of the cultivator against demands for revenue in "a season of calamity," however, was the only advantage to the communal system recognized by Munro, and even this applied only under repressive regimes. The great disadvantage of both communal tenure and payment of rent in kind was that they discouraged the individual cultivator from putting in the extra effort required to accumulate wealth.[18]

There is a surprising similarity between Indian land tenure at this time and Scotland's traditional land tenure systems, which by the late eighteenth century were regarded as a hindrance to agricultural improvement. Writing in 1814, Sir John Sinclair explained that a century earlier all Scottish landholders with legal rights had been tenants either directly of the king or of one of the king's great vassals, a situation similar to sirkar (state) and zamindari (landholder) forms of tenure found in India. Within this framework three tenurial systems existed in Scotland. In one, which went by the name of "steel bow" and which resembled the Indian practice of "taccavi," the landlord provided his tenants with seeds in addition to the use of his land. Writing in 1801 to Read, who had returned to Britain, Munro remarked, "I suppose you have ere now encountered Arthur Young, and had some debates with him on sagwulli [cultivation] and taccavi." Adam Smith mentions, disapprovingly, that steel-bow tenure is still in use in Scotland. In the second Scottish system, Highland or clan tenure, a "tacksman" held land cheaply from his chief in return for military service, while he sublet it at a relatively high rent even though he in turn required military service from his tenants. As long as military service was required, the tacksman could justify his position. But when economic considerations became more important than military ones, he was seen by agricultural reformers as an expensive and dispensable anachronism: the

type of quasi-feudal poligar Munro tried to eradicate in South India, and
the type of clan "middleman" that was a frequent victim of the contemporary Scottish Highland "clearances." The third system, communal
tenure, known in India as "mirasi" and in Scotland as "run-rig," had been
the most prevalent and still existed around Glasgow in the 1750s and in
many other parts of Scotland throughout the eighteenth century. A *Survey
of Argyllshire* published in 1798 states that as run-rig was phased out, "every
man was late and early at his work, and performed twice as much work as
when the work was common." Communal tenure is "perhaps the most serious obstacle to progress in agriculture."[19] Munro saw communal (mirasi) tenure in India as similarly antiprogressive.

Prior to taking office as governor of Madras in 1820, Munro consistently advocated measures designed to reduce the power and influence of
local lords and often that of the prebendary jagir and inam holders as
well.[20] This is generally seen as an attempt to enhance the company's revenue by abolishing intermediaries so that their portion of the produce of
the land would revert to the company state. But it should rather be seen as
an attempt to eradicate unproductive and, in the case of poligars, potentially troublemaking groups who inhibited progress. Munro's efforts to
abolish this type of lordship and any land tenure form he saw as standing
in the way of agricultural improvement, together with his preference for
numerous small landholders and graduated social ranks, were consistent
with eighteenth-century Scottish explanations of the progress of agriculture which had provided the foundation for Europe's transition from medieval confusion to its contemporary, relatively superior stage of development.

During his short term in Kanara in 1799 and 1800, Munro continued
to try to eradicate the obstacles to progress he identified in local social
and economic institutions, but his terms of employment and the conditions in Kanara were different. In the Baramahal, Read and his assistants
had enjoyed relative independence and had had plenty of time to survey
the land. The importance of irrigation had complicated the assessment of
land values but the predominance of sirkar tenure, in which the cultivator
held his land directly from the state, the absence of private property
rights in the land, and the rarity of petty rajas, poligars, or zamindars, had

provided relatively uncomplicated conditions. In Kanara, Munro was instructed to make the company's first revenue collection according to the existing system set up by the previous rulers, Haidar Ali and Tipu Sultan of Mysore, but he was also to suggest the quickest and most effective means of introducing the Bengal zamindari revenue system into the region. He had neither time nor money for a detailed survey, and the climate, terrain, and social and economic structure—intricately interrelated and analyzed by Munro in materialist terms—were quite different from those of the Baramahal.

In two papers, both entitled "On the Condition and Assessment of Kanara," Munro explains to the government that Kanara's economy rests on the cultivation and exportation of rice. The region receives regular and plentiful rain, so the "dependent" types of land tenure he associates with the need to irrigate in other parts of the subcontinent are unnecessary. As neither government, wealthy landholder, nor community capital have been required for building and maintaining water tanks, over the centuries the land, which is held by innumerable small proprietors, has become private property, and the only ground that could possibly be described as sirkar land is what Munro calls, probably incorrectly, "unclaimed waste." In almost every district, however, there are "pretenders, either open or concealed," to ancient poligar domains. These potentially disruptive members of society are anathema to Munro, but numerous small landholders with private property rights to their land are precisely what he wants to encourage, although the cultivators in Kanara are often members of warrior castes and more volatile than those of the Baramahal. The problem is that the "established system" he is supposed to utilize first involves "oppressive exactions" which he claims are crushing the economy of Kanara, devaluing the land, and may lead to "the extinction of the class of ancient proprietors," while the introduction of the zamindari system will turn his cherished small private properties into a few large, artificially formed estates.[21]

Although his terms of reference leave him little room for maneuver, Munro manages, by skillful use of language, to promote his own system while apparently following the government's directives. He presents a persuasive argument showing that both government and people will benefit by retaining a system requiring small proprietors to pay a moderate fixed revenue as they had during the supposedly prosperous and stable period before Haidar Ali's usurpation. This, of course, was the foundation of the ryotwari system, although Munro never mentions it by name. He warns potentially predatory British authorities against copying the type of military fiscalism introduced by Haidar Ali and Tipu Sultan: "A highly improved country" had been ravaged by Haidar Ali's use of it as a "fund from which he might draw, without limit, for the expenses of his military operations in other quarters." Munro also claims that "historical evidence" shows that "previous to the conquest of Kanara by Haidar, all lands were private property, and the rents were fixed and moderate." Stein's meticulous research on Kanara, however, has failed to discover this evidence, in the form of the books used to register the public revenue and transfers of land that Munro cited in support of his claims. As Bayly mentions, British officials found it difficult to understand a society in which there were no absolute proprietary rights in land. Munro, believing that agricultural improvement could only be achieved where farmers had security of tenure protected by law, may have exaggerated or fabricated evidence to suit his own purposes. It is also possible that as Edmund Burke had endorsed Cornwallis's zamindari system because he believed it to be the "traditional" system in Bengal, Munro may have felt that claims of historical authenticity would strengthen his case for supporting small private property holders.[22]

Having demolished the pretensions of Haidar Ali and Tipu Sultan's "established system" in order to promote his own preference for private property in land and fixed, moderate assessments, Munro turns his attention to the introduction of the zamindari system. He begins, tactfully, by conceding that in a country where the cultivators are too poor to improve their land and where there is no private property, dividing the land into larger units "may possibly have some advantages." In Kanara, however, where almost all land is private property, large estates cannot be formed without injustice to the present landowners, nor would they provide any advantage. He discounts the claim that the owners of small properties are unable to improve their land and proceeds to his first explanation of what he terms "the arrangement of nature" so far as Indian property is concerned. Where there is no entail and no primogeniture, where early marriage and adoption in the absence of a natural heir are normal practice, and where there is an abundance of food, "every great estate must in a short time be divided into a number of small ones." Only "violent regulations" can prevent a widely extended division of property. Extra industry might hold together a few large estates, but, in general, small ones will be continually formed "by the operation of unrestrained transfer, and of division among all the sons of every succeeding generation." Small estates, Munro argues, are the natural condition; to divide Kanara into great estates would be regressive, carrying the region backwards a century or two.[23]

Two more statements of "economic principle"—along the line that "where estates are small . . . the aggregate produce of the land may be, and probably always is, greater than when the whole belongs to a few principal landholders"—are followed by a further affirmation of the importance of incentive. In the *Wealth of Nations*, Adam Smith had commented that "a small proprietor . . . who knows every part of his little territory, who views it with all the affection which property, especially small property, naturally inspires, . . . is generally of all improvers the most industrious, the most intelligent and the most successful." Munro echoes him. Whatever advantage great landowners might seem to derive from their wealth is more than counterbalanced by the deep feelings every small proprietor has for "looking after his little spot, and by the unremitting attention which both his attachment to it, and his necessity, impel him to exert, in order to extract from it its greatest possible produce."[24]

Although Munro strongly favors small proprietors, he recognizes his "duty" to explain how the zamindari system may be introduced to Kanara. What actually emerges from his explanation, however, are subtle warnings of the probably dire consequences of its introduction, the flaws in the arguments for its supposed benefits and, by a careful use of language, the link between great proprietors and feudalism. Even the humble potail (village headman) will become "a kind of lord of the manor," while no estates worth more than five thousand pagodas should be formed because the proprietors might become "a kind of petty poligars." Munro warns that "All past events in this country show that great landed property has . . . a tendency to excite a turbulent spirit in the possessor. . . . An estate of ten thousand pagodas in most parts of Kanara . . . would place under the land-lord so large a district, furnished with retreats so strong, that were he to become refractory, it would be difficult to reduce him to obedience."[25] Great landed property in India meant armed retainers, not improving landlords.

From November 1800 to October 1807, Munro was responsible for the settlement of districts ceded to the company by the nizam of Hyderabad. The Ceded Districts were more like the Baramahal than Kanara in that they were arid and relatively flat, their produce was millet, cotton, and pulses rather than rice, and there was little of Kanara's potential to prosper; the people were constantly threatened by famine. But unlike the Baramahal, they were surrounded by potentially hostile neighbors and there were numerous, militant poligar chiefs. When Munro began his term as chief collector of the Ceded Districts, the governor-general, Lord Wellesley, was hoping these could be turned into zamindari landlords, thus achieving two major objectives at the same time: pacification and the introduction of a clearly defined administrative system. Munro thought this goal unrealistic and was hoping to find an opportunity to get rid of the poligar chiefs. Although severely criticized at first for his ruthlessness in sequestering their estates, his success in subordinating the chiefs to company rule eventually vindicated him with most authorities.

Munro had acquired some support by this time for his opposition to the zamindari system in both the Home and the Madras governments. On 15 August 1807, in a minute entitled "On the Relative Advantages of the Ryotwar and Zamindar Systems" (the minute referred to by the Madras board of revenue when praising Munro for his knowledge of political economy) he restates his case against zamindari's antiprogressive tendencies to a more receptive audience. He explains again how the ryotwari system will promote law, order, prosperity, and "attachment"— meaning loyalty for reasons of interest rather than tradition or emotion. It will require "no artificial restraints, contrary to custom and the laws of inheritance, to prevent the division of estates." It permits "all gradations of large and small farms," and it is conducive to good order because everyone, as the proprietor of his own land, has an interest in stability and in supporting the government.[26]

Both Adam Smith and Lord Kames favored the subdivision of land. Describing the acquisition of great tracts of land by barbarian chiefs after the fall of Rome, Smith observed that this "great evil" should have been merely a temporary hindrance to progress. Under natural law the vast estates would have been quickly subdivided by succession or alienation, but the introduction of laws of primogeniture and entail prevented their dismemberment and a wider distribution of the land. According to Smith,

When land . . . is considered as the means only of subsistence and enjoyment, the natural law of succession divides it . . . among all the children. . . . But when land was considered as the means . . . of power and protection, it was thought better that it should descend undivided to one. In those disorderly times, every great landlord was a sort of petty prince. His tenants were his subjects. . . . He made war according to his own discretion, frequently against his neighbours, and sometimes against his sovereign. The security of a landed estate, therefore, . . . depended upon its greatness. To divide it was . . . to expose every part of it to be oppressed and swallowed up by the incursions of its neighbours.

Entail, a natural consequence of primogeniture, was introduced, according to Smith, to preserve a particular line of succession and to prevent the alienation of any part of a great estate through "the folly, or by the misfortune of any of its successive owners." It still existed throughout Europe because it was believed necessary to the maintenance of aristocratic control of the great offices of the state: "that order having usurped one unjust advantage over the rest of their fellow-citizens, lest their poverty should render it ridiculous, it is thought reasonable that they should have another." In other words, entail, in Smith's view, allowed a few individuals to monopolize power and use it in their own, but not necessarily the state's, interest. It also undermined the family and, as a result, social cohesion: "nothing can be more contrary to the real interest of a numerous family, than a right which in order to enrich one, beggars all the rest of the children." England had less entailed land than elsewhere in Europe, but more than a third of Scottish land was still entailed. Lord Kames opposed entail because it had converted "one of the greatest blessings of life," landed property, "into a curse." It constituted an easily identifiable obstacle to Scottish improvement.[27]

Munro believed that small farms were natural in India and that using land as a source of political power would both impede economic progress and create a potential threat to the stability of the company state. Al-

though the British might expect local chiefs to be grateful for being allowed to keep their lands, "the love of distinction and independence," as
he points out, "is a much stronger and more universal passion than gratitude." Although fear of failure and self-interest might deter a chief from
opposing British authority, "men . . . do not always maturely weigh distant consequences." The British would be wiser to avoid the risk of a land
settlement which rested for security on the gratitude of a few large landholders.[28]

In one of his first minutes as governor of Madras, dated September
1820, Munro changes direction dramatically on the subject of entail. Considering his earlier pronouncements on the subject of subdivision, it is
startling to read an opening paragraph which states that the company has
mistakenly broken down the entail by which the estates of different classes
of zamindar and government servant "were protected from division and
descended entire to a single heir," causing so much injury to both individuals and the public that "we ought to revert to the ancient usage and confirm it by law." He claims, partly no doubt to justify his own earlier attitude but also with truth, that when British power was weak and the great
zamindars could offer formidable resistance, the division of their lands
was probably desirable. Now that the company's position is virtually unas-
sailable, however, ancient families of rank should be preserved. If all of
them are swept away, power and distinction will be monopolized by Europeans, creating a resentment among Indians that may spread rapidly
through a society in which everyone has been reduced to a similar level of
subordination.[29]

The company's regulations, Munro states, were intended to protect
the rights of all the people, "but they are too much calculated to facilitate
the minute division of property, and the descent of society to its lowest
level." He explains that under Indian governments this tendency was
counteracted by allowing lands held by officials to descend undivided to a
single heir, and by grants of land to civil servants and army officers who
remained in their districts rather than "retiring with their wealth to a distant country, like the European servants of the company, who have succeeded them." By the 1820s, Munro was acknowledging the importance of
the "richer gentry" to the local economy and also the dangers, recognized

by Adam Smith, of the situation described by Indian nationalist historians as "the drain" of wealth. Under Indian governments, Munro observes
in a different minute, rich jagirdars, inamdars, higher civil servants and
army officers, prominent merchants and cultivators—in other words, local
notables—provided a "supply of men whose wealth enabled them to encourage cultivation and manufactures." These advantages were likely to be
lost under British rule, because all senior civil and military posts were
filled by Britons whose savings "go to their own country." In a commentary on the *Wealth of Nations* made after his return to Britain, Elphinstone
also claims that the drain of Indian wealth to Britain is, "Of all the objections made by Adam Smith against the Government of India, . . . the only
one now in force."[30]

In his minute on entail, Munro expresses regret that the lands of village and government officials as well as those of high-ranking families are
being divided, and warns that unless steps are taken to prevent this, "every
land-owner will be reduced to the state of a common cultivator." The fall
of the higher ranks will lower the character of the whole people. They
will become less attached to the government, which will lose the opportunity to "improve" them, and the task of government will become more
difficult. Munro proposes regulations (which were not adopted) governing all lands traditionally passed to a single heir. They would ensure the
continuance of a class of Indian gentry and "preserve those graduations
in society, through which alone it can be improved."[31]

This apparent contradiction of his earlier opinions on entailed estates
may be attributed not only to the greater stability of the company state
but also to Munro's greater understanding, by the 1820s, of Indian social
structure. From his earliest days in the Baramahal, Munro's chief objective
had been the creation of middle ranks in the Indian countryside. Apparently seeing rural society—inaccurately—in Hume's terms of two widely
separated groups, he had expected an intermediate group to emerge as a
result of the provision of security and incentives for improvement. Later,
realizing that rural Indian society already had its own graduated ranks
made up of minor notables and service gentry, and recognizing that Hindu laws governing inheritance and the subdivision of land would prohibit
the formation of the sort of groups he had envisaged, he began to pro-

mote the Indian service gentry, advocating its employment by the British
in more, and more responsible, positions. Munro's abrupt turn on entail is
consistent with his desire for a strong Indian rural middle "class"; he has
simply changed his views on how this may be obtained.

The minute on entail was laid before the Madras government four
months after Munro visited Elphinstone at Bombay in May 1820, and it is
tempting to assume that Elphinstone, whose bias in favor of a traditional
aristocracy is well known, influenced Munro's new outlook. Munro, however, had instructed Elphinstone two years earlier—as the younger man
began his administrative career—on the importance of supporting the
great jagirdars, pointing out at the same time that, "though the people of
India have not what we call gentry, they have what they respect as such
themselves." He identified this group as village potails and curnams
(headmen and accountants), and various revenue officials. Munro's letter
was dated 8 March 1818. Four months later, Elphinstone sent a circular
letter to British officials serving under him in the peshwa's former territories directing them to support the authority of the potails. They must
never be displaced, except for treason against the state.[32]

Although Malcolm and Elphinstone shared Munro's general assumptions about landownership and agricultural progress, neither had the opportunity, nor probably the inclination, to become as expert on Indian
land tenure and revenue systems as Munro. Their works on administration—Elphinstone's *Report on the Territories Conquered from the Peshwa* and
Malcolm's *Memoir of Central India*—include largely descriptive chapters on
revenue, providing information obtained from Indian sources on the
probable origins of established systems.[33] They recommend the continued
use of these systems, pruned of their worst defects and under careful supervision.

Malcolm, who describes revenue assessment and collection as one of
the most important aspects of government, remarks of the Bengal zamindari system that, although it is pleasant to see a rich landowner spending
his money on agricultural improvement, general prosperity will not be
achieved "unless the frugal and industrious of the cultivating class have
the path open to obtain property, as well as to preserve what they already
possess." He discusses the arguments for and against ryotwari without

committing himself to that system, and suggests that "nations so various as those under our dominion in India" should not be subjected to a uniform method of revenue collection. He also warns that as the well-being of nine-tenths of the Indian population depends solely on the company's revenue, rather than its political or judicial policies, crime rates and litigation will depend largely on the success of the revenue settlement. He believes it would be "politic" to raise "a superior class of natives," drawn from distinguished army officers, meritorious judges or presidents of panchayats, and hard-working and deserving heads of districts and villages, to help with local government. But any system must also "admit the rise of the frugal and industrious cultivator."[34] Like Munro he is concerned with the role he wants middle-ranking Indians to play and also with the need to protect the interests of the ordinary cultivator.

For Elphinstone the maintenance of order should be the priority of government, but judicial and revenue settlement policies are also important. The rights of the different classes must be recognized so that all may obtain the share in the produce of the soil to which they are entitled; the "best plan" will be "to improve on the institutions of the country instead of making new ones, or importing those of distinct and dissimilar countries." Despite claiming that he is not democratic enough to insist on ryotwari, Elphinstone nevertheless encouraged all his subordinates in the peshwa's territories to work on "the principle of the ryotwar settlement." He recommended that the country's notables, whether the heads of villages or the heads of zamindaris, should be supported and their various rights defined, but the rights of the cultivators should also be protected, even against the demands of their social superiors.[35]

The assessment and collection of revenue was not always arranged according to the precepts of the Munro system, owing to local resistance, practical difficulties, company policies, and even different interpretations of what constituted a ryotwari settlement. But Munro's form of ryotwari aimed, in principle, at providing opportunities and incentives for individual cultivators to help themselves and at replacing the subsistence economy with more market-oriented practices in order to promote a greater distribution of wealth throughout the community, to the benefit of both state and individual. It was also intended to encourage the development of a more prominent middle rank of prosperous and independent cultivators who would recognize that their improved wealth and status was dependent upon the continued provision of order and opportunity by the company state.[36] Malcolm and Elphinstone differed with Munro on some details but were in broad agreement with his approach to land tenure and revenue collection issues. They closely agreed with his views on the administration of justice and the employment of Indians by the government—the third and fourth components of the Munro system.

There were three main objectives behind Munro's judicial recommendations. He wanted to use traditional legal forms that would be familiar to the people. He wanted to protect the cultivator from corrupt officials and oppressive social superiors, not only to ensure the effective working of his revenue system, but also because, like David Hume and William Robertson, he believed that a sense of security was an essential prerequisite for economic and social improvement. As Roberston had put it, "If men do not enjoy the protection of regular government, together with the certainty of personal security which naturally flows from it, they never attempt to make progress in science, nor aim at attaining refinement in taste or in manners."[37] Munro's third objective was to use Indians in the administration of justice, not only because they would understand local customs and attitudes better than Europeans but also because participation in the public service, he believed, would be of benefit to Indians for psychological and moral reasons.

As commissioner for the Ceded Districts during the years 1800 to 1807, Munro was expected to introduce not only the zamindari revenue system but also the Bengal judicial system, which derived from English ideas about judicial process. Although the laws it administered were Indian, taken over from the previous Mughal administration, it required the separation of the executive and legal branches of government and the implementation of a British-style court system with British judges and written depositions. Its "first principle" was to enable private individuals to protect their rights and their property against other individuals and the state. Most Englishmen at the time saw these English legal principles as universally valid and likely to have beneficial effects wherever they were adopted. But in his first statement on judicial matters, one brief paragraph in a letter to Read written in 1797, Munro points out that the main argument in favor of separating the judicial and executive functions of government—that the administration of justice might be used to destroy the liberty of the people—is irrelevant in India because a people under foreign rule do not possess "liberty." As there is little "property" in the country to go to law about, suits in India are concerned mainly with stray cattle, laborers' wages, or the shares of farming partners. They often have some connection with revenue matters and, according to Munro, the collector and his tahsildars (Indian revenue officers) or a panchayat (Indian jury) would settle them more easily and quickly than a British judge. British judges would be no more likely to protect the cultivators than British collectors, while, knowing less about local affairs, they would be less likely than collectors to make "true" judgments. He recommended, however, that a superior British court should be available to hear appeals against the decisions of the collector and complaints against "acts of oppression."[38]

Munro enlarged on the grounds of his objection to English legal procedures and his preference for magisterial powers for collectors in 1824. "We suppose that our laws are founded upon just principles, and that they must therefore have the same beneficial operation here as at home; but we forget that one great first principle, the freedom of the people, from which they derive their influence, does not exist here. Our institutions here, not resting on the same foundation as those of a free country, cannot be made to act in the same way." In Britain people resist oppression, and their spirit gives efficacy to the law; "in India the people rarely resist oppression, and the law intended to secure them from it can therefore derive no aid from themselves." As they will not protect themselves, the government must try to protect them through laws which would be unnecessary in England, or in any other country not under foreign dominion. For Munro this means investing the person most interested in the welfare of the cultivators, the collector, with the power of a magistrate.[39] As most government income derives from land revenue, the collector, as the government's representative, is bound to protect those who pay most of the taxes, the cultivators, from being forced to pay extra, unofficial levies to local notables with traditional influence and authority.

Like Munro, Malcolm believes it to be "among the first and greatest objects of a rational and just government (freedom can enter little into a rule of conquerors) to be fully understood by those it governs for." In the *Memoir of Central India* he states the same "first principle": that no system can be good that is not thoroughly understood and appreciated by those for whose benefit it is intended. He advocates the use of panchayats, spending fourteen pages discussing the way they work and anticipating objections to their use. Elphinstone, similarly, warns the Supreme govern-ment to remember that "even just government will not be a blessing if at variance with the habits and character of the people." Later, he describes panchayats as an excellent institution for dispensing justice, and for up-holding the principles of justice, "which are less likely to be observed among a people to whom the administration of it is not at all entrusted." Panchayats, however, will not be able to handle all cases. "Numerous na-tive judges with European super-intendance" will also be needed.[40]

Munro's first official minute on judicial issues, "Trial by Panchayat," was written in August 1807 at the end of his term of office in the Ceded Districts. It opens with some musings on Indian social morality: the "strange mixture of fraud and honesty in the natives of India, and even in the same individuals, in different circumstances," that makes it difficult for outsiders to comprehend the ramifications of Indian disputes. A British judge, with his limited command of the native language, cannot detect "the minute points by which truth and falsehood are often separated." Under these circumstances no legal system will be entirely satisfactory, but the most effective will be trial by panchayat, which is "as much the common law of India in civil matters as that by jury is in England. No native thinks that justice is done where it is not adopted."[41]

Most Britons, too, felt that justice could not be done without a jury. William Blackstone, famous for his *Commentaries on the Law of England* (1765–69), referred to juries as the "grand bulwark" of English liberties. A contributor to the *Gentleman's Magazine* in 1777 wrote that nothing "shines more eminently conspicuous than trial by jury. This invaluable prerogative is the birthright of every Englishman, and distinguishes the laws of this happy country from the arbitrary decisions of other states."[42] Both would have been surprised that an institution the British proudly thought they had invented was traditional practice in several parts of India.

British legal processes changed considerably during the second half of the eighteenth century in both the Scottish and English systems.[43] Under the "old" system in Scotland there were at least ten different types of court, most of them private or ecclesiastical. These were somewhat similar to the zamindari jurisdictions and caste arrangements for the enforcement of acceptable standards of social behavior that existed in India, although the laws and customs and practices they dealt with were, of course, less similar. In Scotland sheriffs and burgh courts, which dealt mainly with debt, property actions, minor crime, and "good neighbour" offenses, and the high court, which dealt with treason and crimes of violence, all used juries. Private barony and regality courts had powers similar to those of the sheriffs courts over certain lands. Various church courts handled poor relief and social discipline, which meant sexual offenses, "sabbath breach," "unseemlie behaviour" (swearing and drunkenness), and slander. The old system was very decentralized; large areas were beyond the control of the central government and justice was administered by private individuals rather than paid government officials. Unlike England, there were other law-making bodies beside Parliament: in particular, the general assembly of the Church of Scotland and local regality courts. Custom and usage were more important than statute law.[44]

Historically, Scotland's legal system had developed differently from England's. What statutes there were derived from Roman legal concepts, brought to Scotland by law students who attended French and Dutch universities during the sixteenth and seventeenth centuries. Most legal decisions, however, were based on "practicks," printed collections of decisions arranged in alphabetical order by subject, although inadequate records meant that in many areas precedents were lacking. Lord Stair, as important in Scottish legal history as Blackstone is in English, pointed the way to reform. In his *Institutes of the Law of Scotland* (1681) he presented a compendium of established usage that also demonstrated how usage derived from principles of equity as well as precedent. Stair subscribed to the idea of natural law as expressed by Grotius and Pufendorf: "Law is the dictate of reason." But while sometimes speaking of legal *rights*, he saw law as a series of *obligations* that limited both the freedom to be found in the natural state and the sanctity of private property. For Stair, rights in property might be restricted in the public interest: "the holder of property . . . was theoretically almost a trustee of his property on behalf of the community."[45]

The old system supervised the economic as well as the social life of the community and was supposed to maintain order and social stability rather than protect individual rights. Local courts in which jurors, judges, and church elders alike knew the usages and personalities involved as well as the community's needs worked quite effectively in both civil and criminal cases until the mid–eighteenth century. But the system was in decline by the time rapid political and economic change, and the abolition of private jurisdictions after the Jacobite rebellion of 1745, led to prolonged debate and new legislation. Anyone who had read Smith, Millar, or Kames knew that the object of the debate was to reform the law to make it relevant to the needs of a changing society. The old system, which had been suitable for an earlier stage in the progress of Scotland, was becoming obsolete.[46]

In 1740, David Hume had argued that laws had emerged because they were a social convenience, like the development of language and the use of money, and that particular laws followed from the needs and contrivances of mankind, not from the dictates of kings, the "absolutes" of "the natural state," or even from God. Lord Kames, whose writings on law fit comfortably within the Scottish Enlightenment tradition in that they trace the historical origins of laws and the relationship between legal and social change, recognized the irrelevance of much Scottish law to modern society: "The law of a country is in perfection when it corresponds to the manners of the people, their circumstances, their government. And as those are seldom stationary, the law ought to accompany them in their changes." Munro echoes Kames in pointing out that in Britain, laws had been introduced gradually during several centuries in a way that matched the increasing knowledge and level of civilization of the people. Kames also maintained that if the two principles "justice" and "social utility" were in conflict, justice might be sacrificed: "Equity when it regards the interest of a few individuals only, ought to yield to utility when it regards the whole society."[47] In promoting his judicial recommendations, Munro stated that "We must . . . frame gradually from the existing institutions, such a system as may advance the prosperity of the country, and be satisfactory to the people." He felt the British Indian judicial system should regulate economic and social stability rather than protect the rights of individuals by strict adherence to European notions of what was just. The system may be stigmatized as expediency because it happened to suit the company's authoritarian form of government. But it mixed principle with earlier Scottish practice and, most important, was thought suitable to the present stage in the progress of India.

While on leave in Edinburgh in 1808, Munro wrote a paper on the problems of the company's judicial system, which he describes as having grown rapidly into "the most expensive judicial system in the world." This might have been acceptable if it worked in the public interest, but Indians preferred their own system which was "free of expense in its principles" and speedy. The company system was complex and slow; it encouraged litigation because native pleaders brought everything to court; not one in ten European judges could understand his pleaders without an interpreter; the backlog of cases in one Bengal court alone exceeded a hundred thousand, and more courts of the same type would not help. The judicial code should be amended "to return to the heads of villages their ancient jurisdictions in petty causes"; all important cases should be tried by panchayats; and as far as possible, the administration of justice should be given "into the hands of intelligent natives" rather than to inadequately qualified European judges. Finally, as Indian collectors had also acted as magistrates, the offices of magistrate and collector, separated under the Bengal system, should be "reunited." Munro concludes with a list of the courts to be abolished, claiming "the whole saving in India would probably amount to nearly half a million Sterling."[48] A convincing case for retrenchment could be expected to attract favorable attention from the company directorate; this paper was no doubt in part an exercise in self-promotion by Munro. His opinions, however, remained constant. Judicial powers for village headmen, Indian juries, and a magistrate's powers for the collector are mentioned in every paper he wrote on the judicial system.

On his appointment as judicial commissioner for Madras in 1813, Munro submitted a minute on "The Administration of Justice" in which he reiterates these points and assesses the positive and negative effects of the company's existing system. It is good in that it provides protection to the persons and property of Indians and in that Indians seem to recognize that "it is the wish of the Government that its power should be founded on justice." Its harm lies in justice being more difficult to obtain than previously owing to a "collision of authorities," a need for a more summary process in petty suits, the abolition of the traditional jurisdiction of potails, and the fact that Indians perceive the system to be good in intention rather than effect. The body of the minute is devoted to an account of the viability of the judicial forms used by precolonial governments. Although corruption was rampant under weak rulers, Munro believes it had declined immediately prior to British rule as a result of the use of panchayats and by the "check" of public opinion. If the powers of magistrate and control of police are given back to collectors, and if panchayats are used in civil cases, the Indian system will work effectively in conjunction with the superior courts and criminal justice system introduced by the company. The union of the powers of magistrate and collector might be unacceptable in Britain, "but as the municipal institutions of India are calculated for those duties being vested in the same person, it is much better that they should remain united in him. . . . We are not to consider English maxims as always applicable to India but to follow those rules which are most applicable to the country, as it now is." Munro's key point was that a system at variance with the feelings and beliefs of the people will have "no moral force to uphold it." Adam Ferguson expressed a similar idea: "If forms of proceeding, written statutes, or other constituents of law, cease to be enforced by the very spirit from which they arose; they serve only to cover, not to restrain, the iniquities of power."[49]

Munro was still calling for a reduction in the number of British-style courts in 1827, maintaining that "the people would be much more solidly protected by abolishing the expensive establishments, and remitting the amount in their [revenue] assessment."[50] Although naturally aware of the company's urgent need for revenue, Munro nevertheless believed that any reduction in the cost of the judicial system should go to benefit the local economy. Extra wealth distributed throughout society rather than appropriated by the state would, in the long run, create more wealth for both individuals and the state.

The importance of allowing Indians to play a part in the administration of justice, for reasons of principle as well as expediency, is the central theme of Munro's last minute, entitled "Trial of Criminal Cases by Jury or Panchayat." Written a few days before his death in July 1827, it was also his last official paper. Panchayats are practical because they act quickly and efficiently; they have moral value because "the character of the people will inevitably be raised by being employed in distributing justice"; and they may be justified on the principle that, even if the decisions of a European judge are technically more "correct," this will not compensate for "the evil of excluding the people" from the process. "It would merely be executing strict justice among men whom we had degraded; for nothing so certainly degrades the character of a people as exclusion from a share in the public affairs of the country, and nothing so certainly raises it as public employment being open to all."[51]

The two concepts—that legal systems should be suited to the nature of the society they are to serve, and that the interests of the whole society should take precedence, if necessary, over individual rights—were particularly well suited to the purposes of the Munro system. Although, unlike Munro's revenue policies, his judicial recommendations contained in themselves no principles of improvement, they were intended to provide a setting in which the most important of all his principles of improvement, personal enterprise, and moral development—on which all other areas of progress, he believed, depended—could be fostered. Munro saw the pursuit of individual self-improvement as beneficial for society as a whole, but he also believed in "public spirit," in what appears to be the classical sense of "civic virtue." In the civic humanist tradition, participation in public affairs was part of the way in which man achieved moral fulfillment; if Indians could not legislate for their own society, they must at least be permitted to administer the legislation of their rulers. Munro's system seems thus to combine the eighteenth-century conception of the civic tradition, in which there was declining interest by the end of the century, with intimations of the individualism and emphasis on self-help that were to be important in nineteenth-century liberal thought.[52]

The employment of Indians in government—the fourth component of his system—had become a major preoccupation for Munro by the 1820s. Because it was neither possible nor desirable that the company state should rest indefinitely on military force, policies must be directed to the

attachment of the people by providing better government and, for both
practical and philosophical reasons, by employing Indians as officials. In
his minute "On the Employment of Natives in the Public Service,"
Munro claims that even if it were practicable to employ only Europeans,
excluding Indians from both high and subordinate offices, it should not
be done because it would be both politically and morally wrong.[53] If Indians submitted passively to European domination, "they would sink in
character . . . [and] would degenerate into an indolent and abject race." In
a passionate plea on behalf of Indians, Munro derides the advocates of
improvement who fail to recognize "the great springs on which it depends." They place no confidence in Indians, give them no authority and
exclude them from office, "but they are ardent in their zeal for enlightening them by the general diffusion of knowledge." Books alone can do
nothing; literature cannot improve the character of a nation for, in every
age and country, the great stimulus to the pursuit of knowledge is the
prospect of fame, wealth, or power. Great attainments have no value if
they cannot "be devoted to their noblest purpose, the service of the community."

Munro believes this to be true of all countries, not only India: "Let
Britain be subjugated by a foreign power to-morrow; let the people be excluded from all share in the Government, from public honours, from
every office of high trust and emolument, and let them in every situation
be considered as unworthy of trust, and all their knowledge and all their
literature, sacred and profane, would not save them from becoming, in another generation or two, a low-minded, deceitful, and dishonest race." For
Munro it would be better for the British to be expelled from India than to
debase a whole people, "for in proportion as we exclude them from the
higher offices and a share in the management of public affairs we lessen
their interest in the concerns of the community and degrade their character."[54] It is a very different critique of empire from the widely held and often cited eighteenth-century view that the wealth and power of empire
would corrupt the imperial nation, but it bears a marked resemblance to
William Robertson's analysis of Rome.

Robertson argued that the Romans, having "desolated" Europe, tried
to civilize it. They set up a despotic but not arbitrary government in the
conquered territories, preserved public "tranquillity" and, "As a consola-

tion for the loss of liberty, they communicated their arts, sciences, language, and manners, to their new subjects." Their rule, however, was neither happy nor favorable to "the improvement of the human mind." "The martial and independent spirit, which had distinguished their ancestors, became extinct among all the people subjected to the Roman yoke; they lost not only the habit but even the capacity of deciding for themselves, . . . and the dominion of the Romans, like that of all great Empires, degraded and debased the human species." Similarly, for Adam Ferguson "final corruption" lay in policies that deprive "the citizen of occasions to act as the member of a public; that crush his spirit; that debase his sentiments, and disqualify his mind for affairs."[55]

Malcolm and Elphinstone agreed with these sentiments but gave their recommendations a practical gloss. In *The Government of India*, Malcolm states that unless Indians are treated with more confidence and distinction and given access to higher office, Britain cannot hope to retain her position in India for long. If the most active and eminent Indians are treated generously, however, they will be raised in their own estimation and that of others. They will become attached and, through them, the population at large will become attached "to a government which, daring to confide in its own justice and wisdom, casts off the common narrow and depressing rules of foreign conquerors." Writing to Munro in 1822, Elphinstone stresses that in its own interest, Britain must permit Indians to play a role in the government of their own country. It may take fifty years but the system of government and education "must some time or other work such a change on the people . . . that it will be impossible to confine them to subordinate employments." If they are denied opportunities to satisfy their ambition, "we may expect an explosion which will overturn our government."[56]

Although there is broad agreement between the three men on the general form of government, true to character, Malcolm emphasizes rewards and recognition while Munro emphasizes opportunities for self-help, as the best way of fostering progress. Elphinstone, also characteristically, emphasizes education. In 1818 he stated that Britain's best course in seeking the moral improvement of the inhabitants of the peshwa's former territories would be to improve their education, but he was uncertain as to method. The establishment of free schools by the company might create a

suspicion of concealed designs. In his minute on education of 1823, Elphinstone's views on education reflect those of Adam Smith. Smith believed that the state derived considerable advantage from the education of
the poor. The better educated they were, the less liable they would be to
"the delusions of enthusiasm and superstition, which, among ignorant nations, frequently occasion the most dreadful disorders." An educated people were always more decent and orderly than an ignorant one. "They feel
themselves, each individually, more respectable, and more likely to obtain
the respect of their lawful superiors, and they are therefore more disposed
to respect those superiors . . . they are less apt to be misled into any wan-
ton or unnecessary opposition to the measures of government." Elphinstone observes that it is now agreed that the well-being of the poor depends on education, because only by education can they acquire "those
habits of prudence and self-respect from which all other good qualities
spring." He points out that even Smith, "the political writer of all others
who has put the strictest limits to the interference of executive government, especially in education," admits that the instruction of the poor
should be "among the necessary expenses of the sovereign." Although not
always in full agreement with Smith, Elphinstone seems to have consulted
his writings for guidance on questions of government and administration
and, in regard to education, accepted Smith's claim of a connection between self-respect and respect for authority.[57]

The central ideas of the school of thought on Indian government associated with the names of Munro, Malcolm, and Elphinstone are discussed by Munro in three minutes: "General Remarks on the Judicial Administration and on the Police," "On the Employment of Natives in the
Public Service," and "On the State of the Country and the Condition of
the People," all dated 31 December 1824, after Munro had submitted his
resignation as governor of Madras and was expecting to leave India shortly for the last time. Although he stayed on for two and a half years during
the First Burma War, these three papers should be seen, as Munro intended, as his final statement of the ideas on colonial administration he had
developed and expressed during the previous thirty years.

In a detailed exegesis of the minute "On the State of the Country and
the Condition of the People," the most important statement made by

Munro on his main interests and most firmly held beliefs in regard to administration, Burton Stein, who refers to it as "the Great Minute," points out rightly that more than half of it is given to a discussion of land tenure and revenue, and that other important topics include "the pragmatic and moral foundation for a greater role for Indians in the internal administration of the country," the judicial system and the police, and "the nature and purpose of British rule in India." Stein claims that Munro's "review of tenurial forms, especially of mirasi tenure, and his insistence that ryotwar encompassed all other systems as well as pre-dating most is unexpected," because Munro had been appointed governor of Madras in 1819 partly "in recognition of the triumph of his administrative principles." He adds that other subjects one might have expected Munro to discuss, such as the army and trade, are not mentioned.[58] The "Great Minute," however, should be seen as Munro's last exposition of *his own system*, not as a general statement on British rule, and the core issues of the Munro system were land tenure and revenue collection, the judicial system and the police, and the inclusion of Indians in the process of government. The army, defense, and trade were of only peripheral importance to him as an administrator and therefore largely irrelevant to the subject matter of this minute. It is also possible that to Munro, in the 1820s, "the triumph of his administrative principles" was less obvious than it appears a century and a half later, for his warnings against innovation are more pronounced in the papers from his governorship than in ones written earlier in his career. Despite the apparent triumph represented by his high appointment, Munro was aware of the challenge, posed by new ideas gathering support in Britain and British India, to the system of political economy he had developed to suit the needs of a colonized people whose stage of political, economic, and social development, he believed, was less advanced than that of the British people.

PART III

REPRESENTATIONS

CHAPTER 12

Orientalist Representations

> *Orientalist: one versed in Oriental languages and literature.*
> —*Samuel Johnson*

An entire book could be devoted to an analysis of the place of Munro, Malcolm, and Elphinstone in the current scholarly debate on Orientalism, but it is an issue that is too complex to examine in depth in a book about a different aspect of their role in history. Munro, Malcolm, and Elphinstone, however, were Orientalists in both Samuel Johnson's contemporary definition of the word, and in a more recent and more specialized sense: they viewed Asian history and culture through a screen of preconceptions derived from western intellectual discourse. This makes it necessary to look briefly at a few of the issues encompassed by the term "Orientalism."

Prior to the publication in 1978 of Edward Said's immensely stimulating but controversial book, *Orientalism*, the term "orientalism," expanding slightly on Johnson's definition, generally referred to the study of eastern cultures through a sufficient command of the relevant languages to give access to the great religious and literary texts of Asia. "Orientalists" were generally appreciative and respectful would-be scholars whose aim was to both preserve and make accessible to the Western world what they saw as

valuable ancient "knowledge." In Bayly's felicitous phrase: they were attempting "to make room in European mentalities for the great kingdoms
of the east."[1] In Said's interpretation, however, "Orientalism" refers to
Western colonial representations of "the Orient" (Asia and Islamic North
Africa), which gain credence as "authoritative knowledge" but which are,
in fact, merely artificial constructions of Asian history and cultures intended to provide intellectual reinforcement for political, economic, and
military domination. The significance of colonialism is the key element in
this definition. "Orientalists" are writers whose unsympathetic interpretations of Asian and Islamic cultures are made from a position of Western
intellectual superiority. Thomas R. Trautmann in *Aryans and British India*
(1997), his thoughtful and enlightening study of the role of India in the
development of British ethnology, has "tagged" these meanings, for the
sake of convenience, "Orientalism/1" and "Orientalism/2" respectively,[2]
and these designations will be used, also for the sake of convenience, in
this chapter.

Since 1978, however, numerous studies of Western writing on Asia—
more, perhaps, by social scientists and literary critics than by historians—
have demonstrated, through their weaknesses as well as their strengths,
that there are at least five major problems with Said's thesis. First, Said
oversimplifies the colonial relationship. As John M. MacKenzie points
out, recent works highlighting the "mutual complicity and the interpene-
trations of imperial and indigenous culture" have demonstrated that the
relationship was far more complex than the simple domination/subordi-
nation model indicates; there were "reversals in apparent power relationships."[3] Second, as Nicholas Thomas has demonstrated, the wonderful diversity of orientalisms cannot be confined within a single "consistent
discourse."[4] Third, Said failed to give sufficient weight to differing historical contexts. Orientalisms can only be fully understood when analyzed in
relation to their own time and place.[5] Fourth, Said failed to acknowledge
that the historical context, in many cases, is that of contemporary European intellectual debate rather than agendas of colonial oppression. As
Bayly observes, "colonial ideologies were varied, unstable and contradicto-
ry" and "owed as much to debates in European intellectual history as they
did to particular Indian circumstances."[6] A fifth problem, as Rosane

Rocher notes, is that the discipline of Indology for much of the nine-teenth and twentieth centuries was dominated by German scholars with no direct links to colonialism at all.[7]

In regard to Orientalism/1, Munro, Malcolm, and Elphinstone proba-bly had sufficient command of Persian to gain access to many of the great religious and literary texts of Islamic India and Persia if they chose, as well as to the fables and stories they probably preferred. None of them seem to have made any effort to learn Sanskrit, probably because the type of knowledge to which Sanskrit gave access was largely irrelevant to their interests. Ancient knowledges—expositions of religious and philosophi-cal beliefs—were of less interest to them than the *effects* of religious and philosophical beliefs on man and society. Malcolm and Elphinstone had an adequate knowledge of spoken Marathi and Hindustani to carry out their diplomatic duties, and Munro, who clearly felt he had a flair for lan-guages, was sufficiently fluent in several south Indian vernacular languages to communicate verbally with Indians in the course of his work.

How competent they were at reading and writing Indian scripts is difficult to determine; Malcolm and Elphinstone certainly used munshis (secretaries or writers) to help them with their research as authors as well as with their work as diplomats and administrators. Munro could work with written Persian in cursive script and, in the 1780s, while still only an ensign, he sent to a friend a translation he had made of a Persian manu-script which contained the story of Shylock. The translation, formally at-tributed to Munro, was included in the notes at the end of *The Merchant of Venice* in Edmund Malone's edition of *The Plays of William Shakespeare*, of which there were several editions between the 1780s and 1830s.[8] But this, perhaps, is as close as any of them came to being Orientalists of this type. Malcolm and Elphinstone read Persian history for the facts it supplied, not for its literary merits, and Munro was no admirer of Persian litera-ture:

The Persian writers have always been fond of long, pompous periods; and Abul-Fazel [Akbar's secretary], who seems to have thought that the essence of all good writing consisted in this, has been so eminently successful, that his nominatives and verbs are often posted at the distance of three pages from each other; and the space within is oc-cupied with parentheses within parentheses, where the sense, if any, lies concealed behind such a number of intrenchments [sic], that the Council of Trent would be more puzzled to discover it, than they were to settle the meaning of Grace.

He also observes that, judging by his translations of Abul-Fazel, Alexander Dow, the respected author of *The History of Hindostan* (1770), "appears to have been but a poor Persian scholar," which suggests that Munro felt he could do better. Munro was similarly unimpressed with Persian histories: "[They] are faithful; but are written in a dull, heavy style, like the genealogical chapters in the Bible. They contain but two descriptions of men—the good and the bad. The former are, without exception, as strong as elephants, as brave as Alexander, and as wise as Solomon; the latter oppressed their subjects, depised men of letters, and are gone to hell." Munro adds, "Of all their writings, none are more ridiculous, affected, and quaint, than their letters." Persian stories are "their best style of writing" because they are relatively simple in form.[9]

No one, as yet, has cast doubts on Munro's competency as a linguist. M. E. Yapp, however, suggests that Malcolm's admission that he received help from his Persian secretary in reading an old and obscure Persian manuscript may indicate that he had problems reading Persian. Old and obscure manuscripts, however, can be a much more demanding proposition than manuscripts written in the copperplate hand of a professional secretary, whether using European or Asian cursive scripts, and it seems likely that by the time Malcolm's career as a diplomat ended, he was reasonably proficient at reading official correspondence and at composing official letters using what Bernard Cohn terms "the epistolatory practices of professional scribes."[10]

Bayly mentions Elphinstone, together with Neil Edmonstone, Lord Wellesley's Persian secretary, and the Kirkpatrick brothers, as among the few British officials who, during the twenty years after 1790, "appear to have mastered the art of reading cursive Persian and familiarised themselves with the specialised forms of official letter writing." Elphinstone's command of languages, however, was played down by a contemporary. In a farewell address to Elphinstone given at the Bombay Literary Society in November 1827—a type of occasion which usually drew forth eulogies— Colonel Vans Kennedy, secretary of the society and himself a respected Oriental scholar, observed that Elphinstone, "if not a profound classical scholar . . . was sufficiently master of Greek and Latin . . . to enable him to appreciate and enjoy the matchless works of antiquity. . . . His active life, however, and public duties restricted his knowledge of the numerous languages of Asia to a conversancy with Persian and prevented him from prosecuting even that language."[11] Despite this disparaging assessment, however, Elphinstone, like Malcolm, was probably capable of reading and composing official correspondence in Persian.

Munro, Malcolm, and Elphinstone studied Indian languages to give them access to certain types of employment and to certain types of knowledge that would help further both their careers and their intellectual reputations as experts on Asia. Much of their research, although not all in the case of Munro, was done as a means to an end, not as an end in itself. Although they certainly tried to make accessible to the Western world what they saw as valuable information on Asian societies and cultures, it was factual information on the way things had been, and were now being, done, not "ancient knowledge" that they sought, and their writings were all overtly political in character. Most of the "true" practitioners of Orientalism/1, men like Sir William Jones, who is often cited as the archetypal Orientalist, were interested in languages for career purposes and the pursuit of intellectual renown as well. But much of their research and writing was done from curiosity and as a sideline to their professional employment, and, despite the utility to the government of Jones's work on Hindu law, the material they circulated or published had fewer direct implications for the exercise of British power within India than the public papers of Munro, Malcolm, and Elphinstone.[12]

While the political character of the three Scotsmen's writings on Asia probably bars them from classification as Orientalists of the first type, it appears to set them up as prime candidates for castigation as the fabricators of "Orientalist constructions" of Asia according to the definition of Orientalism/2. Yet a relationship between their texts on India and other Asian societies and Said's definition of Orientalism is difficult to sustain despite the fact that works of philosophical and conjectural history are believed to have played a significant part in the development of this type of interpretation of Asian cultures.

According to Said, an Orientalist is one who teaches, writes about, or researches the Orient, while Orientalism is a way of thinking that is founded on a metaphysical conception of the nature of being and on epistemological beliefs and makes a clear distinction between "the East" and "the West". It is also "a corporate institution for dealing with the Orient"—for describing it, making statements about it, ruling over it, and establishing authoritative opinions on it. Ronald Inden, following Said, discusses the relationship of knowledge to power and what he calls commentative, explanatory, and hegemonic accounts, all of which play central roles in the development and teaching of Orientalism. Specialized knowledge, which allows those who possess it to speak with authority, to instruct, and to exert leadership, provides the foundation stone of Orientalism. Knowledge is transmitted by description, in which the thoughts and acts of subjects are represented to the reader. Commentative accounts provide a framework in which the thoughts and acts are classified according to some accepted system. Explanatory, or interpretive, accounts represent what is "strange and incoherent" in the subject in a way to make it seem rational or normal. Hegemonic accounts are the texts used "by scholars and their administrative doubles" to establish their authority and maintain the precedence of their "knowledge" over the knowledge of rivals. Said claims that for most of the nineteenth century the Orient was studied mostly from books and manuscripts, particularly from texts from what was regarded as "the classical period" of whatever society was being examined. But this is inaccurate. On-the-spot official reports, surveys, and submissions to parliamentary inquiries, as Gyan Prakash points out, joined translations of Persian and Sanskrit literature and historical interpretations to bolster the canon of literature which represented the Orient to the West.[13]

By these criteria, Munro, Malcolm, and Elphinstone are Orientalists according to the definitions of Said and Inden. They acquired knowledge on Asian topics largely in order to establish themselves as authorities for career purposes. They researched, wrote about, and hoped to teach Western audiences about Asia and, as cultural mediators, they passed on their knowledge by means of their own written texts. Malcolm and Elphinstone both used commentative and explanatory accounts in their works of history, classifying subjects and ordering them according to the methods of the genre known as philosophical history and the ideology of late eighteenth-century moral philosophy. Their texts were hegemonic in the sense that they presented their knowledge of India and other parts of Asia with didactic purpose. But, and this is a key point, their texts never achieved hegemonic status because their knowledge of the Orient, which represented late eighteenth-century principles and assumptions, was quickly superceded (in the case of Elphinstone's *History of India* before it was written) and their interpretations, by the mid–nineteenth century, had failed to take precedence over the "knowledge" of their rivals. The challenge to the hegemony of Mill's *History of British India* posed by Elphinstone's *History of India*, as Inden points out, was easily repulsed.[14]

The organizing principle of Orientalism/2 was essentialism—the Orient as object, separate from and different from the Occident, "the other" to the West's "self." This central dichotomy, the concept of self and other, encompasses three other important binary classifications: static-progressive, unitary-diverse, material and rational as against emotional and spiritual.[15] If these categories are inherent in Orientalist discourse, then Munro, Malcolm, and Elphinstone cannot be classified as Orientalists in Said's sense for, although they recognized cultural differences, their organizing principle was the universality of human nature. They did not see Indian and Western society in opposition to one another. Elphinstone complimented Malcolm on the "eminent degree" to which his *History of Persia* demonstrated a "knowledge of human nature and of Asia"—not of the nature of Asia.[16]

In *Oriental Imaginings*, Javed Majeed discusses what might be termed the catch-22 of Edward Said's analysis of Orientalism. Western writers on Asia are condemned by Said whether they depict the Orient as an unknown and unknowable "other" or try to "translate" it into terms that will make it comprehensible to the West. Majeed points out that Said fails to make it clear whether he believes a sound understanding of another culture is possible.[17] Munro, Malcolm, and Elphinstone believed it was, although, unlike Mill, they thought first hand experience—empiricism—was necessary. They are not guilty of applying the model of the Orient as unknowable "other," as defined by Inden, but they do belong to the "translator" group. Their sociological and anthropological interests led them to explain Asia to their Western audience in universal terms.

Comparisons feature prominently in Orientalist constructions. Analogies provided a convenient if misleading way of explaining aspects of an Asian society's beliefs and practices to an audience with no firsthand experience of Asian life, and Munro, Malcolm, and Elphinstone used them frequently. Where Orientalists/2 tended to emphasize differences, however, they stressed similarities. Like William Robertson in his popular and widely read histories, their comparisons were intended to bring two cultures closer together,[18] although Malcolm and Elphinstone tended to compare the Indians, Afghans, and Persians of their own day with the people of an earlier stage in European civilization. Munro, however, acknowledged similarities between contemporary Indians and Britons. His statement that "The more intelligent brahmins in their knowledge of politics and finance—and in ideas of justice—differ little from Europeans"[19] does not belong in a discourse of cultural domination.

The existence of a dichotomy between the rational and material West and the emotional and spiritual essence of Hinduism is entirely absent from Munro, Malcolm, and Elphinstone's representations of India, because they did not see the West as essentially rational nor India as much less materialist than Britain. A secular approach to religion in general and an interest in protosociological explanations of the origins, purpose, and institutional organization of religion deflected their attention from anything more spiritual than a vaguely defined monotheism or deism, while their apparent acceptance of Scottish Enlightenment views on the relative importance of feelings or emotions over rational decision as the motive force for human action precluded a perception of India as a spiritual and emotional "other." In his recommendations of policies that were intended to lead to economic improvement, Munro, at least, seems to have assumed that Indian cultivators would be as motivated by self-interest and material considerations as any Lowland Scottish yeoman farmer.

Munro, Malcolm, and Elphinstone did not see India as homogenous in opposition to Western heterogeneity. They recognized and recommended the preservation of many of the different regional forms of administration that hindered the British from imposing their own practical manifestation of a unitary state, and compared the Indian subcontinent with continental Europe in its diversity of peoples.

Although Inden argues that "caste" came to be seen by Orientalists as the governing element in an "homogeneous world," and as a somehow substantialized alternative to human agency in Indian history, Munro, Malcolm, and Elphinstone gave it less weight. Munro, who was interested in the phenomenon of caste but who, like many westerners, probably underestimated its pervasiveness in Hindu culture, believed that "The influence of caste in India, however great, is insignificant compared to that which the head men of the villages possess from their hereditary station as chiefs of the municipality."[20] Although all three men acknowledged the importance of caste in Indian society, they certainly did not see it as either the governing element in India, or as an alternative to human agency in determining the course of Indian history.

In regard to progress, as opposed to the representation of Indian stasis, Elphinstone believed that, at the time of the death of the great Akbar, India had been on the threshold of progress similar to that of early modern Europe, but fortuitous events had interrupted the "liberal spirit of inquiry" that was Akbar's legacy. Munro, who at the time still feared Mysore as an enemy, nevertheless saw Tipu Sultan's regime as capable of bringing progress to his state.

Munro, Malcolm, and Elphinstone made sweeping generalizations about individuals and groups which reflect stereotyped characterizations of Muslims and Hindus, and Malcolm and Elphinstone were typical philosophical historians, commenting on and explaining Asian societies and forms of government according to their own ideological beliefs. However, in regard to India, which they knew well, their opinions do not reflect the Orientalist classifications of Said and Inden.

Munro, Malcolm, and Elphinstone share some of the attributes of the practitioners of both Orientalism/1 and Orientalism/2, but do not closely fit the mold of either designation. They do, however, have much in common with the model that David Ludden has called "Orientalist Empiricism." The key to understanding Orientalist empiricism is historical context, and three particular features of late eighteenth- and early nineteenth-century India are useful in identifying Munro, Malcolm, and Elphinstone as empiricists. These are, first, the East India Company's transformation from merchant into ruler, which provided the practical setting for the working lives of the empiricists; second, the socialization and educational considerations which determined differences in the character of the Orientalisms of first and second generation colonial officials; and third, the question of power, that is, the relative insecurity of the company's hold on India prior to 1818 when compared to the strength of its position after the declaration of British paramountcy by the marquis of Hastings.

Although Warren Hastings had been struggling since 1772 to establish a regular form of government for the East India Company's Bengal territories, when Munro began his career in 1780, commercial considerations remained the company's main preoccupation. But between the 1780s and 1820s, its small and scattered possessions in the south and west of India were transformed into two powerful imperial provinces, and company officials, who had been recruited with only commercial or military service in mind, found they were now expected to function as colonial administrators and diplomats.[21] Prior to the 1780s, most company servants' knowledge of India was restricted to technical information on commercial matters. Their understanding of Indian culture, forms of government, and administrative practices was derived, as Bayly points out, from impressions and hearsay rather than from their own observations and was abysmally inadequate for their new responsibilities.[22] "Indian knowledge" was at a premium and, as Ludden claims, the foundations of Orientalism can be found in the desperate need for Indian knowledge of this first generation of administrators and diplomats. The type of knowledge these people needed, of course, was not the "ancient knowledge" contained in the Persian and Sanskrit texts beloved of earlier Orientalists. They could manage without knowing the finer points of Indian religion and philosophy; what they needed to know was how Indian rulers collected revenues, administered the law, fought wars, and conducted their foreign relations. The new information, obtained largely from Indian sources but also from personal observation, was produced "under the Enlightenment rubric of objective science." It was regarded as scientific "fact," supposedly verified by the accepted methodologies of contemporary scientific practice, and Ludden believes that although Orientalism as a body of knowledge was nurtured by colonialism, the "scientific" claims that surrounded its inception allowed it to be passed down to future generations as a formation of factual statements about Indian reality that existed, and could be known, "independent of any subjective, colonizing will."[23] Munro, Malcolm, and Elphinstone were leading empirical Orientalists who gathered "facts" about India, Persia, and Afghanistan from local sources and their own observations and used the proto-social science methodologies—the "rough, common sense empiricism" favored by the Scottish moral philosophers—to give authority to their representations of Asia.

The nature of their representations, however, was shaped by the values and assumptions they had inculcated from the socialization and educational processes of late eighteenth-century Scotland. Where the following generation of administrators spent several of their most susceptible formative years at Haileybury and Fort William Colleges in training to be rulers and imbibing knowledge and values—including those of contemporary Utilitarianism and Evangelicalism—that assumed the superiority of Western civilization, the empiricist generation in India, most of whom had no expectation of becoming rulers, were exposed to the relatively tolerant and cosmopolitan knowledge and values of the Englightenment in both its Scottish and European forms. They were often resistant to the Utilitarian predilection for "system" and to Evangelical Christian "enthusiasm," at least in relation to India. Although the relatively sympathetic approach to Indian culture of Munro, Malcolm, and Elphinstone derived to a considerable extent from the ideas of the Scottish "sentimentalist" school, which seems to have had a particularly powerful appeal for Malcolm, one other element in the historical context of the period may have contributed to the absence of a sense of "self" and "other" in the writings of the empiricist generation. In 1786, Sir William Jones had made known his discovery of the links between European and Indian languages. A minor consideration, perhaps, but taken together with the Englightenment belief in a universal human nature it might have worked to diminish European perceptions of Indian dissimilarity.

Recognition of the relative insecurity of the company's position in India is clearly evident in many of the earlier writings of Munro, Malcolm, and Elphinstone. Lynn Zastoupil draws attention to this aspect of their thought by including them in his "empire of opinion" group. The word "opinion" refers of course to their insistence that the consent of the Indian people must be courted by means of a generous and comprehensible civil administration, as company rule cannot be maintained indefinitely by military power alone. In the last years of their Indian careers, their writings reflect more confidence in British power but still lack the arrogance of conquerors manifest in the writings of many of the succeeding generation of administrators. Although they did not see India in terms of "alienness," the three Scotsmen would probably have endorsed Bayly's view that "India's alienness could never be too crudely asserted by a government dependent on an army of Indian subordinant servants."[24]

In *Empire and Information*, Bayly repeatedly emphasizes the extent to which the company Raj was dependent upon Indians, not only as subordinant servants—soldiers and low-level administrators—but also as sources of expert knowledge. Ludden points out that the facts the empricists sought were "locked away in the minds of Indian commercial, judicial, military, and revenue specialists."[25] Much of the interaction between Indians and colonial officials stemmed initially from the need of the latter for factual information, but it led quite often to what are now referred to as "dialogic encounters," which in turn led to exchanges of ideas from which new formulations of identity emerged.[26] The reliance of Munro, Malcolm, and Elphinstone on oral and written Asian sources has been stressed throughout this book, and it was the persuasive accounts of Indian institutions delivered by Indian revenue, judicial, political, and military specialists during dialogic encounters of this type that helped the three men recognize their viability. But the Indian voices have been distorted by the Scottish gloss their accounts were given as part of the process whereby Munro, Malcolm, and Elphinstone made their policy recommendations both attractive and comprehensible to British authorities. The recovery of these Indian and other Asian voices would be a worthy project but one that would require, of course, the labors of a specialist in Persian and Indian languages.

The writings on Asia of Munro, Malcolm, and Elphinstone provide support for the present emphasis in colonial discourse analysis on the complexity of colonial relationships, the diversity of Orientalisms, the crucial significance of historical context, and the equality of European intellectual debate with agendas of colonial oppression as formative influences on the nature of Orientalist representations.

The three Scotsmen were Orientalists and, when generalizing, their approach can be placed, usefully, within the paradigm of Orientalist empiricism. Their writings, however, contain both elements that relate their work to other definitions of the word Orientalism and elements that are unique to them, sometimes as a group and sometimes as individuals; caution needs to exercised when attaching a more specific subtitle to their Orientalism.

CHAPTER 13

Historiographical Representations

> *We . . . receive, with caution, the traditionary histories of . . .*
> *[the] founders of states.*
> *—Adam Ferguson*

The misrepresentation of one group of agents of colonialism by another is of less interest, in the present so-called postcolonial era, than the misrepresentation of one society and culture by members of another, particularly when inequities of power are involved. But if "colonial discourse analysis," as Dane Kennedy defines it, "refers to the examination and interpretation of particular colonial texts,"[1] the various biographies of Munro, Malcolm, and Elphinstone that were written in the nineteenth century, as well as their own writings on Asia, should be classified as "colonial texts."

The orthodox representation of the lives and work of Munro, Malcolm, and Elphinstone—key players in the founding of the British Indian state—was established by their first biographers, the Reverend George Gleig, Sir John Kaye, and Sir T. E. Colebrooke, and reaffirmed and more widely disseminated by J. S. Cotton and John Bradshaw in their short biographies of Elphinstone and Munro in the cheap, widely read, and popular late nineteenth-century *Rulers of India* series. It is a representation that needs to be treated with the caution recommended by Ferguson, however, because it has had a durable but misleading impact on the way the three men have been perceived by later historians.

Nineteenth-century biographies were used as agents of socialization, part of the process by which the middle ranks reinforced the moral, ethical, and religious attitudes of their own generation and attempted to pass them on to the next. They were a sweeter pill to swallow than sermons, their messages similar but more easily digested. Traditional values were being challenged in the mid–nineteenth century by ideas that had generated and justified the American and French Revolutions, by changing attitudes to social and economic issues associated with industrialization, and by advances in scientific knowledge. It was firmly believed that a new, secure world would eventually manifest itself; philosophical liberalism had converted many to an implicit belief in human progress. But in the meantime there was confusion and anxiety, and writers were expected not only to inform and entertain but also, and more important, to suggest solutions to the intractable problems of the day. Growing religious skepticism generated a religion of conduct to take the place of faith in the revealed will of God as the basis of moral and ethical standards. Public figures, great men, became the new "saints" whose example would lead Victorians from "Doubting Castle." Thomas Carlyle, one of the most admired conservative writers of the mid–nineteenth century, regarded hero worship as "the basis of all possible good, religious or social, for mankind."[2]

In turning their subjects into icons for Anglo-Indian civil and military officials, as well as venerated proconsuls for the general reading public, Cotton and Bradshaw as well as Gleig, Kaye, and Colebrooke overemphasized the devotion to duty, moral rectitude, and religious orthodoxy of their subjects and played down their vigorous pursuit of wealth and status—their career-building strategies. More important, they misrepresented Munro, Malcolm, and Elphinstone as the heroes and chief spokesmen of the approach to Indian government to which they themselves subscribed. By highlighting the conservative but playing down the liberal and progressive elements and emphasizing the practical but ignoring, or failing to discern, the principles that lay behind the three Scotsmen's school of thought, they reconstructed it as a Conservative Anglo-Indian approach to Indian government—an alternative to that of the westernizing reformist Utilitarian and Evangelical groups, which are usually referred to collectively as Anglicists. The Scottish school, however, should be located between the Conservative and Anglicist approaches; it has affinities with, as well as differences from, both.

In the sense that the ideas of the Scottish moral philosophers were "conservative," so too were those of Munro, Malcolm, and Elphinstone. But the three men retained throughout their careers the belief that the human nature of Indians was essentially the same as that of Europeans and equally capable of improvement if the system of government provided the right framework for progress. Although they rejected the idea that Indians could—or should—be turned into imitation Englishmen, the regime they envisaged for India nevertheless resembled late eighteenth- and early nineteenth-century Europe; the scope of their imagination, like that of most people, was limited by their experience. By the 1820s, however, the challenge presented by the more radical proposals for reform by the Anglicists was producing increasingly strident protests from Munro, Malcolm, and Elphinstone against systems and innovations they saw as speculative and mechanical and, therefore, less suitable for bringing progress to India than their own empiricist and organic approach. These protests allowed the next generation of Conservatives to adopt the three Scotsmen as allies in their own campaign against westernization.

Nineteenth-century Conservative administrators believed, like Munro, Malcolm, and Elphinstone, that the British should utilize traditional Indian institutions in governing India. But where the three Scotsmen, who neither wanted nor expected Indian institutions to remain unchanged, advocated their use as a springboard to improvement, Conservatives did not regard them as potential agents of progress. Increasingly doubtful about the universality of human nature, increasingly likely to perceive Indians in terms of oriental/occidental difference, and often convinced that Indians were unwilling or, perhaps, incapable of responding positively to British efforts to promote progress, they tended to advocate Indian forms of administration because they could preserve stability and require less effort on the part of British officials.

Both the Conservative and the Scottish school's approaches have been termed "paternalist," but the nature of their paternalism differed. Munro, Malcolm, and Elphinstone saw paternalism as a relationship between mentor and acolyte, as a well-intentioned limitation of the freedom of the governed, but with the objective, as Elphinstone put it, of guiding "the natives into a state that will admit of their governing themselves."[3] By the time their biographers were writing, however, the brand of paternalism favored by Conservatives—fatherly control of the affairs of their Indian "children"—was acquiring intimations of permanence and increasingly racist connotations that are absent from the Scotsmen's writings. By the mid–nineteenth century, Haileybury-educated Conservative public servants—supposedly upright, manly, Christian, and therefore capable of deciding what was best for Indians on a practical basis without the help of either philosophers, politicians, or Indians—would supervise the traditional (read static and unenlightened) way of life of the majority of the Indian people, complacent that the blessings of the Pax Britannica, when compared with the supposed horrors of the supposed disorder of precolonial India, justified their presence. Although Munro, Malcolm, and Elphinstone would have shared some of the concerns of the Conservative service gentry and, no doubt, many of the underlying elements of self-interest, their conservatism emphasized continuity with the past, not preservation of the past.

The objectives of the Scottish school were as principled, as progressive in intent, and, in Munro's case during the early years as a revenue collector, probably as innovative, as those of the Utilitarian reformers. But all three men expected Indian improvement to come slowly and organically from within Indian society, rather than quickly as a result of introducing British ways of doing things. Like Hume, they expected that

A long course of time, with a variety of accidents and circumstances, are requisite to produce those great revolutions, which so much diversify the face of human affairs. And the less natural any set of principles are, which support a particular society, the more difficulty will a legislator meet with in raising and cultivating them. It is his best policy to comply with the common bent of mankind, and give it all the improvements of which it is susceptible.[4]

Unlike the Anglicists, they believed history proved beyond doubt that successful reformers had taken into consideration the nature of the societies they intended to change and, like good teachers, had taken the people with them rather than forcing them, reluctantly and perhaps rebelliously, to accept innovations incomprehensible in the light of their historical experience.

From the 1830s until Indian independence in 1947, the historiography of British India was dominated by Anglo-Indian Conservative writers who were mostly members of what has been described as an "imperial service gentry"—men from a political and social stratum that was a by-product of Britain's imperial expansion. They owed their financial well-being and social status to India: salaries, investments, titles, decorations, and often an aristocratic style of life that would have been beyond their reach in Britain. They were carefully recruited and organized, held all but a few of the most important Indian appointments, had considerable influence on policy making, and controlled the executive machinery for putting policy into practice.[5] Although their political affiliations ranged across the spectrum of British conservative and liberal thought and they often differed on specific issues, they shared a vision that saw India through a distorting screen of middle-class Victorian and Edwardian cultural values and the traditions, shared experiences, and corporate self-interest of their own caste. This vision informed their interpretations of British Indian history and the role in British Indian history of Munro, Malcolm, and Elphinstone. Apparently impervious to new developments in international historiography, they were largely successful in isolating the study of British Indian history from the application of new ideas and methodologies. It was, in fact, Indian nationalist historians who both appropriated the new methodologies and identified the more progressive and liberal elements in the Scottish school of thought.

As Jawaharlal Nehru bitterly lamented while writing in a British Indian prison cell, "History is almost always written by the victors and conquerors and gives their view."[6] It is hardly surprising, therefore, that the generally uncritical nature of British historical writing should have allowed the reputations of Munro, Malcolm, and Elphinstone as wise and sympathetic empire builders to remain unchallenged for over a century. What is more surprising is the relative lack of criticism from the other side, a consideration that is interesting in relation to the issue of "colonial discourse." For many years before and after 1947, the history of British India was enmeshed in a sometimes vituperative debate between Indian scholars, politicians, and writers who were concerned with the issues of nationalism and economic exploitation, and the Anglo-Indian Conservatives, now known as the "Imperialist" school, who mounted a sturdy defense of the British Raj. Munro, Malcolm, and Elphinstone were long-revered heroes for the Imperialists, but for many western-educated Indians, their value as propagandists for the nationalist cause often outweighed their disadvantages as agents of colonial oppression.

Although R. Palme Dutt, in his Marxist analysis of the condition of India in 1940, traces the deterioration of Indian society to the introduction by Munro of the concepts of private property and individualism, claiming that the two concepts had undermined the natural communism of the traditional "village republics," Munro and Elphinstone gained the respect of many Indians whose attitudes and values had been influenced by western liberalism. The irony in this is magnificent, because liberal thought had been transmitted to India originally by the Anglicists, and Indian liberals were now using what in essence were Anglicist criteria to assess, quite favorably, the views on India of Munro and Elphinstone which the Anglicists had condemned as conservative.

Nehru cites Munro's indignant assertion that no previous foreign conqueror of India had treated the whole population as untrustworthy, dishonest, and "fit to be employed only where we cannot do without them [which] seems . . . not only ungenerous, but impolitic," and quotes a letter to Lord Hastings in which Munro regrets that the advantages to India of British rule have been so dearly bought by the sacrifice of Indian independence and national character. B. S. Baliga, in 1942, acknowledged what he saw as Munro's beneficial influence in extending the ryotwari system to the Madras presidency. Baliga saw the ryotwari system as progressive— perhaps because, as Palme Dutt had claimed, under Munro's supervision it had introduced the concepts of private property and individualism to India. K. N. Sastri Venkatasubba in 1939 identified Munro as the founder of a "liberal school of Indian administration" and traced the Montagu Declaration of 1917 to Munro's views on Indian governance. The views Venkatasubba admired are evident in a letter he quotes, written by Munro in 1794 in response to a request from Colonel Alexander Allan, later a company director, for information on "Law, Commerce, Agriculture." In this letter Munro states that although the inhabitants of the Baramahal region, unlike those of Bengal, had no written legal codes, "they have enough of tradition to make a very good common law. On this tradition and on common sense their decisions are grounded—and . . . they are just as good as any we could have were we to go for them as far as England." Asking, rhetorically, how English law could possibly be administered through interpreters, Munro announces that he "would as soon see the Inquisition among us as a corps of judges turned loose in the country, led by such banditti." He adds that "we are so vain of our laws that we suppose all nations are impatient to share in the Blessings." This letter, which had been excluded from Gleig's careful selection, had an obvious appeal for Indian nationalists in the 1930s.[7] In addition, the often-quoted statements of Munro, Malcolm, and Elphinstone depicting British rule in terms of a temporary trusteeship, their equally often-quoted opposition to the exclusion of Indians from positions of responsibility, Munro and Elphinstone's acknowledgment of "the drain" of Indian resources to Britain, and Munro's support for free access to British markets for Indian goods were all put to good use in the campaign for Indian self-government.

Throughout the period when Indian historiography was dominated by Anglo-Indian, or Imperialist, writers, the careers and writings of Munro, Malcolm, and Elphinstone were made to fit a congratulatory discourse of great imperial leadership along what by the mid–twentieth century were being termed "Conservative-Orientalist" lines. But even after independence in 1947, little effort was made to reassess their roles. Two works, one by a British writer and one by an Indian, continued to perpetuate the misleading Conservative-Orientalist representation. Philip Mason's *Men Who Ruled India* (1954) remains firmly in the hero-worshipping, paternalist camp. He uses the concept of trusteeship as the framework for his teleological thesis—from an aim "glimpsed by Munro and Elphinstone . . . explicitly proclaimed in 1917 . . . it is clear that the change from government for Indians to government by Indians has been carried through successfully"—as though Britain had always been committed to that end. Evidence indicating that between the 1850s and the First World War few Anglo-Indians paid more than lip service to the concept of trusteeship is overlooked. Munro, Malcolm, and Elphinstone feature as "founders" of a British Raj dedicated to trusteeship, and their work is extolled in a section glowingly entitled "The Golden Age, 1798–1858": "the flowering, the highest peak perhaps in the lofty range of what the *English* [my italics] have done, when a handful of our countrymen, by the integrity of their character and with not much else to help them, gave to many millions for the first time for many centuries the idea that a ruler might be concerned with their well-being."[8] Mason relied on nineteenth-century biographies, personal accounts, and secondary sources. In association with the nostalgic sentiments and loyalties derived from his own distinguished Indian career, the result was a restatement, in glowing terms, of a very familiar historical representation.

R. D. Choksey's study of Elphinstone probably developed out of his work on the history of the Marathas and the Bombay Deccan during Elphinstone's period. His object is to provide insight into Elphinstone, not just as an official but as a man, and he makes good use of Elphinstone's often almost illegible journals, which unlike the journals of many prominent men were not intended for public consumption and permit a relatively intimate view of their author's personality. Choksey, whose approach seems to owe something to the contemporary influence of psychohistory, examines Elphinstone's attitudes towards money, patronage, personal relationships, his struggles with ill health, and in particular, his equivocal attitude towards India and his career. He portrays him as ambitious for recognition but not ambitious enough—or, perhaps, not sufficiently self-confident or energetic—to really drive for it as Malcolm did. The biography contains much interesting, sometimes gossipy, detail on Elphinstone, his family, his friends, and his contacts with other British Indian officials, and it records failures as well as successes and mentions less praiseworthy aspects of Elphinstone's character and career. But in the end, Choksey's portrayal fails to escape from the nineteenth-century genre of hero-worshipping biography, and Elphinstone appears again as a late nineteenth-century Englishman, not as an early nineteenth-century Scotsman.[9]

A growing interest in social and economic history by academic historians in the 1950s and 1960s finally challenged the near monopoly of Anglo-Indian historiography and produced fresh and interesting insights
into Munro's and Elphinstone's work as administrators. Fine studies by
Ballhatchet, Mukherjee, Frykenberg, and Beaglehole added much to our
knowledge of the way in which the Scotsmen's policies affected the social,
economic, and cultural life of India and to our understanding of the nature of the company state. They demonstrated also that many of the developments Munro, Malcolm, and Elphinstone hoped would occur as a
result of their policy recommendations did not come to pass.[10] In the
1980s and 1990s several scholars, while working on other issues, have made
interesting points about the work and ideas of Munro, Malcolm, and Elphinstone.[11] But postindependence studies of British Indian intellectual
history—like this book, concerned with ideas, theories, and assumptions
and with recommended, not implemented policies—have added little that
is new to the Conservative-Orientalist, Burkean, pragmatic representation
of the Scotsmen's approach to government.[12] This does not mean that this
representation is accurate; it merely indicates that the one crucial source
has been overlooked. Connections between their eighteenth-century Scottish sociocultural roots and the careers and thought of Munro, Malcolm,
and Elphinstone are still largely ignored, and the three men are still, for
the most part, treated as though they had been raised in England.

CHAPTER 14

British Scotland, British India

A bridge of significant proportions was created between Scotland and British India in the late eighteenth and early nineteenth centuries by the conjunction of three developments: the socioeconomic position of the middle ranks of Scottish society and their rising ambitions for betterment, their interest in education and the new initiatives it produced in terms of a more practical curriculum, and the increasing demand for relatively well-educated men to fill new diplomatic and administrative positions in India. Most of the many youthful Scotsmen who went to India as company writers or cadets at this time came from middle-ranking but poor families. They lacked the "interest" necessary to obtain the remunerative and relatively high-status appointments that were increasingly available in Britain, but they generally knew at least one person in Scotland who could provide access to similarly increasing but lower-status Indian appointments. The relative poverty of Scotland's more privileged classes, which sent a high proportion of men from well-educated gentry and professional families to India, their perception of education and the acquisition of knowledge as worthwhile exercises in career self-interest, and the number of Scotsmen who made their names in positions requiring technical skills, an above-basic knowledge of mathematics, or an ability to analyze and present information indicate a significant connection between the benefits of a Scottish education and the number of Scotsmen, including Thomas Munro, John Malcolm, and Mountstuart Elphinstone, who rose to prominence in the East India Company's military and civil services at this time.

The fact that they were countrymen helped bring Munro, Malcolm, and Elphinstone together during the earlier stages of their careers. Scotland was a small country with a small population and among the middle and upper ranks of society everyone knew or knew of everyone else. Munro and Malcolm's sisters had met in Scotland before their brothers' paths crossed in India, and the Malcolm and Elphinstone families were acquainted before the two men went to India. When Munro and Malcolm met in the Baramahal in 1796 and Malcolm and Elphinstone met at Pune in 1803 they had acquaintances as well as interests in common to discuss. Malcolm provided the initial link between the three men. He corresponded regularly with the other two, visited them when his peripatetic career brought him within reach, and praised their abilities to influential men in the company and government. Munro and Elphinstone met only twice, in May 1818 and May 1820, and their relationship was sustained almost entirely by correspondence on matters of policy. However, after the mainly social visit of Munro and his wife to Elphinstone in Bombay in 1820, the letters become less formal and occasionally refer to personal matters. Until the Third Maratha War, Malcolm was the most prominent of the three men and may have seen himself in some respects as Munro and Elphinstone's patron. But in the 1820s, when the three men became presidency governors and Indian government focused on efficient administration, not foreign relations, Munro emerged as the leading member of the group. Although Eric Stokes sees their ideas on government as the dominant school of thought prior to 1818, the decade between 1814 and 1824 is probably the period in which their views had the most influence, and it is from 1817, when Malcolm and Elphinstone joined Munro as administrators, that the three men are clearly identifiable as a leadership cadre.

Munro, Malcolm, and Elphinstone are rarely seen as military and civil bureaucrats; more often they are regarded as the archetypes of what B. B. Misra calls rule by "executive interposition," the antithesis of bureaucratic system, described by Munro as "acting without interference, and authorized to pursue whatever measures I thought best for the settlement of the country."[1] They all certainly found the periods in which they enjoyed a relatively unrestricted freedom to introduce their own policies to be the most satisfying episodes in their careers. Yet the bureaucratic technique of acquiring the specialized knowledge necessary for a particular type of appointment served Munro and Malcolm better than the more conventional paths to high office—seniority and patronage—and even Elphinstone found it useful. Lord Wellesley's policies as governor-general allowed, indeed required men who had acquired some local expertise to obtain challenging, powerful, and prestigious positions. No amount of Indian knowledge would have aided their careers if they had failed to produce practical results. In early nineteenth-century India, however, when civil administrators and diplomats worked for long periods of time with Indian cultivators or Indian rulers, in isolation from British centers of power and decision making, the ability to understand and speak Indian languages, to obtain intelligence from Indian informants, to interpret Indian culture, and to communicate information and recommendations in articulate reports were useful tools which could play a major role in determining whether or not an official achieved high office.

Many British officials wrote letters and reports presenting their own activities in the most favorable light while communicating information, opinions, and recommendations to the Supreme and Home governments. Many published books, pamphlets, and journal articles to defend their actions, canvass support for cherished policies, or merely to make their names known to the general public. But of all the early nineteenth-century writer-officials whose careers were spent entirely in India, none used the written word to better effect in building their careers and promoting their thought on government than Munro, Malcolm, and Elphinstone. Their writings are extensive, and when examined in the context of the Scottish culture in which they were raised, they establish the ideological foundations of a "Scottish school of thought" on Indian governance. The "bridge" between Scotland and India, constructed initially from career-building techniques defined by financial and status objectives, educational skills, and employment opportunities, was reinforced when these men turned to the cultural "luggage" they had brought with them—theories about man and society that were popular in Scotland when they were growing up—to help them analyze and prescribe solutions for the problems of governing India.

Like many of Scotland's most influential thinkers, Munro, Malcolm, and Elphinstone saw systems of government as the most important determinants of national character and, therefore, as the arbiters of political, economic, and social progress. In political terms, the main inhibitors of progress for them, as they had been for William Robertson in his analysis of the progress of Europe, were the quasi-feudal local lords—Munro's "poligar chiefs" or Malcolm's "Rob Roys"—with their armed retainers, destabilizing feuds, and repressive agricultural vassalage. In terms of modes of production the inhibitors of progress were traditional land tenure practices. Communal landholding in India, as in Scotland, provided no incentive for individual cultivators to improve production and, therefore, their own and the state's prosperity. Large landholdings cultivated by numerous tenant farmers with insecure tenure of the land they worked similarly lacked the necessary incentives for progress. The "Scottish school of thought"—or the Munro system as it was endorsed by Malcolm and Elphinstone—should be seen primarily as a clearly articulated system of political economy on lines specified by Adam Smith, David Hume, and other Scottish writers. It was meant to provide "a plentiful revenue or subsistence for the people, or more properly to enable them to provide such a revenue or subsistence for themselves; and . . . to supply the state or common-wealth with a revenue sufficient for the public services." Everyone, hopefully, would "enjoy the fruits of his own labour," because this would increase the wealth of numerous individuals and, through them, the wealth of the state.[2] These objectives, however, required an efficient military organization to support the authority of the state and ensure its security and political stability; they required land tenure and revenue collection systems that encouraged rather than inhibited progress; they required the creation of economically and politically active "middling" social groups to function as the agents of improvement; and they required, as a counterpoise to the inevitably authoritarian nature of imperial rule, liberty for Indians to participate in the administration, if not the legislation, of their own country—particularly the administration of justice. Progress, Munro, Malcolm, and Elphinstone believed, would come from within Indian society as a result of the provision of security, economic prosperity, personal economic and social opportunity, and the regeneration of the institutions with which Indians were familiar.

Munro, Malcolm, and Elphinstone were both "conservative" and "orientalist" in the sense that they saw Indian institutions as viable and resisted the introduction of government systems and laws that they believed were relevant to the stage of development Britain, but not India, had reached. But the school of thought that they developed envisioned greater social and political change than either Warren Hastings or Burke would have favored and was more progressive in intent than any neoabsolutist, sultanist, militarist, or Jacobite "model" was likely to be. While Burke and the Scottish philosophes were all, in philosophical terms, late eighteenth-century Whig thinkers, Burke's writings helped define the form taken by mid–nineteenth century conservatism, while Adam Smith's work had an equally profound influence on the development of nineteenth-century liberalism. And the intellectual divergence implicit in these two legacies is crucial to an understanding of the "Scottish school of thought."

The progressive policies of one generation of rulers, however, often appear conservative to the next, and it was easy for the many Anglicist reformers who followed Munro, Malcolm, and Elphinstone to India to present the ideas of the three men in an overly conservative light. It is also easy to fail to recognize principles as such when they differ from one's own. To the following generation of administrators, the three Scotsmen's sympathy for Indian usages and manners, their belief in the viability of many of India's traditional institutions, their insistence that administrative systems must be comprehensible and relevant to Indians, and their conviction that Indian progress must and would be achieved through the efforts of Indians themselves did not appear to be based on valid principles. These men believed, with increasing conviction, that Britain's supposedly superior forms of government and religion, and the morality, enterprise, industry, and knowledge of its people gave it a divine mandate to bring about the improvement of others in its own image. "Inferior" religions could not be left to reform themselves; they required the dedicated labors of British missionaries. Nor could the British be seen to administer a despotic form of government—it had to be renamed "paternalism."

And the relationship between wealth and virtue was no longer debated: the wealth—and power—of empire was the natural reward for the virtue, which included the enterprise, of a British "chosen people." When, in the aftermath of the Great Mutiny Rebellion of 1857–58, the Anglo-Indian Conservatives enjoyed a resurgence of influence, they appropriated Munro, Malcolm, and Elphinstone's school of thought, pruned of its more progressive and principled elements, and passed it on to posterity as Conservative, Orientalist, and pragmatic. This was a portrayal—and betrayal—that had a lasting impact not only on the way the history of the Indian empire has been written but also, because the three men were presented as role models, on the way the Indian empire was actually governed. Several generations of teleologically minded historians, who treated the adjectives "conservative," "paternalist," "humanitarian," and "utilitarian" as though they had been captured by the great intellectual movements of the nineteenth century and transformed into capitalized nouns with highly specific meanings, perpetuated a misleading representation of Munro, Malcolm, and Elphinstone's school of thought. Its conservatism was progressive in intent. Its paternalism was mentorist rather than proscriptive. Its humanitarianism derived from ideas about human psychology and empathy, not the patronizing penchant for "good works" of Victorian Evangelical philanthropists. Their so-called pragmatism— their practicality—which rejected out of hand Utilitarian and rationalist "system," was nevertheless subjected, on the principle of common sense, to the touchstones of utility and reason. All this was the legacy, not of Victorian England, but of Enlightenment Scotland.

Abbreviations

Bentinck	*The Correspondence of Lord William Cavendish Bentinck, Governor-General of India, 1828–1835*
IO	India Office Records, British Library
Mss. Eur.	British Library, Oriental and India Office Collections, European Manuscripts
H/	India Office Records, Home Miscellaneous Series
J/	India Office Records, Haileybury Records
MM	*Sir Thomas Munro: Selections from his Minutes and Other Writings*
NLS	National Library of Scotland, Edinburgh
ECN	*Elphinstone Correspondence, 1804–1808*
PRC	*English Records of Maratha History: Poona Residency Correspondence*
Parl. Paps.	*Parliamentary Papers*
Wellesley	*The Despatches, Minutes, and Correspondence of the Marquess Wellesley, K.G., during his Administration in India*
WD	*The Dispatches of Field Marshal the Duke of Wellington during his Various Campaigns from 1799–1818*
WND	*Despatches, Correspondence, and Memoranda of Field Marshal Arthur, Duke of Wellington, K.G.*
WSD	*Supplementary Despatches, Correspondence and Memoranda of Field Marshal Arthur, Duke of Wellington, K.G.*

Notes

Introduction

1. Eric Stokes, *The English Utilitarians and India* (Oxford, 1963), p. 9. Stokes and many other historians include Charles Metcalfe (1785–1846) in this group. Metcalfe, who also enjoyed a distinguished career in India, was a generation younger than Munro but admired and was influenced by Munro's administrative policies. He was acquainted with Malcolm and Elphinstone.

2. A. P. Thornton, "Essay and Reflection: Third Thoughts on Empire," *International History Review* 10 (1988), p. 582. H. T. Dickinson, *Liberty and Property: Political Ideology in Eighteenth-Century Britain* (London, 1977), pp. 2–4.

3. Cumming, a clerk at the board of control who became a valued ally of Munro, acquired an extensive and influential expertise on Indian revenue and judicial affairs. M'Culloch attracted the directors' attention with an impressive series of articles on trade in the *Morning Chronicle*, and was appointed from outside India House to a senior position in the London secretariat in 1809. Mill was hired to fill an important office two years after the publication of his *History of British India* in 1817 had brought him to the attention of the directors.

4. According to Dugald Stewart, professor of moral philosophy at Edinburgh University from 1785 to 1810, moral philosophy was concerned with any subjects which, when described in works of history, could be attributed to human causes. They included what would now be called sociology and anthropology, psychology, and political science as well as religion, law, and history. Dugald Stewart cited in L. Schneider, *The Scottish Moralists on Human Nature and Society* (Chicago, 1967), p. xiv.

5. Colin Kidd, "The Ideological Significance of Robertson's *History of Scotland*," in *William Robertson and the Expansion of Empire*, ed. Stewart J. Brown (Cambridge, 1997), p. 122. David Allan, "'This Inquisitive Age': Past and Present in the Scottish Enlightenment," *Scottish Historical Review* 76. 1, no. 201 (April 1997), p. 85. Callender quoted in John D. Brims, "The Scottish 'Jacobins', Scottish Nationalism and the British Union," in *Scotland and England, 1286–1815*, ed. Roger A. Mason (Edinburgh, 1987), p. 253. In *The Eclipse of Scottish Culture: Inferiorism and the Intellectuals* (Edinburgh: Polygon, 1989), Craig Beveridge and Donald Turnbull provide an interesting examination of the cultural effects of the Union on Scotland, using the concept of "inferiorisation" that Frantz Fanon applied to his study of colonized peoples in *The Wretched of the Earth* (1967).

6. See C. A. Bayly, *Indian Society and the Making of the British Empire, The New Cambridge History of India*, part 2, vol. 1 (Cambridge, 1988); Frank Perlin, "State Formation Reconsidered," *Modern Asian Studies* 19 (1985), pp. 415–80; Burton Stein, "State Formation and Economy Reconsidered," *Modern Asian Studies* 19 (1985), pp. 387–413; D. A. Washbrooke, "Progress and Problems: South Asian Economic and Social History c. 1720–1860," *Modern Asian Studies* 22 (1988), pp. 57–96.

7. P. J. Marshall, *Bengal: The British Bridgehead, Eastern India 1740–1828, The New Cambridge History of India,* part 2, vol. 2 (Cambridge, 1987), p. 77. Marshall's meticulous scholarship has added much to our understanding of the East India Company's activities during the eighteenth and early nineteenth centuries.

8. See John Cannon, *The Aristocratic Century: The Peerage of Eighteenth Century England* (Cambridge, 1984); Linda Colley, "Whose Nation? Class and National Consciousness in Britain, 1750–1830," *Past and Present* 113 (1986), pp. 97–117; W. D. Rubenstein, "The End of 'Old Corruption' in Britain, 1780–1860," *Past and Present* 101 (1983), pp. 55–86; Lawrence Stone and Jeanne C. Fawtier Stone, *An Open Elite? England 1540–1880* (Oxford, 1984).

9. John Brewer, *The Sinews of Power: War, Money and the English State, 1688–1783* (Cambridge, Mass., 1990).

10. Linda Colley, *Britons: Forging the Nation, 1707–1837* (New Haven and London, 1992), pp. 120–32.

11. Ibid., p. 127.

12. For the sake of convenience, only the senior titles of the governors-general will be used in this work. Lord Mornington became Marquis Wellesley on 2 December 1799. Lord Minto became the earl of Minto on 24 February 1813. Lord Moira became the marquis of Hastings on 13 February 1817.

13. Edward Ingram, *Britain's Persian Connection, 1798–1828: Prelude to the Great Game in Asia* (Oxford, 1992).

14. Vincent Harlow, "The New Imperial System, 1783–1815," in *The Cambridge History of the British Empire, 1783–1870,* vol. 2, *The Growth of the New Empire,* ed. J. Holland Rose, A. P. Newton, and E. A. Benians (Cambridge, 1940). Vincent Harlow, *The Founding of the Second British Empire, 1763–1793* (London, 1952).

15. C. A. Bayly, *Imperial Meridian: The British Empire and the World, 1780–1830* (London, 1989). Douglas M. Peers, *Between Mars and Mammon: Colonial Armies and the Garrison State in India, 1819–1835* (London, 1995). Stein, "State Formation." Colley, *Britons,* pp. 131–32. C. A. Bayly, in "The First Age of Global Imperialism, c. 1760–1830," *Journal of Imperial and Commonwealth History* 26 (1992), pp. 28–47, also emphasizes militarism. He claims that the "predominant, though not the only, motive force" behind the East India Company's territorial expansion in India between 1760 and 1856 "was the need to finance its army," p. 33.

16. John M. MacKenzie, "Essay and Reflection: On Scotland and the Empire," *International History Review* 15 (1993), pp. 661–80.

Chapter 1. Scottish Families, 1760s–1790s

Note to epigraph: Munro to his mother, Jan. 1796, Mss. Eur., F/151/142.

1. N. T. Phillipson and R. Mitchison, eds., *Scotland in the Age of Improvement: Essays in Scottish History in the Eighteenth Century* (Edinburgh, 1970), p. 4.

2. Munro to his mother, Aug. 1783, Mss. Eur., F/151/140. Elphinstone, journal entry, 10 May 1820 quoted in Sir T. E. Colebrooke, *Life of the Honourable Mountstuart Elphinstone,* 2 vols. (London, 1884), 2:110.

3. T. M. Devine, "Glasgow Colonial Merchants and Land, 1770–1815," in *Land and Industry: The Landed Estate and the Industrial Revolution,* ed. J. T. Ward and R. G. Wilson (New York, 1971). Alexander Munro worked as a teller at the Glasgow Arms Bank; see T. M Devine, *The Tobacco Lords: A Study of*

the Tobacco Merchants of Glasgow and their Trading Activities, c. 1740–90 (Edinburgh, 1975), p. 182. The bank had been founded in 1750 by a group of tobacco merchants: C. R. Fay, *Adam Smith and the Scotland of His Day* (Cambridge, 1956), p. 61.

4. Lord Clive to Henry Strachey, 19 Oct. 1799, Mss. Eur., F/128/6.

5. John Gibson Lockhart, *Memoirs of the Life of Sir Walter Scott, Bart . . .* (Edinburgh, 1845), 3:17–18 n. Malcolm to Scott, July 1822, NLS, Ms. 3895.

6. Sir William Fraser, *The Elphinstone Family Book of the Lords Elphinstone, Balmerino and Coupar,* 2 vols. (Edinburgh, 1897), 2:41; Bruce Lenman, *Integration, Enlightenment, and Industrialization: Scotland 1746–1832* (Toronto, 1981), p. 81. John Johnstone had retired to Scotland in the 1760s with a fortune of £300,000 made in India. He bought three estates and established a parliamentary interest. Thomas Somerville, *My Own Life and Times, 1741–1814* (Edinburgh, 1861), pp. 97–98, 261. John Rae, *Life of Adam Smith* (1895; with an introduction by Jacob Viner, New York, 1965), p. 255. In 1772, Pulteney recommended Adam Smith, Adam Ferguson, and Andrew Stuart to the court of directors of the East India Company as possible members of a proposed Special Commission of Supervision. Ibid., pp. 253–54.

7. Cannon, *Aristocratic Century*, p. 28.

8. Lord Ellenborough, journal entry, n.d., quoted in Colebrooke, *Elphinstone*, 2:276.

9. Fraser, *Elphinstone Family Book*, 1:309. George Keith Elphinstone (1746–1823) entered navy, 1761; served in American Revolutionary War, 1781; Prince William Henry was placed under Elphinstone's care, 1780–90; MP for Dumbarton, 1796–1801; MP for Stirlingshire; returned to navy 1793 as captain; rear admiral, 1794; commander in chief of expedition against the Dutch at the Cape of Good Hope, 1795; vice admiral, 1797; made Baron Keith, 1801; admiral; May 1803 appointed commander in chief, North Sea fleet; Feb. 1812, appointed commander in chief, Channel fleet; May 1814, viscount. See Keith, George Elphinstone, Viscount, Navy Records Society: *The Keith Papers: Selected from the Letters and Papers of Admiral the Viscount Keith,* ed. H. G. Perrin and C. Lloyd, 3 vols. (London: 1927–55). William Fullerton Elphinstone became a director of the East India Company in 1786 and served as chairman in 1804, 1806, and 1814; see C. H. Philips, *The East India Company, 1784–1834* (1941; reprint, Manchester: Manchester University Press, 1961), pp. 7, 338.

10. Ronald M. Sunter, *Patronage and Politics in Scotland, 1707–1832* (Edinburgh, 1986), chaps. 3 and 6. Writers Petitions, 1775–1806, IO, J/1/9–J/1/21. See also G. J. Bryant, "Scots in India in the Eighteenth Century," *Scottish Historical Review* 64 (April 1985), pp. 22, 26–27.

11. Fraser, *Elphinstone Family Book*, 2:28–29.

12. Donald J. Withrington, "Education and Society in the Eighteenth Century", in *Age of Improvement*, ed. Phillipson and Mitchison, pp. 172–73.

13. W. M. Mathew, "The Origins and Occupations of Glasgow Students, 1740–1839," in *Past and Present* 33 (1966), p. 82. Mathew compares the occupations of the fathers of Cambridge and Glasgow University students from the 1750s to 1840. More than 66 percent of the Cambridge fathers were from the nobility or gentry or had church careers, compared to under 23 percent of the Glasgow fathers. In contrast, more than 61 percent of Glasgow fathers were employed in industry, business, or as tenant farmers, as compared to only 7 percent of Cambridge fathers. Adam Smith, *An Inquiry into the Nature and Causes of the Wealth of Nations,* 2 vols. (Glasgow ed., Oxford, 1976). Munro to Kirkman Finlay, 15 Aug. 1825, quoted in Gleig, *Munro*, 3:427–28.

14. Munro to his sister Erskine, 15 Sept. 1795, quoted in Gleig, *Munro*, 1:170. Munro to his father, 30 March 1780, quoted in ibid., 3:7, 8–9.

15. Munro to his father, 6 Jan. 1785, Mss. Eur., F/151/140. Munro to his mother, 21 Feb. 1782, Mss. Eur., F/151/140. Malcolm to his mother, 1792, quoted in Sir John William Kaye, *The Life and Correspondence of Major-General Sir John Malcolm, G.C.B., Late Envoy to Persia, and Governor of Bombay; from Unpublished Letters and Journals,* 2 vols. (London, 1856), 1:42.

16. Gillian Sutherland, "Education," in *Cambridge Social History of Britain, 1750–1950,* vol. 3, *Social Agencies and Institutions,* ed. F. M. L. Thompson (Cambridge, 1990), pp. 137–38.

17. Jane Rendall, "Scottish Orientalism: From Robertson to James Mill," *Historical Journal* 25 (1982), p. 45. In December 1803, Elphinstone refers to a meeting with a Mr. McLean "who remembered me at college [in Edinburgh]," Colebrooke, *Elphinstone,* 1:102. Elphinstone to his mother, n.d., quoted in ibid, 1:9.

18. Bryant, "Scots in India," p. 22. Cannon, *Aristocratic Century,* p. 34.

19. Burton Stein, *Thomas Munro: The Origins of the Colonial State and His Vision of Empire* (Delhi, 1989), pp. 6–23.

20. Twelve was a more normal age for entry into the navy. The India Act of 1784 made fifteen the minimum and eighteen the maximum age for entry into the company's service. The maximum was raised to twenty-two in 1793.

21. Gerald Bryant, "Officers of the East India Company's Army in the Days of Clive and Hastings," *Journal of Imperial and Commonwealth History* 6 (May 1978), pp. 203–25. Edward Ingram, *In Defence of British India: Great Britain in the Middle East, 1775–1842* (London, 1984), chap. 3, "The Role of the Indian Army at the End of the Eighteenth Century." These two works present interesting accounts of the way in which the company army was organized and the many problems which company, rather than Crown, officers faced. Munro to his father, 29 July 1783, quoted in Gleig, *Munro,* 3:45.

22. Elphinstone, journal, 30 May 1813, Mss. Eur., F/88, Box 3A5.

Chapter 2. India, 1780–1801

Note to epigraph: Sir John Kaye, *Lives of Indian Officers,* 2 vols. (London, 1867), 1:xii.

1. Raymond Callahan, *The East India Company and Army Reform, 1783–1798* (Cambridge, Mass., 1972), p. xi.

2. Michael Fisher, "Indirect Rule in the British Empire: The Foundations of the Residency System in India (1764–1858)," *Modern Asian Studies* 18 (1984), p. 414.

3. Munro to his mother, 1780, quoted in Gleig, *Munro,* 3:9. Munro to his father, 23 Jan. 1784, Mss. Eur., F/151/140.

4. Bernard Cohn, "The Command of Language and the Language of Command," in *Subaltern Studies IV: Writings on South Asian History and Society,* ed. Ranajit Guha (Delhi, 1985), p. 301.

5. Munro to his mother, 21 Aug. 1783, Mss. Eur., F/151/140; Munro to his father, 6 Jan. 1785, Mss. Eur., F/151/140; Munro to his father, 23 Jan. 1784, Mss. Eur., F/151/140. Bernard Cohn, "The Command of Language," traces the development of Hindustani, through a process of dialogue between Indians (both Hindus and Muslims) and British in the late eighteenth and nineteenth centuries, into the British "language of command" in India.

6. Cornwallis to the court of directors, 5 April 1792, quoted in *Correspondence of Charles, First Marquis Cornwallis,* 3 vols., ed. Charles Ross (2nd ed., London, 1859), 2:539.

7. T. H. Beaglehole, *Thomas Munro and the Development of Administrative Policy in Madras, 1792–1818: Origins of "The Munro System"* (Cambridge, 1966). Eugene F. Irschick, *Dialogue and History: Constructing South India, 1795–1895* (Berkeley, 1994), p. 6.

8. Beaglehole, *Thomas Munro*, p. 10.

9. For Munro's account of how Read and Munro obtained their appointments, and for Munro's high opinion of Read's character and ability, see Munro to his father, 14 April 1793, quoted in Gleig, *Munro*, 1:145–48. See Stein, *Munro*, pp. 39–49, for a discussion of the historiography on Munro and Read in the Baramahal. For recent scholarship on the issue of "dialogic encounters" between colonial officials and Indians, see C. A. Bayly, *Empire and Information: Intelligence Gathering and Social Communication in India, 1780–1870* (Cambridge, 1996); Irschick, *Dialogue and History*; Lynn Zastoupil, "India, J. S. Mill, and 'Western' Culture," in *J. S. Mill's Encounter with India*, ed. Martin I. Moir, Douglas M. Peers, and Lynn Zastoupil (Toronto, 1999). Munro's administrative methods are examined in some detail in chap. 11, below.

10. Irschick, *Dialogue and History*, pp. 195–96.

11. Munro to his father, 14 April 1793, quoted in Gleig, *Munro*, 1:147; Dykes, quoted in Beaglehole, *Munro*, p. 20 and in Stein, *Munro*, p. 40. Munro quoted in ibid., p. 53.

12. Munro to his mother, 21 Feb. 1782, Mss. Eur., F/151/140.

13. R. H. Phillimore, *Historical Records of the Survey of India*, 3 vols. (Dehra Dun, 1950), p. 1. Bryant, "Scots in India," p. 23. David Kopf, *British Orientalism and the Bengal Renaissance: The Dynamics of Indian Modernization, 1773–1835* (Berkeley and Los Angeles, 1969), p. 95.

14. Revenue letter from Fort St. George, 12 Aug. 1814, quoted in Gleig, *Munro*, 3:244.

15. Munro to his father, 23 April 1781, Mss. Eur., F/151/140. On Andrew Stuart, see Rae, *Adam Smith*, pp. 391–92. Erskine Munro to Thomas, 1 Nov. 1781, Mss. Eur., F/151/146. Munro to his brother Alexander, n.d., 1811, Mss. Eur., F/151/144.

16. Bayly points out that although the company's political intelligence improved between 1779 and 1785, "its military intelligence remained inadequate," *Empire and Information*, p. 66.

17. Munro to his brother Alexander, 2 May, 6 June and 2 Dec. 1795, Mss. Eur., F/151/142.

18. Munro to his father, 18 April 1796, Mss. Eur., F/151/142. Munro to his sister Erskine, 7 Feb. 1798, Mss. Eur., F/151/142. Malcolm to his sister Mina, 6 Aug. 1796, quoted in Kaye, *Malcolm*, 1:50.

19. Kaye, *Lives of Indian Officers*, 1:194.

20. Malcolm, n.d., quoted in Kaye, *Malcolm*, 1:31–33. Adam Smith, *The Theory of Moral Sentiments*, ed. D. D. Raphael and A. L. Macfie (Glasgow ed., Oxford, 1976), p. 9. Malcolm, quoted in Kaye, *Malcolm*, 1:32.

21. Malcolm to his brother Gilbert, 22 Feb. 1795, quoted in Kaye, *Malcolm*, 1:40. Malcolm to his mother, n.d., written before he left India in 1794, ibid., 1:42.

22. Malcolm to his brother Gilbert, 22 Feb. 1795, quoted in ibid., 1:40. Malcolm to his sister Agnes, 16 Oct. 1797, quoted in ibid., 1:58–59. Thomas Reid, *Thomas Reid's Inquiry and Essays*, ed. Keith Lehrer and Ronald E. Beanblossom (Indianapolis, 1975).

23. Munro to his father, 6 Feb. 1780, quoted in Gleig, *Munro*, 3:3.

24. Elphinstone to his mother, n.d., quoted in Colebrooke, *Elphinstone*, 1:11. Elphinstone to his mother, 22 April 1796, quoted in ibid., 1:13. James Elphinstone to Lady Elphinstone, quoted in Fraser, *Elphinstone Family Book*, 1:311.

25. Elphinstone, journal, n.d., 1812, Mss. Eur., F/88 Box 3A5.

26. Munro to his sister Erskine, 23 Jan. 1789, quoted in Gleig, *Munro*, 1:73–74. Munro to his sister Erskine, n.d., 1780, Mss. Eur., F/151/140. Munro to his father, n.d., 1782, Mss. Eur. F/151/140.

27. Elphinstone, journal entries from 6 March 1801 to 14 Nov. 1801, quoted in Colebrooke, *Elphinstone,* 1:23–40; Elphinstone arrived at Pune early in 1802. Elphinstone to John Adam, Sept. 1803, quoted in ibid., 1:72.

28. Munro to his brother Alexander, 15 July 1796, Mss. Eur., F/151/142.

29. Malcolm to his nephew John Malcolm, 15 Sept. 1828, IO H/734; Malcolm to Duncan Malcolm, 26 Oct. 1828, IO H/734; Malcolm to George Malcolm, n.d., ibid.

30. Elphinstone quoted in Fraser, *Elphinstone Family Book,* 2:30, from a letter in the Elphinstone family charter chest, 1 July 1811. Mountstuart Elphinstone, *An Account of the Kingdom of Caubul,* 2 vols. (1815; reprint, with an introduction by Sir Olaf Caroe, Karachi: Oxford University Press, 1972). Elphinstone to Edward Strachey, 29 Nov. 1816, quoted in Colebrooke, *Elphinstone,* 1:347. Elphinstone to Lord Keith, 3 Oct. 1818, quoted in ibid., 2:49.

31. Bayly, *Empire and Information,* p. 10.

32. John Malcolm, *The Political History of India, 1784–1823,* 2 vols. (1826; reprint, edited and introduced by K. N. Pannikar, New Delhi: Associated Publishing House, 1970), 1:xxvii.

33. Elphinstone, journal, 6 April 1801, quoted in Colebrooke, *Elphinstone,* 1:26.

Chapter 3. India, 1798–1812

Note to epigraph: Malcolm, *Political History,* 2:378.

1. Colley, *Britons,* p. 128.

2. Kopf, *British Orientalism,* p. 19 and note; P. J. Marshall, ed. *The British Discovery of Hinduism in the Eighteenth Century* (Cambridge, 1970), p. 2; B. B. Misra, *The Bureaucracy in India* (Delhi, 1977), pp. 60, 68–69; Ainslie Embree, *Charles Grant and British Rule in India* (London, 1962), p. 178; Kopf, *British Orientalism,* p. 18 n.

3. On Wellesley's ambitions see Edward Ingram, *Commitment to Empire: Prophecies of the Great Game in Asia, 1797–1800* (Oxford, 1981), pp. 115–24; Elizabeth Longford, *Wellington: The Years of the Sword* (London, 1971), pp. 64–75, 81–82.

4. Arthur Wellesley, who had been in India since February 1797, and the adjutant general at Bengal explained this to Lord Wellesley. Ingram, *Commitment to Empire,* p. 135.

5. See "Statutes of the College of Fort William, Bengal," in Wellesley, Richard Colley, Marquis, *The Despatches, Minutes, and Correspondence of the Marquess Wellesley, K.G., during his Administration in India.* 5 vols., ed. R. Montgomery Martin (1836–37; reprint, New Delhi: Inter-India Publications, 1984), 2:732–34; "The Governor-General's Notes with respect to the foundation of a College at Fort William," in Wellesley, Richard Colley, Marquis, *A Selection from the Despatches, Treaties, and other Papers of the Marquis Wellesley, K.G. during his Government of India,* ed. Sidney J. Owen, (Oxford, 1877), p. 718; Kopf, *British Orientalism,* p. 46; Misra; *Bureaucracy,* pp. 66–69. Kopf, *British Orientalism,* pp. 96–97. Lord Wellesley, quoted in Cohn, "The Command of Language," p. 306.

6. Munro to his sister Erskine, 7 Feb. 1798, Mss. Eur., F/151/142.

7. Clarke to Malcolm, n.d., quoted in Kaye, *Malcolm,* 1:52 n. Malcolm to Kennaway, 16 Oct. 1797, quoted in ibid., 1:61 n.

8. Wellesley to Malcolm, 20 Sept. 1798, *Wellesley,* 1:264. Wellesley to Dundas, 11 Sept. 1798, in Edward Ingram, ed., *Two Views of British India. The Private Correspondence of Mr. Dundas and Lord Wellesley: 1798–1801* (Bath, 1970), p. 100.

9. Kaye, *Malcolm,* 1:79–82, 36–37, and Longford, *Wellington,* p. 95. Longford describes Malcolm as one of Wellington's closest friends.

10. Bayly, *Indian Society,* pp. 97–98.

11. Wellesley to Montresor, 27 Dec. 1802, Arthur Wellesley, 1st Duke of Wellington, *Supplementary Despatches, Correspondence, and Memoranda of Field Marshal Arthur, Duke of Wellington, K.G.,* (London: 1858–64), 3:499.

12. Malcolm to his sister Mina, 6 Aug. 1796, quoted in Kaye, *Malcolm,* 1:50–51.

13. For the details of the Mysore settlement see A. S. Bennell, "Wellesley's Settlement of Mysore, 1799," *Journal of the Royal Asiatic Society* (1952): 124–32. Munro to his sister Erskine, 30 June 1799, Mss. Eur., F/151/142.

14. Harris to Lord Wellesley, quoted in Kaye, *Malcolm,* 1:86–87. A. Wellesley to H. Wellesley, 9 March 1799, *WSD,* 1:200.

15. Wellesley, quoted in M. E. Yapp, *Strategies of British India: Britain, Iran and Afghanistan, 1798–1850* (Oxford, 1980), p. 29. Wellesley to Elgin, 17 Oct. 1801, *Wellesley,* 2:588.

16. H. Wellesley to Malcolm, 28 March 1801, quoted in Kaye, *Malcolm,* 1:150.

17. Munro to his father, 6 Aug. 1799, Mss. Eur., F/151/142; Malcolm to Munro, 19 Sept. 1799, quoted in Gleig, *Munro,* 1:233–34.

18. Munro to Wellesley, 29 June 1799, *Wellesley,* 2:58–59.

19. Malcolm to Wellesley, 9 Feb. 1803, quoted in Kaye, *Malcolm,* 1:204–5.

20. Government of Fort St. George to the court of directors, Gleig, *Munro,* 2:237.

21. See Wellesley to Dundas, 26 Oct. 1800, Ingram, *Two Views,* p. 310; Josiah Webbe, chief secretary to the Madras government, to Munro, and enclosure, Clive to Webbe, 27 Sept. 1800, and Munro to his brother Alexander, 22 Nov. 1800, quoted in Gleig, *Munro,* 1:308–11; Stein, *Munro,* p. 73.

22. Longford, *Wellington,* p. 124. Wellesley to Munro, 20 Aug. 1800, Mss. Eur., F/151/1. Munro to Read, 6 March 1804, quoted in Gleig, *Munro,* 3:190. Munro was unaware that Read had died at Malta in 1803.

23. Bayly, *Empire and Information,* p. 155.

24. Stein, *Munro,* pp. 89–90, 98. Revenue letter from Fort St. George to court of directors, 21 Oct. 1807, quoted in Gleig, *Munro,* 2:244. See ibid., 2:238–46, appendix 2, for other expressions of the Madras and Home governments' approval of Munro's administration of the Ceded Districts.

25. Dundas to Lady Elphinstone, Jan. 1798, cited in Colebrooke, *Elphinstone,* 1:20. Elphinstone, journal, 23 Jan. 1801, quoted in ibid., 1:22.

26. Charles R. Sanders, *The Strachey Family, 1588–1932* (New York, 1968), pp. 67–73.

27. Elphinstone, journal, n.d., 1802, cited in Colebrooke, *Elphinstone,* 1:40–42.

28. Ibid., pp. 6–7. See U. N. Chakravorty, *Anglo-Maratha Relations and Malcolm, 1798–1830* (New Delhi, 1979), chap. 1, for an account of inter-Maratha relations. See Enid M. Fuhr, "Strategy and Diplomacy in British India under the Marquis Wellesley: The Second Maratha War, 1802–1805" (Ph.D. dissertation, Simon Fraser University, 1994), and A. S. Bennell, "The Anglo-Maratha Confrontation of June and July 1803," *Journal of the Royal Asiatic Society* (October, 1962), pp. 107–31, for different views on Lord Wellesley's Maratha policies. Collins to Lord Wellesley, 12 June 1803, Arthur Wellesley, 1st Duke of Wellington, *The Dispatches of Field Marshal the Duke of Wellington during His Various Campaigns from 1799–1818,* ed. Lt. Col. John Gurwood (London, 1834–38), 3:172–73; A. Wellesley to Collins, 18 July 1803, ibid., 2:99–100.

29. Elphinstone to Strachey, 9 Oct. 1803, quoted in Colebrooke, *Elphinstone,* 1:77–78.

30. Bayly, *Empire and Information,* p. 68.

31. Elphinstone, journal, n.d., quoted in Colebrooke, *Elphinstone,* 1:115. Wellesley to A. Wellesley, 9 Jan. 1804, *WD,* 2:14. Elphinstone journal, n.d., quoted in Colebrooke, *Elphinstone.* 1:115–16.

32. Major Merrick Shawe to Malcolm, 29 April 1804, quoted in Kaye, *Malcolm,* 1:275.

33. Malcolm to John Pasley, 10 Feb. 1804, quoted in ibid., 1:258. Malcolm to his mother, n.d., quoted in ibid., 1:293 n. Ibid., 1:261.

34. Wellesley to Malcolm, 14 March 1804, *WSD,* 3:166. A. Wellesley to H. Wellesley, 13 May 1804, ibid, 4:383–86.

35. Bayly, *Indian Society,* p. 98.

36. Fuhr, "Strategy and Diplomacy," pp. 232–33.

37. Editor's introduction, Malcolm, *Political History,* 1:xxii; Kaye, *Malcolm,* 1:363. Chakravorty, *Anglo-Maratha Relations,* chap. 4, and Fuhr, "Strategy and Diplomacy," chaps. 5 and 6, provide details of Malcolm's role in the diplomatic and military maneuvering that took place between the company and the Marathas between 1804 and 1806 and the change of company policy under Cornwallis and Barlow.

38. Yapp, *Strategies,* p. 53. Fuhr, "Strategy and Diplomacy," pp. 170, 99. A. Wellesley to Close, 5 Aug. 1803, *WD,* 3:258–59. A. Wellesley to Malcolm, 31 Jan. 1804, *WD,* 3:38. Elphinstone to John Adam, 15 Nov. 1817, quoted in Colebrooke, *Elphinstone,* 2:5.

39. Zastoupil, "India, Mill and 'Western' Culture," pp. 131–34, provides an interesting discussion of Malcolm's views on the value of maintaining at least the ceremonial status of Indian rulers as a prop to the legitimacy of the British regime.

40. Blair, quoted in John Dwyer, "Clio and Ethics: Practical Morality in Enlightened Scotland," *Eighteenth Century* 30 (1989), p. 59. See Hugh Blair, *Sermons* (Edinburgh, 1777), 2: sermon 10 and ibid., 3: sermon 18.

41. Malcolm to Colonel Lake, Jan. 1807, quoted in Kaye, *Malcolm,* 1:378. Malcolm to Elliot, 29 June 1807, quoted in ibid., 1:384–85. Minto to Malcolm, n.d., quoted in ibid., 1:385–86.

42. Malcolm to Minto, 26 July 1807, cited in Yapp, *Strategies,* pp. 49–50; Bentinck to Malcolm, 9 July 1828, acknowledges receipt of Malcolm's "very interesting paper on dramatis personae." Bentinck to Malcolm, 30 Sept. 1828, comments on Malcolm's accuracy. Lord William Cavendish Bentinck, *The Correspondence of Lord William Cavendish Bentinck, Governor-General of India, 1828–1835,* 2 vols., ed. C. H. Philips (Oxford, 1977), 1:47–49, 1:83.

43. Minto to Dundas, n.d., 1808, quoted in Gilbert Elliot, Earl of Minto, *Lord Minto in India: Life and Letters of Gilbert Elliot, First Earl of Minto from 1807–1814,* ed. Countess of Minto (London, 1880), p. 108; Minto to Hewett, 30 July 1808, ibid., pp. 114–15.

44. Memorandum by Malcolm, 20 Oct. 1804, NLS, Ms. 11719. Charlotte Malcolm to Minto, 6 June 1808, NLS, Ms. 11148. Elphinstone to Strachey, 23 April 1808, Mss. Eur., F/128/7.

45. John Malcolm, *Sketch of the Political History of India* (London, 1811); *Observations on the Disturbances in the Madras Army in 1809* (London, 1812); *Sketch of the Sikhs . . .* (1812; reprint, under the title, *Sketch of the Sikhs: Their Origin, Customs and Manners,* Chandigarh: Vinay Publications, 1981). G. Khurana, *British Historiography on the Sikh Power in the Punjab* (London and New York, 1985), pp. 138, 17–31.

46. Malcolm, *The History of Persia from the Most Early Period to the Present Time . . . ,* 2 vols. (London, 1815). See Edward Ingram, "Family and Faction in the Great Game in Asia: The Struggle over the Persian Mission, 1828–1835," *Middle Eastern Studies* 17 (1981), pp. 291–309, for an account of how Malcolm exploited and protected his unofficial but professionally valuable status as Persian expert.

47. Edmonstone to Elphinstone, 15 June 1804, *Elphinstone Correspondence, 1804–1808,* ed. R. M.

Sinha and A. Avasthi (Nagpur, 1961), p. 51. Edmonstone to Elphinstone, 31 Dec. 1804, ibid., pp. 156–59. Elphinstone to Strachey, 13 April 1805, quoted in Colebrooke, *Elphinstone*, 1:128.

48. A. Wellesley to Agnew, 13 Jan. 1805, *WSD*, 4:479–81.

49. Bayly, *Empire and Information*, p. 149.

50. Elphinstone to Strachey, 23 April 1808, Mss. Eur., F/128/165.

51. Court of directors to Supreme government, 5 June 1805, quoted in J. S. Grewal, *Muslim Rule in India: The Assessments of British Historians* (Oxford, 1970), p. 110. Malcolm to Edmonstone, 5 March 1811, NLS, Ms. 11717; Kaye, *Malcolm*, 2:60 n.

52. Elphinstone, journal, 7 Feb. 1812, quoted in Colebrooke, *Elphinstone*, 1:244–45.

53. Elphinstone to his sister Elizabeth, 6 Oct. 1813, Mss. Eur., F/88, Box 3A5.

54. Rendall, "Scottish Orientalism," p. 45. For a discussion of Vans Kennedy's work see Grewal, *Muslim Rule in India*, chap. 6.

55. Mackintosh, journal, 30 Aug. 1811, cited in Kaye, *Malcolm*, 2:62. Elphinstone, journal, 14 March 1812, Mss. Eur., F/88, Box 3A5.

Chapter 4. Britain, 1808–1817

Note to epigraph: Munro to his sister Erskine, 5 Aug. 1807, quoted in Gleig, *Munro*. 1:371.

1. Wellington to Lord Melville, 12 March 1812, quoted in Kaye, *Malcolm*, 2:90 n. Wellington to Malcolm, 118 Aug. 1813, *WSD*, 8:196.

2. Elphinstone, journal, 21 Aug. 1817, quoted in Colebrooke, *Elphinstone*, 1:366–67. Munro to Peter Bruce, 6 Jan. 1809, Mss. Eur., F/151/12.

3. The opening lines of Jane Austen's *Pride and Prejudice.* Letters from Munro to different correspondents, Mss. Eur., F/151/144, passim.

4. Munro to his sister Erskine, 5 Aug. 1807, quoted in Gleig, *Munro*, 1:370. Munro to George Brown, 29 Aug. 1805, Mss. Eur., F/151/151. Gleig, *Munro*, 1:297. Munro to his sister Erskine, quoted in Mss. Eur., F/151/144. For the philosophes on marriage see David Hume, quoted in Gladys Bryson, *Man and Society: The Scottish Inquiry of the Eighteenth Century* (Princeton, 1945), p. 181; Francis Hutcheson, cited in ibid., pp. 179, 178; see also William C. Lehmann, *John Millar of Glasgow, 1735–1801: His Life and Thought and His Contributions to Sociological Analysis* (Cambridge, 1960), p. 219.

5. Munro to Wellington, 26 April 1811, *WSD*, 7:113. Munro to his sister Erskine, 27 July 1811, Mss. Eur., F/151/144. Munro to his brother, Alexander, 12 Sept. 1811, Mss.Eur., F/151/144. Spencer Percival headed a Tory administration from 1809 to 1812 and was succeeded by Lord Liverpool, also a Tory, from 1817 to 1827.

6. John Sullivan was nephew to Laurence Sulivan although they spelled their names differently. Philips, *East India Company*, p. 102 n. Ibid., p. 195. Stein, *Munro*, p. 158.

7. Munro, memorandum, Sept. 1808, NLS, Ms. 12. Robert Dundas to Munro, 30 April 1810, Mss. Eur., F/151/152. M'Cullock, to Munro, 16 Jan. 1812, Mss. Eur., F/151/21. Thomas Munro, *Selections from His Minutes and Other Official Writings*, edited and introduced by Sir A. J. Arbuthnot, 2 vols. (London, 1881), 1:92–101; 2:3–6. See Beaglehole, *Munro*, pp. 88–91, on Cumming's interest in Munro's work.

8. *Parl. Paps.* (Commons), 1812–13, vol. 7, passim.

9. Malcolm to Elphinstone, n.d. quoted in Kaye, *Malcolm*, 2:313 n. Grant denied having obstructed Malcolm's advancement. Grant to unnamed correspondent, 14 Oct. 1810, quoted in ibid., 1:449 n.

10. For Munro's views on free trade see Munro to Kirkman Finlay, 15 Aug. 1825 and 10 May

1827, quoted in Gleig, *Munro*, 3:427–29, 434–35. Anonymous, *Opinions ... of ... Mountstuart Elphinstone upon some of the Leading Questions Connected with the Government of British India—Compared to those of Sir Thomas Munro and Sir John Malcolm, as taken from their Evidence before Parliament, ... By the Author of "An Enquiry into the Causes of the Stationary Condition of India,"* Political Tracts no. 3 (London, 1831), p. 3; see also Philips, *East India Company*, pp. 202–3.

11. See chapters 10 and 11 for Munro's views on the administration of justice.

12. See official letters, 1800–1811, Gleig, *Munro*, appendix 2, 2:237–50.

13. Stein, *Munro*, p. 163. The papers written by Munro on Indian matters in 1813 are to be found in Mss. Eur., F/151/125.

14. Beaglehole argues that the Home government, knowing little of the problems of administering a vast foreign territory, endorsed Munro's system for its apparent superiority in unearthing Indian resources, not from a preference for it principles. Beaglehole, *Thomas Munro*, pp. 95, 93.

15. Ibid., p. 91.

16. Munro to Malcolm, 10 June 1818, Gleig, *Munro*, 3:257.

17. Notes, Malcolm for Buckinghamshire, summer 1813, quoted in Kaye, *Malcolm*, 2:77–78. Scott to J. B. S. Morritt, 12 Oct. 1812, Lockhart, *Sir Walter Scott*, 3:17.

18. Malcolm, journal, extracts 24 July to 11 Sept. 1815, provide an account of Malcolm's French visit. Quoted in Kaye, *Malcolm*, 2:100–30. Mackintosh to Malcolm, n.d., quoted in ibid., 2:94. Elphinstone to Captain Close, 8 June 1816, quoted in Colebrooke, *Elphinstone*, 1:317. Kaye, *Malcolm*, 2:137 n.

19. Malcolm quoted in Kaye, *Malcolm*, 2:138.

20. Fraser, *Elphinstone Family Book*. For a short "memoir" of John, Twelfth Lord Elphinstone, see 1:130–36, and for Charles Elphinstone see 1:305–6. Munro to his sister Erskine, 30 June 1799; Webbe to Munro and enclosure, Clive to Webbe, 27 Sept. 1800; Munro to his mother, 20 Aug. 1804; quoted in Gleig, *Munro*, 1:228, 309–10, 355–56. Elphinstone to William Elphinstone, 2 April 1817, quoted in Fraser, *Elphinstone Family Book*, 2:30.

Chapter 5. India, 1812–1819

Note to epigraph: Malcolm, *Political History*, 2:61.

1. Elphinstone to Edmonstone, 26 Oct. 1811, *English Records of Maratha History: Poona Residency Correspondence*, 15 vols., ed. G. S. Sardesai et al. (Bombay, 1936–51), 12:80–110; see p. 86.

2. Edward Strachey, Letterbooks, "On the Governor-General's desire to arbitrate differences between the Peshwa and his Southern Jagirdars." See Mss. Eur., F/128/173 and F/128/161 for the correspondence between Strachey, Lord Wellesley, Close, and Arthur Wellesley. Extract from minute of the governor-general, 3 April 1812, *PRC*, 12:152. Elphinstone to Strachey, 12 July 1813, quoted in Colebrooke, *Elphinstone*, 1:252. Elphinstone to Montresor, 26 Nov. 1812, *PRC*, 12:229–30.

3. P. C. Gupta, *Baji Rao and the East India Company, 1796–1818* (Bombay, 1939), chap. 6. Bayly, *Empire and Information*, p. 89. Elphinstone to Hastings, 16 Aug. 1815, *PRC*, 12:384. Ibid., 12:386.

4. John Adam, government secretary, to Elphinstone, 10 Sept. 1815, *PRC*, 12:426.

5. Elphinstone to Lady Hood, 27 April 1816, quoted in Colebrooke, *Elphinstone*, 1:314.

6. Munro, "Memorandum of the services of Sir T. Munro, written by himself," quoted in John Bradshaw, *Sir Thomas Munro and the British Settlement of Madras Presidency*, Rulers of India Series, general editor W. W. Hunter (Oxford, 1894), appendix, p. 220. Munro to Cumming, 1 March 1815, quoted in Gleig, *Munro*, 1:426–27.

7. Biswanath Ghosh, *British Policy Towards the Pathans and the Pindaris in Central India, 1805–1818* (Calcutta, 1966), p. 324. Dirk H. A. Kolff, "The End of an Ancien Régime: Colonial War in India, 1798–1818," in *Imperialism and War: Essays on Colonial Wars in Asia and Africa*, ed. J. A. de Moor and H. C. Wesseling (Leiden, 1989), pp. 23–24.

8. Ghosh, *Central India*, p. 321.

9. Elphinstone, cited in Colebrooke, *Elphinstone*, 1:306–7. Munro to his brother Alexander, 6 April 1818, quoted in Gleig, *Munro*, 3:242.

10. Malcolm to unnamed correspondent, May 1817, quoted in Kaye, *Malcolm*, 2:154. Gleig, *Munro*, 1:455, 458.

11. Malcolm to John Adam, 6 July 1817, quoted in Kaye, *Malcolm*, 2:158–59. Munro to Hastings, 12 Aug. 1817, quoted in Gleig, *Munro*, 1:461; Malcolm, *Political History*, 2:274–330.

12. Elphinstone, journal, 16 June 1817, quoted in Colebrooke, *Elphinstone*, 1:361. Elphinstone, journal, 31 July, 8 Aug. 1817, quoted in ibid., 1:364–65.

13. Malcolm to William Elphinstone, 6 Aug. 1817, quoted in Kaye, *Malcolm*, 2:167–68. Elphinstone, journal, 9 Aug. 1817, quoted in Colebrooke, *Elphinstone*, 1:365.

14. Bayly, *Empire and Information*, p. 69.

15. Elphinstone, journal, 12 Aug. 1817, quoted in Colebrooke, *Elphinstone*, 1:365. Elphinstone to Smith, 5 Oct. 1817, quoted in ibid., 1:372.

16. Munro to Elphinstone, 5 Feb. 1818, quoted in Gleig, *Munro*, 3:234.

17. Malcolm to John Adam, 17 Feb. 1818, quoted in ibid., 1:503.

18. See Stein, *Munro*, chap. 6, pp. 218–45 for a detailed account of Munro's role in the Third Maratha War. Grant, quoted in Kenneth Ballhatchet, *Social Policy and Social Change in Western India, 1817–1830* (London, 1957), p. 15.

19. Dunlop to Munro, 29 Dec. 1810, Mss. Eur., F/151/152. Munro to his father, on the Third Mysore War, January 1790 to July 1791, quoted in Gleig, *Munro*, 1:79–125, passim; Munro to his father, on general strategic and military matters, 30 Sept. 1796 to 10 Feb. 1799, ibid., 3:102–10, passim; correspondence between Arthur Wellesley and Munro on the Fourth Mysore War and the Second Maratha War, 17 Sept. 1799 to 24 May 1804, ibid., 3:123–97, passim; correspondence on the First Burma War, mainly between Munro and Lord Amherst, 18 Sept. 1824 to 17 May 1826, ibid., 2:90–177; Sixteen official minutes by Munro on the First Burma War, 18 June 1824 to 28 Feb. 1826, *MM*, 2:169–202.

20. Munro to Wellesley, 14 Oct. 1803, quoted in Gleig, *Munro*, 3:177–79. Wellesley to Munro, 1 Nov. 1803, *WSD*, 3:210–13. Munro to Wellesley, 28 Nov. 1803, quoted in Gleig, *Munro*, 3:182–84.

21. Wellington to Wynn, 24 March 1825, Wellington, Arthur Wellesley, 1st Duke of, *Despatches, Correspondence, and Memoranda of Field Marshal Arthur, Duke of Wellington, K.G.*, edited by the 2nd Duke of Wellington (1868; reprint, New York: Kraus, 1973), 2:429–30. The minute referred to is no. 3, 24 Aug. 1824, in *MM*, 2:174–75.

22. Munro had outlined his strategy in a letter to the governor-general prior to the campaign, hoping it would help him obtain a military command. Hastings, however, had already dispatched his commission as brigadier general. See Munro to Hastings, 28 Nov. 1817, quoted in Gleig, *Munro*, 1:473.

23. Malcolm to Adam, 17 Feb. 1818, quoted in ibid., 1:503. Elphinstone to Captain Close, 16 April 1818, quoted in Colebrooke, *Elphinstone*, 2:42.

24. Munro to George Canning, 1 May 1823, quoted in Gleig, *Munro*, 2:67.

25. Elphinstone, journal, 10 Feb. 1818, quoted in Colebrooke, *Elphinstone*, 2:27.

26. Malcolm's official report to the adjutant general of the army, 22 Dec. 1817, is printed in Kaye, *Malcolm*, 2:212–15. Munro to Malcolm, 26 Jan. 1818, quoted in Gleig, *Munro*, 3:307.

27. See "Memorandum of the Proceedings of Brigadier Sir John Malcolm from 16th January till the 29th of June 1818 including those connected with the submission of the Peshwa Badjirow", n.d., Mss. Eur., F/151/62. Malcolm to chief secretary of government, n.d., quoted in Kaye, *Malcolm*, 2:240.

28. Malcolm to his wife, n.d., quoted in Kaye, *Malcolm*, 2:250.

29. Munro to his brother Alexander, 30 Sept. 1818, quoted in Gleig, *Munro*, 3:284.

30. Munro to Malcolm, 19 June 1818, quoted in ibid., 3:261–62. Munro to Elphinstone, 28 June 1818, quoted in ibid., 3:263.

31. Munro's problem with his sight was probably due, merely, to a need for a new pair of reading glasses. See Stein, *Munro*, p. 244 n.

32. Elphinstone to Munro, 30 May 1818, Mss. Eur., F/151/29.

33. J. S. Cotton credited Munro with teaching Elphinstone "the duty of investigating thoroughly the indigenous institutions," and Kenneth Ballhatchet, examining the ideas behind the system of government in Bombay, points out that Elphinstone studied Munro's published writings as well as seeking his advice on the day-to-day problems of administration. J. S. Cotton, *Mountstuart Elphinstone and the Making of South-Western India*, Rulers of India Series (Oxford, 1885), p. 128. Ballhatchet, *Western India*, p. 32.

34. Munro to Elphinstone, 8 March 1818, quoted in Gleig, *Munro*, 3:239–40. Munro to Malcolm, 10 June 1818, quoted in ibid., 3:258. Munro to Elphinstone, 25 Jan., 26 April, and 5 May 1818, quoted in ibid., 3:230, 250, 251.

35. Elphinstone journal, June 1818, quoted in Cotton, *Elphinstone*, p. 127.

36. Elphinstone to Munro, 22 June, 30 June, 17 July 1818, Mss. Eur., F/151/29. Elphinstone to Munro, 17 July 1818, Mss. Eur., F/151/63. Munro to Elphinstone, "On the State of the Southern Maratha Country," 28 Aug. 1818, quoted in Gleig, *Munro*, 2:266–81. Munro's private letters to Elphinstone during the period 1817–1819 are in Mss. Eur., F/88, Box 9F26.

37. Mountstuart Elphinstone, *Report on the Peshwa's Territories* (1822; reprint, under the title *Territories Conquered from the Paishwa: A Report*, introduction by J. C. Srivastava, Delhi, 1973), pp. 20, 44, 43.

38. John Malcolm, *A Memoir of Central India, including Malwa and Adjoining Provinces. With the History . . . of the Past and Present Condition of that Country*, 2 vols. (1823; reprint, New Delhi: Sagar Publications, 1970), 1:3–4. Malcolm to Scott, 26 April 1818, NLS, Ms. 3889, no. 210, pp. 256–59.

39. Canning, quoted in Philips, *East India Company*, p. 222.

Chapter 6. 1819–1830

Note to epigraph: Elphinstone to Lord Keith, 3 Oct. 1818, quoted in Colebrooke, *Elphinstone*, 2:48.

1. Elphinstone, journal, 1801, Mss. Eur., F/88, Box 13E16 (i). Elphinstone to his sister Elizabeth, 6 Oct. 1813, Mss. Eur., F/88, Box 3A5. Elphinstone to Lord Keith, 3 Oct. 1818, quoted in Colebrooke, *Elphinstone*, 2:49.

2. Elphinstone to Malcolm, 4 Dec. 1819, quoted in R. D. Choksey, *Mountstuart Elphinstone: The Indian Years, 1796–1827* (Bombay, 1971), p. 274. Elphinstone, journal, 10 Feb. 1822, quoted in ibid., p. 277. Elphinstone, journal, n.d., quoted in ibid., p. 447.

3. Munro to Lady Liston, 12 March 1826, NLS, Ms. 5676. Munro to his sister Erskine, 12

Dec. 1819, quoted in Gleig, *Munro*, 2:8–9. Munro to George Brown, 11 Aug. 1821, Mss. Eur., F/151/174. Accounts of the estates in Britain and India of Sir Thomas Munro at his death, Mss. Eur., F/151/203.

4. Malcolm to Munro, 11 May 1820, Mss. Eur., F/151/62. Malcolm to Wellington, 6 Feb. 1827, Mss. Eur., F/151/62. William Elphinstone to Munro, 10 Sept. 1828, Mss. Eur., F/151/73.

5. Philips, *East India Company*, p. 222.

6. Kaye, *Malcolm*, 2:459. Malcolm to his wife, 1820, quoted in ibid., 2:316 n.

7. Ravenshaw to Munro, 13 July 1820, Mss. Eur., F/151/73. Gleig, *Munro*, 2:4. Stein, *Munro*, pp. 329–30.

8. Elphinstone to Malcolm, n.d., quoted in Colebrooke, *Elphinstone*, 2:105. Stein, *Munro*, p. 248. Munro to Canning, 30 June 1821, 1 May 1823, quoted in Gleig, *Munro*, 2:57–67.

9. Malcolm to his wife, 1820, quoted in Kaye, *Malcolm*, 2:316 n. Malcolm to Captain Tod, 1819, quoted in Kaye, *Lives of Indian Officers*, 1:301.

10. Hastings to Elphinstone, 2 July 1819, quoted in Colebrooke, *Elphinstone*, 2:102–4.

11. Elphinstone to Hastings, n.d., 1819, quoted in ibid., 2:103–4. The letter was written in reply to Hastings's letter of 2 July 1819. Elphinstone, quoted in Ballhatchet, *Western India*, p. 138.

12. Elphinstone to Hastings, n.d., 1819, quoted in Colebrooke, *Elphinstone*, 2:104.

13. Malcolm to John Adam, n.d., 1820, quoted in Kaye, *Malcolm*, 2:320. Malcolm to Hastings, 4 Aug. 1820, Mss. Eur., F/151/62; this file includes many letters from Malcolm to Munro on the subject of the lieutenant governorship. Munro to Canning, 15 May 1820, quoted in Gleig, *Munro*, 2:51. Canning to Malcolm, Nov. 1820, quoted in Kaye, *Malcolm*, 2:327 n. William Elphinstone to Munro, 10 Sept. 1820, Mss. Eur., F/151/73. Ravenshaw to Munro, 13 July 1820, Mss. Eur., F/151/73.

14. Malcolm to Canning, n.d., quoted in Kaye, *Malcolm*, 2:374–75. Wellington to Wynn, 25 Dec. 1825, *WSD*, 2:592.

15. Malcolm to his wife, n.d. 1820, quoted in Kaye, *Malcolm*, 2:316.

16. Zastoupil, "India, Mill, and 'Western' Culture," p. 133.

17. Munro to George Brown, 11 Aug. 1821, Mss. Eur., F/151/174. Malcolm to Munro, n.d., 1819, Mss. Eur., F/151/62. Munro to Malcolm, 15 Oct. 1820, and 15 April 1821, quoted in Gleig, *Munro*, 2:75–76.

18. John Malcolm, *Sketches of Persia: From the Journals of a Traveller in The East*, 2 vols. (London, 1827).

19. James Morier, *The Adventures of Hajji Baba of Isfahan*, 2 vols. (First published 1824; London, 1895). Malcolm, *Sketches of Persia*, 1:xiv. M. E. Yapp, who argues that Malcolm disliked Persia and the Persians, sees the *Sketches* as a caricature of Persia. See *Strategies*, p. 31.

20. Malcolm to Scott, 1825, NLS, Ms. 3901. Munro to Malcolm, 15 June 1826, quoted in Gleig, *Munro*, 2:163.

21. Editor's preface, Malcolm, *Political History*, 1:v. Sir John Shore, *The Private Record of a Governor-Generalship: the Private Correspondence of Sir John Shore, Governor-General, with Henry Dundas, President of the Board of Control, 1793–1798*, ed. Holden Furber (Cambridge, Mass., 1933), p. vii n. Callahan, *East India Company Army*, p. 2.

22. See Douglas M. Peers, "The Duke of Wellington and British India during the Liverpool Administration 1819–27," *Journal of Imperial and Commonwealth History* 17 (1988), pp. 5–25, for an interesting account of conflict between the directorate and the British government and the impor-

tant role played by Wellington in Indian affairs over the selection of the presidency governors at this time. See also Philips, *East India Company*, pp. 251–54.

23. Munro to Malcolm, 15 June 1826, quoted in Gleig, *Munro*, 2:165.

24. Elphinstone to Munro, 27 Aug. 1820, Mss. Eur., F/151/63. Elphinstone to Munro, 27 Oct. 1822, quoted in Colebrooke, *Elphinstone*, 2:142–43. Elphinstone to Munro, n.d., 1820, Mss. Eur., F/151/63.

25. Munro to Elphinstone, 19 April 1823, quoted in Gleig, *Munro*, 3:414. Stein, *Munro*, pp. 326–27.

26. See Gleig, *Munro*, 2:110–43, for a selection of the correspondence between Munro and Lord Amherst on the First Burma War.

27. Liverpool to Wellington, 6 Oct. 1825, Wellington to Liverpool, 10 Oct. 1825, *WND*, 2:514–15. Wynn to Wellington, 27 Oct. 1825, ibid., 2:549–53. Munro to Wellington, 26 April 1826, ibid., 3:308; Munro to Ravenshaw, 18 July 1825, 17 May 1826, quoted in Gleig, *Munro*, 2:175–77. Peers, "Wellington and British India," pp. 10–13.

28. Munro to Ravenshaw, 17 May 1826, quoted in Gleig, *Munro*, 2:176–77.

29. Hill to Mackenzie, 7 Nov. 1827, NLS, Ms. 6370.

30. Elphinstone, journal, 15 Feb. 1830, quoted in Colebrooke, *Elphinstone*, 2:292.

31. John Malcolm, "General Observations on the Administration of the Bombay Presidency," in John Malcolm, *The Government of India* (London, 1833), appendix A, p. 92. Ibid., p. 41.

32. Zastoupil, "India, Mill, and 'Western' Culture," p. 120.

33. Malcolm to John Bax, 23 July 1830, *WSD*, 7:227.

34. For the differences between Elphinstone and West, see Choksey, *Elphinstone*, chap. 22, and F. G. D. Drewitt, *Bombay in the Days of George IV; Memoirs of Sir Edward West, Chief Justice of the King's Court during Its Conflict with the East India Company* (London, 1907).

35. Drewitt, *Bombay in the Days of George IV*, p. 324.

36. Colebrooke, *Elphinstone*, 2:177–95. Malcolm to Bentinck, 6 July 1830, *Bentinck*, 1:467–68. Munro, "On Altamgha Inams," 1 Feb. 1822, *MM*, 1:136–63, see pp. 140–44.

37. Malcolm, *Political History*, 2:173.

38. Kaye, *Lives of Indian Officers*, 1:430. See also Yapp, *Strategies*, p. 53. Choksey, *Elphinstone*, p. 284. Douglas M. Peers, "Between Mars and Mammon: The Military and the Political Economy of British India at the Time of the First Burma War, 1824–1826" (Ph.D. dissertation, London, 1988), p. 139.

39. Ravenshaw to Bentinck, 1 Dec. 1828, 18 Feb. 1829, *Bentinck*, 1:108.

40. Munro to Wellington, 6 Feb. 1827, quoted in Kaye, *Malcolm*, 2:479. Charlotte Malcolm to Wellington, 13 Feb. 1828, *Bentinck*, 1:10. Bentinck to Melville, 12 Jan. 1829, ibid., 1:141.

41. Ellenborough to Lord Bentinck, 15 May 1830, ibid., 1:439; 11 Aug. 1830, 1:495. Ellenborough, journal, n.d. quoted in Colebrooke, *Elphinstone*, 2:276.

42. Fraser, *Elphinstone Family Book*, 1:316. Mountstuart Elphinstone, *The History of India* (London, 1841); *The Rise of British Power in the East*, ed. by Sir Edward Colebrooke (London, 1887).

Chapter 7. Philosophical Historians

Note to epigraph: Hume, *History of Great Britain*, p. 251.

1. C. H. Philips, *Historians of India, Pakistan and Ceylon* (London, 1961), and Grewal, *Muslim Rule in India*, both include chapters on Elphinstone as an historian. Khurana, *British Historiography*, dis-

cusses Malcolm's account of the Sikhs. M. E. Yapp, "Two British Historians of Persia," in *Historians of the Near and Middle East*, ed. B. Lewis and P. M. Holt (Oxford, 1962), assesses Malcolm's Persian history. T. P. Peardon, *The Transition in English Historical Writing, 1760–1830* (New York, 1933), has a paragraph on Malcolm, pp. 263–64, and R. Sencourt, *India in English Literature* (London, 1925), briefly describes both Malcolm's and Elphinstone's works, pp. 411–14.

2. Hume, *History of Great Britain*, p. 251. Hume was referring to Camden's history of Queen Elizabeth, which he regarded with cautious approval. William Robertson, *The Progress of Society in Europe: A Historical Outline from the Subversion of the Roman Empire to the Beginning of the Sixteenth Century*, edited and with an introduction by Felix Gilbert (Chicago, 1972); Robertson, cited in editor's introduction, p. xviii. Robertson, quoted in Karen O'Brien, *Narratives of Enlightenment: Cosmopolitan Histories from Voltaire to Gibbon* (Cambridge, 1997), p. 135. Sir James Mackintosh, *Memoirs of the Life of the Rt. Hon. Sir James Mackintosh*, ed. Robert James Mackintosh (London, 1836), p. 90. Malcolm, *History of Persia*, 1:276. Gibbon, quoted in Adam Smith, *Correspondence of Adam Smith*, ed. E. C. Mossner and I. S. Ross (Oxford, 1977), p. 317. Malcolm, *History of Persia*, 1:xi–xii.

3. Nicholas Phillipson, "Providence and Progress: An Introduction to the Historical Thought of William Robertson," in *William Robertson and the Expansion of Empire*, ed. Stewart J. Brown (Cambridge, 1997), p. 59.

4. Dugald Stewart, quoted in Peardon, *Transition in English Historical Writing*, pp. 13–14.

5. Adam Ferguson, *An Essay on the History of Civil Society* (1767; edited and with an introduction by Duncan Forbes, Edinburgh, 1966). John Millar, "Origin of the Distinction of Ranks," in *John Millar of Glasgow, 1735–1801: His Life and Thought and His Contributions to Sociological Analysis*, ed. William C. Lehmann (Cambridge: Cambridge University Press, 1960), pp. 175–322.

6. Elphinstone to William Erskine, 7 June 1847, quoted in Colebrooke, *Elphinstone*, 2:371. Ferguson, *Civil Society*, p. 71. Malcolm, *History of Persia*, 1:xi.

7. Elphinstone, *India*, 1:564–69.

8. Malcolm, *History of Persia*, 1:231–33, 263.

9. Ibid., 1:209.

10. Elphinstone, *India*, 1:98–99.

11. The information on Hugh Blair and "sensibility" in this paragraph comes from Dwyer, "Clio and Ethics."

12. Smith, *Theory*, part 1, pp. 9–66. Hume, quoted in O'Brien, *Narratives of Enlightenment*, p. 61.

13. Blair, quoted in Dwyer, "Clio and Ethics," p. 59.

14. See Elphinstone, *India*, 1:532–77, for Elphinstone's description and observations on Mahmud's reign.

15. Elphinstone to Malcolm, 11 Sept. 1816, quoted in Colebrooke, *Elphinstone*, 1:323. Malcolm, *History of Persia*, 1:555. Ferguson, *Civil Society*, p. 263.

16. Elphinstone, fragment written in 1833, quoted in Colebrooke, *Elphinstone*, 2:331. Mackintosh, journal, 30 Aug. 1811, quoted in Kaye, *Malcolm*, 2:62 n.

17. Elphinstone to William Erskine, 24 Oct. 1840, quoted in Colebrooke, *Elphinstone*, 2:351. Kaye, *Lives of Indian Officers*, 1:442–43. J. Majeed, "James Mill's 'The History of British India' and Utilitarianism as a Rhetoric of Reform," *Modern Asian Studies* 24 (1990), p. 212.

18. Elphinstone, journal, 5 June 1840, quoted in Colebrooke, *Elphinstone*, 2:355, 353. Elphinstone, quoted in Philips, *Historians*, p. 223. Elphinstone to William Erskine, 22 Aug. 1833, quoted in Colebrooke, *Elphinstone*, 2:341. Elphinstone, journal, 7 June 1840, quoted in ibid., 1:355. See chap. 10 be-

low for a discussion of the differences between Mill's ideological assumptions and those of Munro, Malcolm, and Elphinstone.

19. O'Brien, *Narratives of Enlightenment*, p. 237. Elphinstone, journal, 5 June 1840, quoted in Colebrooke, *Elphinstone*, 2:354.

20. Yapp, "Historians of Persia," p. 346. Forbes introduction, Hume, *History of Great Britain*, pp.10–11. William Creech, *Letters, addressed to Sir John Sinclair, Bart . . .* (1793; reprint, New York: AMS Press, 1982), p. 12. "David Hume received £5000 for the remainder of his History of Britain; and Dr. Robertson, for his second work, received £4500." See also Richard B. Sher, "Charles V and the Book Trade: An Episode in Enlightenment Print Culture," in *William Robertson and the Expansion of Empire*, ed. Stewart J. Brown (Cambridge, 1997).

21. Malcolm, *History of Persia*, 1:276.

Chapter 8. Moral Philosophers

Note to epigraph: Dugald Stewart, *Outlines of Moral Philosophy for the Use of Students in the University of Edinburgh* (Edinburgh and London, 1793, new edition with a Memoir and Supplement, and Questions, by James M'Cosh, London, 1897), p. 2.

1. Bryson, *Man and Society*, pp. 17–18.

2. There is an enormous canon of literature on the place of the Scottish Enlightenment in the history of ideas. See Bryson, *Man and Society*; Charles Camic, *Experience and Enlightenment: Socialization for Cultural Change in Eighteenth Century Scotland* (Chicago, 1983); Forbes, introduction to Ferguson, *Civil Society*; Millar, "Origin of the Distinction of Ranks"; Robert Bierstedt, "Sociological Thought in the Eighteenth Century," in *A History of Sociological Analysis*, ed. Tom Bottomore and Robert Nisbet (New York, 1978), pp. 3–38; S. A. Grave, *The Scottish Philosophers of Common Sense* (Oxford, 1960); David Kettler, *The Social and Political Thought of Adam Ferguson* (Columbus, 1965); J. Ralph Lindgren, *The Social Philosophy of Adam Smith* (The Hague, 1973); Donald G. MacRae, "Adam Ferguson 1723–1816," in *The Founding Fathers of Social Science*, ed. Timothy Raison (Harmondsworth, 1969, revised edition by Paul Barker, London, 1979), pp. 26–35; Schneider, *The Scottish Moralists*; Richard Sher, *Church and University in the Scottish Enlightenment: The Moderate Literati of Edinburgh* (Princeton, 1985); M. A. Stewart, ed., *Studies in the Philosophy of the Scottish Enlightenment* (Oxford, 1990). See also O'Brien, *Narratives of Enlightenment*, which contains an important new interpretation of Hume and Robertson as historians. For Robertson and human agency see O'Brien, in *Narratives of Enlightenment*, p. 135.

3. O'Brien, *Narratives of Enlightenment*, p. 135.

4. Bryson, *Man and Society*, pp. 17–19, 83–84. Robertson, *Progress of Society*, pp. 22, 25.

5. Malcolm, *History of Persia*, 2:620. Malcolm, *Political History*, 2:386. Malcolm, *History of Persia*, 1:413, 194.

6. Munro, "On the Employment of Natives in the Public Service," 31 Dec. 1824, *MM*, 2:319; Munro, memorandum, 1820–1, quoted in Gleig, *Munro*, appendix 5, 2:263.

7. Elphinstone, *Rise of British Power*, p. 31. Malcolm, *Political History*, 1:1. Smith, *Theory*, p. 234.

8. Elphinstone, *Caubul*, 1:284 n, 1:332.

9. David Hume, *Philosophical Works*, 4 vols., ed. T. H. Green and T. H. Grose (1882–86; reprint, Darmstadt, 1964), 3:244–52.

10. Malcolm, *History of Persia*, 1:263. Ibid., 2:621, 623.

11. Munro to his father, 10 May 1796, Mss. Eur., F/151/142.

12. Elphinstone, *India*, 1:370–1, 2:491.

13. Hume, *History of Great Britain*, 1:219. Malcolm, *History of Persia*, 1:263. Blair, quoted in Dwyer,

"Clio and Ethics," p. 59. Munro, "General Remarks on the Judicial Administration and on the Police," 31 Dec. 1824, *MM*, 2:29. James Melvil to Munro, n.d., 1796, Mss. Eur., F/151/152. Bills and Accounts, 12 April 1814, Mss. Eur., F/151/159.

14. Munro to his sister Erskine, 30 Dec. 1815, quoted in Gleig, *Munro*, 3:212.

15. John Malcolm, Review of "An Account of the Rise and Progress of the Bengal Native Infantry" *Quarterly Review* 18 (1818) pp. 423, 415, 386.

16. Stokes, *The English Utilitarians*, p. 23; George D. Bearce, *British Attitudes Towards India, 1784–1858* (London, 1961), p. 306; Stein, *Munro*, p. 96. Thomas R. Metcalf, *Ideologies of the Raj* (Cambridge, 1994).

17. Stokes, *The English Utilitarians*, p. 15. Bearce, *British Attitudes Towards India*, p. 306. Stein, *Munro*, p. 196–97. Ibid., p. 294. Bills and Accounts, 1814, Mss. Eur., F/151/159.

18. Leslie Stephen, *History of English Thought in the Eighteenth Century.* 2 vols. (1881; reprint, New York: Harcourt, Brace and World, 1962), 1:59. Bryson, *Man and Society*, p. 5. Munro to his sister Erskine, 15 Sept. 1795, quoted in Gleig, *Munro*, 1:170.

19. Hume, quoted in Bryson, *Man and Society*, p. 156. The statement appeared in Hume's *Treatise on Human Nature*, which was first published in 1739. Smith, *Theory*, p. 231.

20. Burke to Smith, quoted in the introduction to Smith, *Theory*, p. 28.

21. Hutcheson, quoted in Nicholas Phillipson, "Adam Smith as Civic Moralist," in *Wealth and Virtue: The Shaping of Political Economy in the Scottish Enlightenment*, ed. Istvan Hont and Michael Ignatieff (Cambridge, 1983), p. 179.

22. Munro to Foulis, Dec. 1788, quoted in Gleig, *Munro*, 3:47. Munro to Foulis, 2 April 1790, quoted in ibid., 3:49.

23. Munro to Andrew Ross, 17 Feb. 1792, quoted in ibid., 3:77. Charles Parkin, *The Moral Basis of Burke's Political Thought* (Cambridge, 1956).

24. Munro to his mother, n.d., 1794, Mss. Eur., F/151/142. Munro to George Brown, 1817, Mss. Eur., F/151/174. Munro to Brown, 4 July 1823, quoted in Gleig, *Munro*, 2:83.

25. Malcolm, *Political History*, 1:20–21.

26. Elphinstone, journal, 7 Feb. 1802, quoted in Colebrooke, *Elphinstone*, 1:44.

27. Henry Craik, quoted in Bryson, *Man and Society*, p. 7.

Chapter 9. Religious Moderates

Note to epigraph: Robertson, *Progress of Society*, p. 40.

1. Ian D. L. Clark, "From Protest to Reaction: The Moderate Régime in the Church of Scotland, 1752–1805," in Phillipson and Mitchison, *Age of Improvement*, p. 205. Alexander Fergusson, *The Honourable Henry Erskine, Lord Advocate For Scotland* (Edinburgh, 1882), p. 156.

2. "English Chapel" was the term used for places of worship set up on an Anglican model by Scottish Episcopalians trying to avoid the stigma of the association of episcopalianism with Jacobitism after the 1745 rebellion. Munro to his sister Erskine, 7 Feb. 1798 and 25 April 1793, quoted in Gleig, *Munro*, 1:197, 153. Gleig quoted in *Munro*, 2:225–27. Munro to Erskine, 9 Sept. 1791, 15 Sept. 1795, 7 Feb. 1798, quoted in ibid., 3:68; 1:169, 196.

3. Hume, *Philosophical Works*, 3:149. See the essay, "Of Superstition and Enthusiasm," pp. 144–50. In regard to eastern religions, Munro would have accepted the first but not the second part of Hume's contention that superstition was "an enemy to civil liberty and enthusiasm a friend to it."

4. Munro, minute, 15 Nov. 1822, quoted in Gleig, *Munro*, 2:37–45.

5. Munro, memoranda, dated 1812–13, quoted in ibid., 2:255.

6. Munro to Erskine, 30 Dec. 1815, 15 Sept. 1795, quoted in ibid., 3:213; 1:166.

7. Kaye, *Malcolm*, 1:57, 31.

8. Malcolm, *History of Persia*, 2:339–42. Malcolm, *Sikhs*, p. 117. Malcolm, *History of Persia*, 2:383.

9. Malcolm, *Sikhs*, pp. 138–39. Hume, *Philosophical Works*, 4:334. Malcolm, *Sikhs*, p. 40.

10. Malcolm, *Sikhs*, pp.120, 58.

11. Malcolm, *History of Persia*, 2:319.

12. The seventh Lord Elphinstone married the daughter of the archbishop of Glasgow in 1667, indicating that during the later seventeenth century the family had been Episcopalian. Fraser, *Elphinstone Family*, 1: frontispiece, 13, 220.

13. Elphinstone to Adam, 8 Sept. 1819, quoted in Choksey, *Elphinstone*, p. 257. Colebrooke, *Elphinstone*, 2:410. Cotton, *Elphinstone*, p. 216. Colebrooke, *Elphinstone*, 1:8.

14. For a discussion of the influence of Stoicism on the moderate clergy see Richard Sher, *Church and University*, pp. 175–86. Editor's introduction, Smith, *Theory*, pp. 5–10.

15. Hume, *Philosophical Works*, 4:309. Ibid., 4:309–63.

16. Elphinstone, journal, 1801, Mss. Eur., F/88, Box 13.

17. Elphinstone, journal, 6 April 1846, quoted in Colebrooke, *Elphinstone*, 2:410. Ibid., 2:410.

18. Smith, *Wealth of Nations*, 2:292, 280–313. Malcolm, *History of Persia*, 1:272. Elphinstone to Strachey, 18 Sept. 1804, Mss. Eur., F/128/164. Munro to his sister Erskine, 5 March 1795, quoted in Gleig, *Munro*, 1:165. Hume, *Philosophical Works*, 4:309–63, see p. 319. Elphinstone, diary entry, 6 April, 1846, quoted in Colebrooke, *Elphinstone*, 2:410–11.

19. Elphinstone, *India*, 1:186, 161, 187.

20. Ibid., 1:88. *Parl. Paps.* (Commons), *1812–13*, 7:132.

21. Malcolm, *History of Persia*, 2:622, 587.

22. Munro to his brother Alexander, 2 May 1795, Mss. Eur., F/151/142. Yapp, "Historians of Persia," p. 351.

23. H. Grey Graham, *The Social Life of Scotland in the Eighteenth Century* (London, 1899; 4th ed., illustrated, 1937), p. 108.

24. Hume, *Philosophical Works*, 3:258; Hume, quoted in Bryson, *Man and Society*, p. 181. Francis Hutcheson, cited in ibid., pp. 179, 178 and quoted, p. 179. Millar, *Ranks*, p. 219.

25. Malcolm, *Sikhs*, pp. 27–29. Malcolm, *History of Persia*, 1:317–19.

26. Elphinstone, *Peshwa's Territories*, quoted in Colebrooke, *Elphinstone*, 2:95.

27. Quoted in Choksey, *Elphinstone*, p. 456.

Chapter 10. Systems of Government

Note to epigraph: Hume, *Philosophical Works*, 3:116.

1. Ferguson, *Civil Society*, p. 71. Hume, *History of Great Britain*, pp. 20, 22.

2. O'Brien, *Narratives of Enlightenment*, p. 142. Hume, *History of Great Britain*, pp. 18–24, 30, 83, 221–22, 226. Robertson, *Progress of Society*, pp. 78–82. Hume, *Philosophical Works*, 3:306, 161; *History of Great Britain*, p. 230. Smith, *Wealth of Nations*, provides a theoretical explanation, with much historical evidence, of the economic and political "progress of mankind." In Book 3, chapter 4, Smith mentions that he believes Hume to be the first writer to notice the relationship between commerce and manufactures on the one hand and the introduction of order, good government, and the liberty and security of individuals on the other. See also John Robertson, "The Scottish Enlightenment at the Limits of the Civic Tradition," in Hont and Ignatieff, *Wealth and Virtue*, pp. 163–66.

3. Malcolm, *Sikhs*, pp. 1, 4, 86–87. Elphinstone, *Caubul*, 2:280.

4. Malcolm, *Sikhs*, pp. 3, 38–84.

5. Ibid., pp. 36–37, 40–41.

6. Ibid., pp. 58, 36, 81–82.

7. Elphinstone, quoted in Bayly, *Empire and Information*, p. 134.

8. Elphinstone, *Caubul*, 2:281–83.

9. Ibid., 2:282–83, 298–99.

10. Ibid., 1:230.

11. Ibid., 1:231. Ibid., 1:232.

12. Ibid., 1:233–35.

13. Malcolm, *History of Persia*, 2:621–22, 627. Ervand Abrahamian, in "Oriental Despotism: The Case of Qajar Iran," *Journal of Middle East Studies* 5 (1974), p. 9, calls the shahs "despots without the instruments of despotism"; the lack of a central administrative structure circumscribed their power. Ann Lambton, in "Persia: the Breakdown of Society," *Cambridge History of Islam*, 1: chap. 6, argues that the authority of the shah was undermined by divisions within the Qajar family and by ineffective financial and military organization. Malcolm, *History of Persia*, 2:486–90. Ibid., 2:637–38, 494, 622–23.

14. Ibid., 2:493, 619. Ferguson, *Civil Society*, pp. 7–8.

15. Malcolm, *History of Persia*, 2:619–20. Ferguson, *Civil Society*, p. 167.

16. Stewart, *Outlines of Moral Philosophy*, p. 6. Munro to his sister Erskine, 21 Jan. 1800, quoted in Gleig, *Munro*, 1:280.

17. Bayly, *Imperial Meridian*, pp. 8–9, 157.

18. Ibid., p. 54. Washbrooke, "South Asian Economic and Social History," p. 68. Ibid., p. 72.

19. See Stein, "State Formation"; *Munro*; and "Idiom and Ideology in Early Nineteenth Century South India," in *Rural India; Land, Power and Society under British Rule*, ed. Peter Robb (London, 1983).

20. Stein, "State Formation," p. 410. Ibid., p. 401. Regulations for the administrative organization of Omalur in Salem were translated by Sir William Jones and published in 1795. Munro to his father, 6 Aug. 1799, quoted in Gleig, *Munro*, 1:214–15, 220–22; Munro, "On the Condition and Assessment of Kanara," 31 May 1800, MM, 1:55–79. Stein, "State Formation," pp. 405–6.

21. Malcolm, *Political History*, 2:63–73. Munro, quoted in Gleig, *Munro*, 2:307.

22. Stein, *Munro*, p. 349.

23. Ibid., pp. 351, 391.

24. Editor's introduction, Robertson, *Progress of Society*, p. xxiv. Robertson's *History of Scotland* (1759) and *The History of America* (1777) were also both critically acclaimed and widely read.

25. Gleig, *Munro*, 1:5–8.

26. Robertson, *Progress of Society*, p. 31. Stein notes that the earliest use by Munro of the term dates from June 1806. Stein, *Munro*, p. 130 n.

27. Robertson, *Progress of Society*, pp. 68–69, 82–83.

28. Ferguson, *Civil Society*, pp. 24, 219.

29. Munro to Hastings, 12 Aug. 1817, quoted in Gleig, *Munro*, 1:465. Munro, memorandum, n.d., 1823, quoted in ibid., 2:264–65. Munro, "On the Employment of Natives in the Public Service," MM, 2:327. Munro to Hastings, 12 Aug. 1817, quoted in Gleig, *Munro*, 1:465–67.

30. Munro, memorandum, n.d., 1823, quoted in Gleig, *Munro*, 2:264–65. Munro to Canning, 1 May 1823, quoted in ibid., 2:67. Rosalind O'Hanlon and D. A. Washbrooke use the phrase "prin-

ciple vehicle of human liberation" in a discussion of recent work by Indian historians on colonialism and capitalism. See "Histories in Transition: Approaches to the Study of Colonialism and Culture in India," *History Workshop* 32 (1991): pp. 118–19.

31. P. J. Marshall, "A Free Though Conquering People: Britain and Asia in the Eighteenth Century," inaugural lecture in Rhodes Chair of Imperial History, University of London (1981), p. 3. Ingram, *Commitment to Empire*, pp. 117, 145–46, 154.

32. Elphinstone, *India*, 1:512–13.

33. See Ibid., 2:1–92 for Elphinstone's account of this period of Indian history.

34. Ibid., 2:554.

35. Ibid., 2:259–60, 315.

36. Ibid., 2:330–35.

37. Ibid., 2:86, 189, 272, 551–52, 564.

38. Horace Hayman Wilson, quoted in Philips, *Historians*, p. 226.

39. Malcolm's views on Aurangzeb's reign are stated in *Central India*, 1:50–57. Zastoupil, "India, Mill and 'Western' Culture," pp. 131–35.

40. Malcolm, *Central India*, 1:50.

41. Ibid., pp. 157–95. See pp. 194, 176, 174, 182, 177, 194–95, 174.

42. Douglas M. Peers, "Between Mars and Mammon: The East India Company and Efforts to Reform its Army, 1796–1832," *Historical Journal* 33 (1990), p. 389. Ibid., p. 387.

43. Peers, "Wellington and British India," p. 16. Peers, "Military and Political Economy," pp. 119, 122–24.

44. Peers, "Military and Political Economy," p. 120. Malcolm, *Government of India*, p. 272. Peers, "Military and Political Economy," pp. 119–20. Munro, quoted in Beaglehole, *Munro*, p. 116. Munro, "Address to Students at the College of Fort St. George," n.d., 1820, quoted in Gleig, *Munro*, 2:12.

45. Peers, "Military and Political Economy," p. 128. Munro to Canning, 14 Oct. 1820, quoted in Gleig, *Munro*, 2:51–52.

46. Peers, "Military and Political Economy," see chap. 5, pp. 130–79. Malcolm, *Political History*, 2:122–33; ibid., review article, "Bengal Native Infantry", pp. 386, 404, 420.

47. Peers, "Military and Political Economy," p. 123. Munro to Malcolm, 29 Sept. 1825, quoted in Gleig, *Munro*, 2:156.

48. Peers, "Wellington and British India," p. 19. Munro, memorandum, n.d., 1812–13, quoted in Gleig, *Munro*, 2:259–60. See also Munro, *MM*, 2:142–43, 153. Munro, "Regarding an Insubordinate Letter Addressed to the Government by the Military Board," 10 May 1822, ibid., 2:141–43. "On Unauthorized Changes in the Dress of the Native Army," 19 Dec. 1823, ibid., 2:153–54. See also "On the Same Subject," 20 April 1825, ibid., 2:155–56. Elphinstone to Villiers, 19 Aug. 1832, quoted in Peers, "East India Company and its Army," pp. 385–86.

49. Peers, "Military and Political Economy," p. 202. Munro to his brother Alexander, 6 Dec. 1794, Mss. Eur., F/151/142. Munro, memorandum, n.d., quoted in Gleig, *Munro*, 2:309, appendix 8. See Munro, "Minutes on the War with Burma," no.1, 18 June 1824, *MM*, 2:169, 171; no. 2, 3 Aug. 1824, ibid., 2:173, 52; no. 3, 24 Aug. 1824, ibid., 2:175.

50. Malcolm, *Political History*, 1:5.

51. Lynn Zastoupil, *John Stuart Mill and India* (Stanford, 1994), chap. 3.

52. James Mill, *The History of British India*, 6 vols. (1817; 3rd ed., London, 1826), 1:283.

53. James Mill, *The History of British India*, abridged and with an introduction by William Thomas (Chicago, 1975), p. xxi.

54. Elphinstone to Malcolm, quoted in Philips, *Historians*, p. 223. Anonymous, *Opinions . . . of . . . Mountstuart Elphinstone*.

55. Munro, memorandum, n.d., quoted in Gleig, *Munro*, 2:308, appendix 8.

56. Malcolm, *Central India*, 2:282. Malcolm often repeated verbatim in his writings on Indian government statements which he considered particularly important. This one also appears in the *Political History*, 2:83–84.

57. Hume, *Philosophical Works*, 3:10.

58. Elphinstone, *India*, 1:385.

Chapter 11. A Scottish School of Thought

Note to epigraph: Adam Smith quoted in Bryson, *Man and Society*, p. 208.

1. Beaglehole, *Munro*, p. 11. Stein, *Munro*, p. 358.

2. Munro to Canning, 1 May 1823, quoted in Gleig, *Munro*, 2:66.

3. Ranajit Guha, *A Rule of Property for Bengal: An Essay on the Idea of Permanent Settlement* (Paris, 1963); Tapan Raychaudhuri, "Permanent Settlement in Operation: Bakorganj District, East Bengal," in *Land Control and Social Structure in Indian History*, ed. Robert Frykenberg (Madison, 1969), p. 90.

4. David Ludden, "Orientalist Empiricism: Transformations of Colonial Knowledge," in *Orientalism and the Postcolonial Predicament: Perspectives on South Asia*, ed. Carol A. Breckenridge and Peter van der Veer (Philadelphia, 1993), p. 262.

5. E. J. Hobsbawm, "Scottish Reformers of the Eighteenth Century and Capitalist Agriculture," in *Peasants in History. Essays in Honour of Daniel Thorner*, ed. E. J. Hobsbawm et al. (Oxford, 1980), pp. 4–5, 18.

6. On James Anderson see, Rae, *Adam Smith*, p. 421. Devine, "Glasgow Colonial Merchants and Land," pp. 205–6. Fay, *Adam Smith*, pp. 71–72. Fay provides an interesting study of Smith and the Scotland in which he lived and worked, tracing Scottish influences on Smith and Smith's influence on the members of his own society. Robert Burns, quoted in ibid, p. 72.

7. Munro, "Settlement of Salem," 18 July 1797, *MM*, 1:17. Munro, "Notes on Ricardo's Political Economy, 1820," quoted in Gleig, *Munro*, 2:282. David Ricardo's highly influential *Principles of Political Economy and Taxation* appeared in 1817, twenty years after James Anderson and then Read and Munro had concerned themselves with the questions of soil fertility and labor.

8. Revenue Letter from Fort St. George, 12 Aug. 1814, quoted in Gleig, *Munro*, 2:244–45, appendix 2. When published by Arbuthnot in 1881, Munro's minutes were given titles and dates, but in several instances papers have only the heading, "On Same Subject." Where there are two or more papers on the same subject they have been identified here by date.

9. Munro to his brother James, 9 June 1792, quoted in Gleig, *Munro*, 3:81. Hobsbawm, "Scottish Reformers," p. 5.

10. Smith, *Theory*, p. 233–34.

11. See Stein, *Munro*, pp. 39–49, for a discussion of the historiography on the origins of the Munro system. Webbe to Munro, 24 Nov. 1802, Mss. Eur., F/151/2.

12. Munro, "On the Revenue Settlement of Salem District," 5 Sept. 1797, *MM*, 1:36–37, 54.

13. Munro, "On the Revenue Settlement of the Salem District," 15 Nov. 1796, ibid., 1:22. Munro, "Settlement of Salem," 5 Sept. 1797, ibid., 1:35–36.

14. Smith, *Wealth of Nations*, 2:386.

15. Hume, *Philosophical Works*, 3:296–97. Ibid., 3:306. See also Ferguson, *Civil Society*, p. 70 on two-class societies.

16. Munro, "On the State of the Country and Condition of the People," 31 Dec. 1824, *MM*, 1:254; Munro, "The Position of the Ryot and of the Zamindar," 15 April 1812, ibid., 1:105. Munro, evidence before the House of Commons, April 1813, *Parl. Paps.* (Commons), *1812–13*, 7:143.

17. Elphinstone, *India*, 2:189.

18. Stein, *Munro*, pp. 49–50, 101, 204–7, 271, 343. Munro, "State of the Country," 31 Dec. 1824, *MM*, 1:245–46.

19. Sinclair, cited in Hobsbawm, "Scottish Reformers," p. 7. Brown's *History of Glasgow* and Smith's *Survey of Argyllshire, 1798*, cited in Graham, *Social Life of Scotland*, pp. 156–57, 202.

20. Loosely speaking, jagir holders, who were usually from prominent families, had been granted rights to revenue from certain lands in return for military and administrative services; inams were similar grants made for religious or charitable purposes, or to provide an income for village officials.

21. Munro, "On the Condition and Assessment of Kanara," 31 May 1800, *MM*, 1:55–79; 19 Nov. 1800, ibid., 1:80–88. See Munro, "State of the Country," 31 Dec. 1824, ibid., 1:240. Munro, "Assessment of Kanara," 31 May 1800, ibid., 1:72, 60. Stein, *Munro*, p. 71. Munro, "Assessment of Kanara," 31 May 1800, *MM*, 1:69.

22. Munro, "Assessment of Kanara," 31 May 1800, 1:65, 68. Stein, *Munro*, pp. 68–72. Bayly, *Empire and Information*, p. 49.

23. Munro, "On a Permanent Settlement of Kanara," 31 May 1800, *MM*, 2:354. This is a section of the first minute, "On the Condition and Assessment of Kanara," which Munro's editor, Arbuthnot, extracts and prints separately. *MM*, 2:353–60.

24. Smith quoted in Phillipson, "Adam Smith as Civic Moralist," in Hont and Ignatieff, *Wealth and Virtue*, p. 192. Munro, "Permanent Settlement of Kanara," 31 May 1800, *MM*, 2:353–55.

25. Ibid., 2:356–57.

26. Beaglehole, *Munro*, p. 8. Munro, "On the Relative Advantages of the Ryotwar and Zamindar Systems," 15 Aug. 1807, *MM*, 1:94–95.

27. Smith, *Wealth of Nations*, 1:382–85. Lord Kames, cited in David Lieberman, "The Legal Needs of a Commercial Society: The Jurisprudence of Lord Kames," in Hont and Ignatieff, *Wealth and Virtue*, p. 215.

28. Munro, "Permanent Settlement of Kanara," 31 May 1800, *MM*, 2:357.

29. Munro, "On the Expediency of Introducing Entails," 19 Sept. 1820, ibid., 1:117–20; another minute on the same subject is dated 25 Feb. 1823, ibid., 1:121–23.

30. Ibid., 1:118–19. Munro, "On the Employment of Natives in the Public Service," 31 Dec. 1824, ibid., 2:319–27, 324–25. Elphinstone, "Abstracts of Adam Smith, Ricardo and Malthus," n.d., Mss. Eur., F/88, Box 16D14.

31. Munro, "Introducing Entails," 19 Sept. 1820, *MM*, 1:119.

32. Munro to Elphinstone, 8 March 1818, quoted in Gleig, *Munro*, 3:239. Elphinstone, cited in Ballhatchet, *Western India*, p. 106.

33. See Perlin, "State Formation Reconsidered," p. 416, on the importance of land revenue arrangements in pre-British India.

34. Malcolm, *Political History*, 2:90, 93, 95.

35. Elphinstone to William Erskine, 1 Nov. 1818, quoted in Colebrooke, *Elphinstone*, 2:51–52. El-

phinstone, *Peshwa's Territories*, p. 44. Elphinstone to Edward Strachey, 10 March 1822, quoted in Colebrooke, *Elphinstone*, 2:132.

36. Malcolm describes one of the features of the Munro system as "raising rent in proportion to industry," but this was not meant to happen under Read and Munro's original plan, which recommended a "permanent settlement." See Malcolm, *Political History*, 2:96. Read, "District of Tripatur," 10 Dec. 1796, *MM*, 2:341–44; Munro, "Settlement of Salem," 5 Sept. 1797, ibid., 1:54.

37. Robertson quoted in O'Brien, *Narratives of Enlightenment*, p. 136.

38. Munro, "Settlement of Salem," 5 Sept. 1797, *MM*, 1:52–53.

39. Munro, "State of the Country," 31 Dec. 1824, ibid., 1:270–72.

40. Malcolm to William Erskine, October 1821, Mss. Eur., D/32. Malcolm, *Central India*, 2:281; 2:283–97. Elphinstone, quoted in *Selections from the Minutes and other Official Writings of The Honourable Mountstuart Elphinstone, Governor of Bombay*, ed. George Forrest (London, 1884), p. 57. Elphinstone to Edward Strachey, 21 April 1821, quoted in Colebrooke, *Elphinstone*, 2:124.

41. Munro, "Trial by Panchayat," 15 Aug. 1807, *MM*, 2:4.

42. Quoted in J. M. Beattie, *Crime and the Courts in England, 1660–1800* (Oxford, 1986), p. 314.

43. This account of Scotland's legal system prior to the mid–eighteenth century comes from Stephen Davies, "The Courts and the Scottish Legal System 1600–1747: The Case of Stirlingshire," in *Crime and the Law: The Social History of Crime in Western Europe since 1500*, ed. V. A. C. Gartrell, Bruce Lenman, and Geoffrey Parker (London: 1980), pp. 120–54. Beattie, *Crime and the Courts*, examines in detail similar trends in England in the eighteenth century.

44. Davies, "The Courts and the Scottish Legal System," p. 121.

45. Peter Stein, "Law and Society in Eighteenth Century Scottish Thought," in Phillipson and Mitchison, *Age of Improvement*, pp. 148, 149, 152.

46. O'Brien, *Narratives of Enlightenment*, p. 133.

47. Hume, *Philosophical Works*, 2:263, 271. Kames quoted in "Preface to Kames's Select Decisions (1780)," printed in an appendix to W. C. Lehmann, *Henry Home, Lord Kames, and the Scottish Enlightenment. A Study in National Character and in the History of Ideas* (The Hague, 1971), p. 320. Munro to Thackeray, n.d., quoted in Gleig, *Munro*, 1:327. Kames quoted in Lieberman, "Legal Needs of a Commercial Society," pp. 206, 229.

48. Munro, memorandum, 10 Sept. 1808, NLS, Ms. 12.

49. Munro, "The Administration of Justice," 1813, *MM*, 2:7–16. Ferguson, *Civil Society*, pp. 263–64.

50. Munro, "Reduction of the Zillah Courts," 20 Jan. 1827, *MM*, 2:55.

51. Munro, "Trial of Criminal Cases by Jury or Panchayat," July 1827, ibid., 2:56.

52. Munro, "Trial of Criminal Cases," July 1827, ibid., 2:56. See J. G. A. Pocock, "Cambridge Paradigms and Scotch Philosophers: A Study of the Relations between the Civic Humanist and the Civic Jurisprudential Interpretation of Eighteenth Century Social Thought," and Robertson, "The Scottish Enlightenment at the Limits of the Civic Tradition," in Hont and Ignatieff, *Wealth and Virtue*, pp. 235–52; pp.137–78.

53. Munro, "Employment of Natives," 31 Dec. 1824, *MM*, 2:319–27.

54. Ibid., 2:322.

55. Robertson, *Progress of Society*, pp. 7–8. Ferguson, *Civil Society*, pp. 213–14.

56. Malcolm, *Government of India*, pp. 57–58. Elphinstone to Munro, 27 Oct. 1822, quoted in Colebrooke, *Elphinstone*, 2:143.

57. Smith, *Wealth of Nations,* 2:788. Elphinstone, n.d., quoted in Colebrooke, *Elphinstone,* 2:149–50. Elphinstone, extract from minute on education, Oct. 1823, quoted in ibid., 2:154–55.

58. Stein, *Munro,* pp. 287–98.

Chapter 12. Orientalist Representations

Note to epigraph: Samuel Johnson, quoted in *The Complete Oxford English Dictionary.*

1. *The Concise Oxford Dictionary.* Bayly, *Empire and Information,* p. 48.

2. Thomas R. Trautmann, *Aryans and British India* (Berkeley, 1997), p. 23.

3. John M. MacKenzie, *Orientalism: History, Theory and the Arts* (Manchester, 1995), p. 20–21. MacKenzie provides an interesting discussion of the Orientalism debate in chap. 1.

4. Nicholas Thomas, *Colonialism's Culture: Anthropology, Travel and Government* (Princeton, 1994).

5. Julie F. Codell and Dianne Sachko Macleod, "Orientalism Transposed: The 'Easterniza- tion' of Britain and Interventions to Colonial Discourse," in *Orientalism Transposed: The Impact of the Colonies on British Culture* (Brookfield, Vt. 1998), p. 2.

6. Bayly, *Empire and Information,* p. 142.

7. Rosane Rocher, "British Orientalism in the Eighteenth Century: The Dialectics of Knowl- edge and Government," in Breckenridge and van der Veer, *Orientalism and the Postcolonial Predicament,* p. 215.

8. Munro's translation is included in Gleig, *Munro,* 1:64–65.

9. Letter from Munro to an unnamed friend, n.d., ibid., 1:58–67.

10. Yapp, "Historians of Persia," p. 347. Cohn, "The Command of Language," p. 283.

11. Vans Kennedy, address to Bombay Literary Society, 26 Nov. 1827, quoted in Choksey, *El- phinstone,* p. 453–54.

12. Bayly, *Empire and Information,* p. 48.

13. Edward Said, *Orientalism* (New York, 1979), p. 3. Ronald Inden, *Imagining India* (Oxford, 1990), pp. 36–48. Ibid., pp. 36, 38, 41–42, 43. Said, *Orientalism,* p. 52. Gyan Prakash, "Writing Post- Orientalist Histories of the Third World: Perspectives from Indian Historiography," *Comparative Studies in Society and History* 32 (1990), p. 384.

14. Inden, *Imagining India,* p. 45.

15. Prakash, "Writing Post-Orientalist Histories," pp. 384–85.

16. Elphinstone to Malcolm, 11 Sept. 1816, quoted in Colebrooke, *Elphinstone,* 1:320.

17. Javed Majeed, *Ungoverned Imaginings: James Mill's 'The History of British India' and Orientalism* (Oxford, 1992), p. 198.

18. Karen O'Brien, "Robertson's Place in the Development of Eighteenth-Century Narrative History," chap. 4 in Brown, *William Robertson.*

19. Munro to his mother, 5 Oct. 1794, Mss. Eur., F/151/142.

20. Inden, *Imagining India,* p. 71. Munro, memorandum, 1808, Mss. Eur., F/151/23.

21. Rocher, "British Orientalism," provides an excellent discussion of the East India Compa- ny's transition from commercial to imperial preoccupations, pp. 216–19.

22. Bayly, *Empire and Information,* p. 44.

23. Ludden, "Orientalist Empiricism," pp. 252–53.

24. Zastoupil, *John Stuart Mill and India,* p. 143. Bayly, *Empire and Information,* p. 142.

25. Ludden, "Orientalist Empiricism," p. 253.

26. Irschick, *Dialogue and History,* p. 4.

Chapter 13. Historiographical Representations

Note to epigraph: Ferguson, *Civil Society,* p. 123.

1. Dane Kennedy, "Imperial History and Post-Colonial Theory," *Journal of Imperial and Commonwealth History* 24 (1996), p. 346.

2. Thomas Carlyle, quoted in Walter E. Houghton, *The Victorian Frame of Mind, 1830–1870* (1957; reprint, New Haven: Yale University Press, 1985), p. 305.

3. Elphinstone, *Caubul,* quoted in Sir Olaf Caroe's introduction, p. xxiii.

4. Hume, *Philosophical Works,* 3:292.

5. John Lowe Duthie, "Some Further Insights into the Working of Mid-Victorian Imperialism: Lord Salisbury, the 'Forward' Group and Anglo-Afghan Relations: 1874–1878," *Journal of Imperial and Commonwealth History* 8 (1980), p. 200.

6. Jawarharlal Nehru, *The Discovery of India* (London, 1951).

7. R. Palme Dutt, *India-Today* (1940; Bombay, 1949), p. 214. Nehru, *Discovery,* p. 236. B. S. Baliga, "Home Government and the End of the Policy of Permanent Settlement in Madras, 1802–1818," *Indian Historical Records Commission Proceedings* 19 (1942), p. 317. K. N. Venkatasubba Sastri, *The Munro System of British Statesmanship in India* (Mysore, 1939). Munro quoted in ibid., pp.1–2.

8. Philip Mason, *The Men Who Ruled India,* 2 vols. (London, 1954; Paperback edition, London, 1985), p. 395.

9. Choksey, *Elphinstone.*

10. See Ballhatchet, *Western India;* Nilmani Mukherjee, *The Ryotwari System in Madras 1792–1827* (Calcutta, 1962); Beaglehole, *Munro;* Robert Frykenberg, *Guntur District, 1788–1848* (Oxford, 1965).

11. These include Peers, *Between Mars and Mammon;* Stein, "State Formation" and "Idiom and Ideology;" Yapp, *Strategies;* and Zastoupil, *John Stuart Mill and India.*

12. Eric Stokes, in his seminal study, *The English Utilitarians and India,* accepts largely unquestioningly the orthodox interpretation of Munro, Malcolm, and Elphinstone's thought, which is only peripheral to the focus of his work. George Bearce in *British Attitudes Towards India* struggles manfully with the apparent contradictions in the three Scotsmen's thought that have led to the conservative liberal, liberal conservative romantic labels, but fails to provide a coherent explanation of their ideology. Thomas R. Metcalf, in *Ideologies of the Raj,* retains the Burkean conservative representation.

Chapter 14. British India, British Scotland

1. Misra, *The Central Administration of the East India Company, 1773–1834* (Manchester, 1959), pp. 80–81. Munro to Cumming, 1 March 1815, quoted in Gleig, *Munro,* 1:4.

2. Adam Smith, quoted in Bryson, *Man and Society,* p. 208. David Hume, *Philosophical Works,* 3:296.

Glossary

amildar	Officer of the government, especially a collector of revenue.
Bheel (Bhil)	Central and western Indian tribal group.
Brahmin	Member of Hindu priestly order. By turn of the eighteenth/nineteenth centuries, employed in many secular occupations.
curnam (kurnam)	Village accountant.
gaekwar	Maratha title.
inam	Land free of rent or revenue; gift from superior to inferior.
inamdar	Holder of rent- or revenue-free land.
jagir	Land, the revenue of which has been made over to an individual, usually as payment for military service.
jagirdar	Holder of jagir land.
mirasi	Coparcenary (communal) land tenure.
munshi	Secretary, writer. Sometimes also an expert in diplomatic practice.
muttadar	New, East India Company-created zamindar.
nizam	viceroy, or governor, of the Mughal emperors. By the late eighteenth century the nizam of Hyderabad was a virtually independent ruler.
panchayat	Jury; traditional five-member council of elders for settling disputes.
peshwa	Maratha title meaning chief minister. By the late eighteenth century the peshwa of Pune was a virtually independent ruler.
Pindari	Traditionally, irregular horsemen serving with Maratha armies. By the early nineteenth century the term was applied by the British to military plunderers operating in the Deccan, sometimes in association with Maratha armies but often on their own behalf.
poligar	South Indian Hindu warrior chief.

potail	Village headman.
raja	Hindu king, ruler.
ryot	Agriculturalist, cultivator, peasant.
ryotwari	Form of land-revenue assessment and collection found particularly in southern and western India. Tax was levied on the fields cultivated by each individual/family and collected directly from the cultivator by a government official rather than by a local middleman.
sagwulli	Cultivation.
Sikh	Member of an Indian religious reform movement that emerged in response to Hindu/Muslim interaction in the Punjab region of India in the sixteenth century. Monotheistic beliefs are based on revelations received by a line of gurus and are recorded in Sikhism's sacred book, the *Guru Granth Sahib.* The term "Sikh" derives from a Hindi word for "disciple".
sirdar	Leader, or commander. Honorary title for eminent men.
sirkar	The state; the government.
taccavi	Form of land tenure under which landlord provides seed to tenant cultivators.
tahsildar	Indian revenue official in charge of a subdivision of a district (tahsil); collector of revenue or rent from a tahsil.
zamindar	Landholder; traditionally one who controls land and is responsible for the payment of the assessed revenue to the government. In Bengal, often a large rentier landowner, but sometimes, as in the northwestern provinces, a peasant owner-occupier.
zamindari	Form of land-revenue assessment and collection found particularly in the Bengal presidency but also in parts of northern India. Under this system, a local zamindar collected and passed on to the government the land revenues due from each cultivator in his district, retaining 10 percent of the amount collected as a return for his services.

Bibliography

Manuscript Sources

British Library, Oriental and India Office Collections, London
Elphinstone Collection, Mss. Eur., F/89.
IO H/-   Home Miscellaneous Series.
IO J/1/9–23   Haileybury Records.
Mountstuart Elphinstone Collection, Mss. Eur., F/88.
Munro Collection, Mss. Eur., F/151.
Sutton Court Collection, Mss. Eur., F/128.

National Library of Scotland, Edinburgh
Elphinstone, Mountstuart. 1803–1854, Family Correspondence.
Malcolm, John. 1822–1833. Correspondence with C. Malcolm. 5899/5900.
Munro, Thomas. Letters and a Memorandum, 1803–1827. 6370.
Scott, Sir Walter. Letters from Sir John Malcolm, Mountstuart Elphinstone, Sir John Macdonald
    Kinneir, William Erskine, et al. 3881/3903.

National Maritime Museum, Greenwich
Malcolm, Charles. MAL/3 Mss. 60/040.

Primary Sources

Anonymous. *Opinions . . . of . . . Mountstuart Elphinstone upon some of the Leading questions
    Connected with the Government of British India—Compared to those of Sir Thomas
    Munro and Sir John Malcolm, as taken from their Evidence before Parliament, . . . By the Au-
    thor of "An Enquiry into the Causes of the Stationary Condition of India." Political Tracts
    No. 3. London: 1831.

Bentinck, Lord William Cavendish. *The Correspondence of Lord William Cavendish Bentinck, Governor-
    General of India, 1828–1835.* 2 vols. Edited and introduced by C. H. Philips. Oxford: Oxford
    University Press, 1977.

Blair, Hugh. *Sermons.* Edinburgh, 1777.

Burke, Edmund. *The Philosophy of Edmund Burke: A Selection from His Speeches and Writings.* Edited and
    with an introduction by Louis I. Bredvold and Ralph G. Ross. Ann Arbor: University of
    Michigan, 1960.

————. *The Writings and Speeches of Edmund Burke.* Vol. 5. *India: Madras and Bengal, 1774–1785.* Edited by P. J. Marshall. Oxford: Clarendon Press, 1981.

Castlereagh, Robert Stewart, Viscount. (Marquess of Londonderry). *Memoir and Correspondence of Viscount Castlereagh, Marquess of Londonderry.* Edited by 2nd Marquess of Londonderry. 12 vols. London: Henry Colburn, 1848–53.

Cockburn, Lord. *Memorials of His Time.* Abridged and edited with notes by W. Forbes Gray. Edinburgh: Robert Grant & Son, 1946.

Colebrooke, Sir T. E. *Life of the Honourable Mountstuart Elphinstone.* 2 vols. London: John Murray, 1884.

Cornwallis, Charles, Marquis. *Correspondence of Charles, First Marquis Cornwallis.* 2nd ed. 3 vols. Edited by Charles Ross. London: John Murray, 1859.

Creech, William. *Letters, addressed to Sir John Sinclair, Bart. Respecting the Mode of Living, Arts, Commerce, Literature, Manners, etc. of Edinburgh in 1763, and since that period.* 1793. Reprint, New York: AMS Press, 1982.

Elliot, Gilbert, Earl of Minto. *Lord Minto in India: Life and Letters of Gilbert Elliot, First Earl of Minto from 1807–1814.* Edited by the Countess of Minto. London: Longmans, Green and Co., 1880.

Elphinstone, Mountstuart. *An Account of the Kingdom of Caubul.* 2 vols. 1815. Reprint, with an introduction by Sir Olaf Caroe, Oxford in Asia Historical Reprints, Karachi: Oxford University Press, 1972.

————. *Elphinstone Correspondence, 1804–1808.* Edited by R. M. Sinha and A. Avasthi. Nagpur: Nagpur University Historical Society, 1961.

————. *The History of India.* 2 vols. London: 1841.

————. *Report on the Peshwa's Territories.* 1822. Reprint, under the title *Territories Conquered from the Paishwa: A Report,* introduction by J. C. Srivastava, Delhi, 1973.

————. *The Rise of British Power in the East.* Edited by Sir Edward Colebrooke. London: John Murray, 1887.

————. *Selections from the Minutes and other Official Writings of The Honourable Mountstuart Elphinstone, Governor of Bombay.* Edited by George W. Forrest, London: Richard Bentley & Son, 1884.

English Records of Maratha History: Poona Residency Correspondence. 15 vols. Edited by G. S. Sardesai et al. Bombay, 1936–1951.

Ferguson, Adam. *An Essay on the History of Civil Society.* 1767. Edited and with an introduction by Duncan Forbes. Edinburgh: Edinburgh University Press, 1966.

————. *The History of the Progress and Termination of the Roman Republic.* 3 vols. Dublin, 1783. New edition, Edinburgh: 1828.

————. *Principles of Moral and Political Science.* 2 vols. Edinburgh, 1792. Reprint, with an introduction by Jean Hecht. Hildesheim: Georg Olms Verlag, 1975.

Gleig, G. R. *Life of Major General Sir Thomas Munro.* 3 vols. London, 1830.

Home, Henry. (Lord Kames). *Elucidations Respecting the Common and Statute Law of Scotland.* Edinburgh, 1777.

————. *The Gentleman Farmer; Being An Attempt to Improve Agriculture, By subjecting it to the Test of Rational Principles.* Edinburgh, 1776.

Hume, David. *The History of Great Britain: The Reigns of James I and Charles I.* 1754. Reprint, edited by Duncan Forbes. Harmondsworth: Penguin, 1970.

————. *Philosophical Works.* 4 vols. Edited by T. H. Green and T. H. Grose. Reprint of the original London edition, 1882–86. Darmstadt, 1964.

Hutcheson, Francis. *An Inquiry concerning Beauty, Order, Harmony, Design.* (1st of two Treatises which together comprise the *Inquiry into the Origin of Our Ideas of Beauty and Virtue.* 1725.) Edited with an introduction and notes by Peter Kivy. International Archives of the History of Ideas, no. 9. The Hague: Martinus Nijhoff, 1973.

Kaye, Sir John William. *The Life and Correspondence of Major-General Sir John Malcolm, G.C.B., Late Envoy to Persia, and Governor of Bombay; from Unpublished Letters and Journals.* 2 vols. London: Smith, Elder, and Co., 1856.

Keith, George Elphinstone, Viscount. Navy Records Society: *The Keith Papers: Selected from the Letters and Papers of Admiral the Viscount Keith.* 3 vols. Edited by H. G. Perrin and C. Lloyd. London, 1927–55.

Lockhart, John Gibson. *Memoirs of Sir Walter Scott, Bart. . . .* Edinburgh: R. Cadell, 1845

Macdonald Kinneir, John. *Geographical Memoir of the Persian Empire.* 1813. Reprint, New York: Arno Press, 1973.

Mackintosh, R. J., ed. *Memoirs of the Life of the Rt. Hon. Sir James Mackintosh.* 2 vols. London: Edward Moxon, 1836.

Malcolm, John. *The Government of India.* London: John Murray, 1833.

———. *The History of Persia from the Most Early Period to the Present Time, Containing an Account of the Religion, Government, Usages and Character of the Inhabitants of that Kingdom.* 2 vols. London, 1815.

———. *A Memoir of Central India, Including Malwa and Adjoining Provinces. With The History, and Copious Illustrations, of the Past and Present Condition of That Country.* 2 vols. 1823. Reprint, New Delhi: Sagar Publications, 1970.

———. "Notes of Instructions to Assistants and Officers Acting under the Orders of Major-General Sir John Malcolm." In John Briggs *Letter Addressed to a Young Person in India: Calculated to Afford Instruction for his Conduct in General, and More especially in his intercourse with Natives.* London: John Murray, 1828.

———. *Observations on the Disturbances in the Madras Army in 1809.* London, 1812.

———. *The Political History of India, 1784 to 1823.* 2 vols. 1826. Reprint, edited and with an introduction by K. N. Pannikar, New Delhi: Associated Publishing House, 1970.

———. Review of "An Account of the Rise and Progress of the Bengal Native Infantry . . ." *Quarterly Review* 18 (1818).

———. *Sketch of the Political History of India.* London: W. Miller, 1811.

———. *Sketch of the Sikhs: A Singular Nation, who Inhabit the Provinces of the Penjab Situated between the Rivers Jumna and Indus.* 1812. Reprint, under the title, *Sketch of the Sikhs: Their Origin, Customs and Manners,* Chandigarh: Vinay Publications, 1981.

———. *Sketches of Persia: From The Journals of a Traveller in The East.* 2 vols. London: Thomas Davison, 1827.

Melville, Henry Dundas, Viscount. *Two Views of British India: The Private Correspondence of Mr. Dundas and Lord Wellesley: 1798–1801.* Edited by Edward Ingram. Bath: Adams and Dart, 1970.

Mill, James. *The History of British India.* 3rd ed. 6 vols. First published 1817. Third edition, London: Baldwin, Critic, and Joy, 1826.

Millar, John. "The Origin of the Distinction of Ranks." In *John Millar of Glasgow, 1735–1801: His Life and Thought and His Contributions to Sociological Analysis,* edited by William C. Lehmann. Cambridge: Cambridge University Press, 1960.

Morier, James. *The Adventures of Hajji Baba of Isfahan.* 2 vols. First published 1824. With an introduction by E. G. Browne. London: Methuen, 1895.

Munro, Sir Thomas. *Sir Thomas Munro: Selections from His Minutes and Other Official Writings.* 2 vols. Edited by Sir Alexander J. Arbuthnot. London: Kegan Paul & Co., 1881.

Parliamentary Papers, House of Commons, 1812–1813, vol. 7.

Pottinger, Henry. *Travels in Beloochistan and Sinde.* London, 1816.

Reid, Thomas. *Thomas Reid's Inquiry and Essays.* Edited by Keith Lehrer and Ronald E. Beanblossom. With an Introduction by Ronald E. Beanblossom. Indianapolis: Bobbs-Merrill, 1975.

Robertson, William. *An Historical Disquisition Concerning the Knowledge Which the Ancients Had of India.* 4th ed. London, 1804.

————. *The History of Scotland.* 2 vols. London, 1759.

————. *The Progress of Society in Europe: A Historical Outline from the Subversion of the Roman Empire to the Beginning of the Sixteenth Century.* 1769. Edited and with an introduction by Felix Gilbert. Chicago: Chicago University Press, 1972.

Scott, David [Royal Historical Society]. *The Correspondence of David Scott, Director and Chairman of the East India Company relating to Indian Affairs, 1787–1805.* 2 vols. Edited and introduced by C. H. Philips. Camden Third Series. London: Royal Historical Society, 1951.

Shore, Sir John. *The Private Record of a Governor-Generalship: The Private Correspondence of Sir John Shore, Governor-General, with Henry Dundas, President of the Board of Control, 1793–1798.* Edited by Holden Furber. Cambridge, Mass.: Harvard University Press, 1933.

Sinclair, Sir John. *The History of the Public Revenue of the British Empire.* 3rd ed. 3 vols. Reprints of Economic Classics. New York: Augustus M. Kelley, 1966.

Smith, Adam. *Correspondence of Adam Smith.* Edited by E. C. Mossner and I. S. Ross. Oxford: Clarendon Press, 1977.

————. *Essays on Philosophical Subjects.* First published 1795. University of Glasgow edition. Edited by W. P. D. Wightman and J. C. Bryce. With "Dugald Stewart's Account of Adam Smith." Edited by I. S. Ross. General editors, D. D. Raphael and A. S. Skinner. Oxford: Clarendon Press, 1980.

————. *An Inquiry into the Nature and Causes of the Wealth of Nations.* 2 vols. First published 1776. University of Glasgow edition. General editors, R. H. Campbell and A. S. Skinner. Textual editor, W. B. Todd. Oxford: Clarendon Press, 1976.

————. *The Theory of Moral Sentiments.* First published 1759. University of Glasgow edition. Edited by D. D. Raphael and A. L. Macfie. Oxford: Clarendon Press, 1976.

Somerville, Thomas. *My Own Life and Times, 1741–1814.* Edinburgh: Edmonstone & Douglas, 1861.

Stewart, Dugald. *Outlines of Moral Philosophy for the Use of Students in the University of Edinburgh.* Edinburgh and London, 1793. New edition with a Memoir and Supplement, and Questions, by James M'Cosh. London, 1897.

Wellesley, Richard Colley, Marquis. *The Despatches, Minutes, and Correspondence of the Marquess Wellesley, K.G., during his Administration in India.* 5 vols. Edited by R. Montgomery Martin. 1836–37. Reprint, New Delhi: Inter-India Publications, 1984.

————. *A Selection from the Despatches, Treaties, and other Papers of the Marquis Wellesley, K.G., during his Government of India.* Edited by Sidney J. Owen. Oxford: Clarendon Press, 1877.

Wellington, Arthur Wellesley, 1st Duke of. *Despatches, Correspondence, and Memoranda of Field Marshal Arthur, Duke of Wellington, K.G.* Edited by the 2nd Duke of Wellington. 1868. Reprint, New York: Kraus, 1973.

————. *The Despatches of Field Marshal the Duke of Wellington during His Various Campaigns from 1799–1818.* 12 vols. Compiled by Lt. Col. John Gurwood. London: John Murray, 1834–38.

————. *Supplementary Despatches, Correspondence, and Memoranda of Field Marshall Arthur, Duke of Wellington, K.G.* Edited by his son, the Duke of Wellington. 11 vols. London, 1858–64.

Secondary Sources

Abrahamian, Ervand. "Oriental Despotism: The Case of Qajar Iran." *International Journal of Middle East Studies* 5 (1974): 3–31.

Allan, David. "'This Inquisitive Age': Past and Present in the Scottish Enlightenment." *Scottish Historical Review*, 76. 1 no. 201 (April 1997): 85.

Bakshi, S. R. "Elphinstone's Mission to Kabul." *Journal of Indian History* 45 (1967): 605–13.

Baliga, B. S. "Home Government and the End of the Policy of Permanent Settlement in Madras, 1802–1818." *Indian Historical Records Commission Proceedings* 19 (1942).

Ballhatchet, Kenneth. "The Elphinstone Professors and Elphinstone College, 1827–1840." In *Indian Society and the Beginnings of Modernisation, c. 1830–1850.* Edited by C. H. Philips and M. D. Wainwright. London: School of Oriental and African Studies, 1976.

———. *Social Policy and Social Change in Western India, 1817–1830.* London: Oxford University Press, 1957.

Banerjee, A. C. "British Relations with Nagpur, 1798–1805." *Journal of Indian History* 28 (1950): 217–25.

Bayly, C. A. *Empire and Information: Intelligence Gathering and Social Communication in India, 1780–1870.* Cambridge: Cambridge University Press, 1996.

———. "The First Age of Global Imperialism, c. 1760–1830." *Journal of Imperial and Commonwealth History* 26 (1992): 28–47.

———. *Imperial Meridian: The British Empire and the World, 1780–1830.* London: Longman, 1989.

———. *Indian Society and the Making of the British Empire. The New Cambridge History of India*, ed. Gordon Johnson, part 2, vol. 1. Cambridge: Cambridge University Press, 1988.

Beaglehole, T. H. *Thomas Munro and the Development of Administrative Policy in Madras, 1792–1818. Origins of "The Munro System."* Cambridge: Cambridge University Press, 1966.

Bearce, George D. *British Attitudes Towards India, 1784–1858.* London: Oxford University Press, 1961.

Beattie, J. M. *Crime and the Courts in England, 1784–1858.* Oxford: Clarendon Press, 1986.

Bennell, A. S. "The Anglo-Maratha Confrontation of June and July 1803." *Journal of the Royal Asiatic Society* (October 1962): 107–31.

———. "Factors in the Marquis Wellesley's Failure against Holkar, 1804." *Bulletin of the School of Oriental and African Studies* 28 (1965): 553–81.

———. "Wellesley's Settlement of Mysore, 1799." *Journal of the Royal Asiatic Society* (1952).

Beveridge, Craig, and Turnbull, Donald. *The Eclipse of Scottish Culture. Inferiorism and the Intellectuals.* Edinburgh: Polygon, 1989.

Bierstedt, Robert. "Sociological Thought in the Eighteenth Century." In *A History of Sociological Analysis*, edited by Tom Bottomore and Robert Nisbet. New York: Basic Books, 1978.

Bradshaw, John. *Sir Thomas Munro and the British Settlement of Madras Presidency.* Rulers of India Series. Oxford: Clarendon Press, 1894.

Breckenridge, Carol A., and Peter van der Veer, eds. *Orientalism and the Postcolonial Predicament: Perspectives on South Asia.* Philadelphia: University of Pennsylvania Press, 1993.

Brewer, John. *The Sinews of Power: War, Money and the English State, 1688–1783.* Cambridge, Mass.: Harvard University Press, 1990.

Brims, John D. "The Scottish 'Jacobins', Scottish Nationalism and the British Union." In *Scotland and England; 1286–1815*, edited by Roger A. Mason. Edinburgh: John Donald Publishers Ltd., 1987.

Bryant, G. J. "Officers of the East India Company's Army in the Days of Clive and Hastings." *Journal of Imperial and Commonwealth History* 6 (May 1978): 203–25.

———. "Pacification in the Early British Raj, 1755–85." *Journal of Imperial and Commonwealth History* 14 (October 1985): 3–19.

———. "Scots in India in the Eighteenth Century." *Scottish Historical Review* 64 (April 1985): 22–41.

Bryson, Gladys. *Man and Society: The Scottish Inquiry of the Eighteenth Century.* Princeton, N.J.: Princeton University Press, 1945.

Cain, Alex M. *The Cornchest for Scotland: Scots in India.* Edinburgh: National Library of Scotland, 1986.

Cain, P. J., and A. G. Hopkins, *Innovation and Expansion, 1688–1914. British Imperialism,* vol. 1. London: Longman, 1993.

Callahan, Raymond. *The East India Company and Army Reform, 1783–1798.* Cambridge, Mass.: Harvard University Press, 1972.

Camic, Charles. *Experience and Enlightenment: Socialization for Cultural Change in Eighteenth Century Scotland.* Chicago: Chicago University Press, 1983.

Campbell, R. H., and A. S. Skinner, eds. *The Origins and Nature of the Scottish Enlightenment.* Edinburgh: John Donald Publishers, 1982.

Cannon, John. *The Aristocratic Century: The Peerage of Eighteenth Century England.* Cambridge: Cambridge University Press, 1984.

Chakravorty, U. N. *Anglo-Maratha Relations and Malcolm, 1798–1830.* New Delhi: Associated Press, 1979.

Chitnis, Anand. *The Scottish Enlightenment: A Social History.* London: Croom Helm, 1976.

Choksey, R. D. *Mountstuart Elphinstone: The Indian Years, 1796–1827.* Bombay: Popular Prakashan, 1971.

Clark, Ian D. L. "From Protest to Reaction: The Moderate Régime in the Church of Scotland, 1752–1805." In *Scotland in the Age Improvement: Essays in Scottish History in the Eighteenth Century,* edited by N. Phillipson and R. Mitchison. Edinburgh: Edinburgh University Press, 1970.

Clark, Jonathon. *English Society, 1688–1832: Ideology, Social Structure and Political Practice during the Ancien Régime.* Cambridge: Cambridge University Press, 1985.

Codell, Julie F., and Dianne Sachko Macleod, eds. *Orientalism Transposed: The Impact of the Colonies on British Culture.* Brookfield, Vt.: Ashgate Publishing Company, 1998.

Cohn, Bernard. *An Anthropologist among the Historians and Other Essays.* Delhi: Oxford University Press, 1987.

———. *Colonialism and Its Forms of Knowledge: The British in India.* Princeton, N.J.: Princeton University Press, 1996.

———. "The Command of Language and the Language of Command." In *Subaltern Studies IV: Writings on South Asian History and Society,* edited by Ranajit Guha. Delhi: Oxford University Press, 1985.

———. "Recruitment and Training of British Civil Servants in India, 1600–1860." In *Asian Bureaucratic Systems Emerging from the British Imperial Tradition,* edited by R. Braibanti. Raleigh, N.C.: Duke University Press, 1966.

Colley Linda. *Britons: Forging the Nation, 1707–1837.* New Haven and London: Yale University Press, 1992.

———. "Whose Nation? Class and National Consciousness in Britain, 1750–1830." *Past and Present* 113.

Cooper, Randolf G. S. "Wellington and the Marathas in 1803." *International History Review* 11 (1989): 31–38.

Cotton, J. S. *Mountstuart Elphinstone and the Making of South-Western India.* Rulers of India Series. Oxford: Clarendon Press, 1885.

Daiches, David. *The Paradox of Scottish Culture: The Eighteenth Century Experience.* London: University of Oxford Press, 1964.

Davie, G. E. *The Scottish Enlightenment.* General Series 99. London: Historical Association, 1981.

Davies, Stephen. "The Courts and the Scottish Legal System, 1600–1747: The Case of Stirlingshire." In *Crime and the Law: The Social History of Crime in Western Europe since 1500,* edited by V. A. C. Gartrell, Bruce Lenman, and Geoffrey Parker. London: Europa Publications, 1980.

Devine, T. M. "An Eighteenth-Century Business Elite: Glasgow-West India Merchants, c. 1750–1815." *Scottish Historical Review* 57 (1978): 40–67.

———. "Glasgow Colonial Merchants and Land, 1770–1815." In *Land and Industry: The Landed Estate and the Industrial Revolution,* edited by J. T. Ward and R. G. Wilson. New York: Barnes & Noble, 1971.

———. *The Tobacco Lords: A Study of the Tobacco Merchants of Glasgow and their Trading Activities, c. 1740–90.* Edinburgh: John Donald Publishers, 1975.

Dickinson, H. T. *Liberty and Property: Political Ideology in Eighteenth-Century Britain.* London: Weidenfeld and Nicolson, 1977.

Dirks, Nicholas B. "Colonial Histories and Native Informants: Biography of an Archive." In *Orientalism and the Postcolonial Predicament. Perspectives on South Asia,* edited by Carol A. Breckenridge and Peter van der Veer. Philadelphia: University of Pennsylvania Press, 1993.

Drewitt, F. G. D. *Bombay in the Days of George IV: Memoirs of Sir Edward West, Chief Justice of the King's Court during Its Conflict with the East India Company.* London: Longmans, 1907.

Duthie, John Lowe. "Some Further Insights into the Working of Mid-Victorian Imperialism: Lord Salisbury, the 'Forward' Group and Anglo-Afghan Relations: 1874–1878." *Journal of Imperial and Commonwealth History* 8 (1980): 181–208.

Dutt, Romesh. *The Economic History of India: Under Early British Rule.* 7th ed. 2 vols. First published 1901. London: Routledge & Kegan Paul, 1950.

Dutt, R. Palme. *India-Today.* 2nd rev. Indian ed. Bombay: People's Publishing House, 1949.

Dwyer, John. "Clio and Ethics: Practical Morality in Enlightened Scotland." *Eighteenth Century* 30 (1989): 45–72.

Dwyer, John, Roger A. Mason, and Alexander Murdoch. *New Perspectives on the Politics and Culture of Early Modern Scotland.* Edinburgh: John Donald, 1982.

Embree, Ainslie. *Charles Grant and British Rule in India.* London: George Allen & Unwin, 1962.

———. "Landholding in India and British Institutions." In *Land Control and Social Structure in Indian History,* edited by R. E. Frykenberg. Madison: University of Wisconsin, 1969.

Fay, C. R. *Adam Smith and the Scotland of His Day.* Cambridge: Cambridge University Press, 1956.

Fergusson, Alexander. *The Honourable Henry Erskine Lord Advocate For Scotland.* Edinburgh: Blackwood & Sons, 1882.

Fisher, Michael. "Indirect Rule in the British Empire: The Foundations of the Residency System in India (1764–1858)." *Modern Asian Studies* 18 (1984): 393–428.

Forbes, Duncan. "Scientific Whiggism: Adam Smith and John Millar." *Cambridge Journal* 7 (1954).

Fraser, Sir William, *The Elphinstone Family Book of the Lords Elphinstone, Balmerino and Coupar.* 2 vols. Edinburgh, 1897.

Freeman, Michael. *Edmund Burke and the Critique of Political Radicalism.* Oxford: Basil Blackwell, 1980.

Fry, Michael. *Patronage and Principle: A Political History of Modern Scotland.* Aberdeen: Aberdeen University Press, 1987.

Frykenberg, Robert., ed. *Land Control and Social Structure in Indian History.* Madison: University of Wisconsin Press, 1969.

———. *Gunthur District, 1788–1848.* Oxford: Clarendon Press, 1965.

Fuhr, Enid M. "Strategy and Diplomacy in British India under the Marquis Wellesley: The Second Maratha War, 1802–1805." Ph.D. dissertation, Simon Fraser University, 1994.

Furber, Holden. *Henry Dundas, First Viscount Melville, 1742–1811. Political Manager of Scotland, Statesman, Administrator of British India.* London: Oxford University Press, 1931.

Gartrell, V. A. C., Bruce Lenman, and Geoffrey Parker, eds. *Crime and the Law: The Social History of Crime in Western Europe since 1500.* London: Europa Publications, 1980.

Ghosh, Biswanath. *British Policy Towards the Pathans and the Pindaris in Central India, 1805–1818.* Calcutta: Punthi Pustak, 1966.

Gilbert, Arthur N. "Recruitment and Reform in the East India Company Army, 1760–1800." *Journal of British Studies* 15 (1975): 89–111.

Graham, H. Grey. *The Social Life of Scotland in the Eighteenth Century.* London: Adam and Charles Black, 1899. 4th ed. illustrated, 1937. Reprint, 1964.

Grave, S. A. *The Scottish Philosophers of Common Sense.* Oxford: Clarendon Press, 1960.

Grewal, J. S. *Muslim Rule in India: The Assessments of British Historians.* Oxford: Oxford University Press, 1970.

Guha, Ranajit. *Dominance without Hegemony: History and Power in Colonial India.* Cambridge, Mass.: Harvard University Press, 1997.

———. *A Rule of Property for Bengal: An Essay on the Idea of Permanent Settlement.* Paris: Mouton & Co., 1963.

Gupta, P. C. *Baji Rao and the East India Company, 1796–1818.* Bombay: Oxford University Press, 1939.

Haakonssen, Knud. *The Science of a Legislator: The Natural Jurisprudence of David Hume and Adam Smith.* New York: University of Cambridge Press, 1981.

Hans, Nicholas. *New Trends in Education in the Eighteenth Century.* London: Routledge & Kegan Paul, 1951. 2nd impression, 1966.

Harlow, Vincent T. *The Founding of the Second British Empire, 1763–1793.* 2 vols. London: Longmans, 1952.

———. "The New Imperial System, 1783–1815." In *The Cambridge History of the British Empire, 1783–1870*, vol. 2, *The Growth of the New Empire*, edited by J. Holland Rose, A. P. Newton, and E. A. Benians. Cambridge: Cambridge University Press, 1929–1940.

Hechter, Michael. *Internal Colonialism: The Celtic Fringe in British National Development, 1536–1966.* London: Routledge and Kegan Paul, 1975.

Hobsbawm, E. J. "Scottish Reformers of the Eighteenth Century and Capitalist Agriculture." In *Peasants in History: Essays in Honour of Daniel Thorner*, edited by E. J. Hobsbawm, Witold Kula, Ashok Mitra, K. N. Ray, and Ignacy Sachs. Calcutta: published for the Sameeksha Trust by Oxford University Press, 1980.

Hont, Istvan, and Michael Ignatieff, eds. *Wealth and Virtue: The Shaping of Political Economy in the Scottish Enlightenment.* Cambridge: Cambridge University Press, 1983.

Hope, V., ed. *Philosophers of the Scottish Enlightenment.* Edinburgh: Edinburgh University Press, 1984.

Houghton, Walter E. *The Victorian Frame of Mind, 1830–1870.* 1957. Reprint, New Haven: Yale University Press, 1985.

Hutchins, Francis. *The Illusion of Permanence.* Princeton, N.J.: Princeton University Press, 1967.

Hutton, W. H. *The Marquess Wellesley and the Development of the Company into the Supreme Power in India.* Oxford: Clarendon Press, 1890.

Ignatieff, Michael. "John Millar and Individualism." In *Wealth and Virtue: The Shaping of Political Economy in the Scottish Enlightenment*, edited by Istvan Hont and Michael Ignatieff. Cambridge: Cambridge University Press, 1983.

Inden, Ronald. *Imagining India.* Oxford: Basil Blackwell, 1990.

———. "Orientalist Contructions of India." *Modern Asian Studies* 20 (1986): 401–46.

Ingram, Edward. "An Aspiring Buffer State: Anglo-Persian Relations in the Third Coalition, 1804–1807." *Historical Journal* 16 (1973): 509–33.

———. *Britain's Persian Connection, 1798–1828: Prelude to the Great Game in Asia.* Oxford: Clarendon Press, 1992.

———. *Commitment to Empire: Prophecies of the Great Game in Asia, 1797–1800.* Oxford: Clarendon Press, 1981.

———. *Empire-building and Empire-builders: Twelve Studies.* London: Frank Cass, 1995.

———. "Family and Faction in the Great Game in Asia: The Struggle over the Persian Mission, 1828–1835." *Middle Eastern Studies* 3 (1981): 291–309.

———. *In Defence of British India: Great Britain in the Middle East, 1775–1842.* London: Frank Cass, 1984.

———. "The Rules of the Game: A Commentary on the Defence of British India, 1798–1829." *Journal of Imperial and Commonwealth History* 3 (1974–75): 257–79.

Irschick, Eugene F. *Dialogue and History: Constructing South India, 1795–1895.* Berkeley: University of California Press, 1994.

Kaye, John William. *Lives of Indian Officers.* 2 vols. London: Strahan, 1867.

Kennedy, Dane. "Imperial History and Post-Colonial Theory." *Journal of Imperial and Commonwealth History* 24 (1996): 345–363.

Kettler, David. *The Social and Political Thought of Adam Ferguson.* Columbus: Ohio State University Press, 1965.

Khurana, G. *British Historiography on the Sikh Power in the Punjab.* London and New York: Mansell Publishing, 1985.

Kidd, Colin. "The Ideological Significance of Robertson's *History of Scotland.*" In *William Robertson and the Expansion of Empire*, edited by Stewart J. Brown. Cambridge: Cambridge University Press, 1997.

———. *Subverting Scotland's Past: Scottish Whig Historians and the Creation of an Anglo-British Identity, 1689–c. 1830.* Cambridge: Cambridge University Press, 1993.

Kolff, Dirk H. A. "The End of an *Ancien Régime:* Colonial War in India, 1798–1818." In *Imperialism and War: Essays on Colonial Wars in Asia and Africa*, edited by J. A. de Moor and H. L. Wesseling. Leiden: Brill, 1989.

Kopf. David. *British Orientalism and the Bengal Renaissance. The Dynamics of Indian Modernization, 1773–1835.* Berkeley: University of California Press, 1969.

Lambton, Ann. "Persia: The Breakdown of Society." In *Cambridge History of Islam*, vol. 1, *The Central Islamic Lands*, edited by P. M. Holt et al. Cambridge: Cambridge University Press, 1970.

Lehmann, W. C. *Henry Home, Lord Kames, and the Scottish Enlightenment. A Study in National Character and in the History of Ideas.* The Hague: Martinus Nijhoff, 1971.

Lenman, Bruce. *An Economic History of Modern Scotland, 1660–1976.* London: B. T. Batsford, 1977.

———. *Integration, Enlightenment, and Industrialization: Scotland 1746–1832.* Toronto: University of Toronto Press, 1981.

Lew, Joseph. "The Necessary Orientalist? *The Giaour* and Nineteenth-Century Imperialist Misogyny." In *Romanticism, Race, and Imperial Culture, 1780–1834,* edited by Alan Richardson and Sonia Hofkosh. Bloomington and Indianapolis: Indiana University Press, 1996.

Lewis, B., and P. M. Holt, eds. *Historians of the Near and Middle East.* London: Oxford University Press, 1962.

Lieberman, David. "The Legal Needs of a Commercial Society: The Jurisprudence of Lord Kames." In *Wealth and Virtue: The Shaping of Political Economy in the Scottish Enlightenment,* edited by Istvan Hont and Michael Ignatieff. Cambridge: Cambridge University Press, 1983.

Lindgren, J. Ralph. *The Social Philosophy of Adam Smith.* The Hague: Martinus Nijhoff, 1973.

Longford, Elizabeth. *Wellington: The Years of the Sword.* London: Panther Books, 1971.

Ludden, David. "Orientalist Empiricism: Transformations of Colonial Knowledge." In *Orientalism and the Postcolonial Predicament. Perspectives on South Asia,* edited by Carol A. Breckenridge and Peter van der Veer. Philadelphia: University of Pennsylvania Press, 1993.

McGuinness, Arthur E. *Henry Home, Lord Kames.* New York: Twayne Publishers, Inc., 1970.

MacKenzie, John M. "Essay and Reflection: On Scotland and the Empire." *International History Review* 15 (1993): 661–80.

———. *Orientalism: History, Theory and the Arts.* Manchester: Manchester University Press, 1995.

McLaren, Martha. "From Analysis to Prescription: Scottish Concepts of Asian Despotism in Early Nineteenth Century British India." *International History Review,* 15 (1993), pp. 469–501.

———. "Philosophical History and Asian Society; The Influence of Scottish Moral Philosophy on the Historical Writing of John Malcolm and Mountstuart Elphinstone," *Indo-British Review,* 20 (1994).

———. "Sir Thomas Munro." Biographical essay for the *New Dictionary of National Biography,* Oxford University Press, forthcoming.

MacRae, Donald G. "Adam Ferguson 1723–1816." In *The Founding Fathers of Social Science,* edited by Timothy Raison. Harmondsworth: Penguin Books, 1969. Revised edition by Paul Barker, London: Scolar Press, 1979.

Majeed, J. "James Mill's 'The History of British India' and Utilitarianism as a Rhetoric of Reform." *Modern Asian Studies* 24 (1990): 209–24.

———. *Ungoverned Imaginings: James Mill's "The History of British India" and Orientalism.* Oxford: Clarendon Press, 1992.

Marshall, P. J. *Bengal: The British Bridgehead. Eastern India 1740–1828. The New Cambridge History of India,* ed. Gordon Johnson, part 2, vol. 2. Cambridge: Cambridge University Press, 1987.

———, ed. *The British Discovery of Hinduism in the Eighteenth Century.* Cambridge: Cambridge University Press, 1970.

———. "'Cornwallis Triumphant': War in India and the British Public in the Late Eighteenth Century." In *War, Strategy, and International Politics: Essays in Honour of Sir Michael Howard,* edited by Lawrence Freedman et al., Oxford: Clarendon Press, 1992.

———. "Empire and Authority in the later Eighteenth Century." *Journal of Imperial and Commonwealth History* 15 (1987): 105–22.

———. "European Imperialism in the Nineteenth Century." *History Today* (May 1982): 49.

———. "A Free Though Conquering People. Britain and Asia in the Eighteenth Century." Inaugural Lecture in Rhodes Chair of Imperial History, University of London, 1981.

———. *Problems of Empire: Britain and India, 1757–1813.* Historical Problems: Studies and Documents No.3. General editor G. R. Elton. London: George Allen and Unwin, 1968.

———. "The Moral Swing to the East: British Humanitarianism, India and the West Indies." In

East India Company Studies: Essays Presented to Sir Cyril Philips, edited by K. Ballhatchet and J. Harrison. Hong Kong: Asian Research Service, 1986.

————, and Glyndwr Williams, *The Great Map of Mankind: British Perceptions of the World in the Age of the Enlightenment.* London: J. M. Dent & Sons, 1982.

Mason, Philip. *The Men Who Ruled India.* 2 vols. London: Jonathon Cape, 1954. Paperback edition, London: Pan Books, 1985.

Mathew, W. M. "The Origins and Occupations of Glasgow Students, 1740–1839." *Past and Present* 33 (1966): 74–94.

Metcalf, Thomas R. *Ideologies of the Raj.* Cambridge: Cambridge University Press, 1994.

Mill, James. *The History of British India.* Abridged and with an introduction by William Thomas. Classics of British Historical Literature, edited by John Clive. Chicago: University of Chicago Press, 1975.

Misra, B. B. *The Bureaucracy in India.* Delhi: Oxford University Press, 1977.

————. *The Central Administration of the East India Company, 1773–1834.* Manchester: Manchester University Press, 1959.

Moir, Martin I., Douglas M. Peers, and Lynn Zastoupil, eds. *J. S. Mill's Encounter with India.* Toronto: University of Toronto Press, 1999.

Moon, Penderel. *The British Conquest and Dominion of India.* London: Duckworth, 1989.

Moore-Gilbert, B. J. *Kipling and "Orientalism."* London: Croom Helm, 1986.

Mukherjee, Nilmani. *The Ryotwari System in Madras, 1792–1827.* Calcutta: Firma K. L. Mukhopadhyay, 1962.

Mukherjee, S. N. *Sir William Jones: A Study in Eighteenth Century British Attitudes to India.* First published 1968. Hyderabad: Orient Longman, 1987.

Murdoch, Alexander. *"The People Above": Politics and Administration in Mid-Eighteenth-Century Scotland.* Edinburgh: John Donald Publishers, 1980.

Nehru, Jawaharlal. *The Discovery of India.* London: Meridian Books, 1951.

O'Brien, Karen. *Narratives of Enlightenment: Cosmopolitan History from Voltaire to Gibbon.* Cambridge: Cambridge University Press, 1997.

————. "Robertson's Place in the Development of Eighteenth-Century Narrative History." In *William Robertson and the Expansion of Empire,* edited by Stewart J. Brown. Cambridge: Cambridge University Press, 1997.

O'Hanlon, Rosalind, and David Washbrooke. "Histories in Transition: Approaches to the Study of Colonialism and Culture in India." *History Workshop* 32 (1991): 110–27.

Osbourne, G. S. *Scottish and English Schools. A Comparative Study of the Past Fifty Years.* Pittsburgh: University of Pittsburgh Press, 1966.

Outram, Dorinda. *The Enlightenment.* Cambridge: Cambridge University Press, 1995.

Owen, J. B. "Political Patronage in Eighteenth Century England." In *The Triumph of Culture: Eighteenth Century Perspectives.* Toronto: A. M. Hakkert, 1972.

Pannikar, K. M. *Asia and Western Dominance.* London: George Allen and Unwin, 1959.

Parkin, Charles. *The Moral Basis of Burke's Political Thought.* Cambridge: Cambridge University Press, 1956.

Pasley, Rodney. *"Send Malcolm!" The Life of Major-General Sir John Malcolm, 1769–1833.* London: British Association for Cemeteries in South Asia, 1982.

Peabody, Norbert. "Tod's *Rajast'han* and the Boundaries of Imperial Rule in Nineteenth-Century India." *Modern Asian Studies* 30, 1 (1996): 185–220.

Peardon, T. P. *The Transition in English Historical Writing, 1760–1830.* New York: Columbia University Press, 1933.

Peers, Douglas M. *Between Mars and Mammon: Colonial Armies and the Garrison State in India, 1819–1835.* London: Tauris Academic Studies, 1995.

———. "Between Mars and Mammon: The East India Company and Efforts to Reform its Army, 1796–1832." *Historical Journal* 33 (1990): 385–401.

———. "Between Mars and Mammon; The Military and the Political Economy of British India at the Time of the First Burma War, 1824–1826." Ph.D. dissertation, London: University of London, 1988.

———. "The Duke of Wellington and British India during the Liverpool Administration, 1819–27." *Journal of Imperial and Commonwealth History* 17 (1988): 5–25.

———. "War and Public Finance in Early Nineteenth-Century British India: The First Burma War." *International History Review* 11 (1989): 628–47.

Perlin, Frank. "State Formation Reconsidered." *Modern Asian Studies* 19 (1985): 415–80.

Philips, C. H. *The East India Company, 1784–1834.* 1941. Reprint, Manchester: Manchester University Press, 1961.

———, ed. *Historians of India, Pakistan and Ceylon.* London: Oxford University Press, 1961.

Phillimore, R. H. *Historical Records of the Survey of India.* 3 vols. Dehra Dun, 1950.

Phillipson, Nicholas. "Adam Smith as Civic Moralist." In *Wealth and Virtue: The Shaping of Political Economy in the Scottish Enlightenment,* edited by Istvan Hont and Michael Ignatieff. Cambridge: Cambridge University Press, 1983.

———. *Hume.* London: Weidenfeld & Nicolson, 1989.

———. "Providence and Progress: An Introduction to the Historical Thought of William Robertson." In *William Robertson and the Expansion of Empire,* edited by Stewart J. Brown. Cambridge: Cambridge University Press, 1997.

———. "Towards a Definition of the Scottish Enlightenment." In *City and Society in the Eighteenth Century,* edited by Paul Fritz and David Williams. Toronto: Hakkert, 1973.

———, and Rosalind Mitchison, eds. *Scotland in the Age of Improvement: Essays in Scottish History in the Eighteenth Century.* Edinburgh: Edinburgh University Press, 1970.

Pocock, J. G. A. "Cambridge Paradigms and Scotch Philosophers: A Study of the Relations between the Civic Humanist and the Civic Jurisprudential Interpretation of Eighteenth-Century Social Thought." In *Wealth and Virtue: The Shaping of Political Economy in the Scottish Enlightenment,* edited by Istvan Hont and Michael Ignatieff. Cambridge: Cambridge University Press, 1983.

———. *Virtue, Commerce and History: Essays on Political Thought and History, Chiefly in the Eighteenth Century.* New York: Cambridge University Press, 1985.

"Politicus." "Sir Thomas Munro." *Modern Review* 14 (July 1913).

Prakash, Gyan. "Writing Post-Orientalist Histories of the Third World: Perspectives from Indian Historiography." *Comparative Studies in Society and History* 32 (1990): 383–408.

Price, J. V. *David Hume.* New York: Twayne Publishers, 1968.

Radcliffe, Lord. *Mountstuart Elphinstone.* The Romanes Lecture, 25 May 1962. Oxford: Clarendon Press, 1962.

Rae, John. *Life of Adam Smith.* First published 1895. With an introduction by Jacob Viner, New York: A. M. Kelley, 1965.

Raychaudhuri, Tapan. "Permanent Settlement in Operation: Bakorganj District, East Bengal." In *Land Control and Social Structure in Indian History,* edited by Robert Frykeberg, Madison: University of Wisconsin Press, 1969.

Razzell, R. E. "Social Origins of Officers in the Indian and British Home Armies, 1758–1962." *British Journal of Sociology* 14 (1963): 248–60.

Rendall, Jane. "Scottish Orientalism: From Robertson to James Mill." *Historical Journal* 25 (1982): 43–69.

———. *The Origins of the Scottish Enlightenment.* London: Macmillan, 1978.

Robertson, John. "The Scottish Enlightenment at the Limits of the Civic Tradition." In *Wealth and Virtue: The Shaping of Political Economy in the Scottish Enlightenment*, edited by Istvan Hont and Michael Ignatieff. Cambridge: Cambridge University Press, 1983.

Rocher, Rosane. "British Orientalism in the Eighteenth Century: The Dialectics of Knowledge and Government." In *Orientalism and the Postcolonial Predicament. Perspectives on South Asia*, edited by Carol A. Breckenridge and Peter van der Veer. Philadelphia: University of Pennsylvania Press, 1993.

Ross, Ian Simpson. *Lord Kames and the Scotland of His Day.* Oxford: Clarendon Press, 1972.

Rubenstein, W. D. "The End of 'Old Corruption' in Britain, 1780–1860." *Past and Present* 101 (1983): 55–86.

Said, Edward W. *Orientalism.* New York: Random House, 1979.

Sajanlal, K. "A Few Unpublished Letters of Sir Thomas Munro." *Indian Historical Records Commission Proceedings* 31 (1955): 106–12.

Sanders, Charles R. *The Strachey Family, 1588–1932: Their Writings and Literary Associations.* New York: Greenwood Press, 1968.

Sardesai, G. S. *New History of the Marathas.* 3 vols. Bombay: Phoenix Publications, 1948.

Schneider, L. *The Scottish Moralists on Human Nature and Society.* Chicago: University of Chicago Press, 1967.

Schofield, Thomas Philip. "Conservative Political Thought in Britain in Response to the French Revolution." *Historical Journal* 29 (1986): 601–22.

Scotland, James. *The History of Scottish Education.* Vol.1. *From the Beginning to 1872.* London: University Press, 1969.

Sencourt, Robert. *India in English Literature.* London: Simpkin, Marshall, 1925.

Sher, Richard. "Charles V and the Book Trade: An Episode in Enlightenment Print Culture." In *William Robertson and the Expansion of Empire*, edited by Stewart J. Brown. Cambridge: Cambridge University Press, 1997.

———. *Church and University in the Scottish Enlightenment: The Moderate Literati of Edinburgh.* Princeton, N.J.: Princeton University Press, 1985.

Smout, T. C. *A History of the Scottish People, 1560–1830.* London: Collins, 1969.

Stanlis, Peter J. *Edmund Burke and the Natural Law.* Ann Arbor: University of Michigan, 1958.

Stein, Burton. "Idiom and Ideology in Early Nineteenth Century South India." In *Rural India: Land, Power and Society under British Rule*, edited by Peter Robb. Collected Papers on South Asia, no. 6. London: Curzon Press, 1983.

———, "State Formation and Economy Reconsidered." *Modern Asian Studies* 19 (1985): 387–413.

———. *Thomas Munro: The Origins of the Colonial State and His Vision of Empire.* Delhi: Oxford University Press, 1989.

Stein, Peter. "Law and Society in Eighteenth Century Scottish Thought." In *Scotland in the Age of Improvement: Essays in Scottish History in the Eighteenth Century*, edited by N. Phillipson and R. Mitchison. Edinburgh: Edinburgh University Press, 1970.

Stephen, Leslie. *History of English Thought in the Eighteenth Century.* 1881. Reprint, New York: Harcourt, Brace and World, 1962.

Stewart, M. A., ed. *Studies in the Philosophy of the Scottish Enlightenment.* Oxford: Clarendon Press, 1990.

Stokes, Eric. *The English Utilitarians and India.* Oxford: Clarendon Press, 1963.

Stone, Lawrence, and Jeanne C. Fawtier Stone. *An Open Elite? England 1540–1880.* Oxford: Clarendon Press, 1984.

Suleri, Sara. *The Rhetoric of English India.* Chicago: University of Chicago Press, 1992.

Sunter, Ronald M. *Patronage and Politics in Scotland, 1707–1832.* Edinburgh: John Donald, 1986.

Sutherland, Gillian. "Education." In *Cambridge Social History of Britain, 1750–1950,* vol 3, *Social Agencies and Institutions,* edited by F. M. L. Thompson. Cambridge: Cambridge University Press, 1990.

Sutherland, Lucy Stuart. *The East India Company in Eighteenth-Century Politics.* Oxford: Clarendon Press, 1962.

Taylor, Stephen, Richard Connors, and Clyve Jones, eds. *Hanoverian Britain and Empire: Essays in Memory of Philip Lawson.* Woodbridge: Boydell Press, 1998.

Teltscher, Kate. *India Inscribed. European and British Writing on India, 1600–1800.* Delhi: Oxford University Press, 1995.

Thomas, Nicholas. *Colonialism's Culture: Anthropology, Travel and Government.* Princeton, N.J.: Princeton University Press, 1994.

Thornton, A. P. "Essay and Reflection: Third Thoughts on Empire." *International History Review* 10 (1988): 579–93.

Trautmann, Thomas R. *Aryans and British India.* Berkeley: University of California Press, 1997.

Varma, Sushma. *Mountstuart Elphinstone in Maharashtra (1801–1827): A Study of the Territories Conquered from the Peshwas.* Calcutta: K. P. Bagchi, 1981.

Venkatasubba Sastri, K. N. *The Munro System of British Statesmanship in India.* Mysore: University of Mysore Press, 1939.

Washbrooke, D. A. "Progress and Problems: South Asian Economic and Social History c. 1720–1860." *Modern Asian Studies* 22 (1988): 57–96.

Winch, Donald. "Adam Smith: Scottish Moral Philosopher as Political Economist." *Historical Journal* 35 (1992): 91–113.

Witherington, Donald J. "Education and Society in the Eighteenth Century." In *Scotland in the Age of Improvement: Essays in Scottish History in the Eighteenth Century,* edited by N. Phillipson and R. Mitchison. Edinburgh: Edinburgh University Press, 1970.

Yapp, M. E. "British Perceptions of the Russian Threat to India." *Modern Asian Studies* 21 (1987): 647–65.

———. "Control of the Persian Mission, 1822–36." *University of Birmingham Historical Journal* 7 (1960): 162–79.

———. *Strategies of British India: Britain, Iran and Afghanistan, 1798–1850.* Oxford: Clarendon Press, 1980.

———. "Two British Historians of Persia." In *Historians of the Near and Middle East,* edited by B. Lewis and P. M. Holt. Oxford: Oxford University Press, 1962.

Zastoupil, Lynn. "India, J. S. Mill, and 'Western' Culture." In *J. S. Mill's Encounter with India,* edited by Martin I. Moir, Douglas M. Peers, and Lynn Zastoupil. Toronto: University of Toronto Press, 1999.

———. *John Stuart Mill and India.* Stanford: Stanford University Press, 1994.

Index

Abercrombie, Sir Robert, 38
Abul-Fazel, 230
Account of the Kingdom of Caubul, An (Elphinstone),
   41, 64, 82, 122
Adventures of Hajji Baba, The (Morier), 105–6
Act of Union (Anglo-Scottish, 1707), 4
Adam, John, 20, 63, 84, 151
Administration of Justice, The (Munro), 217–18
administration, administrative system, 1, 9, 12, 32,
   33, 40, 51, 52, 57, 71, 72, 74, 93, 96, 99, 101,
   106, 108, 113, 168–70 passim, 172, 182, 183, 184,
   187, 189, 190, 192, 195, 197, 199, 214, 217, 223,
   236, 238, 245, 249, 250, 253
Afghan, Afghanistan, 11, 48, 59, 64, 65, 66, 79, 81,
   133, 162, 163–66, 234, 237
agriculture, 4, 161, 169, 173, 193, 194, 246, 252
   improvement, 32, 195, 202, 204 210
   reformers, 201
Ahmad Shah Durani. *See* Durani
Akbar, 176–79, 235
Allan, Sir Alexander, 99, 246
American Revolutionary War, 10, 16, 26, 241
Amherst, William Pitt, 2nd baron, 108, 109, 114
Anderson, James, 194–5
Anglicist reformers, 111, 242, 243, 245, 253
Anglo-Indians, 241, 244–48 passim, 254
Anglo-Maratha Wars, 42, 81
   Second Anglo-Maratha War, 51–2, 54, 57, 63, 87
   Third Anglo-Maratha War, 79, 82, 85, 88, 93,
      96, 98, 99, 100, 250
Anglo-Mysore Wars
   Second Anglo-Mysore War, 16, 39
   Third Anglo-Mysore War, 16, 45
   Fourth Anglo-Mysore War, 16, 34, 35, 47, 53
Annual Register, 139
Arab, Arabic, 122, 134, 149, 166, 176
Argaum, battle of, 55
Army, 11, 24, 29, 30, 36, 52, 55, 72, 106, 174, 182–3,
   185, 223
   Bengal, 35, 90
   Bombay, 110

Crown, 30, 44, 59, 69, 70, 87
Madras, 16, 18, 53, 61, 76, 90, 195.
   See also East India Company, army.
Aryans and British India (Trautmann), 228
Asia(n), 125, 136, 144, 175
   culture, 2, 130, 159, 227, 228, 231
   government, 140, 171, 173, 187
   history, 4, 168, 191, 227, 228
   societies, 130, 133, 140, 161, 187, 231
   sources, 120, 230, 238
Assaye, battle of, 40, 55, 87, 90
Aurangzeb, 177, 178–80
Ava. *See* Burma.

Babur, 65, 177
Baghdad, 59, 66
Baji Rao II, peshwa of Pune. *See* Pune, peshwa
   of
Baliga, B.S., 245
Ballhatchet, Kenneth, 248
Baramahal, 16, 31, 33, 35, 47, 49, 74, 77, 171,
   194–197 passim, 199, 202, 203, 206, 209, 246,
   250
Barlow, Sir George, 57, 61
Baroda, gaekwar of, 54, 81
Bassein, Treaty of, 54
Bayly, C.A., 10, 42, 47, 52, 63, 81, 168, 204, 228,
   230, 236, 238
Beaglehole, T.H., 31, 193, 248, 266n. 14
Bearce, George, 137–38
Beatson, Alexander, 195
Beatson, Robert, 195
Benares, 21, 38, 53, 71
Bengal, 7, 8, 21, 30, 31, 43, 45, 53, 71, 72, 74, 82,
   101, 108, 109, 134, 185, 186, 193, 203, 204, 210,
   212, 217, 236, 246
Bentham, Jeremy, 188, 189
Bentinck, Lord William Cavendish, 59, 108, 109,
   114
Berar, raja of, 21, 40, 54, 55, 57, 58, 63
Bheels (Bhils), 184

299

Blackstone, Sir William, 214
Blair, Rev. Hugh, 37, 58, 124, 125, 135
Board of Control (British Government Board of
    Control for India), 3, 17, 60, 70, 71, 74, 94,
    103, 114, 184
Bombay, 7, 61, 65, 91, 94, 95, 96, 98–102 passim,
    107, 114, 174, 185, 189, 247, 250
    Literary society, 111, 230
    Supreme court, 111–12
Bradshaw, John, 240, 241
Brewer, John, 8
British India, 37, 46, 47, 58, 59, 66
    defense of, 181
    finances, 114, 185
    government, 3, 11, 106, 162, 171, 183, 184, 223,
        240, 244, 245, 246, 249. (see also Govern-
        ment of British India)
    judicial system, 216
    militarism, 182
Brown, George, 97
Bryson, Gladys, 138
Buckinghamshire, earl of. See Hobart, Robert,
    viscount Hobart, 4th earl of Bucking-
    hamshire
bureaucracy, bureaucratization, 3, 66, 182, 250, 251
Burke, Edmund, 2, 12, 34, 137–43, 171, 183, 187,
    204, 248, 253
Burma,
    Ava, 185
    First Burma War, 87, 88, 107, 108–9, 114, 182,
        184, 186
Burns, Robert, 135, 195

Calcutta, 19, 38, 39, 44, 46, 56, 59, 61, 63, 77, 102,
    112, 114, 174, 175, 189
Callahan, Raymond, 29, 106
Callender, James Thomson, 6
Calvin, Calvinism, 37, 145, 146, 148, 151, 188, 189
Cambridge University, 23, 24, 37
Canning, George, 89, 94, 96, 98, 100, 102, 175,
    184, 185, 193
Cannon, John, 25
career building, 3, 61, 103, 231, 241, 251
Carlyle, Thomas, 241
Caste(s), 150, 158, 198, 215, 234–35
Catholic, 146, 147, 148
Ceded Districts, 51, 52, 57, 74, 77, 170, 171, 206,
    212, 214
Central India, 93, 97, 98, 102, 114, 200
Cervantes, Miguel de, 172
Chambers, Sir Charles, 112
Chaplin, William, 92, 108
Charles I (king of England), 124
Charles VII (king of France), 173
Charlotte, of Mecklenburg-Strelitz (queen of
    England), 157

Chaucer, Geoffrey, 122, 133
Choksey, R.D., 113, 247
Christian, Christianity, 146, 148, 151–54 passim
Church of Scotland. 18, 131, 145, 152, 215. See also
    Kirk
civil society, 12, 79, 161, 168, 174, 191
Clapham Sect, 72
Clarke, Sir Alured, 37, 46
Clive, Edward, Lord Clive, 17, 39, 53
Clive, Robert, Lord Clive, 53
Close, Colonel Barry, 45, 47, 54, 80, 143
Cochrane, James, 99
Cohn, Bernard, 31, 230
Colebrooke, Henry, 45
Colebrooke, Sir T.E., 101, 151, 240, 241
College of Fort St. George, 184
College of Fort William. See Fort William Col-
    lege
Colley, Linda, 8, 9, 11
Collins, Colonel John, 56
colonialism, colonial, 10, 192, 228, 229, 236–37,
    238, 240, 44–45
Commentaries on the Law of England (Blackstone), 214
conservatism, Conservative, 2, 12, 78, 140, 143,
    144, 188, 241, 242, 243, 245, 253, 254
Conservative-Orientalist, 246, 248
Cornwallis, Charles, 1st marquis and 2nd earl
    Cornwallis, 16, 31, 37, 43, 57, 71–74 passim,
    127, 193, 194, 204
Cotton, J.S., 151, 240, 241
Court of Directors (of the East India Compa-
    ny), directorate, 10, 29, 31, 37, 48, 69, 72, 94,
    99, 100, 107, 108, 114, 171, 186, 196
Crawfurd, John, 65
Cumming, James, 3, 71, 72, 74, 257n. 3

Dalrymple, Sir James, 1st viscount Stair, 215
Danglia, Trimbakji, 81
Davis, Samuel, 45, 71
Deccan, 79, 80, 84, 89, 113, 158, 184, 247
deism, 149, 234
despotism, 120, 125, 156, 160, 161, 162, 164, 165, 168,
    173, 175, 176, 179, 182, 190, 191, 200, 253
    oriental despotism, 161
"dialogic encounters," 238
Dialogues Concerning Natural Religion (Hume), 152–3
Dickinson, H.T., 2
Don Quixote, 172
Dow, Alexander, 230
"drain, the" (of Indian wealth), 209, 246
Dundas, Henry, 1st viscount Melville, 7, 20, 34,
    37, 46, 48, 53, 142, 188
Dundas, Robert Saunders, 2nd viscount
    Melville, 60
Dunlop, Lieutenant General James, 87
Durani, Ahmad Shah, 162, 163–4, 177

Dutt, R. Palme, 245
Dykes, James, 33

East India Company, 1, 18, 20, 23, 37, 40, 53, 60,
    66, 78, 93, 105, 142, 208, 221
    appointments/recruits, 7, 16, 19–22 passim,
        25–28 passim, 30, 41, 44, 63, 65, 69, 96, 99,
        100, 103, 107, 108, 249, 260n. 20
    army, 24, 29, 30, 35, 61, 72, 75, 85, 89, 103, 141,
        258n. 15, 260n. 21
    & British government, 3, 100, 103, 109
    charter, 71, 76, 147
    civil/military service 29, 33, 60, 68, 69, 98, 250
    commerce, 8, 27, 35, 38, 132, 235, 236
    economy/finance, 8, 10, 102, 110, 182
    expansion, 9, 11, 30, 44, 49, 54, 88, 93, 162
    government/state, 7, 11, 17, 32, 44, 51, 71, 169,
        170, 171, 179, 182, 183, 191, 206, 207, 209,
        212, 217, 219, 236, 235–38 passim
    Haileybury college, 34, 45, 237, 243
    Indian politics/wars, 8, 17, 31, 34, 35, 44, 51, 54,
        80, 83–87 passim, 103, 132, 206
    information/knowledge, 3, 10, 25, 31, 33, 35, 41,
        42, 43, 45, 103, 236, 246, 261n. 16
    missionaries, 71, 147,
    revenue & judicial, 9, 26, 34, 50, 51, 52, 72, 73,
        74, 170, 184, 197, 202, 203, 208, 211, 217,
        218. (see *also* India House & Leadenhall
        Street)
Edinburgh, 37, 125, 135, 156, 217
    university of, 24, 25, 37, 42, 65, 66, 260n. 17
Edmonstone, Neil, 230
education, 2, 5, 21–26, 33, 34, 36, 43, 44–45, 111,
    197, 221–2, 236, 237, 249
Elizabeth (queen of England), 126
Ellenborough, Lord. *See* Law, Edward, earl of El-
    lenborough
Ellichpur, 55, 62
Elliot, Sir Gilbert, 1st earl of Minto, 18, 57, 59,
    60, 64, 66, 70, 79, 80, 258n. 12
Elliot, Hugh (brother and governor of Madras
    1814–20), 100
Elliot, John (son), 59, 61
    Minto, Lady Anna-Maria Amyand (wife), 76
Ellora, 81
Elphinstone, 11th Lord (father), 20
Elphinstone, Charles (brother), 77
Elphinstone, Elizabeth (aunt), 18
Elphinstone, Admiral George Keith (uncle). *See*
    Keith, George, Elphinstone, viscount Keith
Elphinstone, James (brother), 20, 38
Elphinstone, John, (12th Lord Elphinstone,
    brother), 77
Elphinstone, Lady (mother), 20, 53
Elphinstone, Mountstuart,

as administrator, 91–93, 100–2, 110–114 passim,
    Chapter 11 passim, 250
    appointments, 21, 37, 41, 53–54, 55, 62–63, 64,
        79, 80–81, 86, 91, 94, 95, 115
    & E. Burke, 2, 137–38, 143, 252
    as diplomat, 41, 54, 62–64, 77, 84, 86
    education/expert knowledge, 3, 4, 20, 21, 25,
        33–34, 38–39, 41–42, 45, 55, 65–66, 94, 103,
        229–31, 237, 249–50, 251, 260n. 17
    finances, 7, 26, 27, 38, 96–97,
    & Indian influences, 104, 121, 191, 238, 253
    & James Mill, 126–27, 179, 188–90
    & patronage, 20–21, 27–28, 29, 38, 39, 41, 53, 55,
        65, 67, 77
    & Scottish influences, Chapters 7, 8, 9, 10, 11
        passim, 2, 78–79, 94, 120, 127, 130, 133, 140,
        143–44, 146, 152, 153, 157, 164–65, 168, 222,
        234, 237, 248, 252, 253, 254
    & Scottish school of thought, 1, 11–12, 196,
        241, 242–43, 251–52
    Self-promotion/career-building techniques,
        81, 232, 241
    writing, 2, 45, 64–65, 67, 79, 80–82, 107–8, 119,
        162, 175, 182, 238, 240, 251
Elphinstone, William Fullarton (uncle), 18, 20,
    25, 27, 34, 41, 63, 75, 76, 77, 85, 98, 99, 259n. 9
Empire and Information (Bayly), 238
empire building, 124, 244
employment of Indians (natives), 108, 110, 197,
    212, 218–21, 223
England, 4, 6, 9, 77, 78, 93, 194, 200, 206, 246,
    248
    education, 33–4
    law, 214–15
Enlightenment, 5, 236, 237. *See also* Scottish En-
    lightenment
Episcopalians, 146, 151, 273n. 2
Erskine, Henry (brother in law of Munro), 70
Erskine, William, 65, 111, 120, 126
Essay on the History of Civil Society, An (Ferguson),
    121
Eurasians, 112, 113
Europe, Europeans, 8, 12, 44, 45, 47, 59, 61, 62,
    64, 66, 69, 76, 78, 105, 113, 120, 125, 126, 133,
    136, 142, 144, 145, 148, 149, 152, 155, 161,
    167–75 passim, 189, 191, 200, 202, 206, 208,
    214, 217, 219, 221, 228, 230, 234, 237, 242
Evangelicals, 179, 237, 242, 254. *See also* High Fly-
    ers

Ferguson, Adam, 2, 5, 119, 122, 125, 131, 134, 140,
    160, 167, 174–75, 218, 221, 240, 241, 259n. 6
Ferdosi, 122–3
Fifth Report on East India Company Affairs, The (1812),
    71

Fort William College, 21, 33–4, 44–5, 53, 237
France, French, 5, 8, 9, 44, 48, 59, 60, 63, 71, 78,
   120, 160, 173, 241
   French military mission to Persia, 59
   French revolution, 140–42
Free trade, 71, 72
Frykenberg, Robert E., 248
Fuhr, Enid M., 58, 264n. 37
Furber, Holden, 106

Gawilgharh, seige of, 55
*General Remarks on the Judicial Administration and on the
   Police,* (Munro), 222
George, Prince of Wales (later George IV, king
   of England), 49
Ghosh, Biswanath, 82
Gibbon, Edward, 120
Glasgow, 6, 15, 16, 23, 171, 185, 195, 202
   Glasgow Courier, 135
   university of, 22, 24, 34
Gleig, Rev. George, 70, 99, 110, 146, 151, 171, 172,
   186, 240, 241, 246
Government of British India, 2, 3, 64, 66, 71, 72,
   79, 84, 106, 120, 128, 161, 168, 179, 183, 187,
   190, 197, 200, 222, 241. *See also* British India,
   Home government, Indian government,
   Supreme government
Government of India, The (Malcolm), 221
Govind, 162–3
Graeme, Henry, 99
Grant, Charles, 72
Grant, Captain James, 87
Grant, Sir John, 112–13
Greek War of Independence, 89
Grenville, William Wyndham, baron Grenville,
   76
Grotius, Hugo, 63, 215
Gwalior, 56, 61

Haidar Ali of Mysore, 7, 34, 203, 204
Haileybury College, 34, 45, 237, 243
Hamilton, Alexander, 65, 120
Har Govind. *See* Govind
Harlow, Vincent, 10, 168
Harris, Lieutenant General James, 45–48 passim
Hastings, Francis Rawdon, 1st marquis of Hast-
   ings & 2nd earl of Moira, 8, 10, 47, 57, 70,
   79, 81, 83, 84, 88, 91, 100, 101, 109, 174, 236,
   245, 258n. 12
Hastings, Warren, 10, 42, 43, 127, 142–43, 183,
   236, 253
Henry VII (king of England), 161, 173
High Flyers, 145–46, 149, 188. *See also* Evangelicals
Hill, David, 109
Hislop, General Sir Thomas, 79, 83, 84, 86, 89

Hindu, Hinduism, 7, 8, 82, 124 134, 147, 148, 150,
   153–54, 169, 176, 177, 179, 180, 181, 189, 235
   laws, 209, 231
   myths, 122
   religion, 154, 155, 158, 234
History, historians, Chapter 7 passim, 76, 244
   Asian, 41, 168, 191
   conjectural, 5, 121, 231
   European, 123, 124
   Muslim, 124
   philosophical, 5, 120, 121, 126, 128, 231, 232, 235
History of British India, (Mill), 34, 106, 233
History of England (Hume), 126,
History of Great Britain (Hume), 127
History of Hindustan (Dow), 230
History of India (Elphinstone), 115, 122, 127, 153,
   154, 158, 175–79, 233
History of Persia, (Malcolm), 62, 64, 66, 76, 82,
   120, 122, 125, 126, 127, 132, 134, 157, 233
History of the Progress of Society in Europe, (Robert-
   son), 128, 172
History of the Reign of Charles V (Robertson), 172
Hobart, Robert, viscount Hobart, 4th earl of
   Buckinghamshire, 35, 38, 40, 71, 74, 75
Holkar, Ahalya Baee (Ahilyabai), widow of
   Mulhar Rao Holkar, 181–82
Holkar, Jeshwant Rao of Indore, 54, 57, 62, 79,
   83, 89, 90, 93, 102
Holy Alliance, 168, 175
Home government (East India Company), 4, 34,
   57, 59, 77, 82, 83, 87, 100, 103, 111, 114, 196,
   206, 251
House of Commons, 6, 71, 72, 155, 200
House of Hanover, 4, 18
House of Lords, 6, 76
Hudleston, John, 73, 74
Humayan, 177
Hume, David, 2, 66, 70, 119–22 passim, 124, 126,
   127, 128, 130, 133, 134, 138–39, 140, 146, 147,
   150, 152–53, 155, 157, 160, 161, 188, 190, 193, 198,
   199, 209, 212, 216, 243, 252
Hutcheson, Francis, 70, 140, 157
Hyderabad, nizam of, 35–36, 47, 48, 51, 86
Hyderabad, 17, 18, 42, 46, 48, 83, 89

imperial, 9, 168, 175, 180, 228, 236, 244, 246, 252
Imperialist school of thought, 245, 246
India, Indian, 10, 11, 46, 66, 104, 235, 248,
   culture, 45, 236, 237, 248, 257
   "dialogue" 32
   forms of governance, 67–72 passim, 76, 77,
      97, 104, 175, 177, 182, 208, 209, 230
   "voices" 32, 58, 104
India Act (1784), 10, 43, 94
Indian nationalists, 209, 244, 245, 246

Inden, Ronald, 232–35
Indology, 229
India House, 30, 69, 187. *See also* East India Company
Ingram, Edward, 9
Institutes of the Law of Scotland (Stair), 215
Inquiry into the Human Mind on the Principles of Common Sense (Reid), 135
Irschick, Eugene F., 32
Islam, 124, 134, 155, 158, 159, 166, 176, 179, 180, 228, 229

Jacobites, 11, 216, 253
Jamsheed, 123–24
Jehangir, 178
Jenkins, Richard, 45
Johnson, Samuel, 227
John Stuart Mill and India (Zastoupil), 187
Jones, Sir Harford, 59, 60, 61
Jones, Sir William, 231, 237
Johnstone family of Alva, 18, 26
judicial system, law, 71, 73, 82, 99, 107, 109, 110, 111, 113, 197, 211, 217, 219, 223, 252
   Munro system, 213–14, 216–18

Kabul, 64, 163
Kames, Henry Home, Lord Kames, 121, 146, 206, 207, 216
Kanara, 17, 49–51, 147, 168, 170, 202–6
Kaye, Sir John, 29, 125, 126, 148, 151, 240, 241
Keith, George Elphinstone, viscount, admiral, 20, 28, 41, 77, 96
Kennaway, Sir John, 36, 46
Kennedy, Dane, 240
Kennedy, Colonel Vans, 65, 230
Kipling, Rudyard, 7
Kirk, 15, 145, 149, 188. *See also* Church of Scotland
Kirkpatrick, Captain, James, 46, 230
Kirkpatrick, Colonel William, 45, 47, 53, 54, 230
Kopf, David, 33
Koran, 146, 149

Lake, General Gerard, 1st viscount Lake, 57, 58
land tenure, revenue systems, 71, 72, 73, 82, 110, 113, 178, 181, 191, 193, 195, 196, 202, 210, 211, 212, 223, 252
languages (Sanskrit, Persian & other Indian & Asian), 10, 28, 31, 33, 36, 37, 38, 41–46 passim, 50, 52, 54, 55, 65, 66, 73, 178, 214, 229, 230–31, 232, 237, 238, 251, 260n. 5
Law, Edward, earl of Ellenborough, 115
Leadenhall Street, 56. *See also* East India Company and India House
leadership cadre, 78, 94, 250
Leyden, John, 65

liberalism, 2, 12, 219, 241, 244, 245, 253
Life of Major General Sir Thomas Munro (Gleig), 110
"little republics," 172
Liverpool, Robert, 2nd earl of, 107, 108
Lockhart, John, 17
Longford, Elizabeth, 51
Louis, XI, (king of France), 161, 173
Ludden, David, 194, 235, 236–37, 238
Lushington, Stephen, 107, 109, 114
Luther, Martin, 146

Madras, 7, 16–19 passim, 30, 31, 34, 37, 38, 46, 49, 51, 52, 59, 67, 71–75 passim, 77, 82, 83, 84, 88, 95, 96, 97, 99, 100, 107, 114, 174, 185, 189, 245
   board of revenue, 206
   Madras College, 107
   Military board, 186
   Native board of revenue, 107–8
M'Culloch, William, 3, 257n. 3
MacKenzie, Henry, 124
Mackenzie, Holt, 109
MacKenzie, John M., 11, 228
Mackintosh, Sir James, 76, 120, 126, 140
Mahmud of Gazni, 122–23, 124, 158
Malcolm, Charlotte Campbell, Lady Malcolm (wife), 59, 60–1, 100, 103, 114
Malcolm, George (father), 17, 26, 56
Malcolm, Gilbert (brother), 37
Malcolm, Sir James (brother), 68
Malcolm, Sir John,
   as administrator, 93, 104, 110, 112–15 passim, Chapter 11 passim, 250
   appointments, 1, 18–20, 37, 41, 46–47, 48, 55, 56, 59, 61, 79, 84, 93, 95, 1000–2, 107
   & E. Burke, 2, 137–38, 142–43, 252
   as diplomat, 46, 48–49, 55–58, 66, 84, 90–91, 102–3, 125, 137 264n. 39
   education/expert knowledge, 3, 4, 10, 21, 24–25, 33–34, 36, 37, 41–42, 45, 66, 94, 103–4, 229–31, 237, 249–50, 251
   finances, 7, 26, 38, 96, 98
   & Indian influences, 104, 121, 180, 191, 238, 253
   & James Mill, 188–90
   & patronage, 18, 27–28, 29, 38, 40–41, 56, 60, 67, 77, 136
   & Scottish influences, 2, 58, 78–79, 94, Chapters 7, 8, 9, 10, 11 passim, 120, 125–26, 127–28, 130, 133, 140, 143–44, 146, 148, 150, 153, 157, 167, 168, 234, 237, 248, 252, 253, 254
   & Scottish school of thought, 1, 11–12, 196, 241, 242,-43, 251–52
   Self-promotion/career building techniques, 37, 42, 46, 50–51, 59–60, 61, 232, 241, 264n. 46
   as soldier, 35, 47, 48, 83, 89–90

writing, 2, 36, 45, 61–62, 64, 67, 75, 76, 104–6, 119, 162, 179, 182, 221, 238, 240, 251,

Malcolm, Margaret Pasley (mother), 17

Malcolm, Sir Pulteney (brother), 12, 35, 47, 68, 76

Malcolm, Robert (brother), 17, 35, 38, 56

Malcolm, William (brother), 56

Malwa, 93, 94, 101, 102, 104, 180, 181. *See also* Central India

Marathas, 7, 42, 51, 52, 54–58 passim, 63, 77, 80, 82, 83, 85, 88, 89, 92, 92, 102, 170, 179, 189, 247

Marshall, P.J., 175, 258n. 7

Mary (queen of England), 126

Mason, Philip, 246–47

Masulipatam, 61, 75

Mehidpur, battle of, 89

Melvil, James, 135

Memoir of Central India (Report on Malwa, Malcolm), 93, 104–5, 106, 180–82, 210, 214

Men Who Ruled India, The (Mason), 246–47

Mercer, Graeme, 36

Merchant of Venice, The (Shakespeare), 229

Metcalfe, Charles, later baron Metcalfe, 45, 182, 187, 257n. 1

Metcalf, Thomas R., 137

military economy, 187

military fiscalism, 7, 128, 169, 170, 172, 173, 182, 204

Mill, James, 3, 34, 106, 122, 126–27, 179, 188–90, 233, 257n. 3

Mill, John Stuart, 187

Millar, John, 2, 119, 121, 131, 134, 155, 157, 188, 216

Minto, earl of. *See* Elliot, Sir Gilbert, 1st earl of Minto

mirasi (land tenure), 200–1, 202, 223

Misra, B.B., 250

Missionaries, 71, 72, 147, 157, 176, 253

Moderate group, moderatism (Church of Scotland), 5, Chapter 9 passim, 188

Montague Declaration, 245

Montesquieu, 193

moral philosophy, 5, 66, 120, 128, Chapter 8 passim, 233, 237, 242, 257n. 4

Morier, James, 105–6

Mughal empire, 7, 42, 73, 159, 162, 169, 177

Muhammad, 123, 134, 148, 149, 166

Mukherjee, Nilmani, 248

Multan, 175

Munro, Alexander (father), 16, 24, 26, 35, 87, 146

Munro, Alexander (brother), 24, 26, 34, 40

Munro, Daniel (brother), 26, 40, 69

Munro, Erskine (sister), 26, 35, 48, 147, 157

Munro, James (brother), 147, 196

Munro, Jane Campbell, Lady Munro (wife), 75, 82

Munro, John (nephew), 69, 75

Munro, Margaret Stark (mother), 26

Munro, Margaret (sister), 26, 146

Munro, Sir Thomas,
  as administrator (revenue/judicial), Chapter 11 passim, 31–32, 49, 51, 71–75, 82, 99, 136, 217

  appointments, 1, 16–17, 31, 41, 47, 49, 51, 74–75, 79, 82–83, 84, 85–87, 95, 100, 107, 108–9, 217

  & E. Burke, 2, 137–8, 140–42, 143, 252

  education/expert knowledge, 3, 4, 10, 21, 22–24, 31–35, 41–42, 45, 66, 94, 103, 229–31, 237, 249–50, 251

  finances, 7, 26, 75, 96, 97–98

  & Indian influences, 104, 169–70, 173–74, 228, 236, 238, 253

  & military issues, 51–52, 85–89

  & James Mill, 188–90

  & patronage, 16, 27–28, 29, 30, 38, 67, 77, 136

  & Scottish influences, Chapters 7, 8, 9, 10, 11 passim, 1, 2, 78–79, 94, 130, 132, 133, 134, 140, 143–44, 146, 153, 157, 168, 172, 173–74, 175, 193, 194–95, 198–202, 205, 206–7, 209, 212, 216–17, 218, 220–21, 234, 237, 248, 252, 253, 254

  & Scottish school of thought, 1, 11–12, 196, 241, 242–43, 251–52

  Self-promotion/career building techniques, 35, 40, 50–51, 67, 232, 241

  writing, 2, 45, 51, 67, 75, 109–10, 182, 217, 219, 229, 238, 240, 251

Munro, William (brother), 26, 30, 31

Munro system, Chapter 11 passim, 32, 74, 93, 192, 196, 197, 212–13, 219, 223, 252

Murray, Alexander, 65

Muslim(s), 7, 8, 31, 82, 120, 122, 146, 147, 159, 163, 166, 169, 170, 175–78 passim, 180, 235

Mysore, 42, 44, 57, 59, 83, 235

Mysore Commission, 17, 19, 47, 48, 49

Nadir Shah (of Persia), 164

Nagpur, 21, 55, 58, 62, 63, 89

Namier, Sir Lewis, 2

Nanak 149–50, 162

national character, 133, 134, 144, 252

Natural History of Religion (Hume), 152–53, 154

Napoleon (Bonaparte), 48, 64, 142

Nehru, Jawaharlal, 244, 245

neoabsolutism, 10, 168, 169, 253

Newton, Sir Isaac, 130

Newtonian scientific empiricism, 188

O'Brien, Karen, 127

On the Condition and Assessment of Kanara (Munro), 203

On the Employment of Natives in the Public Service (Munro), 174, 221, 222

On the Relative Advantages of the Ryotwar and Zamindar Systems (Munro), 72, 206

On the State of the Country and the Condition of the People, 184, 222–23

Oxford university, 23, 24

Observations on the Disturbances in the Madras Army in 1809 (Malcolm), 61

Origin of the Distinction of Ranks (Millar), 121, 157

Oriental Imaginings, (Majeed), 233

Orientalism (Said), 227–28

Orientalism, Orientalist, 12 passim, 12, 65, 227, 253

Orientalism/1 & /2, 228, 229, 231, 233, 235

Panchayats, 73, 82, 110, 211, 214, 218, 219

Pannikar, K.M., 42, 106

Parkin, Charles, 142

Parliament, 6, 10, 53, 69, 71, 72, 75, 77, 107, 115, 215

Pasley, John, 18, 26

Pasley, Admiral Sir Thomas, 18, 26

Pax Britannica, 143

Peers, Douglas M., 11, 108, 114, 182–86

Permanent settlement (revenue), 196, 279n. 36

Persia, Persian, 9, 11, 48, 59–62, passim, 64, 66, 67, 76, 102, 105–6, 107, 122, 127, 134, 159, 162, 163, 165–68 passim, 176, 178, 185, 229, 232, 234, 237

Persian Gulf, 19, 60

Shah of, 48, 49, 63–64, 102, 107

Peshawar, 64, 163

Petitot, 122

Physiocrats, 194

Pindaris, 79, 82–85 passim, 89, 90, 102

Pitt, William (the younger), 7

Poligars, 52, 200, 202, 203, 205, 206, 252,

political economy, Chapter 11 passim, 5, 74, 144, 191, 192, 195, 196, 206, 223

Political History of India (Malcolm), 105–6, 142, 171, 184

Pope, Alexander, 153

Prakash, Gyan, 232

Prince of Wales. *See* George, Prince of Wales

Progress of Society in Europe. See History of the Progress of Society in Europe (Robertson)

Prophet of Arabia, 158. *See also* Muhammad

Protestantism, 147

Pufendorf, Samuel, 63, 215

Pulteney, Sir William, 18, 259n. 6

Pune, 21, 39, 41, 42, 53, 54, 65, 79, 81, 85, 88, 89, 91, 112, 250

Peshwa of, 80, 81, 83–86 passim, 88–91 passim, 100, 102, 113

Punjab, 7, 124, 162

Rajputana, 35

Ravenshaw, John, 99, 100, 109, 114

Read, Captain, Alexander, 16, 31–34, 49, 52, 74, 169, 194, 195, 196, 198, 201, 213

Reflections on the Revolution in France (Burke), 140–41, 143

Reid, Thomas, 37, 135

Religion, Chapter 9 passim, 4, 5, 15, 62, 129, 139, 144, 166, 176, 178, 179, 180, 182, 188, 189–90, 229, 234, 236, 241, 253

Rendall, Jane, 65

Report on the Territories Conquered from the Peshwa (Elphinstone), 93, 158, 210

Ricardo, David, 194–95

Rise of British Power in the East (Elphinstone), 115, 132

Robertson, Rev. William, 2, 119–122 passim, 128, 129, 131, 145, 161, 212, 221, 234, 252

Rocher, Rosane, 228–29

romanticism, 12

Rulers of India Series, 240

Russia, 10, 59, 62, 76, 160, 175, 185

Ryotwari, 31–33, 73, 82, 107, 109, 110, 194, 196, 197, 206, 210, 211, 223, 245

Safavid empire, 162

Said, Edward, 227–28, 231–32, 235

Satara, 89, 92

Seringapatam, 39, 47

Scotland, 2, 4, 9, 11, 15, 36, 41, 69, 76, 93, 119, 120, 146, 156, 161, 164, 172, 188, 194, 195, 237, 248–51 passim

education, 21–26, 33–34

land tenure, 201, 207

law, 215–16

Scott, Sir Walter, 9, 17, 18, 76, 93, 106

Scottish Enlightenment, 1, 2, 3, 11, 12, 65, 78, 119, 127, 130, 140, 144, 150, 216, 234, 237, 254. *See also* Enlightenment

Scottish school of thought, 12, 79, 136, 192, 222–23, 242, 243, 244, 251, 252, 253

"sensibility," 5, 58, 124, 127, 136, 190. *See also* Sentimentalists

Sentimentalists, 126, 237

Sermons (Blair), 58, 135, 138

service gentry, 169, 209, 210, 243

Shah Nahmah (Ferdosi), 122

Shah Shuja al-Mulk, 21, 64, 163

Shastri, Gangadhar, 81

Sholapur, 89, 90

Shore, Sir John, later 1st baron Teignmouth, 38, 106

Sikhs, Sikhism, 7, 11, 62, 149–50, 162, 179

Sinclair, Sir John, 201

Sindhia, Daulat Rao of Gwalior, 54–57 passim, 62, 83, 85, 89, 93, 102

Sivaji, 179

Sketch of the Political History of India (Malcolm), 61, 105, 143

Sketches of Persia (Malcolm), 105–6, 269n. 19

Sketch of the Sikhs (Malcolm), 61, 122, 157, 162–63

Smiles, Samuel, 30

Smith, Adam, 2, 23, 34, 120, 121, 124, 131, 133, 138–39, 140, 153, 154, 188, 189, 193–96 passim, 198, 199, 201, 205, 206, 207, 209, 216, 222, 252, 253, 259n. 6

Smith, General, 85

Sommerville and Gordon, 26, 87, 185

Sommerville, Thomas, 18

Spain, Spanish, 64, 69, 70, 142, 172

Stadial theory, 130. *See also* stages of civilization

stages of civilization, 121, 124, 133, 136, 144, 161, 193. *See also* stadial theory

Stair, Lord. *See* Dalrymple, Sir James, 1st viscount Stair

state-building, 7, 128, 169, 172, 173

State Formation and Economy Reconsidered (Stein), 171

Stein, Burton, 10, 137–38, 168, 171–72, 174, 193, 204, 223

Stephen, Leslie, 138

Stewart, Dugald, 65, 66, 121, 129, 167–68, 188

stoicism, 152

Stokes, Eric, 137, 250

Strachey, Edward, 53–54, 63, 80

Strachey, Henry, 53

Stratton, George, 99

Stuart, Andrew, 34, 259n. 6

subsidiary alliances, 54, 174

Sufism, 149

Sulivan, Laurence, 26

Sullivan, John, 71, 99

sultanist, sultanism, 11, 169–71, 253

Supreme government (at Calcutta), 59, 80, 82, 84, 88, 90, 102, 114, 175, 214, 251

Survey of India, 33

Swartz, Dr. Christian, 31

systems of government, Chapter 10 passim, 144, 168, 169, 170, 173, 175, 176, 177–182, 183, 188, 190, 242, 252, 253

Tamerlane, 177

Tehran, 48, 61, 66, 107, 115

Thackeray, William, 99

Theory of Moral Sentiments (Smith), 124, 139, 196

Thomas Munro: The Origins of the Colonial State and his Vision of Empire (Stein), 170–72

Thomas, Nicholas, 228

Tipu Sultan of Mysore, 11, 31, 35, 46, 47, 49, 50, 54, 169, 170, 203, 204, 234

Trautmann, Thomas R., 228

Trial by Panchayat (Munro), 214

Trial of Criminal Cases by Jury or Panchayat (Munro), 219

Trimbakji. *See* Danglia, Trimbakji

universal human nature, 131, 136, 144, 233, 237, 242

Utilitarianism, Utilitarian, 2, 12, 72, 179, 237, 242, 243

Unitarian, Unitarianism, 151, 153

Venkattasuba Sastri, K.N., 245–46

Voltaire (Francois-Marie Arouet), 120

Ward, R.P., 63

Wallace, Thomas, 71

Washbrooke, D.A., 169

Wealth of Nations (Smith), 23, 37, 154, 196, 205, 209

Webbe, Josiah, 55, 197

Weber, Max, 11, 169, 169–70

Wellesley, Arthur, 1st Duke of Wellington, 1, 19, 21, 39, 44, 47, 48, 49, 51, 52, 54–58 passim, 62, 63, 68, 69, 70 76, 79, 80, 87–88, 98, 103, 108, 109, 114, 115, 182, 185

Wellesley, Henry, later 1st baron Cowley, 44, 47, 49, 56

Wellesley, Richard, Marquis (formerly 2nd earl of Mornington), 1, 8, 10, 19, 28, 39, 42–51 passim, 53–63 passim, 66, 67, 68, 76, 103, 127, 143, 168, 175, 206, 230, 251, 258n. 12

West, Sir Edward, 111–12

westernizing reformers, 113, 242. *See also* Anglicist reformers

Westminster Confession of Faith, 146

Wilks, Mark, 45

Wilson, H.H., 34, 179

Wynn, Sir Charles, 88, 103, 108, 111

Xenophon, 123

Yapp, M.E., 57, 127, 156, 230

Young, Arthur (agriculturalist), 201

Zamindar, zamindari, 72, 73, 104, 193–94, 200, 202–6 passim, 208, 210, 211, 212, 215

Zastoupil, Lynn, 58, 104, 180, 187–88, 237

Zeman Shah, 48

Zoroaster, Zoroastrianism, 132

ABOUT THE AUTHOR

Martha McLaren is adjunct professor in the Department of History at Simon Fraser University in Burnaby, British Columbia. She specializes in the intellectual history of British colonial South Asia and has written several articles on that subject. She earned her Ph.D. from Simon Fraser University.

ABOUT THE BOOK

British India & British Scotland, 1780–1830: Career Building, Empire Building, and a Scottish School of Thought on Indian Governance was designed and typeset by Kachergis Book Design of Pittsboro, North Carolina. The typeface, Centaur, was originally designed in 1914 for the Metropolitan Museum and released by Monotype in 1929. Designer Bruce Rogers modeled the typeface on letters cut by 15th-century printer Nicolas Jenson.

British India & British Scotland, 1780–1830: Career Building, Empire Building, and a Scottish School of Thought on Indian Governance was printed on 60-pound Glatfelter Supple Opaque Recycled Natural and bound by Thomson-Shore, Inc. of Dexter, Michigan